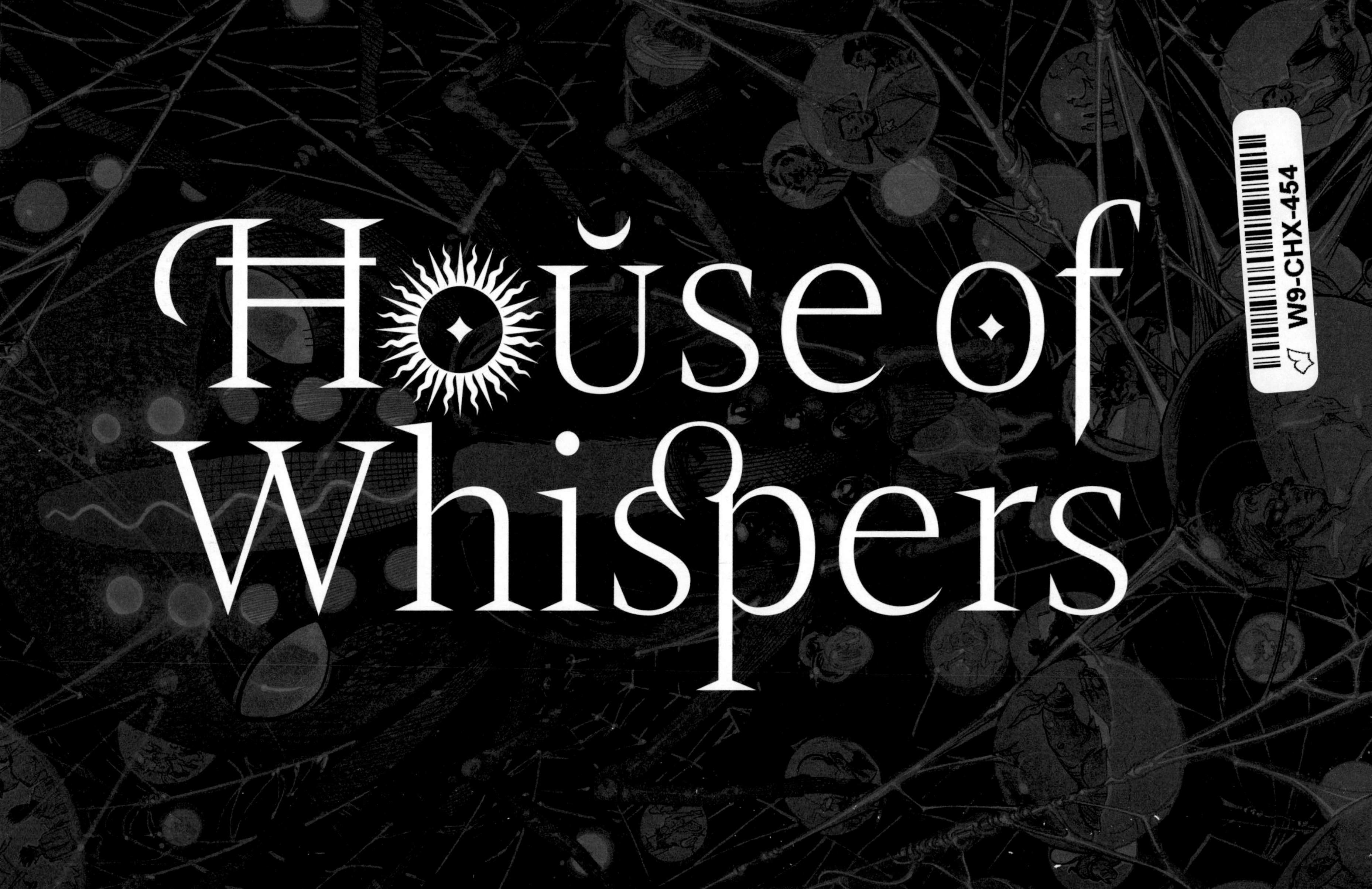
House of
Whispers

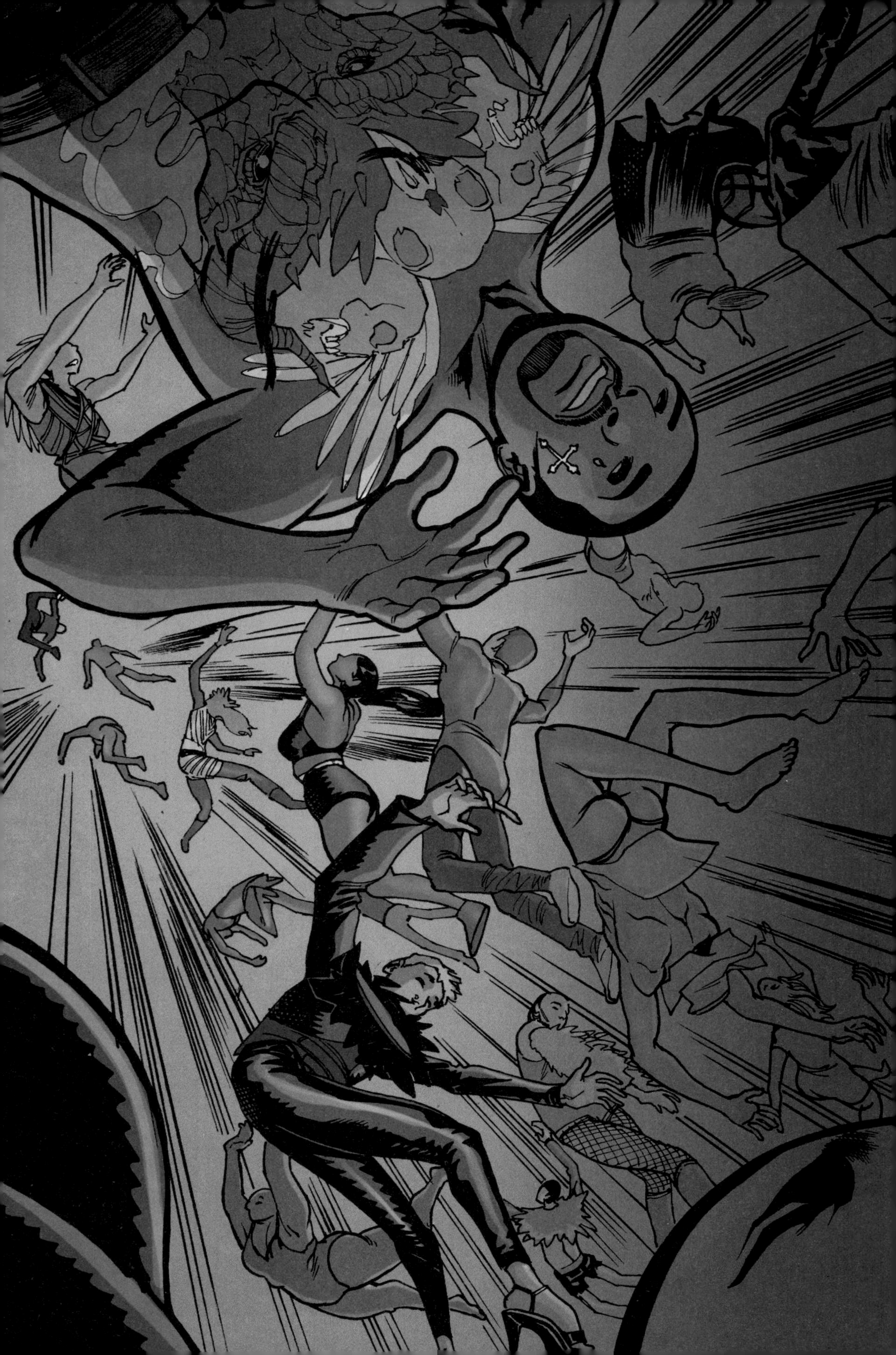

House of Whispers

VOLUME TWO

Ananse

WRITTEN BY
Nalo Hopkinson
and *Dan Watters*

ART BY
*Dominike
"DOMO"
Stanton*
Nelson Blake II
Isaac Goodhart
Amancay Nahuelpan
Aneke

COLORS BY
John Rauch
Zac Atkinson

LETTERS BY
AndWorld Design

COLLECTION
COVER ART AND
ORIGINAL SERIES
COVERS BY
Sean Andrew Murray

The Sandman Universe curated by Neil Gaiman

MOLLY MAHAN
CHRIS CONROY   *Editors – Original Series*
AMEDEO TURTURRO   *Associate Editor – Original Series*
MAGGIE HOWELL   *Assistant Editor – Original Series*
JEB WOODARD   *Group Editor – Collected Editions*
SCOTT NYBAKKEN   *Editor – Collected Edition*
STEVE COOK   *Design Director – Books*
                                  and Publication Design
TOM VALENTE   *Publication Production*

BOB HARRAS   *Senior VP – Editor-in-Chief, DC Comics*
MARK DOYLE   *Executive Editor, Vertigo & Black Label*

DAN DiDIO   *Publisher*
JIM LEE   *Publisher & Chief Creative Officer*
BOBBIE CHASE   *VP – New Publishing Initiatives & Talent Development*
DON FALLETTI   *VP – Manufacturing Operations & Workflow Management*
LAWRENCE GANEM   *VP – Talent Services*
ALISON GILL   *Senior VP – Manufacturing & Operations*
HANK KANALZ   *Senior VP – Publishing Strategy & Support Services*
DAN MIRON   *VP – Publishing Operations*
NICK J. NAPOLITANO   *VP – Manufacturing Administration & Design*
NANCY SPEARS   *VP – Sales*
MICHELE R. WELLS   *VP & Executive Editor, Young Reader*

HOUSE OF WHISPERS VOL. 2: ANANSE

Published by DC Comics. Compilation Copyright © 2020 DC Comics. All Rights Reserved.

Originally published in single magazine form in *House of Whispers* 7-12. Copyright © 2019 DC Comics. All Rights Reserved. All characters, their distinctive likenesses, and related elements featured in this publication are trademarks of DC Comics. The stories, characters, and incidents featured in this publication are entirely fictional. DC Comics does not read or accept unsolicited submissions of ideas, stories, or artwork.
DC – a WarnerMedia Company.

DC Comics, 2900 West Alameda Ave., Burbank, CA 91505
Printed by LSC Communications, Owensville, MO, USA. 1/17/20. First Printing.
ISBN: 978-1-4012-9917-0

Library of Congress Cataloging-in-Publication Data is available.

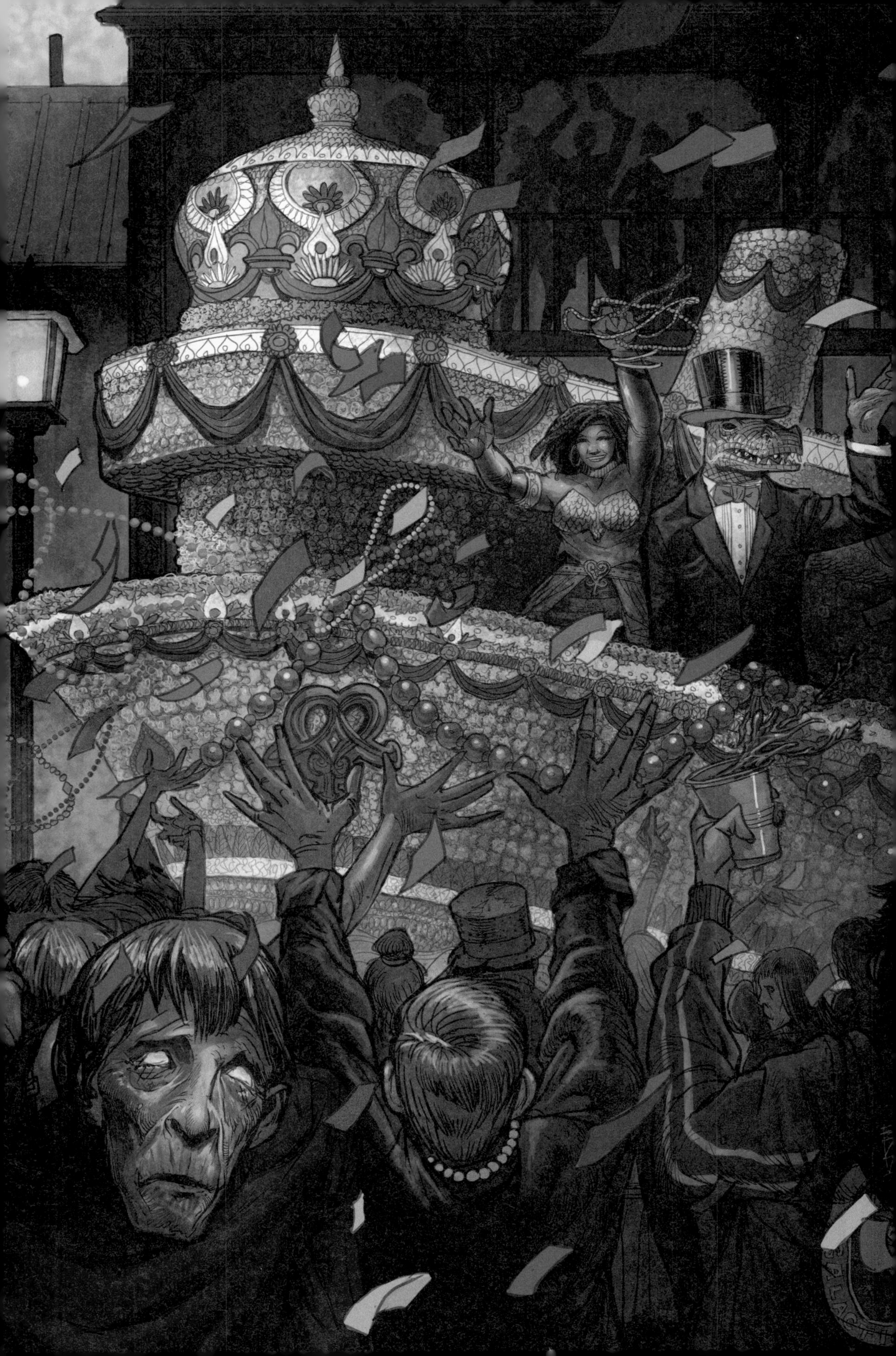

HOUSE OF WHISPERS

The Troubles I've Seen

WRITTEN BY
Nalo Hopkinson
and *Dan Watters*

ILLUSTRATED BY
Dominike "DOMO" Stanton

ADDITIONAL FINISHES BY
Isaac Goodhart (pages 16-17)
Amancay Nahuelpan (pages 21-22)
Aneke (pages 23-24)

COLORS BY
John Rauch

LETTERS BY
AndWorld Design

COVER ART BY
Sean Andrew Murray

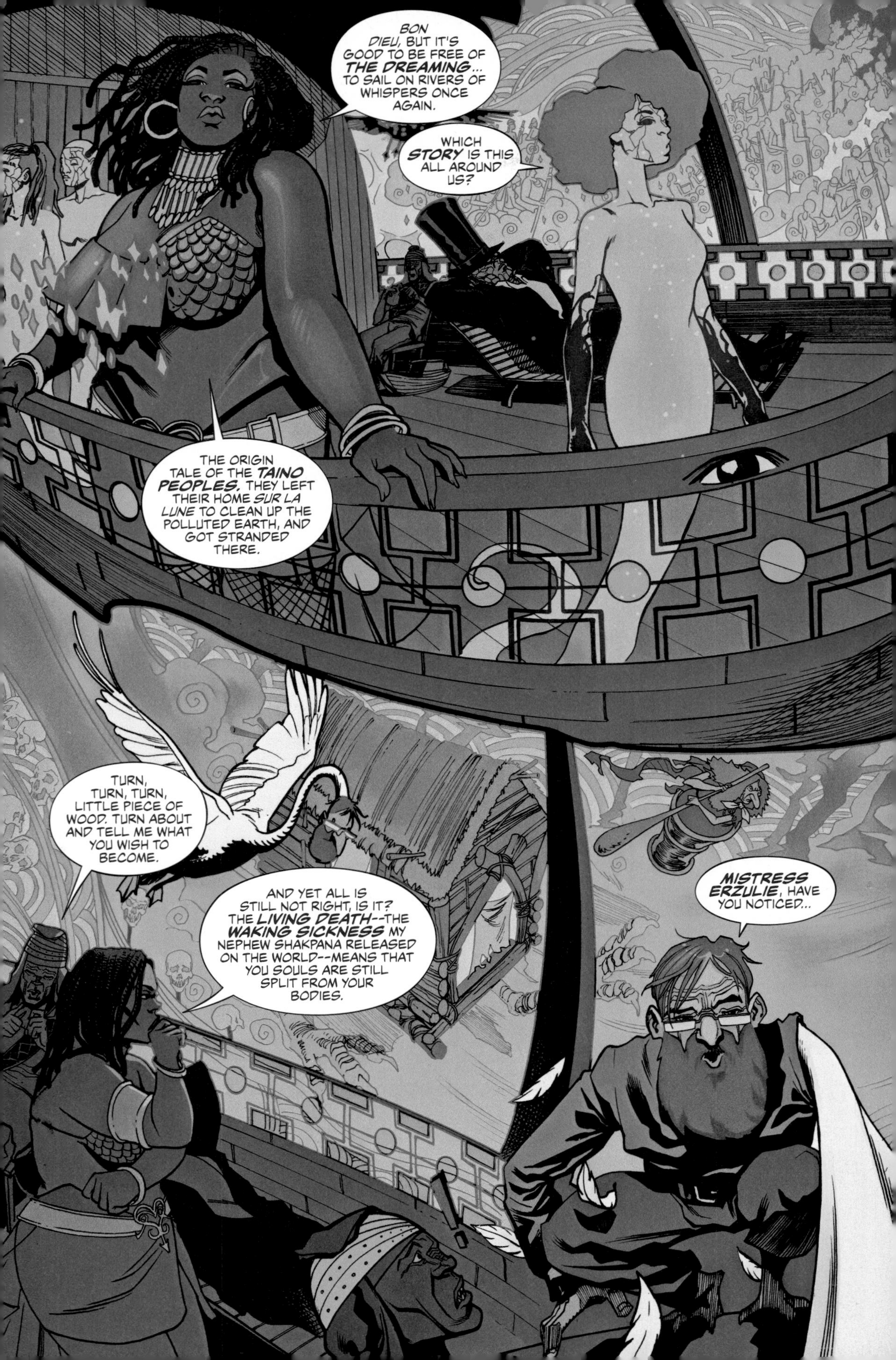
BON DIEU, BUT IT'S GOOD TO BE FREE OF THE DREAMING... TO SAIL ON RIVERS OF WHISPERS ONCE AGAIN.
WHICH STORY IS THIS ALL AROUND US?
THE ORIGIN TALE OF THE TAINO PEOPLES. THEY LEFT THEIR HOME SUR LA LUNE TO CLEAN UP THE POLLUTED EARTH, AND GOT STRANDED THERE.
TURN, TURN, TURN, LITTLE PIECE OF WOOD. TURN ABOUT AND TELL ME WHAT YOU WISH TO BECOME.
AND YET ALL IS STILL NOT RIGHT, IS IT? THE LIVING DEATH--THE WAKING SICKNESS MY NEPHEW SHAKPANA RELEASED ON THE WORLD--MEANS THAT YOU SOULS ARE STILL SPLIT FROM YOUR BODIES.
MISTRESS ERZULIE, HAVE YOU NOTICED...

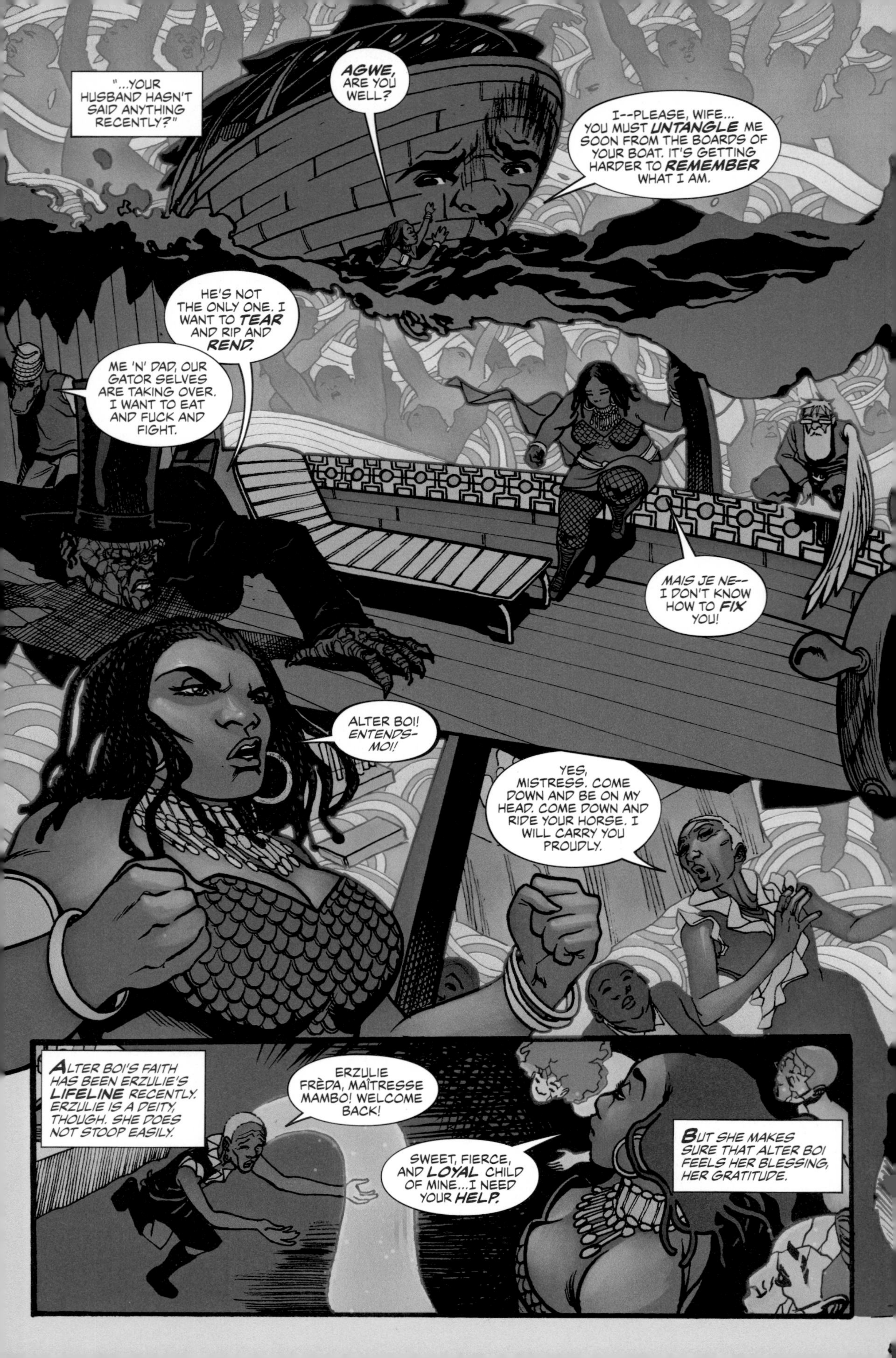
"...YOUR HUSBAND HASN'T SAID ANYTHING RECENTLY?"
AGWE, ARE YOU WELL?
I--PLEASE, WIFE... YOU MUST UNTANGLE ME SOON FROM THE BOARDS OF YOUR BOAT. IT'S GETTING HARDER TO REMEMBER WHAT I AM.
HE'S NOT THE ONLY ONE. I WANT TO TEAR AND RIP AND REND.
ME 'N' DAD, OUR GATOR SELVES ARE TAKING OVER. I WANT TO EAT AND FUCK AND FIGHT.
MAIS JE NE-- I DON'T KNOW HOW TO FIX YOU!
ALTER BOI! ENTENDS-MO!!
YES, MISTRESS. COME DOWN AND BE ON MY HEAD. COME DOWN AND RIDE YOUR HORSE. I WILL CARRY YOU PROUDLY.
ALTER BOI'S FAITH HAS BEEN ERZULIE'S LIFELINE RECENTLY. ERZULIE IS A DEITY, THOUGH. SHE DOES NOT STOOP EASILY.
ERZULIE FRÈDA, MAÎTRESSE MAMBO! WELCOME BACK!
SWEET, FIERCE, AND LOYAL CHILD OF MINE...I NEED YOUR HELP.
BUT SHE MAKES SURE THAT ALTER BOI FEELS HER BLESSING, HER GRATITUDE.

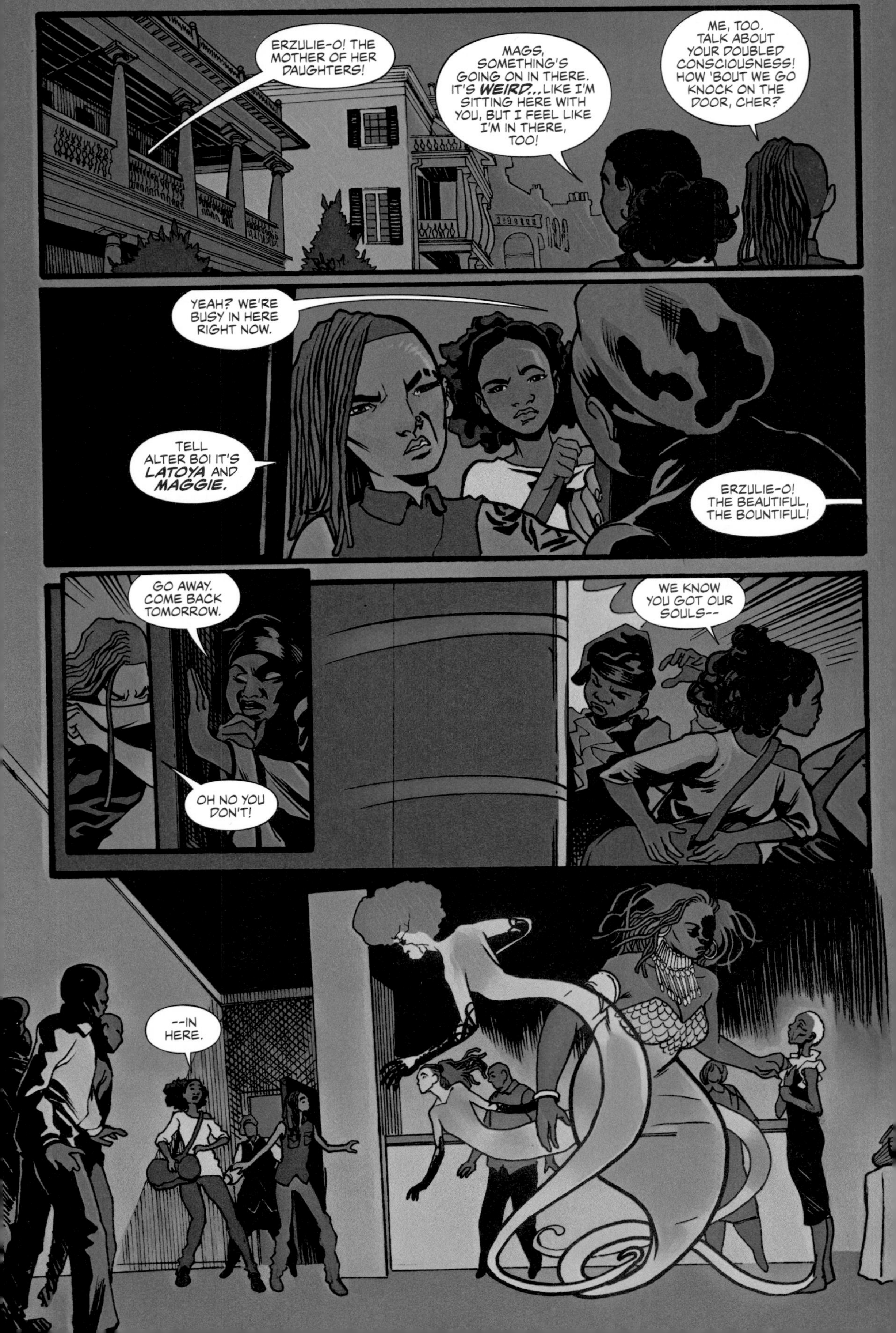
ERZULIE-O! THE MOTHER OF HER DAUGHTERS!
MAGS, SOMETHING'S GOING ON IN THERE. IT'S WEIRD... LIKE I'M SITTING HERE WITH YOU, BUT I FEEL LIKE I'M IN THERE, TOO!
ME, TOO. TALK ABOUT YOUR DOUBLED CONSCIOUSNESS! HOW 'BOUT WE GO KNOCK ON THE DOOR, CHER?
YEAH? WE'RE BUSY IN HERE RIGHT NOW.
TELL ALTER BOI IT'S LATOYA AND MAGGIE.
ERZULIE-O! THE BEAUTIFUL, THE BOUNTIFUL!
GO AWAY. COME BACK TOMORROW.
OH NO YOU DON'T!
WE KNOW YOU GOT OUR SOULS--
--IN HERE.

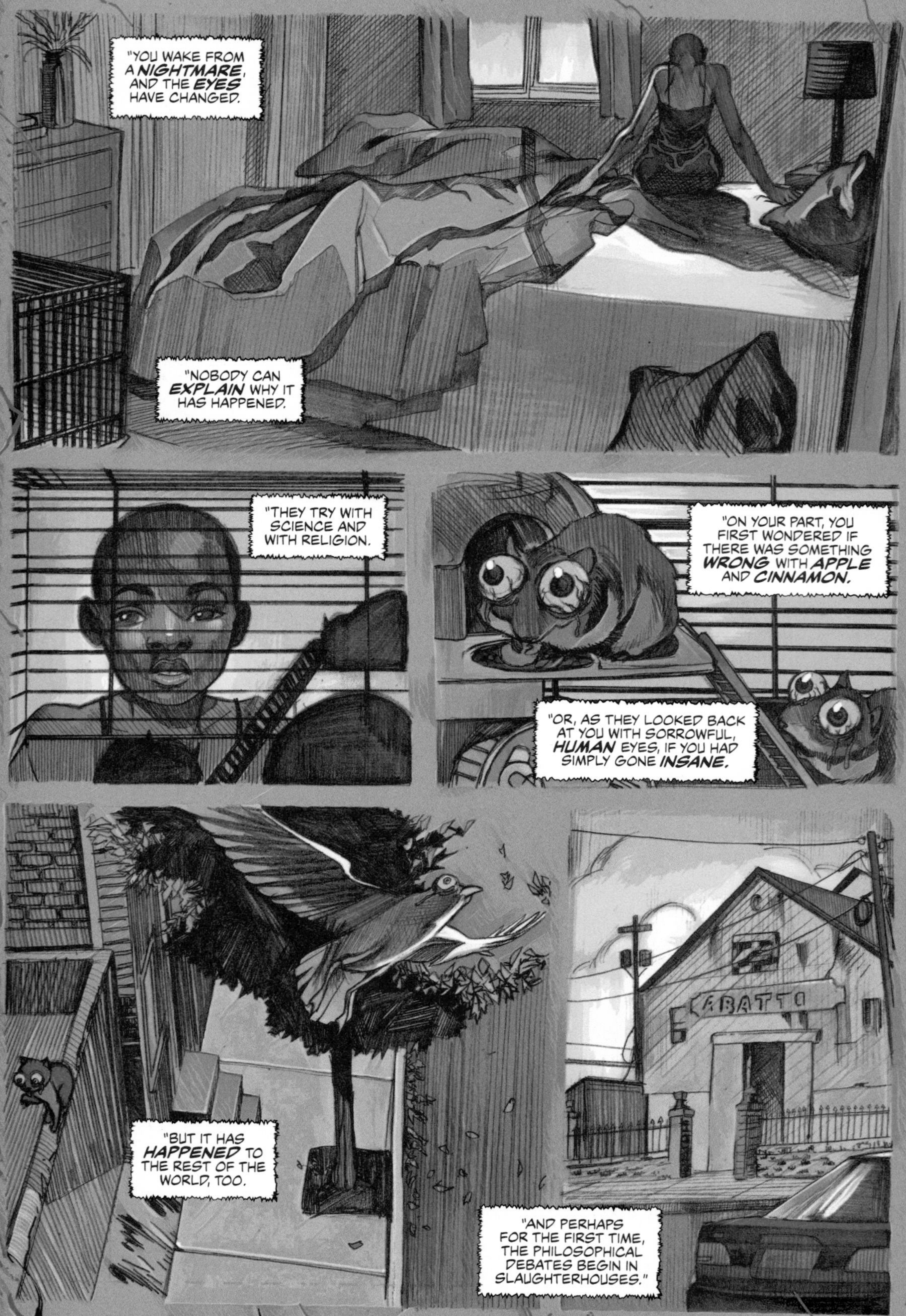
"YOU WAKE FROM A NIGHTMARE, AND THE EYES HAVE CHANGED.
"NOBODY CAN EXPLAIN WHY IT HAS HAPPENED.
"THEY TRY WITH SCIENCE AND WITH RELIGION.
"ON YOUR PART, YOU FIRST WONDERED IF THERE WAS SOMETHING WRONG WITH APPLE AND CINNAMON.
"OR, AS THEY LOOKED BACK AT YOU WITH SORROWFUL, HUMAN EYES, IF YOU HAD SIMPLY GONE INSANE.
"BUT IT HAS HAPPENED TO THE REST OF THE WORLD, TOO.
ABATTO
"AND PERHAPS FOR THE FIRST TIME, THE PHILOSOPHICAL DEBATES BEGIN IN SLAUGHTERHOUSES."

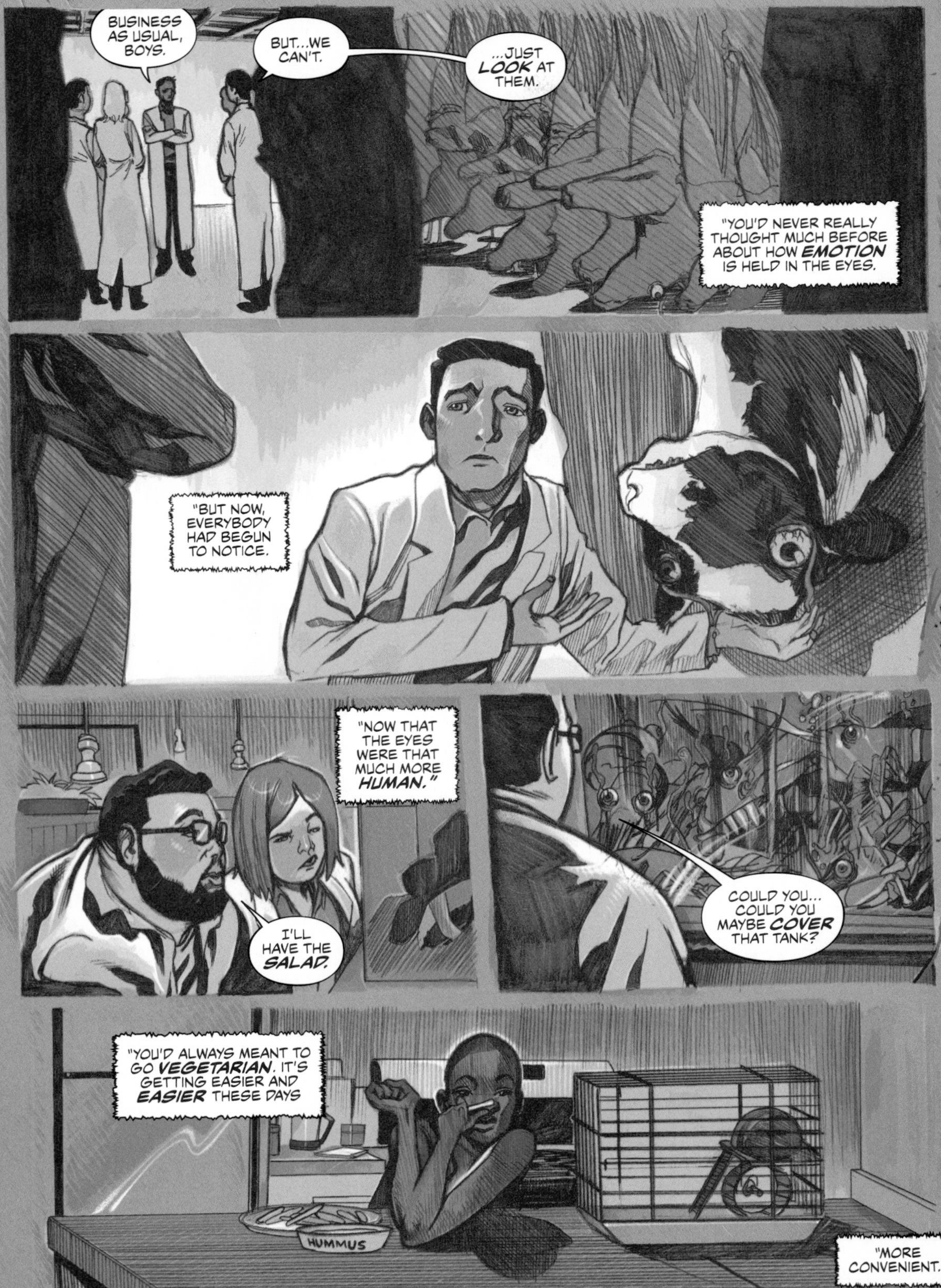
BUSINESS AS USUAL, BOYS.
BUT...WE CAN'T.
...JUST LOOK AT THEM.
"YOU'D NEVER REALLY THOUGHT MUCH BEFORE ABOUT HOW EMOTION IS HELD IN THE EYES.
"BUT NOW, EVERYBODY HAD BEGUN TO NOTICE.
"NOW THAT THE EYES WERE THAT MUCH MORE HUMAN."
I'LL HAVE THE SALAD.
COULD YOU... COULD YOU MAYBE COVER THAT TANK?
"YOU'D ALWAYS MEANT TO GO VEGETARIAN. IT'S GETTING EASIER AND EASIER THESE DAYS
HUMMUS
"MORE CONVENIENT."

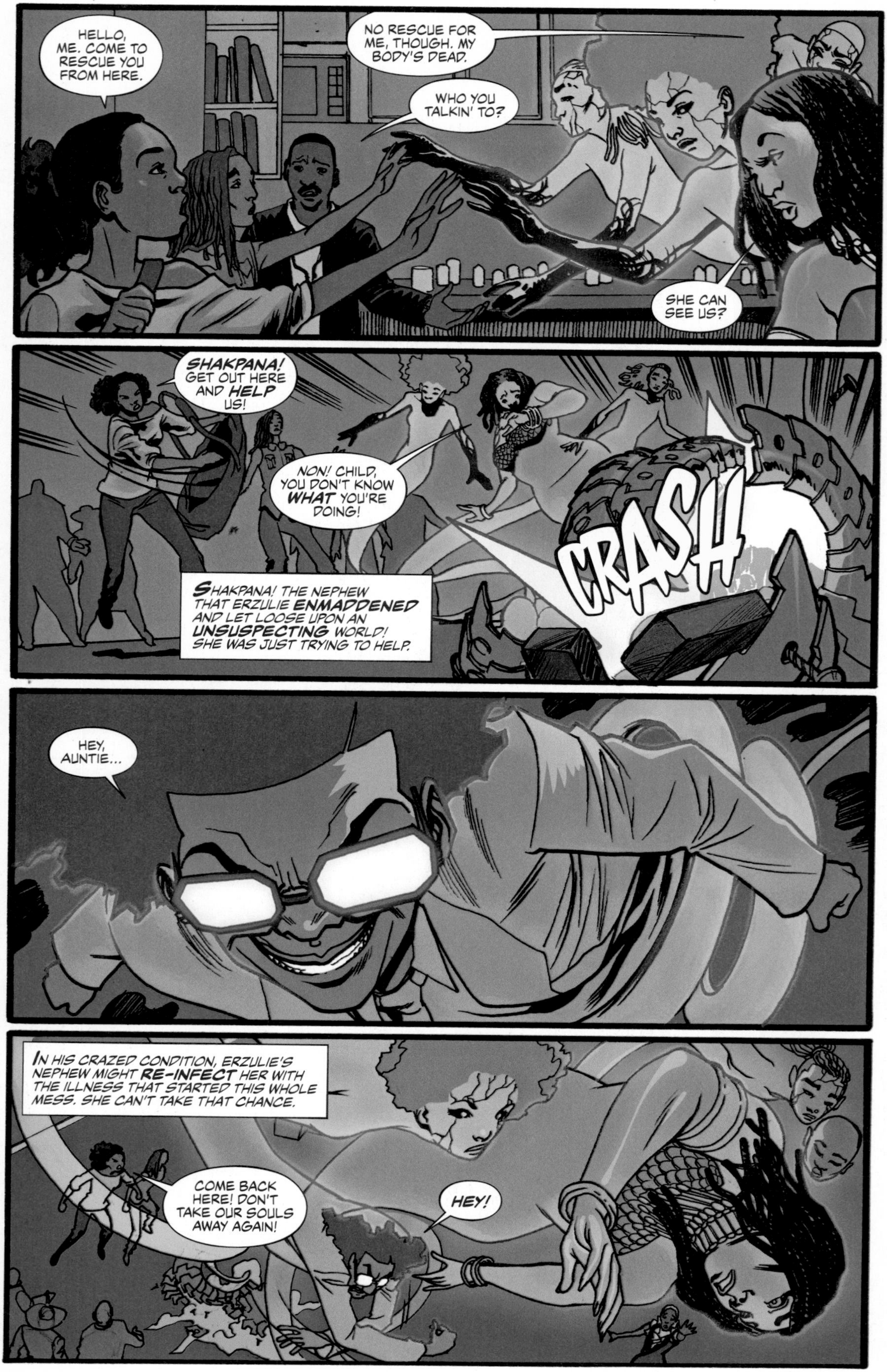
HELLO, ME. COME TO RESCUE YOU FROM HERE.
NO RESCUE FOR ME, THOUGH. MY BODY'S DEAD.
WHO YOU TALKIN' TO?
SHE CAN SEE US?
SHAKPANA! GET OUT HERE AND HELP US!
NON! CHILD, YOU DON'T KNOW WHAT YOU'RE DOING!
CRASH
SHAKPANA! THE NEPHEW THAT ERZULIE ENMADDENED AND LET LOOSE UPON AN UNSUSPECTING WORLD! SHE WAS JUST TRYING TO HELP.
HEY, AUNTIE...
IN HIS CRAZED CONDITION, ERZULIE'S NEPHEW MIGHT RE-INFECT HER WITH THE ILLNESS THAT STARTED THIS WHOLE MESS. SHE CAN'T TAKE THAT CHANCE.
COME BACK HERE! DON'T TAKE OUR SOULS AWAY AGAIN!
HEY!

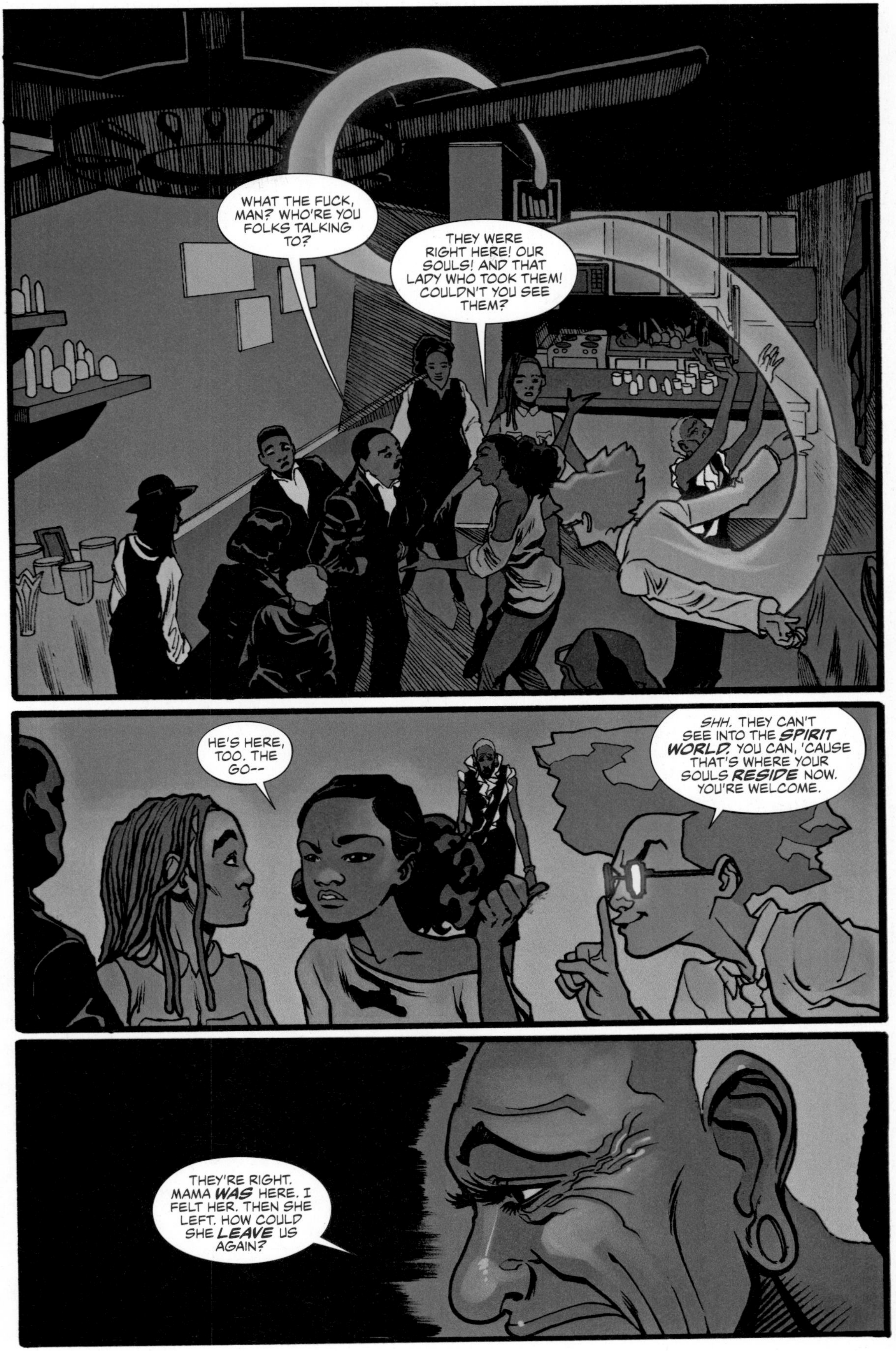
WHAT THE FUCK, MAN? WHO'RE YOU FOLKS TALKING TO?
THEY WERE RIGHT HERE! OUR SOULS! AND THAT LADY WHO TOOK THEM! COULDN'T YOU SEE THEM?
HE'S HERE, TOO. THE GO--
SHH. THEY CAN'T SEE INTO THE SPIRIT WORLD. YOU CAN, 'CAUSE THAT'S WHERE YOUR SOULS RESIDE NOW. YOU'RE WELCOME.
THEY'RE RIGHT. MAMA WAS HERE. I FELT HER. THEN SHE LEFT. HOW COULD SHE LEAVE US AGAIN?

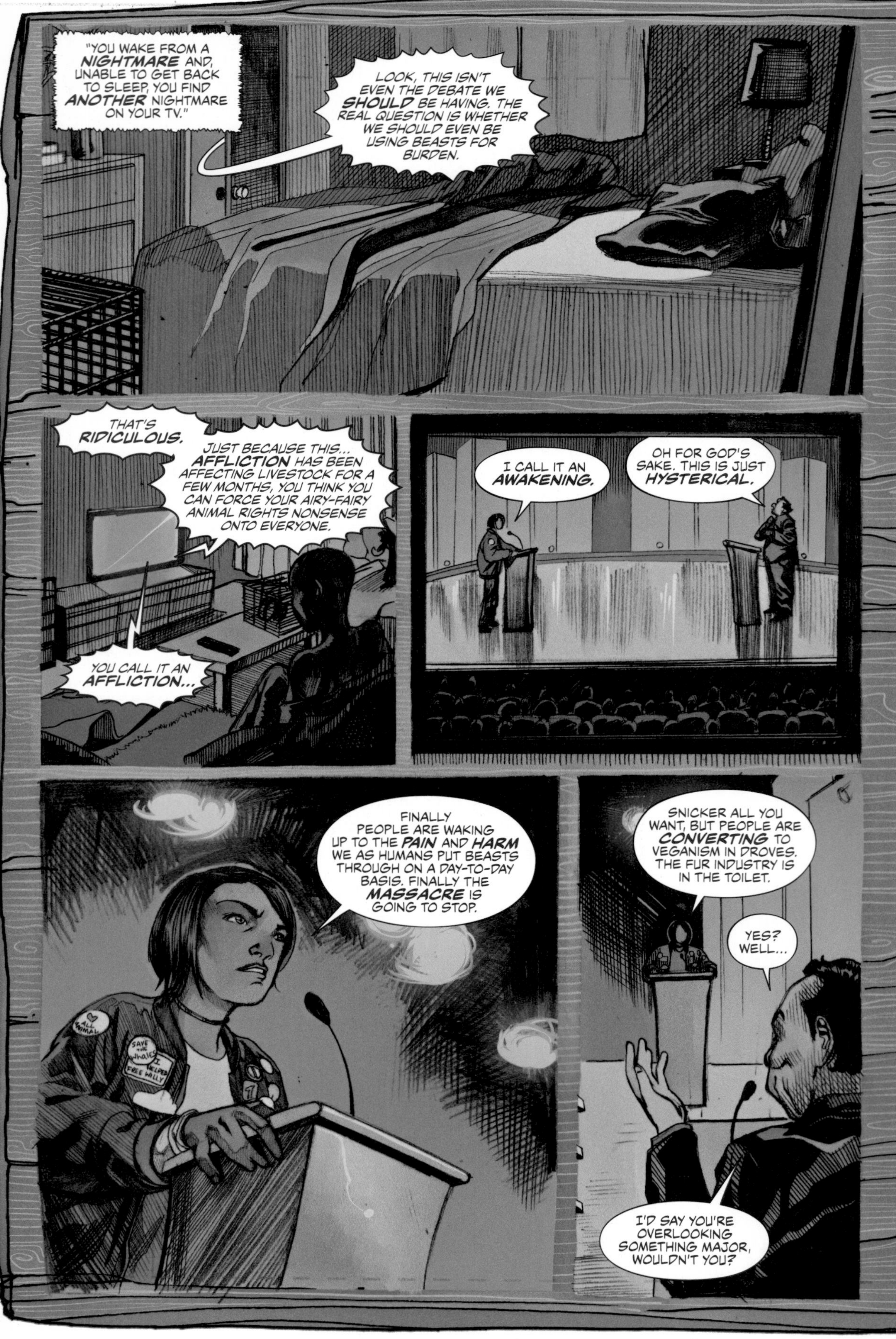
"YOU WAKE FROM A NIGHTMARE AND, UNABLE TO GET BACK TO SLEEP, YOU FIND ANOTHER NIGHTMARE ON YOUR TV."
LOOK, THIS ISN'T EVEN THE DEBATE WE SHOULD BE HAVING. THE REAL QUESTION IS WHETHER WE SHOULD EVEN BE USING BEASTS FOR BURDEN.
THAT'S RIDICULOUS.
JUST BECAUSE THIS... AFFLICTION HAS BEEN AFFECTING LIVESTOCK FOR A FEW MONTHS, YOU THINK YOU CAN FORCE YOUR AIRY-FAIRY ANIMAL RIGHTS NONSENSE ONTO EVERYONE.
YOU CALL IT AN AFFLICTION...
I CALL IT AN AWAKENING.
OH FOR GOD'S SAKE. THIS IS JUST HYSTERICAL.
FINALLY PEOPLE ARE WAKING UP TO THE PAIN AND HARM WE AS HUMANS PUT BEASTS THROUGH ON A DAY-TO-DAY BASIS. FINALLY THE MASSACRE IS GOING TO STOP.
SNICKER ALL YOU WANT, BUT PEOPLE ARE CONVERTING TO VEGANISM IN DROVES. THE FUR INDUSTRY IS IN THE TOILET.
YES? WELL...
I'D SAY YOU'RE OVERLOOKING SOMETHING MAJOR, WOULDN'T YOU?

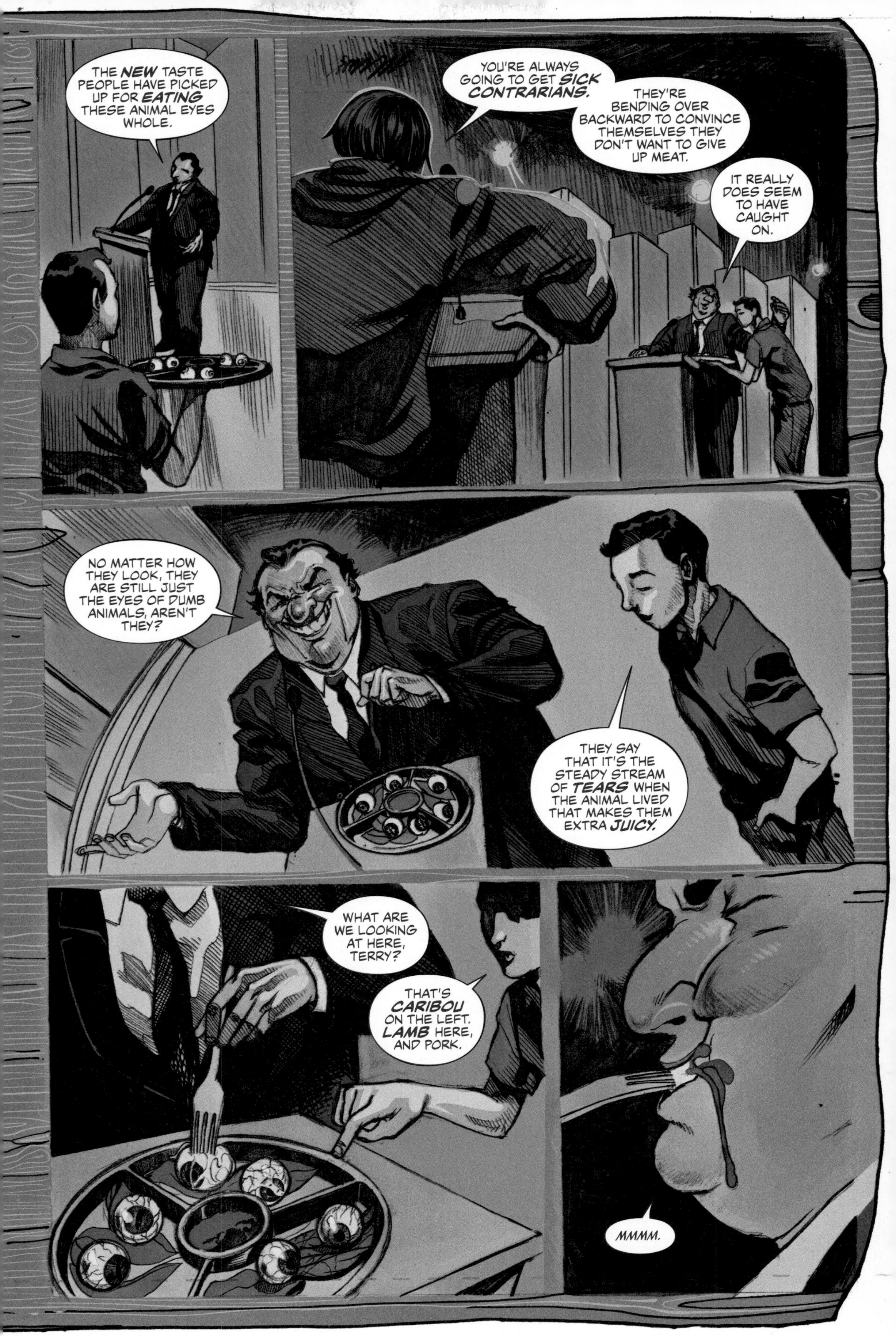
THE NEW TASTE PEOPLE HAVE PICKED UP FOR EATING THESE ANIMAL EYES WHOLE.
YOU'RE ALWAYS GOING TO GET SICK CONTRARIANS.
THEY'RE BENDING OVER BACKWARD TO CONVINCE THEMSELVES THEY DON'T WANT TO GIVE UP MEAT.
IT REALLY DOES SEEM TO HAVE CAUGHT ON.
NO MATTER HOW THEY LOOK, THEY ARE STILL JUST THE EYES OF DUMB ANIMALS, AREN'T THEY?
THEY SAY THAT IT'S THE STEADY STREAM OF TEARS WHEN THE ANIMAL LIVED THAT MAKES THEM EXTRA JUICY.
WHAT ARE WE LOOKING AT HERE, TERRY?
THAT'S CARIBOU ON THE LEFT. LAMB HERE, AND PORK.
MMMM.

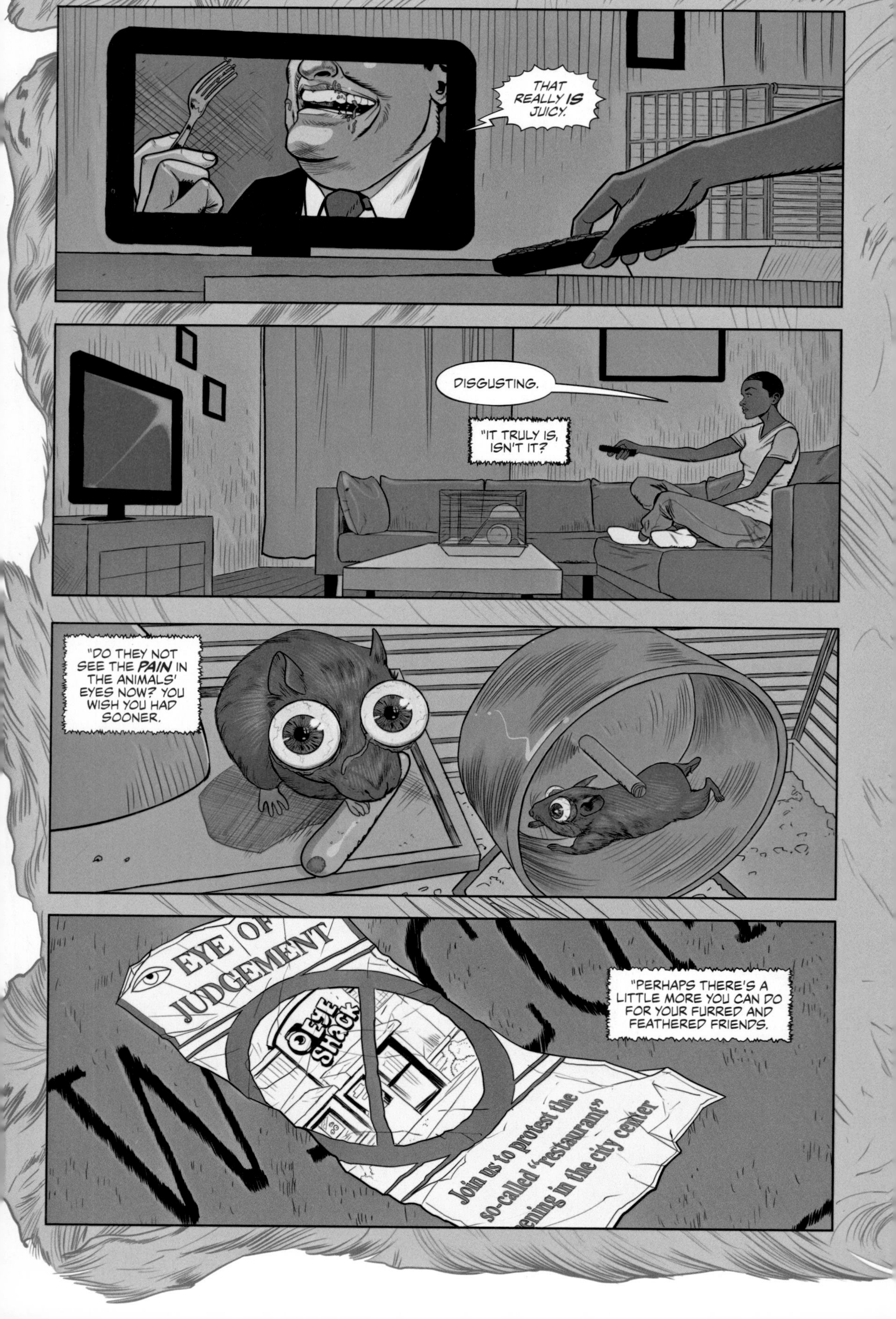
THAT REALLY IS JUICY.
DISGUSTING.
"IT TRULY IS, ISN'T IT?
"DO THEY NOT SEE THE PAIN IN THE ANIMALS' EYES NOW? YOU WISH YOU HAD SOONER.
EYE OF JUDGEMENT
EYE SHACK
Join us to protest the so-called "restaurant" ening in the city center
"PERHAPS THERE'S A LITTLE MORE YOU CAN DO FOR YOUR FURRED AND FEATHERED FRIENDS.

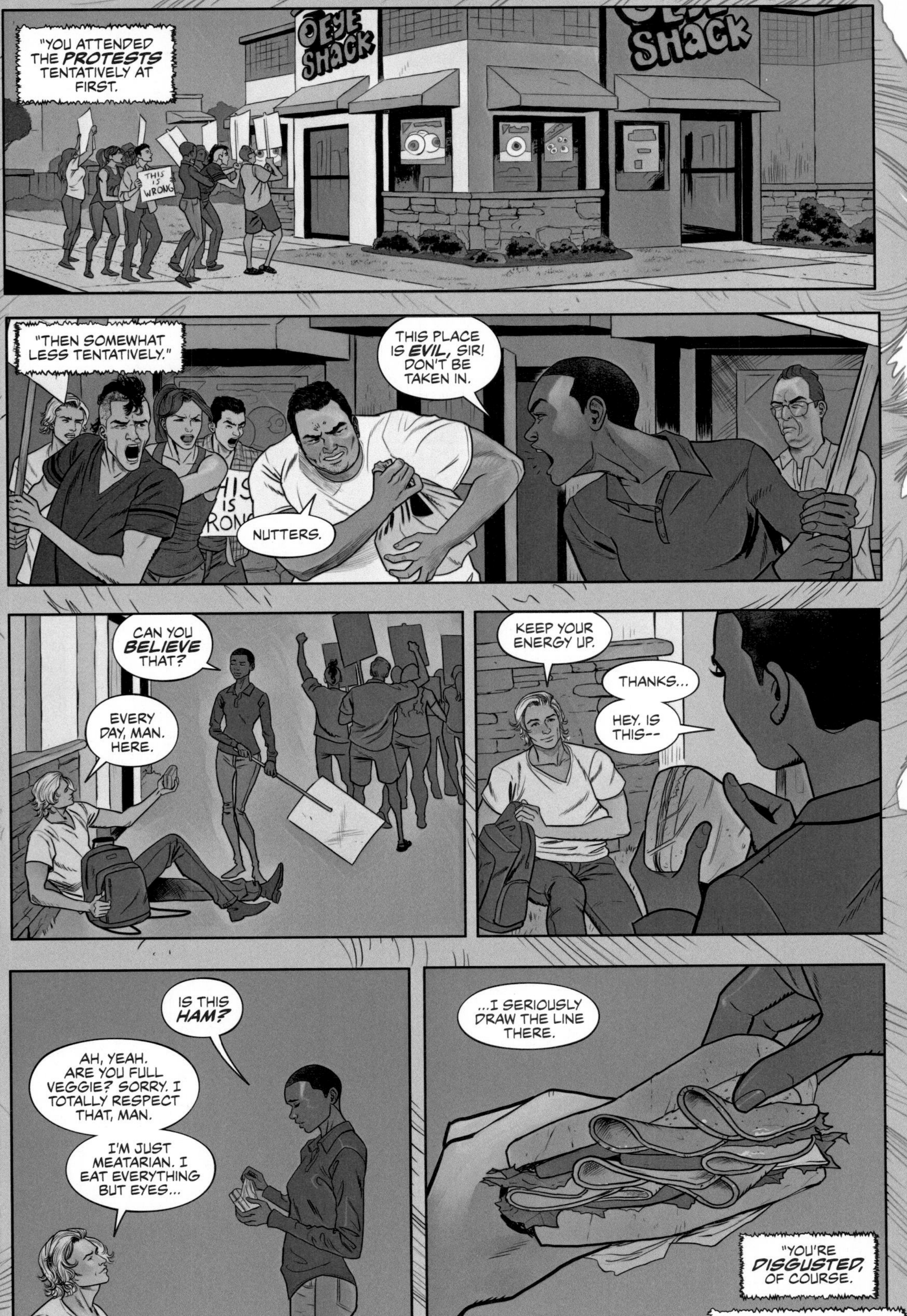
"YOU ATTENDED THE *PROTESTS* TENTATIVELY AT FIRST.
THIS IS WRONG
"THEN SOMEWHAT LESS TENTATIVELY."
THIS PLACE IS *EVIL*, SIR! DON'T BE TAKEN IN.
NUTTERS.
CAN YOU *BELIEVE* THAT?
EVERY DAY, MAN. HERE.
KEEP YOUR ENERGY UP.
THANKS...
HEY. IS THIS--
IS THIS *HAM?*
AH, YEAH. ARE YOU FULL VEGGIE? SORRY. I TOTALLY RESPECT THAT, MAN.
I'M JUST MEATARIAN. I EAT EVERYTHING BUT EYES...
...I SERIOUSLY DRAW THE LINE THERE.
"YOU'RE *DISGUSTED*, OF COURSE.
"HOW CAN EVEN THOSE ON YOUR SIDE SO LACK YOUR CONVICTION?"

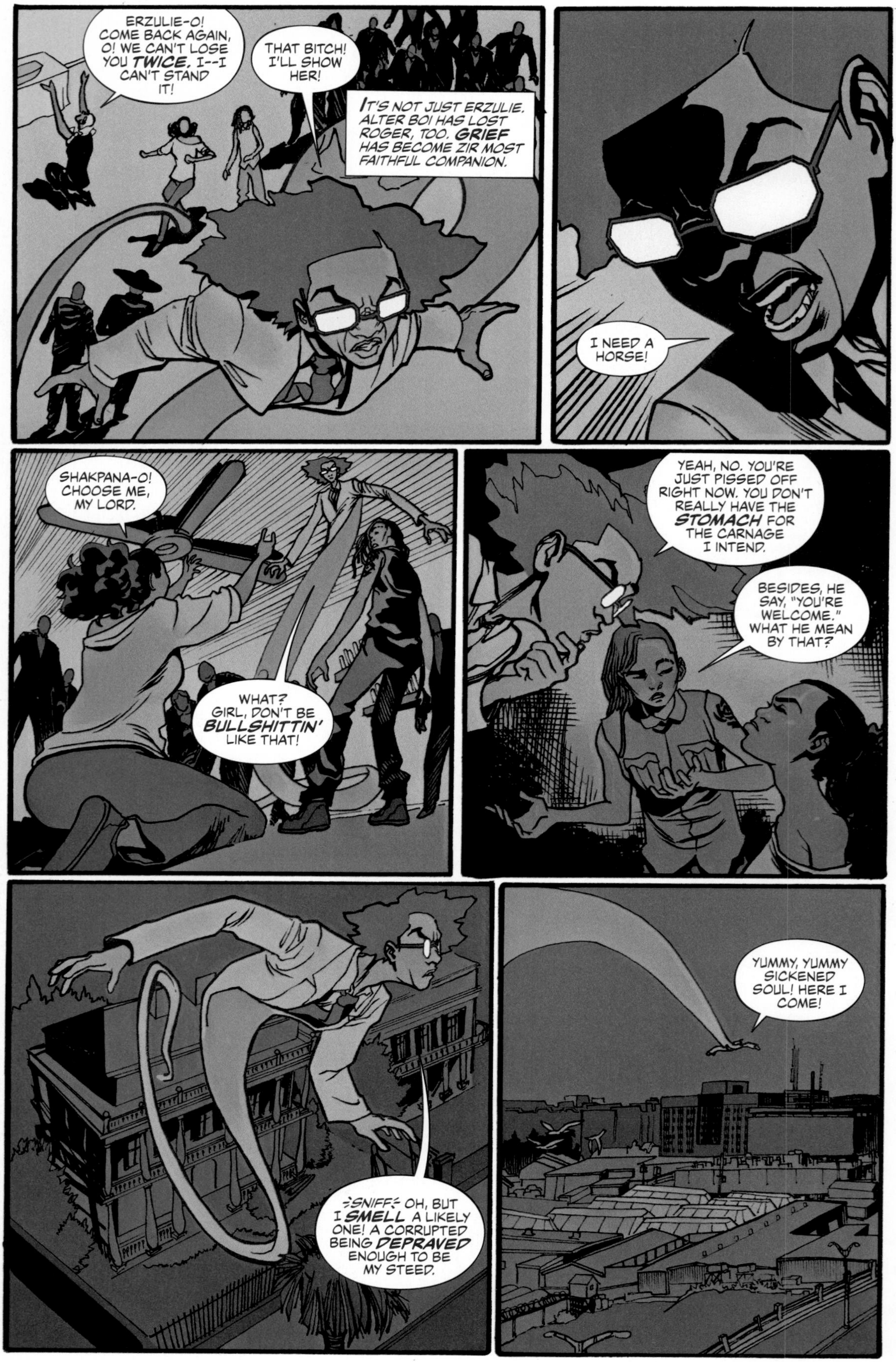
ERZULIE-O! COME BACK AGAIN, O! WE CAN'T LOSE YOU TWICE. I--I CAN'T STAND IT!
THAT BITCH! I'LL SHOW HER!
IT'S NOT JUST ERZULIE. ALTER BOI HAS LOST ROGER, TOO. GRIEF HAS BECOME ZIR MOST FAITHFUL COMPANION.
I NEED A HORSE!
SHAKPANA-O! CHOOSE ME, MY LORD.
WHAT? GIRL, DON'T BE BULLSHITTIN' LIKE THAT!
YEAH, NO. YOU'RE JUST PISSED OFF RIGHT NOW. YOU DON'T REALLY HAVE THE STOMACH FOR THE CARNAGE I INTEND.
BESIDES, HE SAY, "YOU'RE WELCOME." WHAT HE MEAN BY THAT?
SNIFF OH, BUT I SMELL A LIKELY ONE! A CORRUPTED BEING DEPRAVED ENOUGH TO BE MY STEED.
YUMMY, YUMMY SICKENED SOUL! HERE I COME!

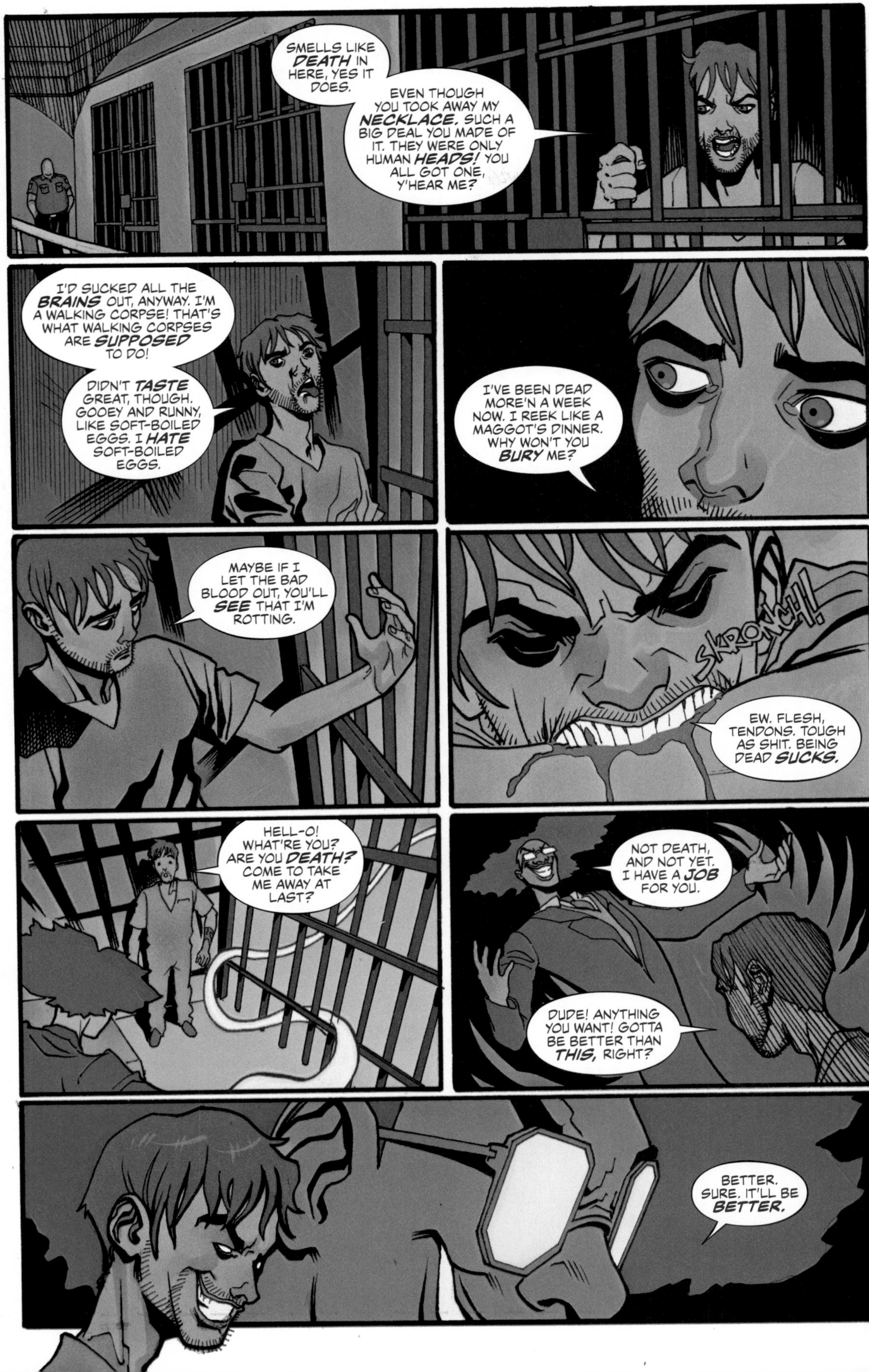
SMELLS LIKE DEATH IN HERE, YES IT DOES.
EVEN THOUGH YOU TOOK AWAY MY NECKLACE. SUCH A BIG DEAL YOU MADE OF IT. THEY WERE ONLY HUMAN HEADS! YOU ALL GOT ONE, Y'HEAR ME?
I'D SUCKED ALL THE BRAINS OUT, ANYWAY. I'M A WALKING CORPSE! THAT'S WHAT WALKING CORPSES ARE SUPPOSED TO DO!
DIDN'T TASTE GREAT, THOUGH. GOOEY AND RUNNY, LIKE SOFT-BOILED EGGS. I HATE SOFT-BOILED EGGS.
I'VE BEEN DEAD MORE'N A WEEK NOW. I REEK LIKE A MAGGOT'S DINNER. WHY WON'T YOU BURY ME?
MAYBE IF I LET THE BAD BLOOD OUT, YOU'LL SEE THAT I'M ROTTING.
SKRONCH!
EW. FLESH, TENDONS. TOUGH AS SHIT. BEING DEAD SUCKS.
HELL-O! WHAT'RE YOU? ARE YOU DEATH? COME TO TAKE ME AWAY AT LAST?
NOT DEATH, AND NOT YET. I HAVE A JOB FOR YOU.
DUDE! ANYTHING YOU WANT! GOTTA BE BETTER THAN THIS, RIGHT?
BETTER. SURE. IT'LL BE BETTER.

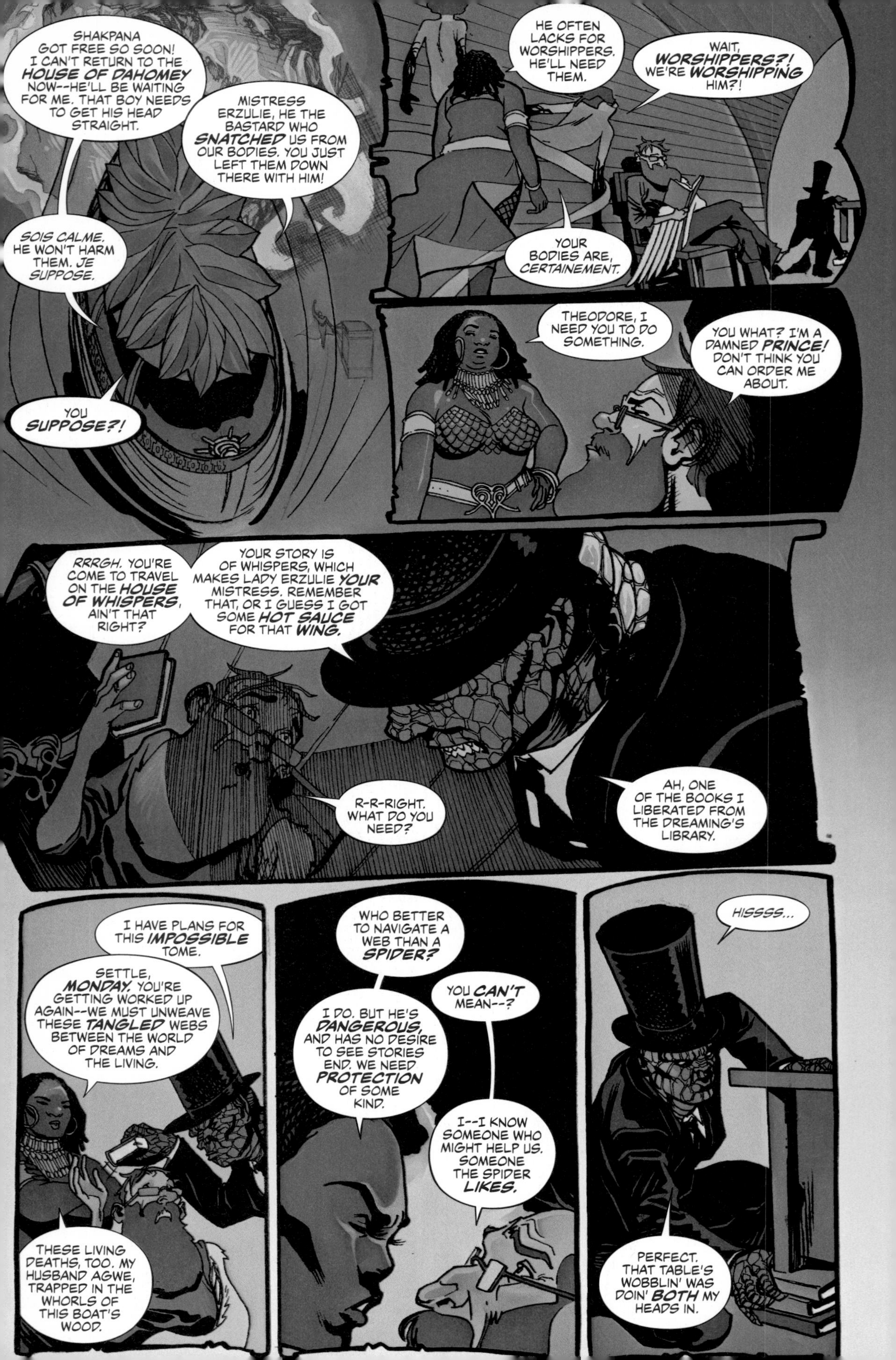
SHAKPANA GOT FREE SO SOON! I CAN'T RETURN TO THE HOUSE OF DAHOMEY NOW--HE'LL BE WAITING FOR ME. THAT BOY NEEDS TO GET HIS HEAD STRAIGHT.
MISTRESS ERZULIE, HE THE BASTARD WHO SNATCHED US FROM OUR BODIES. YOU JUST LEFT THEM DOWN THERE WITH HIM!
SOIS CALME. HE WON'T HARM THEM. JE SUPPOSE.
YOU SUPPOSE?!
HE OFTEN LACKS FOR WORSHIPPERS. HE'LL NEED THEM.
WAIT, WORSHIPPERS?! WE'RE WORSHIPPING HIM?!
YOUR BODIES ARE, CERTAINEMENT.
THEODORE, I NEED YOU TO DO SOMETHING.
YOU WHAT? I'M A DAMNED PRINCE! DON'T THINK YOU CAN ORDER ME ABOUT.
RRRGH. YOU'RE COME TO TRAVEL ON THE HOUSE OF WHISPERS, AIN'T THAT RIGHT?
YOUR STORY IS OF WHISPERS, WHICH MAKES LADY ERZULIE YOUR MISTRESS. REMEMBER THAT, OR I GUESS I GOT SOME HOT SAUCE FOR THAT WING.
R-R-RIGHT. WHAT DO YOU NEED?
AH, ONE OF THE BOOKS I LIBERATED FROM THE DREAMING'S LIBRARY.
I HAVE PLANS FOR THIS IMPOSSIBLE TOME.
SETTLE, MONDAY. YOU'RE GETTING WORKED UP AGAIN--WE MUST UNWEAVE THESE TANGLED WEBS BETWEEN THE WORLD OF DREAMS AND THE LIVING.
THESE LIVING DEATHS, TOO. MY HUSBAND AGWE, TRAPPED IN THE WHORLS OF THIS BOAT'S WOOD.
WHO BETTER TO NAVIGATE A WEB THAN A SPIDER?
YOU CAN'T MEAN--?
I DO. BUT HE'S DANGEROUS, AND HAS NO DESIRE TO SEE STORIES END. WE NEED PROTECTION OF SOME KIND.
I--I KNOW SOMEONE WHO MIGHT HELP US. SOMEONE THE SPIDER LIKES.
HISSSS...
PERFECT. THAT TABLE'S WOBBLIN' WAS DOIN' BOTH MY HEADS IN.

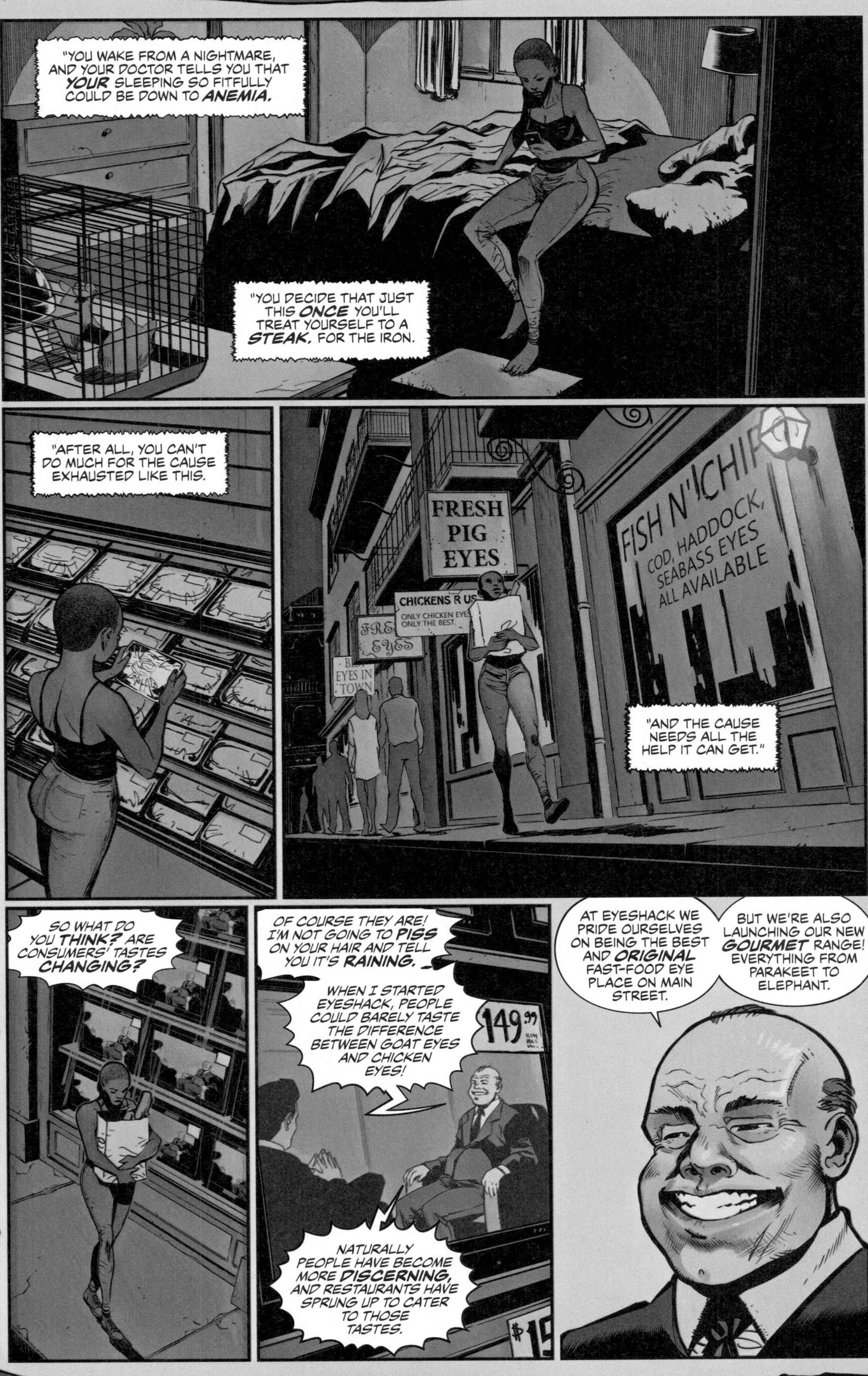
"YOU WAKE FROM A NIGHTMARE, AND YOUR DOCTOR TELLS YOU THAT YOUR SLEEPING SO FITFULLY COULD BE DOWN TO ANEMIA.
"YOU DECIDE THAT JUST THIS ONCE YOU'LL TREAT YOURSELF TO A STEAK. FOR THE IRON.
"AFTER ALL, YOU CAN'T DO MUCH FOR THE CAUSE EXHAUSTED LIKE THIS.
FRESH PIG EYES
CHICKENS R US
ONLY CHICKEN EYES ONLY THE BEST.
FISH N' CHIP
COD, HADDOCK, SEABASS EYES ALL AVAILABLE
"AND THE CAUSE NEEDS ALL THE HELP IT CAN GET."
SO WHAT DO YOU THINK? ARE CONSUMERS' TASTES CHANGING?
OF COURSE THEY ARE! I'M NOT GOING TO PISS ON YOUR HAIR AND TELL YOU IT'S RAINING.
WHEN I STARTED EYESHACK, PEOPLE COULD BARELY TASTE THE DIFFERENCE BETWEEN GOAT EYES AND CHICKEN EYES!
149.99
NATURALLY PEOPLE HAVE BECOME MORE DISCERNING, AND RESTAURANTS HAVE SPRUNG UP TO CATER TO THOSE TASTES.
AT EYESHACK WE PRIDE OURSELVES ON BEING THE BEST AND ORIGINAL FAST-FOOD EYE PLACE ON MAIN STREET.
BUT WE'RE ALSO LAUNCHING OUR NEW GOURMET RANGE! EVERYTHING FROM PARAKEET TO ELEPHANT.

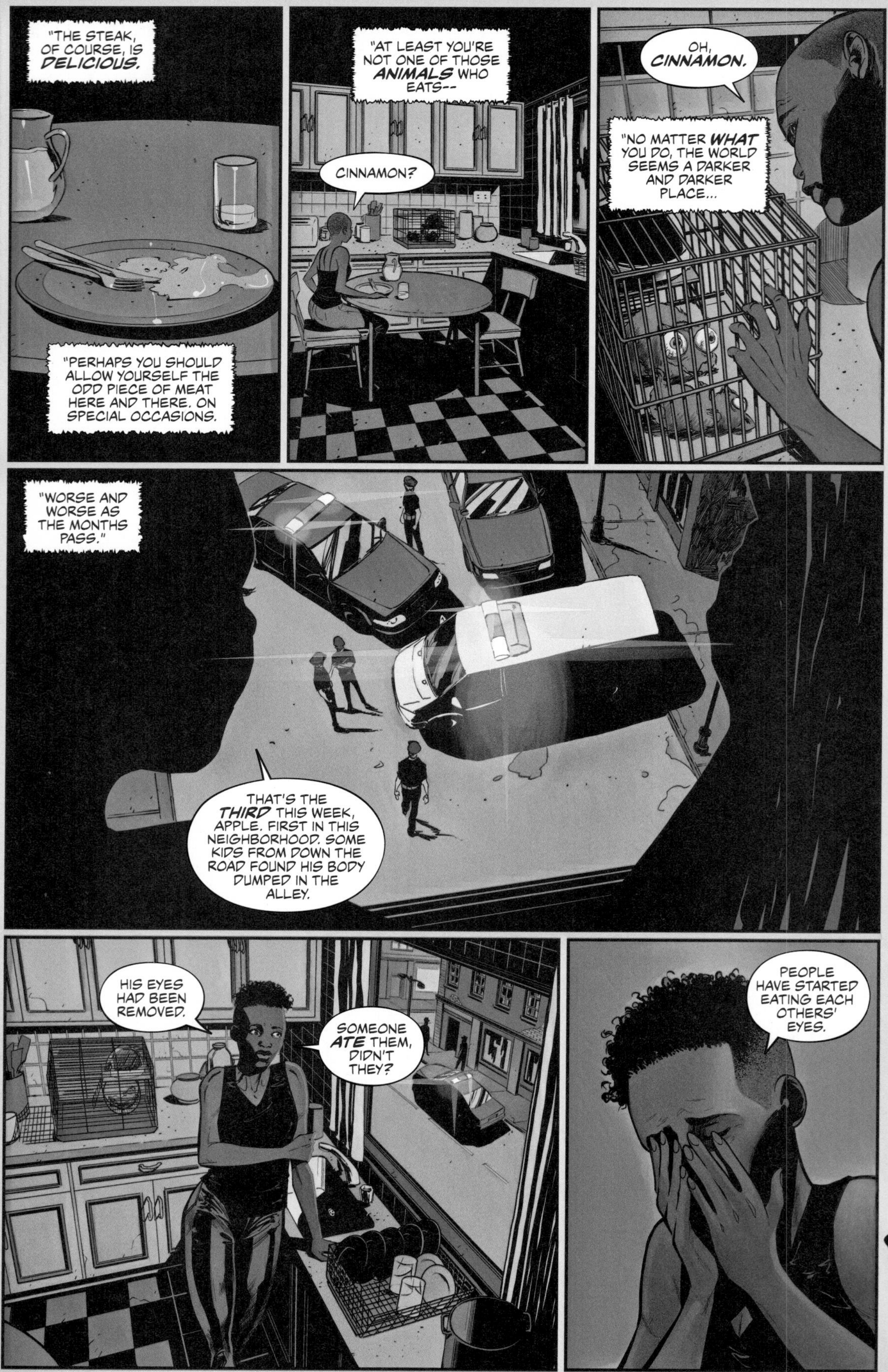
"THE STEAK, OF COURSE, IS DELICIOUS.
"PERHAPS YOU SHOULD ALLOW YOURSELF THE ODD PIECE OF MEAT HERE AND THERE. ON SPECIAL OCCASIONS.
"AT LEAST YOU'RE NOT ONE OF THOSE ANIMALS WHO EATS--
CINNAMON?
OH, CINNAMON.
"NO MATTER WHAT YOU DO, THE WORLD SEEMS A DARKER AND DARKER PLACE...
"WORSE AND WORSE AS THE MONTHS PASS."
THAT'S THE THIRD THIS WEEK, APPLE. FIRST IN THIS NEIGHBORHOOD. SOME KIDS FROM DOWN THE ROAD FOUND HIS BODY DUMPED IN THE ALLEY.
HIS EYES HAD BEEN REMOVED.
SOMEONE ATE THEM, DIDN'T THEY?
PEOPLE HAVE STARTED EATING EACH OTHERS' EYES.

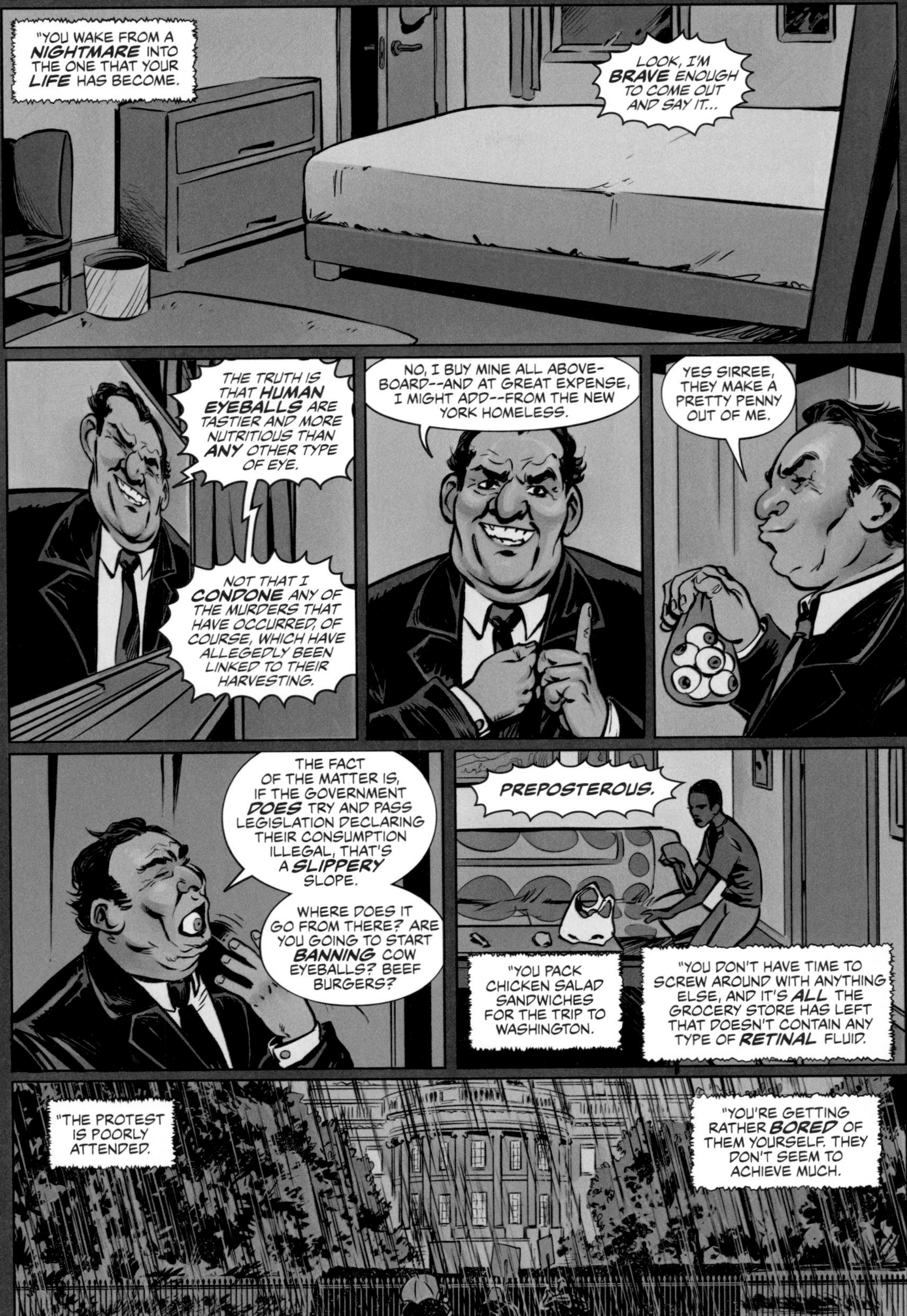
"YOU WAKE FROM A NIGHTMARE INTO THE ONE THAT YOUR LIFE HAS BECOME.
LOOK, I'M BRAVE ENOUGH TO COME OUT AND SAY IT...
THE TRUTH IS THAT HUMAN EYEBALLS ARE TASTIER AND MORE NUTRITIOUS THAN ANY OTHER TYPE OF EYE.
NOT THAT I CONDONE ANY OF THE MURDERS THAT HAVE OCCURRED, OF COURSE, WHICH HAVE ALLEGEDLY BEEN LINKED TO THEIR HARVESTING.
NO, I BUY MINE ALL ABOVE-BOARD--AND AT GREAT EXPENSE, I MIGHT ADD--FROM THE NEW YORK HOMELESS.
YES SIRREE, THEY MAKE A PRETTY PENNY OUT OF ME.
THE FACT OF THE MATTER IS, IF THE GOVERNMENT DOES TRY AND PASS LEGISLATION DECLARING THEIR CONSUMPTION ILLEGAL, THAT'S A SLIPPERY SLOPE.
WHERE DOES IT GO FROM THERE? ARE YOU GOING TO START BANNING COW EYEBALLS? BEEF BURGERS?
PREPOSTEROUS.
"YOU PACK CHICKEN SALAD SANDWICHES FOR THE TRIP TO WASHINGTON.
"YOU DON'T HAVE TIME TO SCREW AROUND WITH ANYTHING ELSE, AND IT'S ALL THE GROCERY STORE HAS LEFT THAT DOESN'T CONTAIN ANY TYPE OF RETINAL FLUID.
"THE PROTEST IS POORLY ATTENDED.
"YOU'RE GETTING RATHER BORED OF THEM YOURSELF. THEY DON'T SEEM TO ACHIEVE MUCH.

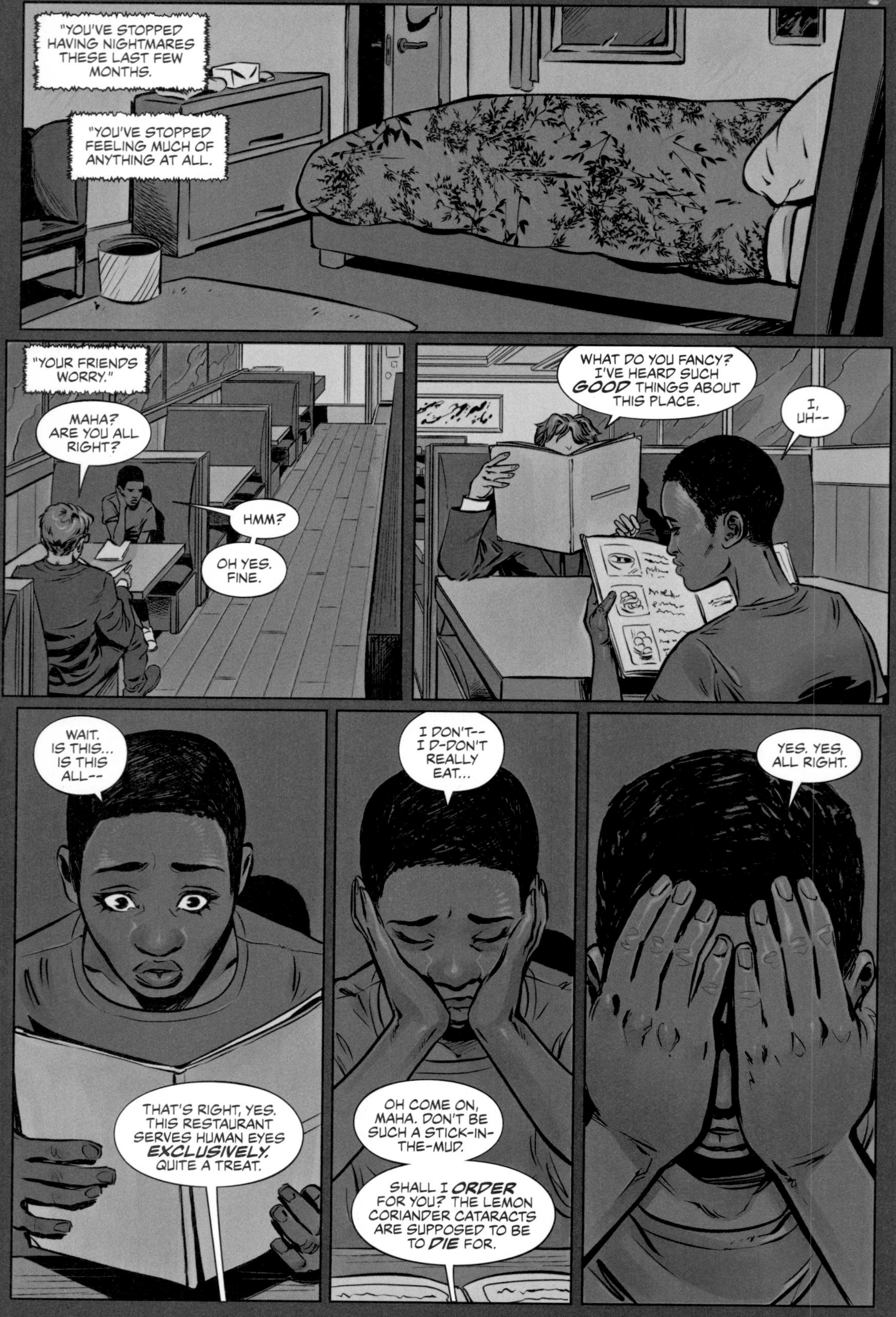
"YOU'VE STOPPED HAVING NIGHTMARES THESE LAST FEW MONTHS.
"YOU'VE STOPPED FEELING MUCH OF ANYTHING AT ALL.
"YOUR FRIENDS WORRY."
MAHA? ARE YOU ALL RIGHT?
HMM?
OH YES. FINE.
WHAT DO YOU FANCY? I'VE HEARD SUCH GOOD THINGS ABOUT THIS PLACE.
I, UH--
WAIT. IS THIS... IS THIS ALL--
THAT'S RIGHT, YES. THIS RESTAURANT SERVES HUMAN EYES EXCLUSIVELY. QUITE A TREAT.
I DON'T-- I D-DON'T REALLY EAT...
OH COME ON, MAHA. DON'T BE SUCH A STICK-IN-THE-MUD.
SHALL I ORDER FOR YOU? THE LEMON CORIANDER CATARACTS ARE SUPPOSED TO BE TO DIE FOR.
YES. YES, ALL RIGHT.

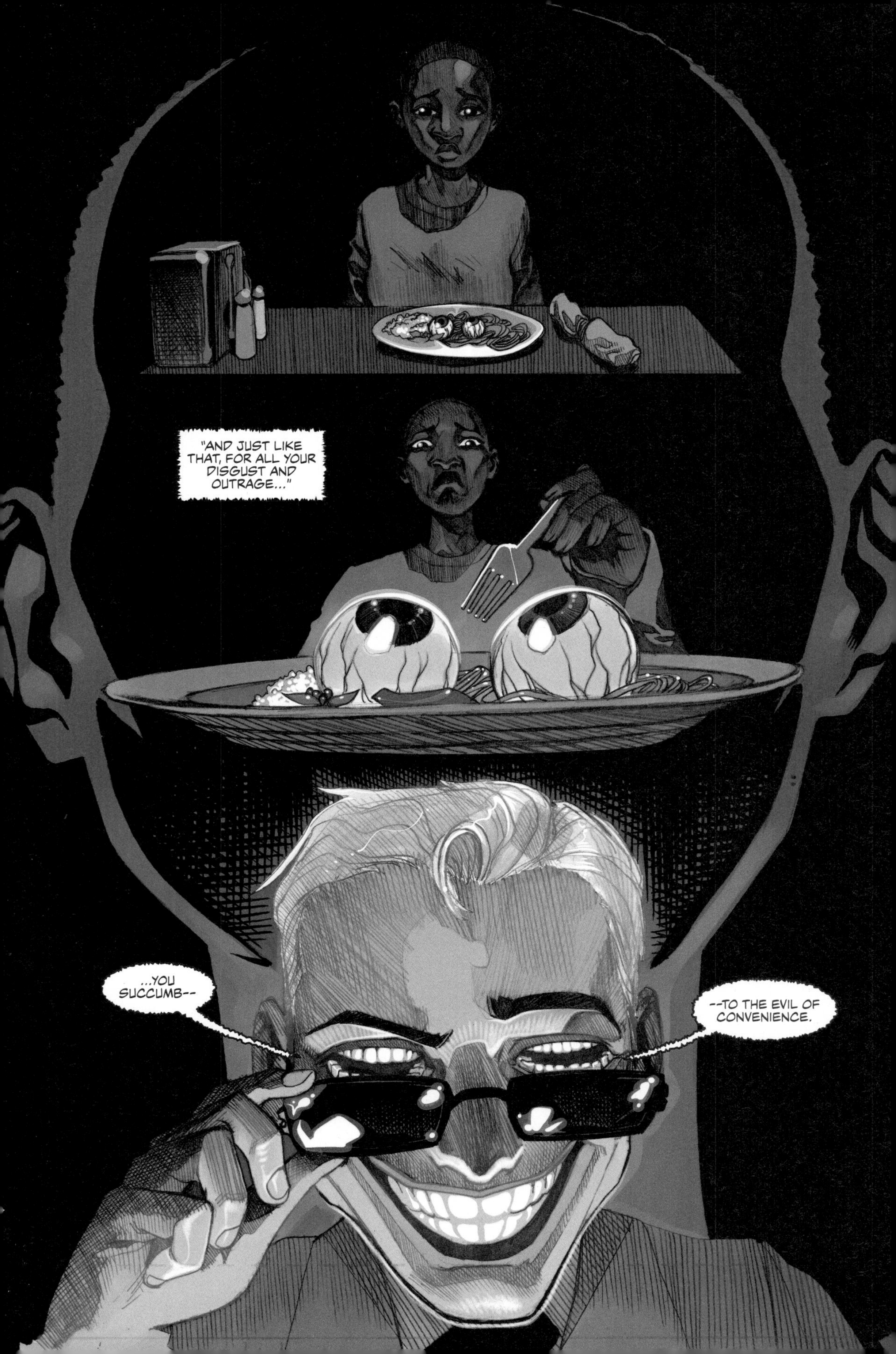
"AND JUST LIKE THAT, FOR ALL YOUR DISGUST AND OUTRAGE..."
...YOU SUCCUMB--
--TO THE EVIL OF CONVENIENCE.

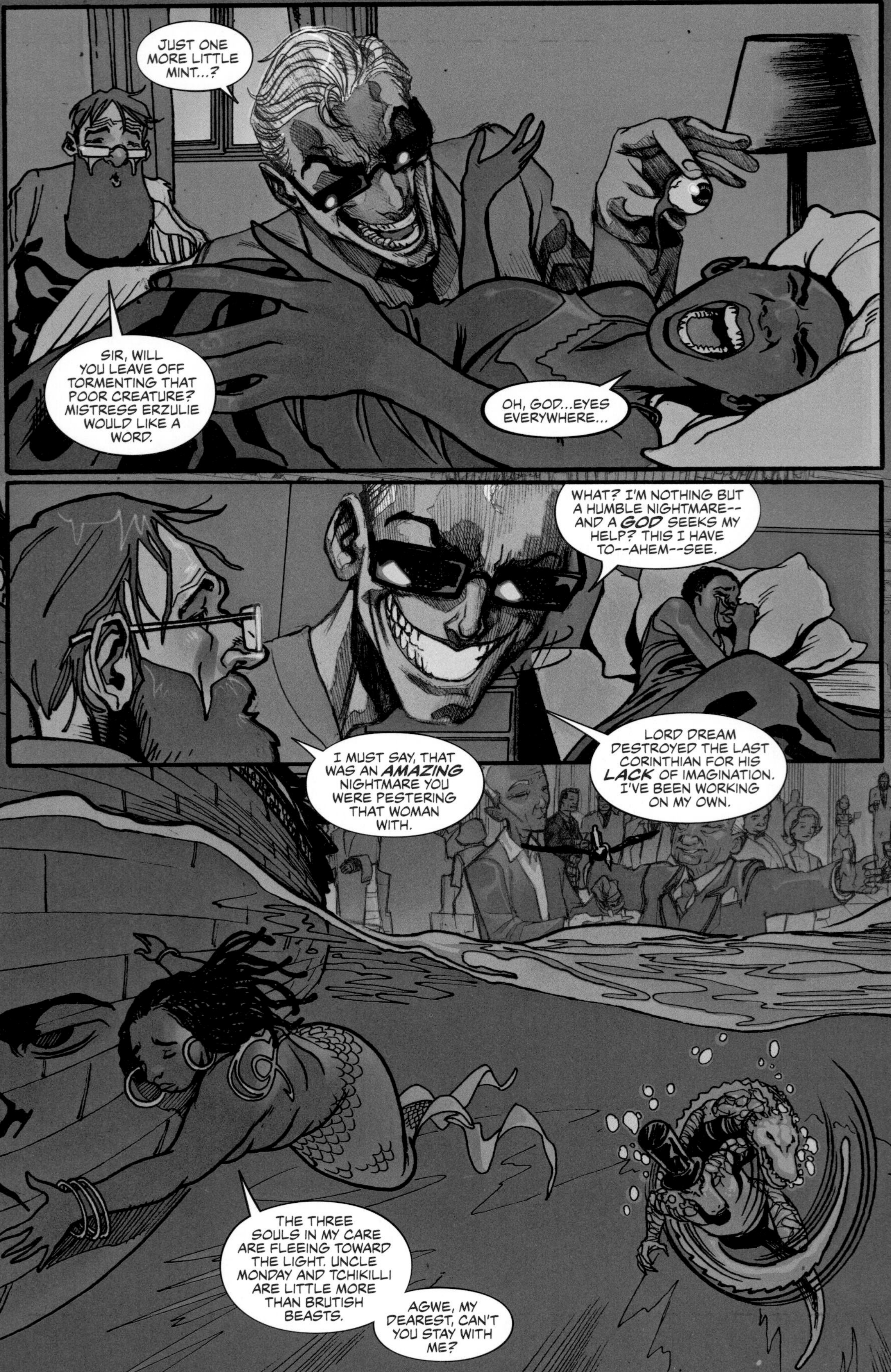
JUST ONE MORE LITTLE MINT...?
SIR, WILL YOU LEAVE OFF TORMENTING THAT POOR CREATURE? MISTRESS ERZULIE WOULD LIKE A WORD.
OH, GOD...EYES EVERYWHERE...
WHAT? I'M NOTHING BUT A HUMBLE NIGHTMARE--AND A GOD SEEKS MY HELP? THIS I HAVE TO--AHEM--SEE.
I MUST SAY, THAT WAS AN AMAZING NIGHTMARE YOU WERE PESTERING THAT WOMAN WITH.
LORD DREAM DESTROYED THE LAST CORINTHIAN FOR HIS LACK OF IMAGINATION. I'VE BEEN WORKING ON MY OWN.
THE THREE SOULS IN MY CARE ARE FLEEING TOWARD THE LIGHT. UNCLE MONDAY AND TCHIKILLI ARE LITTLE MORE THAN BRUTISH BEASTS.
AGWE, MY DEAREST, CAN'T YOU STAY WITH ME?

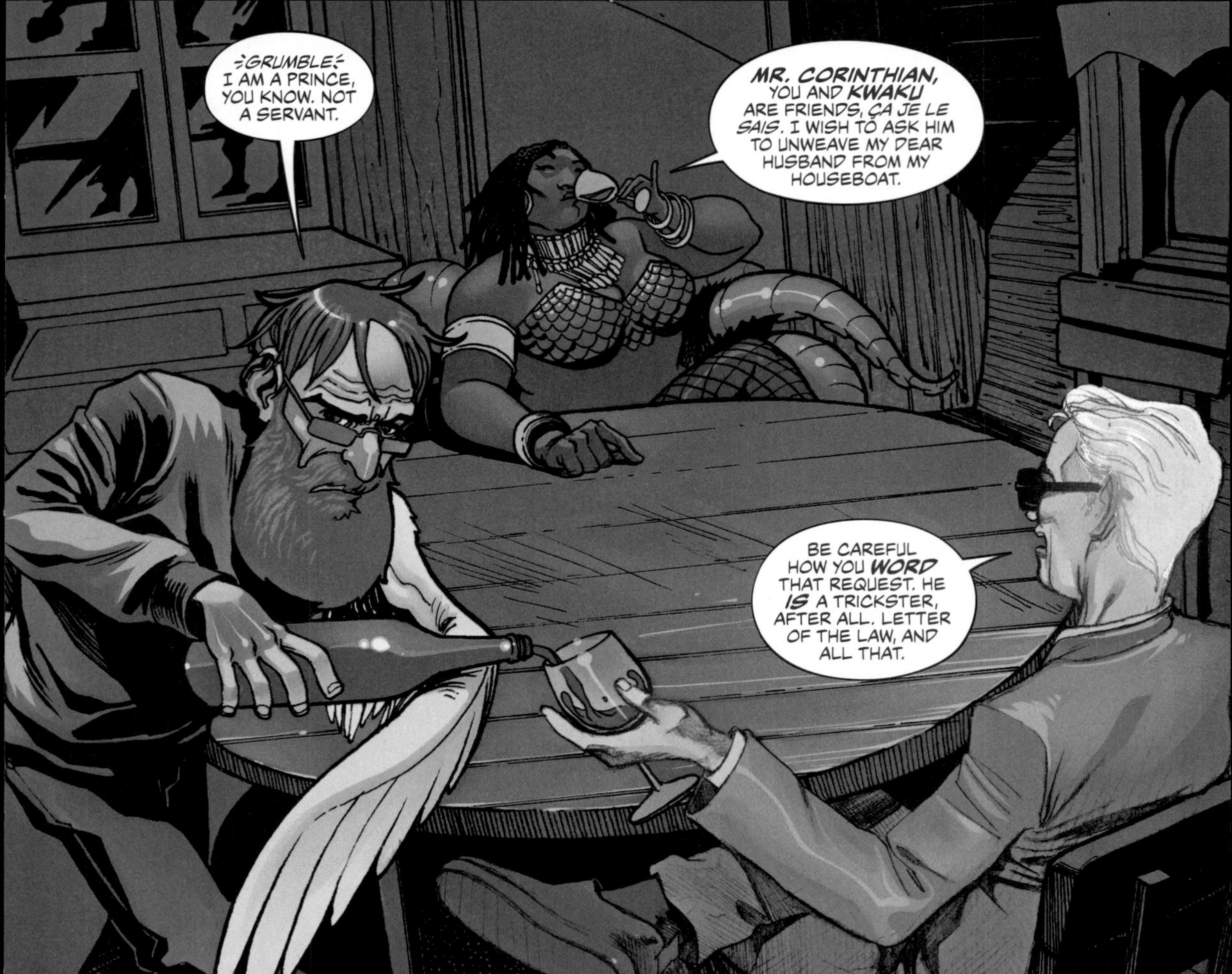
GRUMBLE
I AM A PRINCE, YOU KNOW. NOT A SERVANT.
MR. CORINTHIAN, YOU AND KWAKU ARE FRIENDS, ÇA JE LE SAIS. I WISH TO ASK HIM TO UNWEAVE MY DEAR HUSBAND FROM MY HOUSEBOAT.
BE CAREFUL HOW YOU WORD THAT REQUEST. HE IS A TRICKSTER, AFTER ALL. LETTER OF THE LAW, AND ALL THAT.

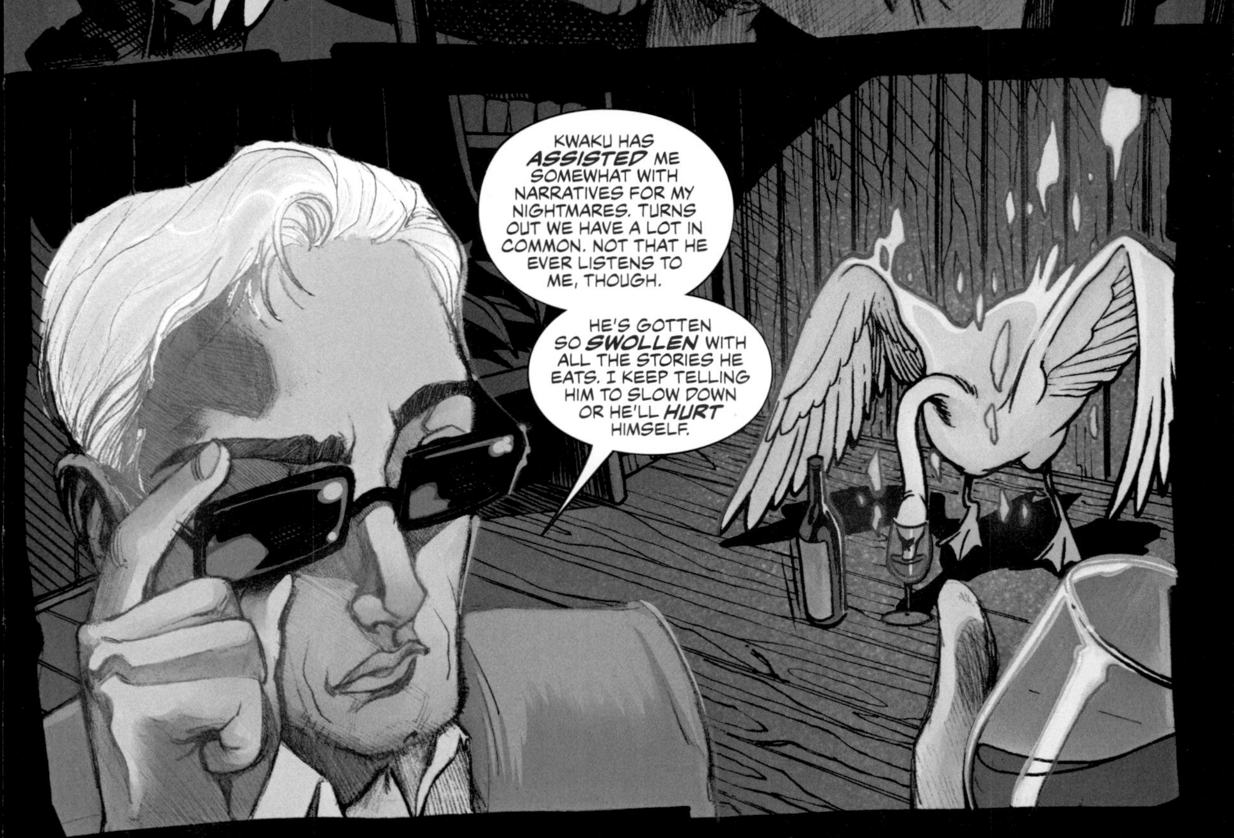
KWAKU HAS ASSISTED ME SOMEWHAT WITH NARRATIVES FOR MY NIGHTMARES. TURNS OUT WE HAVE A LOT IN COMMON. NOT THAT HE EVER LISTENS TO ME, THOUGH.
HE'S GOTTEN SO SWOLLEN WITH ALL THE STORIES HE EATS. I KEEP TELLING HIM TO SLOW DOWN OR HE'LL HURT HIMSELF.

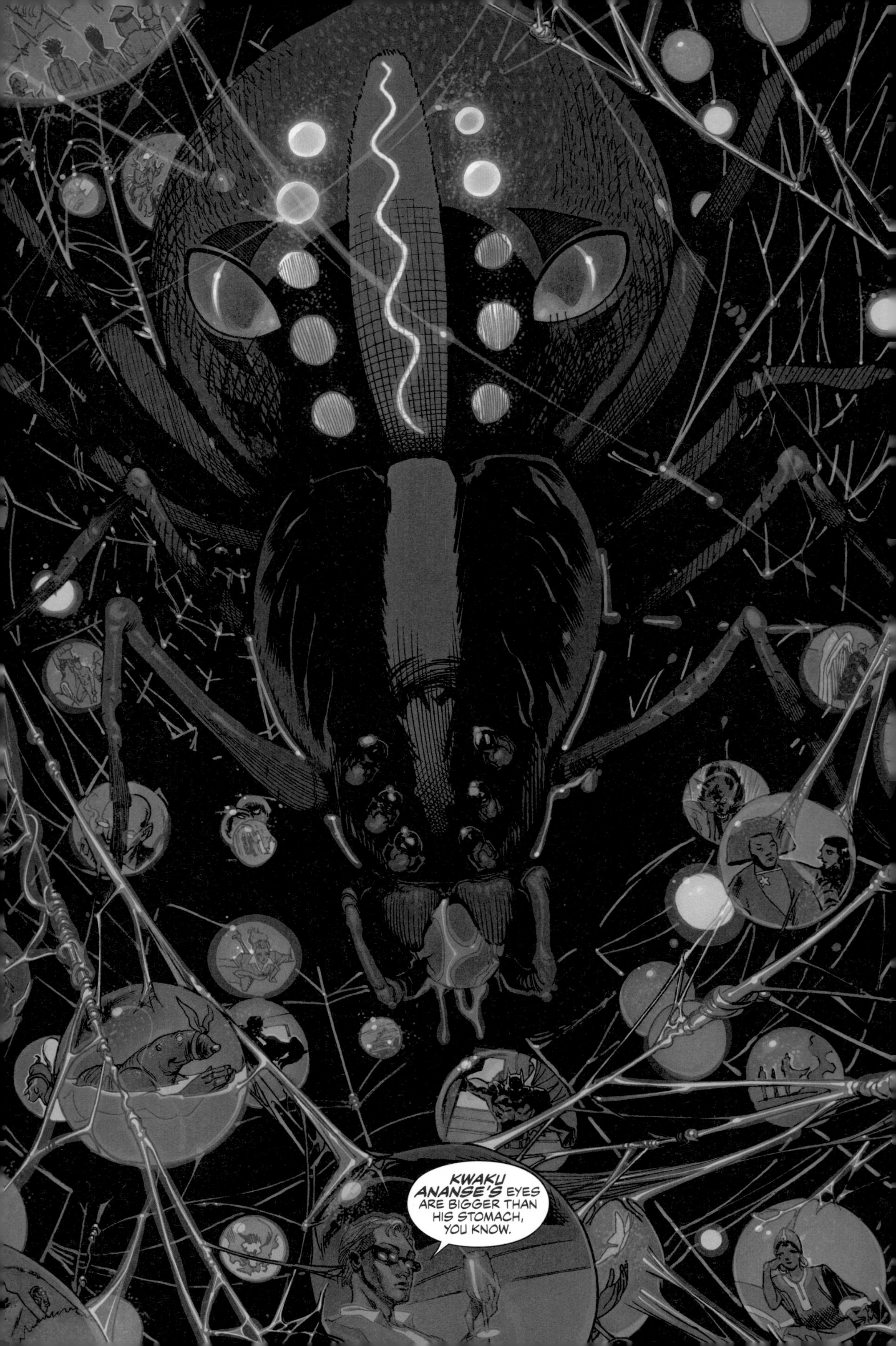
KWAKU ANANSE'S EYES ARE BIGGER THAN HIS STOMACH, YOU KNOW.

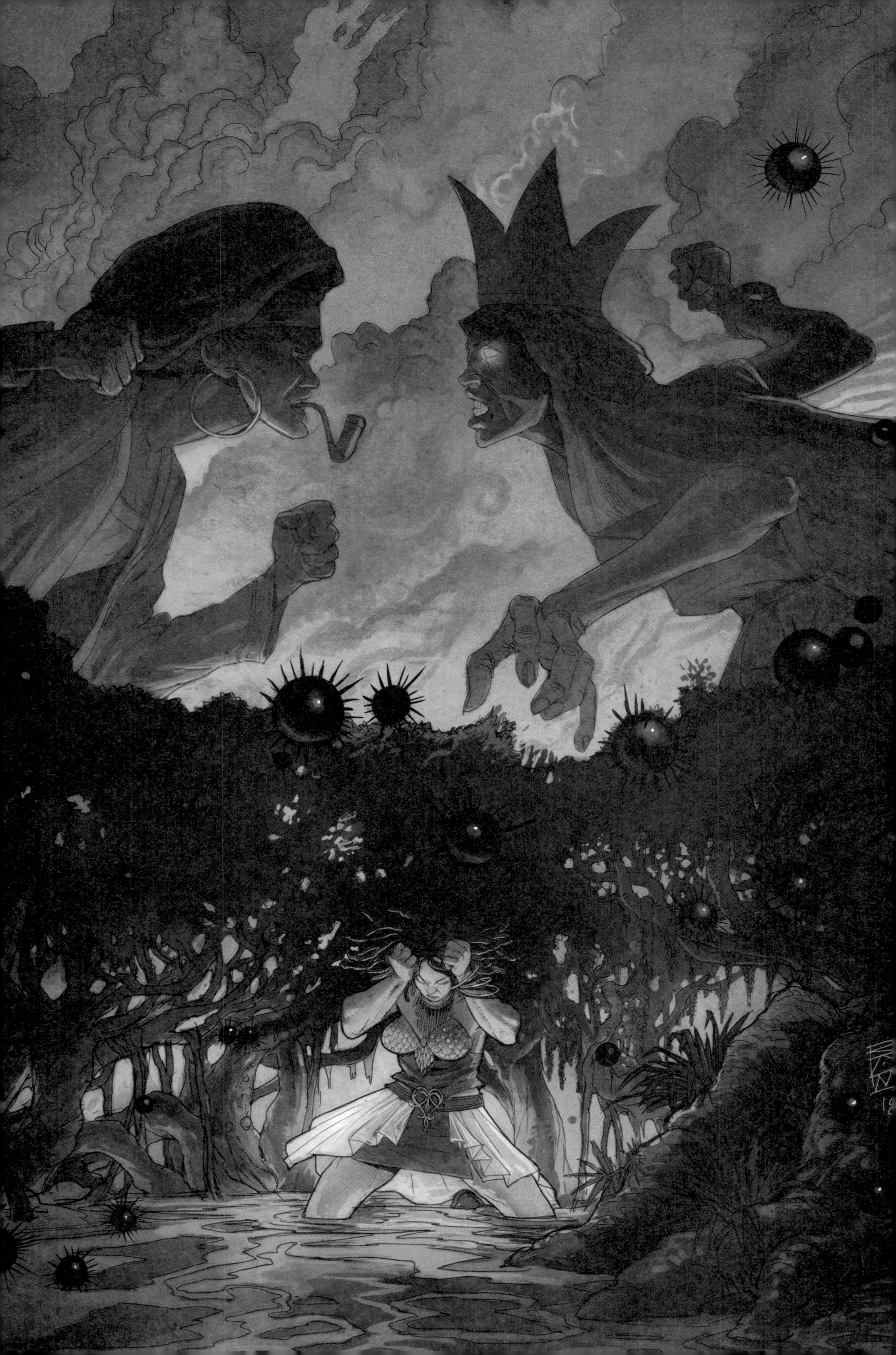

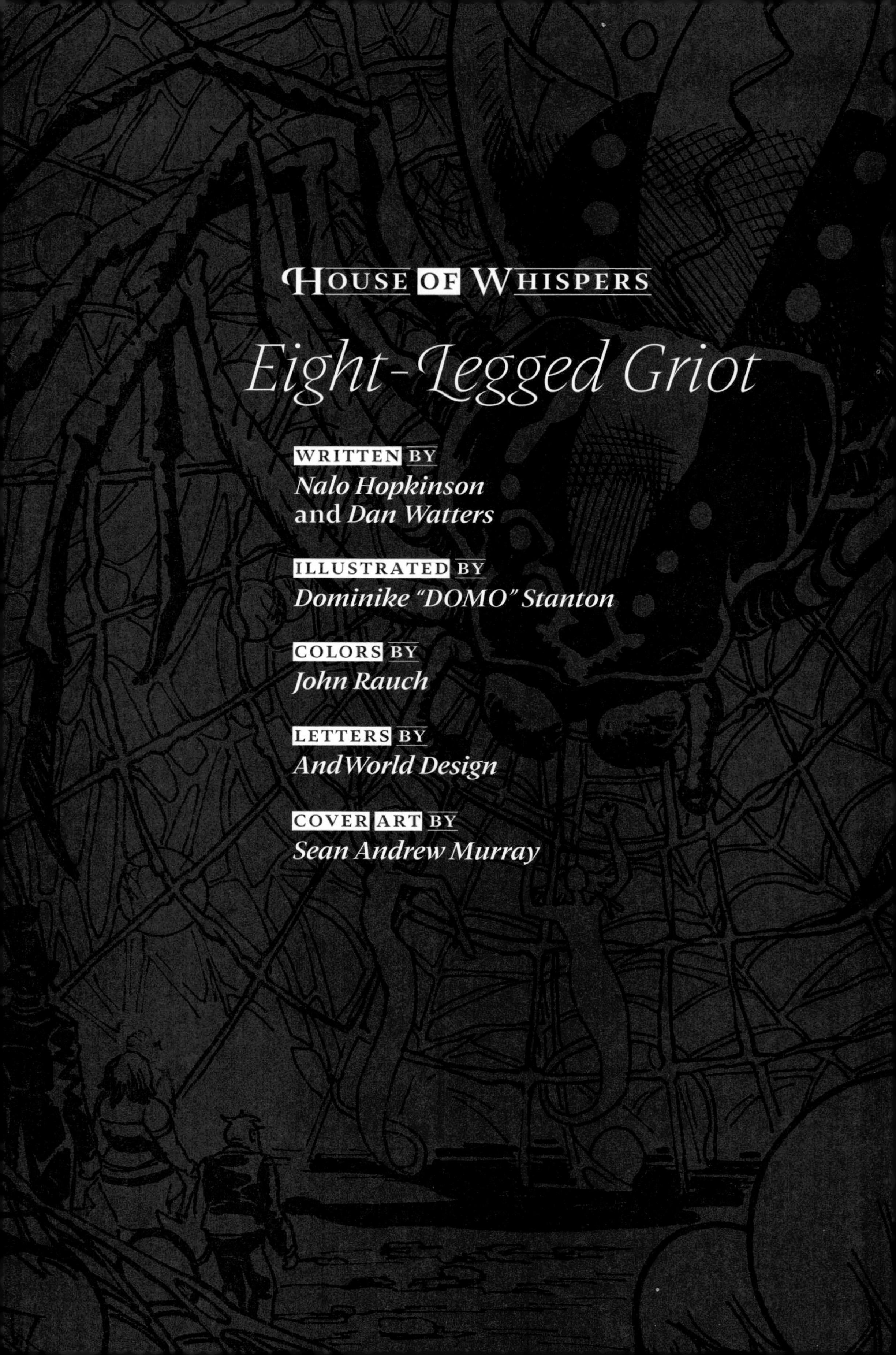

HOUSE OF WHISPERS

Eight-Legged Griot

WRITTEN BY
Nalo Hopkinson
and *Dan Watters*

ILLUSTRATED BY
Dominike "DOMO" Stanton

COLORS BY
John Rauch

LETTERS BY
AndWorld Design

COVER ART BY
Sean Andrew Murray

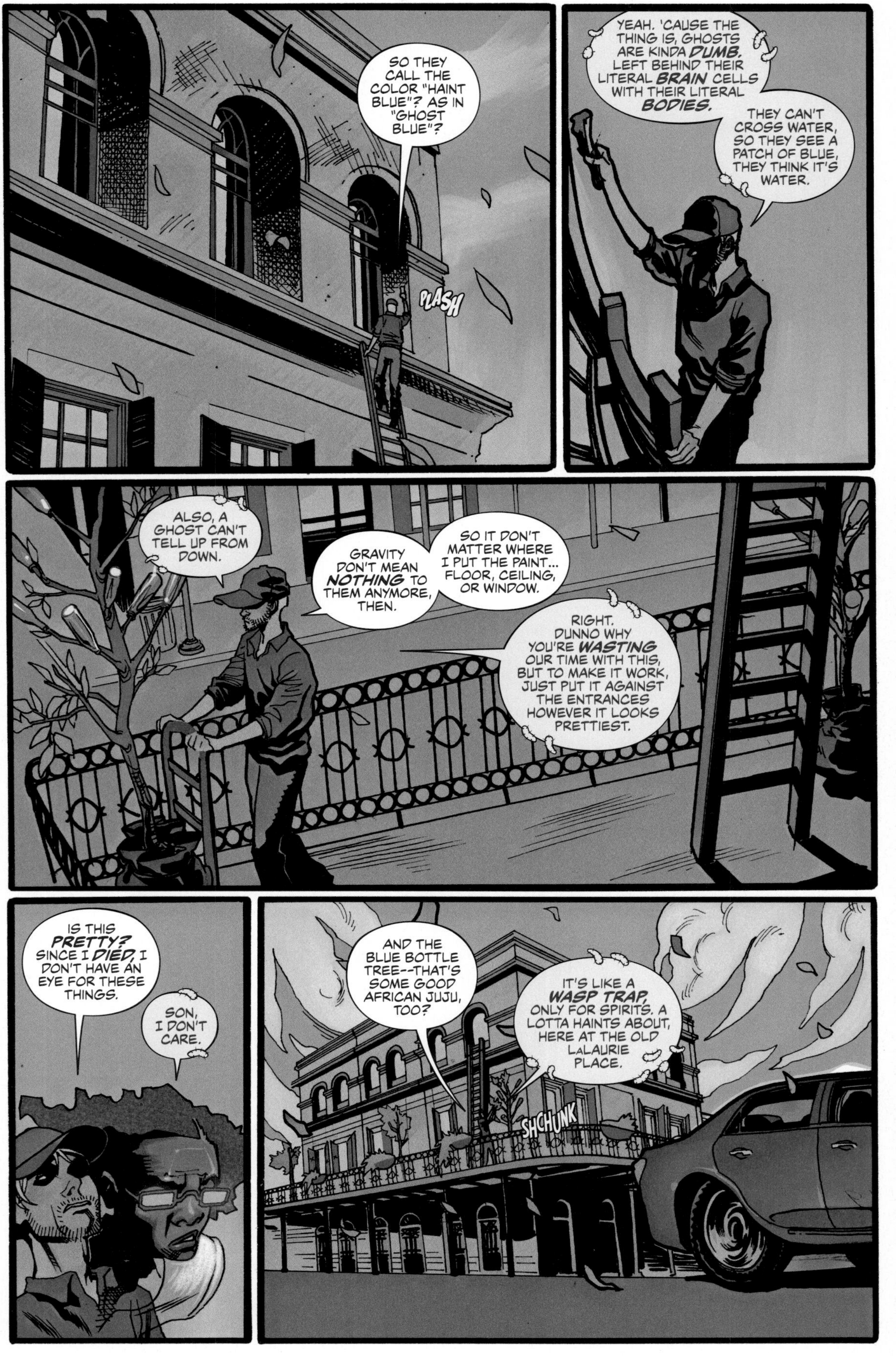
SO THEY CALL THE COLOR "HAINT BLUE"? AS IN "GHOST BLUE"?
PLASH
YEAH. 'CAUSE THE THING IS, GHOSTS ARE KINDA DUMB. LEFT BEHIND THEIR LITERAL BRAIN CELLS WITH THEIR LITERAL BODIES.
THEY CAN'T CROSS WATER, SO THEY SEE A PATCH OF BLUE, THEY THINK IT'S WATER.
ALSO, A GHOST CAN'T TELL UP FROM DOWN.
GRAVITY DON'T MEAN NOTHING TO THEM ANYMORE, THEN.
SO IT DON'T MATTER WHERE I PUT THE PAINT... FLOOR, CEILING, OR WINDOW.
RIGHT. DUNNO WHY YOU'RE WASTING OUR TIME WITH THIS, BUT TO MAKE IT WORK, JUST PUT IT AGAINST THE ENTRANCES HOWEVER IT LOOKS PRETTIEST.
IS THIS PRETTY? SINCE I DIED, I DON'T HAVE AN EYE FOR THESE THINGS.
SON, I DON'T CARE.
AND THE BLUE BOTTLE TREE--THAT'S SOME GOOD AFRICAN JUJU, TOO?
IT'S LIKE A WASP TRAP, ONLY FOR SPIRITS. A LOTTA HAINTS ABOUT, HERE AT THE OLD LaLAURIE PLACE.
SHCHUNK

OOF! DEAD OR ALIVE, I STILL SWEAT THE SAME.

THAT'S 'CAUSE YOU *AIN'T* DEAD, BUCKRA.

YEAH? SHOWS HOW MUCH *YOU* KNOW.

THEY DO KNOW A THING OR TWO, I'M AFRAID.

WE KNOW WHAT *DYING* FEELS LIKE.

WE KNOW WHAT IT'S LIKE TO BE HAULED UP INTO MADAME LaLAURIE'S ATTIC, BEGGING FOR YOUR LIFE, PISS RUNNING HOT DOWN THE INSIDE OF YOUR LEG 'CAUSE YOU KNOW WHAT'S COMING.

WE KNOW ABOUT THE *SMELL* FROM THAT ATTIC--BLOOD. VOMIT. TERROR. IT REEKED IN THERE NO MATTER HOW OFTEN SHE MADE US SLAVES WIPE DOWN THE FLOORS AND TABLES AND WALLS.

I KNOW ABOUT YOUR EYES CROSSING WHEN YOUR BRAINS GET JARRED AS SHE KNOCKS A HOLE IN THE TOP OF YOUR SKULL...

...ABOUT *MEWLING* AND *SHAKING* AS SHE SCRAMBLES YOUR WITS 'CAUSE SHE STUCK A STICK IN YOUR SKULL-PAN AND IS STIRRING YOUR BRAIN MATTER LIKE GUMBO.

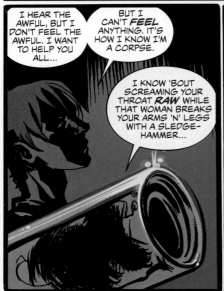

I HEAR THE AWFUL, BUT I DON'T FEEL THE AWFUL. I WANT TO HELP YOU ALL...

BUT I CAN'T *FEEL* ANYTHING. IT'S HOW I KNOW I'M A CORPSE.

I KNOW 'BOUT SCREAMING YOUR THROAT *RAW* WHILE THAT WOMAN BREAKS YOUR ARMS 'N' LEGS WITH A SLEDGE-HAMMER...

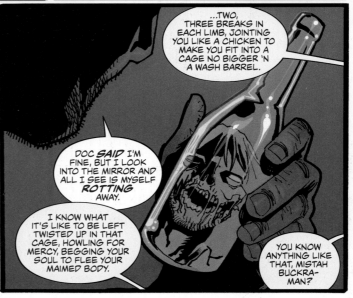

...TWO, THREE BREAKS IN EACH LIMB, JOINTING YOU LIKE A CHICKEN TO MAKE YOU FIT INTO A CAGE NO BIGGER 'N A WASH BARREL.

DOC *SAID* I'M FINE, BUT I LOOK INTO THE MIRROR AND ALL I SEE IS MYSELF *ROTTING* AWAY.

I KNOW WHAT IT'S LIKE TO BE LEFT TWISTED UP IN THAT CAGE, HOWLING FOR MERCY, BEGGING YOUR SOUL TO FLEE YOUR MAIMED BODY.

YOU KNOW ANYTHING LIKE THAT, MISTAH BUCKRA-MAN?

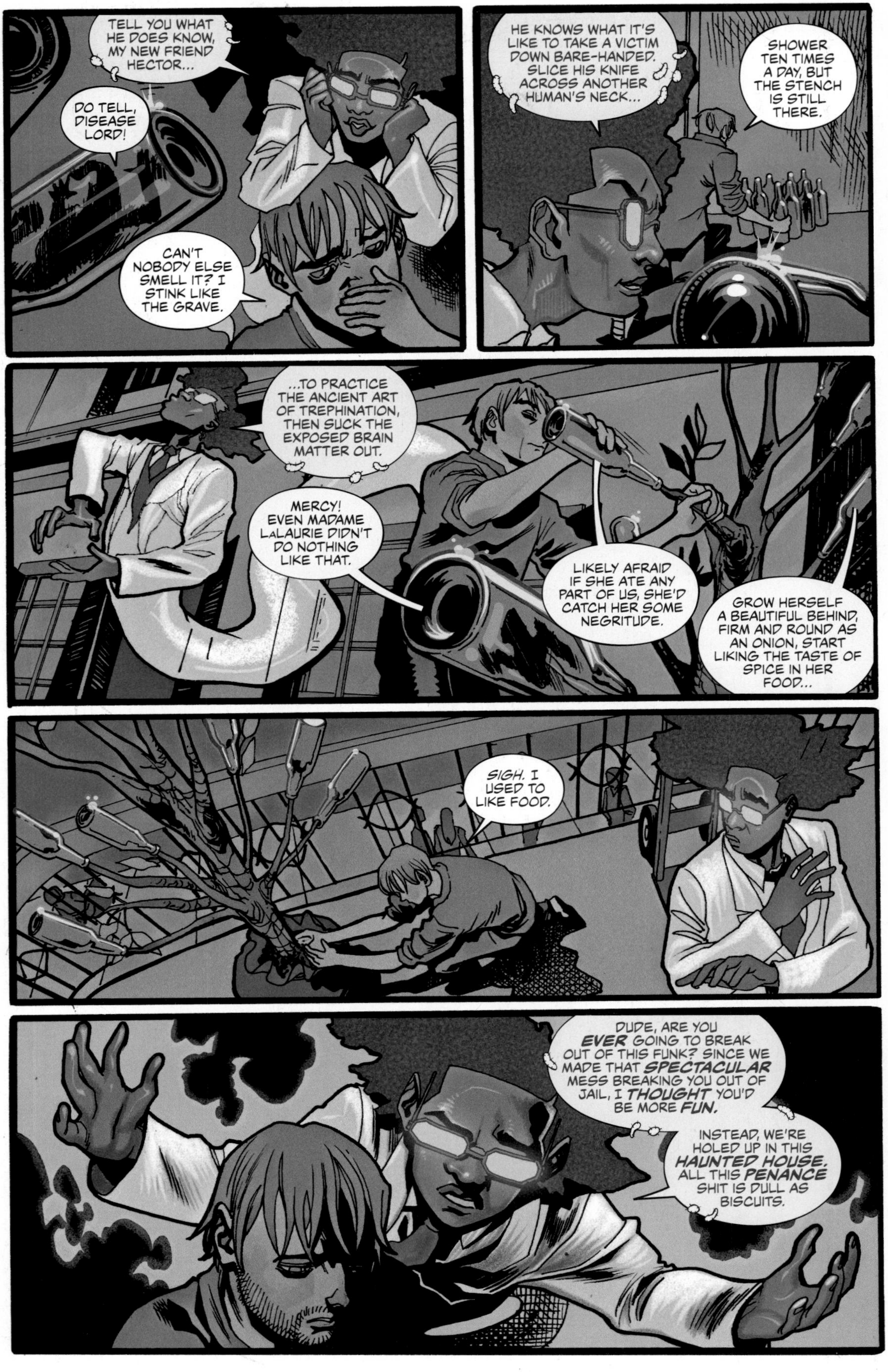

TELL YOU WHAT HE DOES KNOW, MY NEW FRIEND HECTOR...
DO TELL, DISEASE LORD!
CAN'T NOBODY ELSE SMELL IT? I STINK LIKE THE GRAVE.
HE KNOWS WHAT IT'S LIKE TO TAKE A VICTIM DOWN BARE-HANDED. SLICE HIS KNIFE ACROSS ANOTHER HUMAN'S NECK...
SHOWER TEN TIMES A DAY, BUT THE STENCH IS STILL THERE.
...TO PRACTICE THE ANCIENT ART OF TREPHINATION, THEN SUCK THE EXPOSED BRAIN MATTER OUT.
MERCY! EVEN MADAME LaLAURIE DIDN'T DO NOTHING LIKE THAT.
LIKELY AFRAID IF SHE ATE ANY PART OF US, SHE'D CATCH HER SOME NEGRITUDE.
GROW HERSELF A BEAUTIFUL BEHIND, FIRM AND ROUND AS AN ONION, START LIKING THE TASTE OF SPICE IN HER FOOD...
SIGH. I USED TO LIKE FOOD.
DUDE, ARE YOU EVER GOING TO BREAK OUT OF THIS FUNK? SINCE WE MADE THAT SPECTACULAR MESS BREAKING YOU OUT OF JAIL, I THOUGHT YOU'D BE MORE FUN.
INSTEAD, WE'RE HOLED UP IN THIS HAUNTED HOUSE. ALL THIS PENANCE SHIT IS DULL AS BISCUITS.

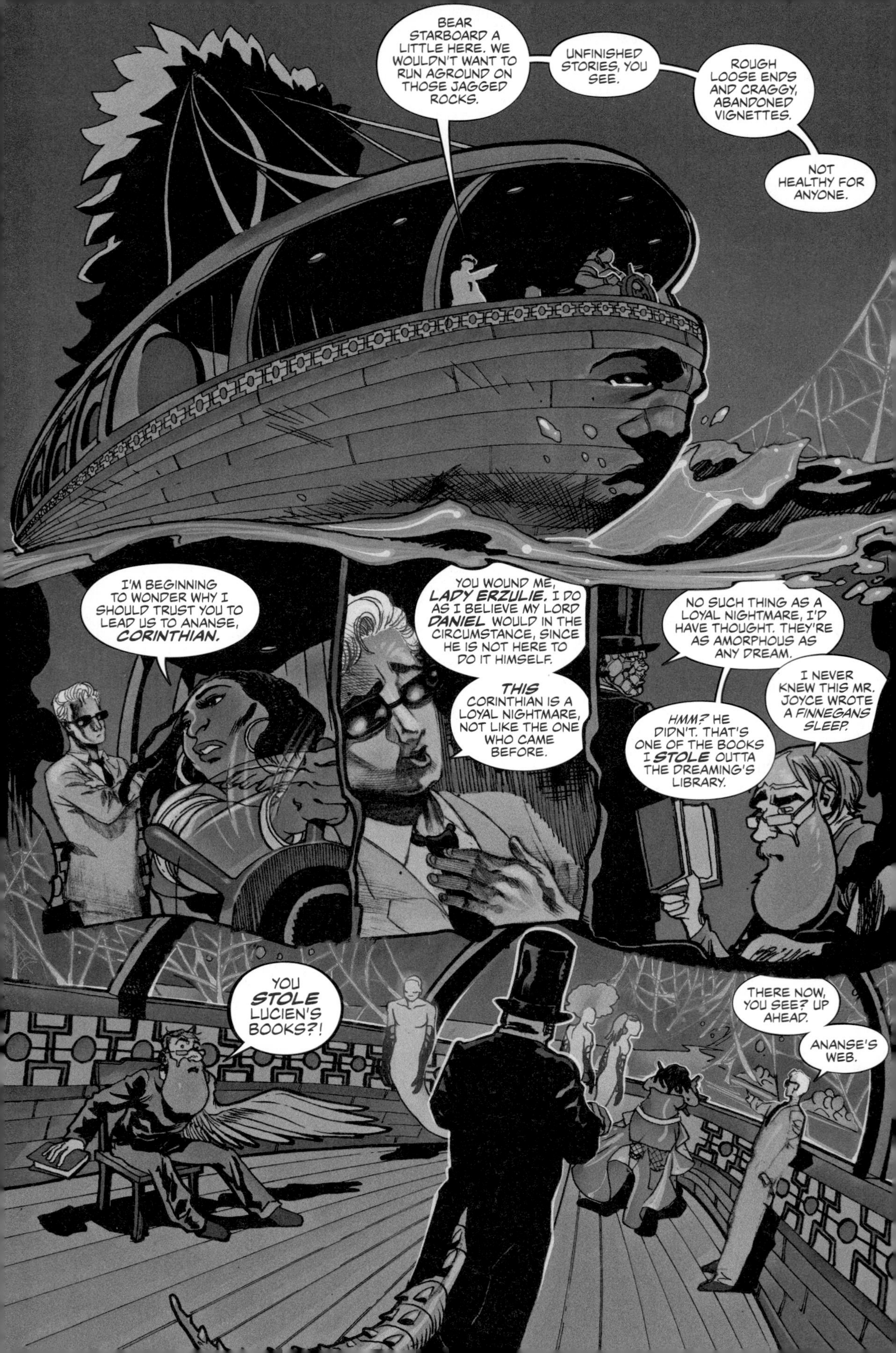
BEAR STARBOARD A LITTLE HERE. WE WOULDN'T WANT TO RUN AGROUND ON THOSE JAGGED ROCKS.
UNFINISHED STORIES, YOU SEE.
ROUGH LOOSE ENDS AND CRAGGY, ABANDONED VIGNETTES.
NOT HEALTHY FOR ANYONE.
I'M BEGINNING TO WONDER WHY I SHOULD TRUST YOU TO LEAD US TO ANANSE, CORINTHIAN.
YOU WOUND ME, LADY ERZULIE. I DO AS I BELIEVE MY LORD DANIEL WOULD IN THE CIRCUMSTANCE, SINCE HE IS NOT HERE TO DO IT HIMSELF.
THIS CORINTHIAN IS A LOYAL NIGHTMARE, NOT LIKE THE ONE WHO CAME BEFORE.
NO SUCH THING AS A LOYAL NIGHTMARE, I'D HAVE THOUGHT. THEY'RE AS AMORPHOUS AS ANY DREAM.
I NEVER KNEW THIS MR. JOYCE WROTE A FINNEGANS SLEEP.
HMM? HE DIDN'T. THAT'S ONE OF THE BOOKS I STOLE OUTTA THE DREAMING'S LIBRARY.
YOU STOLE LUCIEN'S BOOKS?!
THERE NOW, YOU SEE? UP AHEAD.
ANANSE'S WEB.

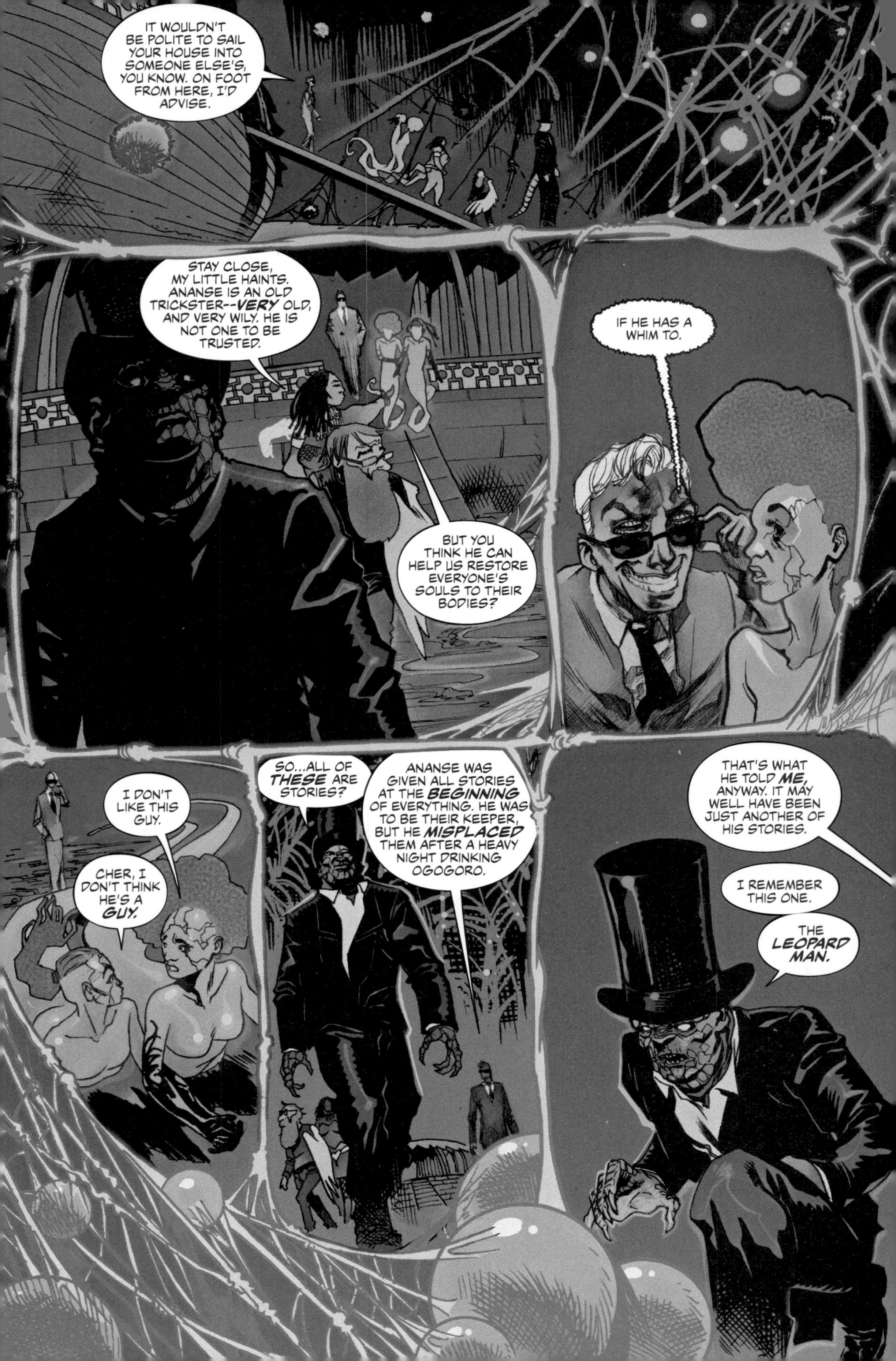
IT WOULDN'T BE POLITE TO SAIL YOUR HOUSE INTO SOMEONE ELSE'S, YOU KNOW. ON FOOT FROM HERE, I'D ADVISE.
STAY CLOSE, MY LITTLE HAINTS. ANANSE IS AN OLD TRICKSTER--VERY OLD, AND VERY WILY. HE IS NOT ONE TO BE TRUSTED.
BUT YOU THINK HE CAN HELP US RESTORE EVERYONE'S SOULS TO THEIR BODIES?
IF HE HAS A WHIM TO.
I DON'T LIKE THIS GUY.
CHER, I DON'T THINK HE'S A GUY.
SO...ALL OF THESE ARE STORIES?
ANANSE WAS GIVEN ALL STORIES AT THE BEGINNING OF EVERYTHING. HE WAS TO BE THEIR KEEPER, BUT HE MISPLACED THEM AFTER A HEAVY NIGHT DRINKING OGOGORO.
THAT'S WHAT HE TOLD ME, ANYWAY. IT MAY WELL HAVE BEEN JUST ANOTHER OF HIS STORIES.
I REMEMBER THIS ONE.
THE LEOPARD MAN.

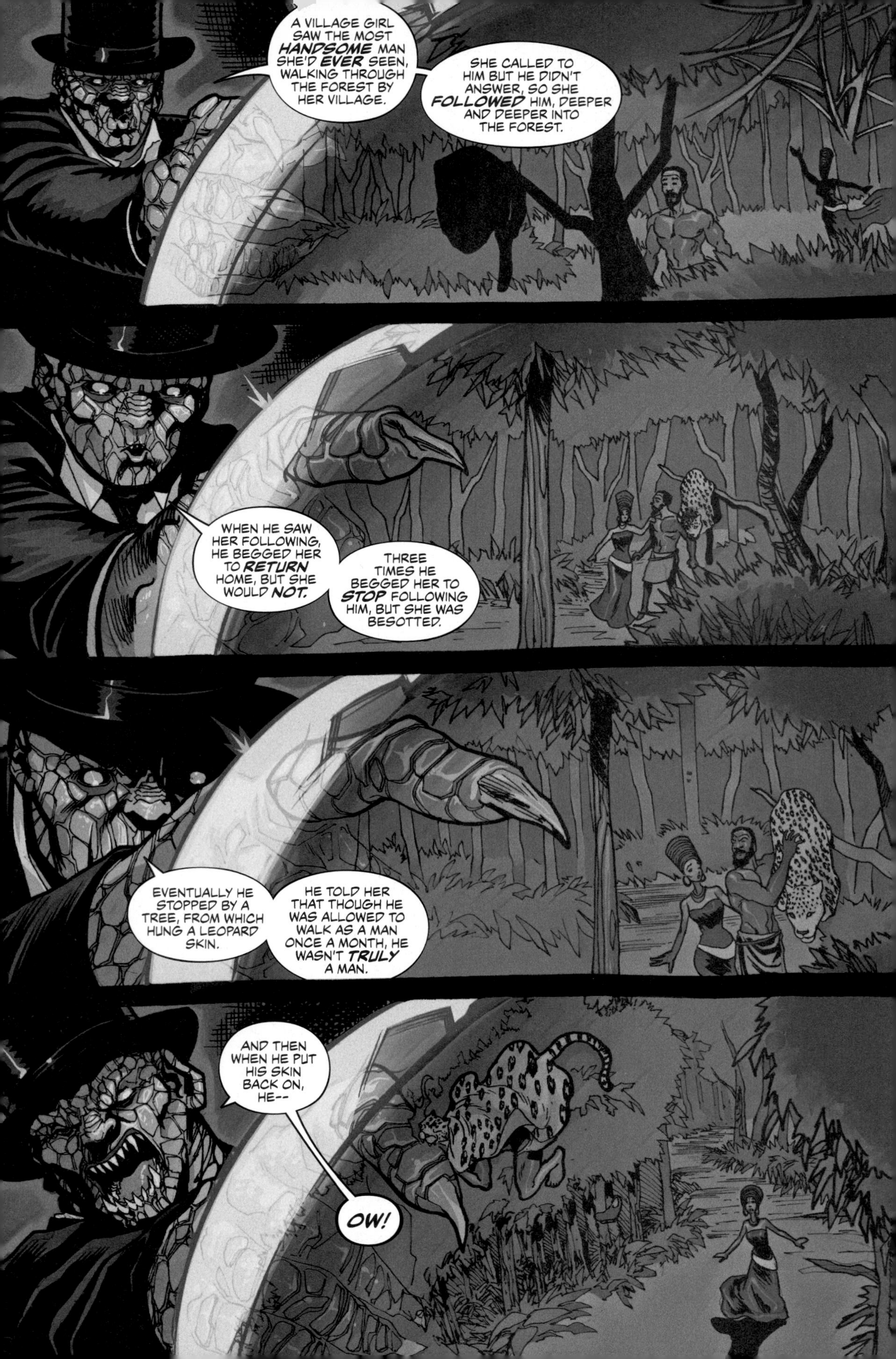
A VILLAGE GIRL SAW THE MOST HANDSOME MAN SHE'D EVER SEEN, WALKING THROUGH THE FOREST BY HER VILLAGE.
SHE CALLED TO HIM BUT HE DIDN'T ANSWER, SO SHE FOLLOWED HIM, DEEPER AND DEEPER INTO THE FOREST.
WHEN HE SAW HER FOLLOWING, HE BEGGED HER TO RETURN HOME, BUT SHE WOULD NOT.
THREE TIMES HE BEGGED HER TO STOP FOLLOWING HIM, BUT SHE WAS BESOTTED.
EVENTUALLY HE STOPPED BY A TREE, FROM WHICH HUNG A LEOPARD SKIN.
HE TOLD HER THAT THOUGH HE WAS ALLOWED TO WALK AS A MAN ONCE A MONTH, HE WASN'T TRULY A MAN.
AND THEN WHEN HE PUT HIS SKIN BACK ON, HE--
OW!

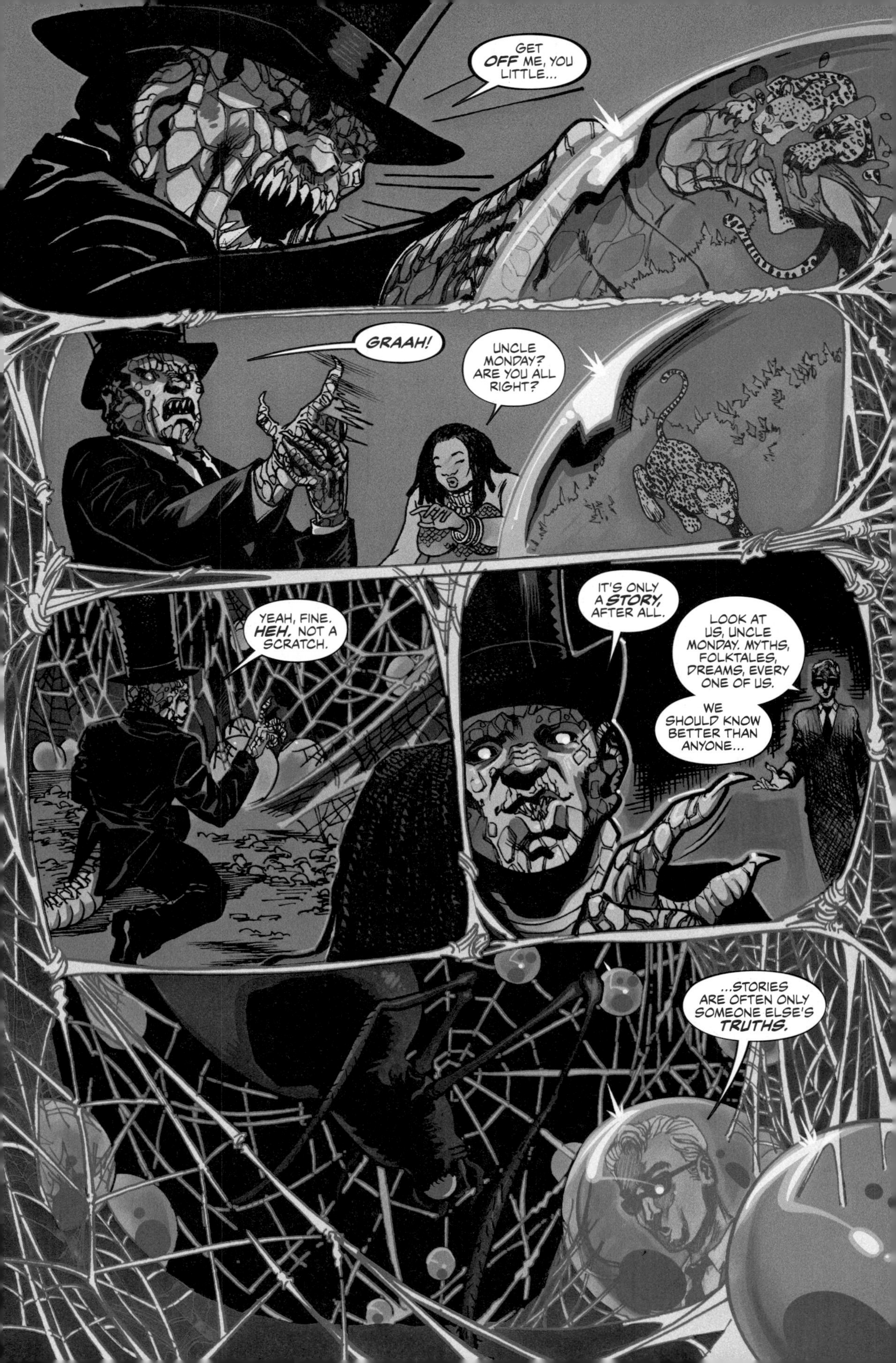
GET OFF ME, YOU LITTLE...
GRAAH!
UNCLE MONDAY? ARE YOU ALL RIGHT?
YEAH, FINE. HEH. NOT A SCRATCH.
IT'S ONLY A STORY, AFTER ALL.
LOOK AT US, UNCLE MONDAY. MYTHS, FOLKTALES, DREAMS, EVERY ONE OF US.
WE SHOULD KNOW BETTER THAN ANYONE...
...STORIES ARE OFTEN ONLY SOMEONE ELSE'S TRUTHS.

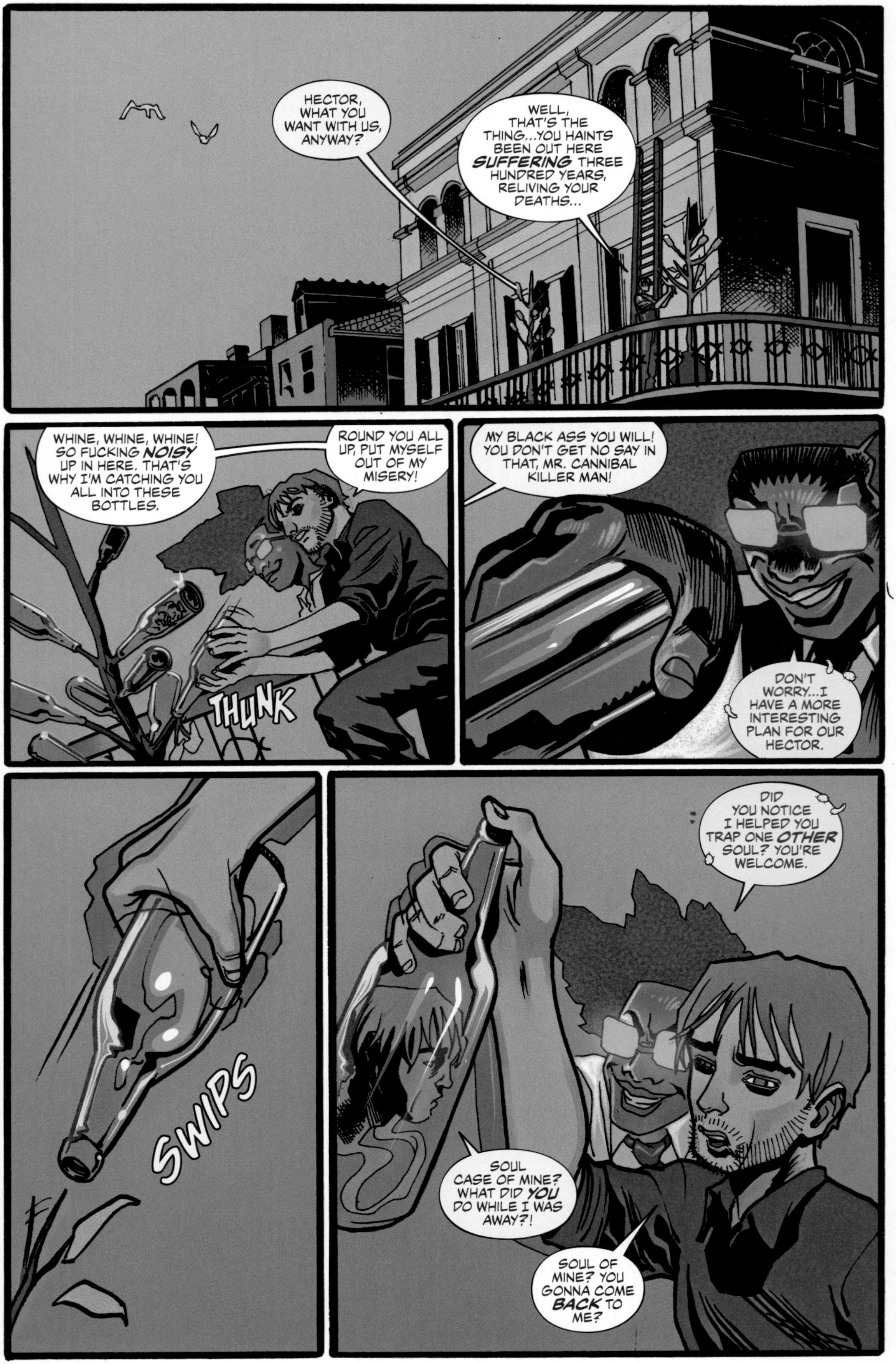
HECTOR, WHAT YOU WANT WITH US, ANYWAY?
WELL, THAT'S THE THING...YOU HAINTS BEEN OUT HERE SUFFERING THREE HUNDRED YEARS, RELIVING YOUR DEATHS...
WHINE, WHINE, WHINE! SO FUCKING NOISY UP IN HERE. THAT'S WHY I'M CATCHING YOU ALL INTO THESE BOTTLES.
ROUND YOU ALL UP, PUT MYSELF OUT OF MY MISERY!
THUNK
MY BLACK ASS YOU WILL! YOU DON'T GET NO SAY IN THAT, MR. CANNIBAL KILLER MAN!
DON'T WORRY...I HAVE A MORE INTERESTING PLAN FOR OUR HECTOR.
SWIPS
DID YOU NOTICE I HELPED YOU TRAP ONE OTHER SOUL? YOU'RE WELCOME.
SOUL CASE OF MINE? WHAT DID YOU DO WHILE I WAS AWAY?!
SOUL OF MINE? YOU GONNA COME BACK TO ME?

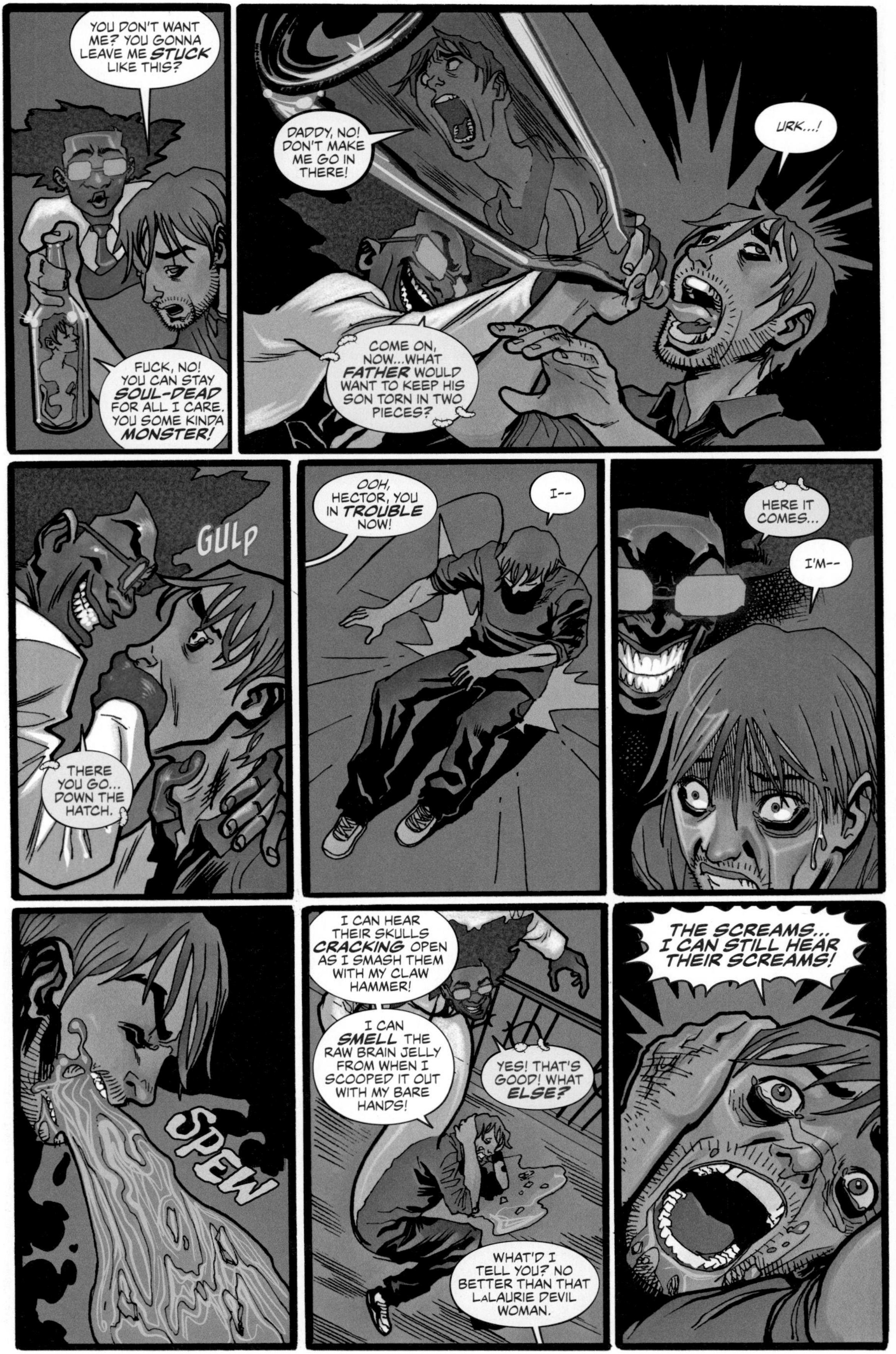
YOU DON'T WANT ME? YOU GONNA LEAVE ME STUCK LIKE THIS?
FUCK, NO! YOU CAN STAY SOUL-DEAD FOR ALL I CARE. YOU SOME KINDA MONSTER!
DADDY, NO! DON'T MAKE ME GO IN THERE!
URK...!
COME ON, NOW...WHAT FATHER WOULD WANT TO KEEP HIS SON TORN IN TWO PIECES?
GULP
THERE YOU GO... DOWN THE HATCH.
OOH, HECTOR, YOU IN TROUBLE NOW!
I--
HERE IT COMES...
I'M--
SPEW
I CAN HEAR THEIR SKULLS CRACKING OPEN AS I SMASH THEM WITH MY CLAW HAMMER!
I CAN SMELL THE RAW BRAIN JELLY FROM WHEN I SCOOPED IT OUT WITH MY BARE HANDS!
YES! THAT'S GOOD! WHAT ELSE?
WHAT'D I TELL YOU? NO BETTER THAN THAT LaLAURIE DEVIL WOMAN.
THE SCREAMS... I CAN STILL HEAR THEIR SCREAMS!

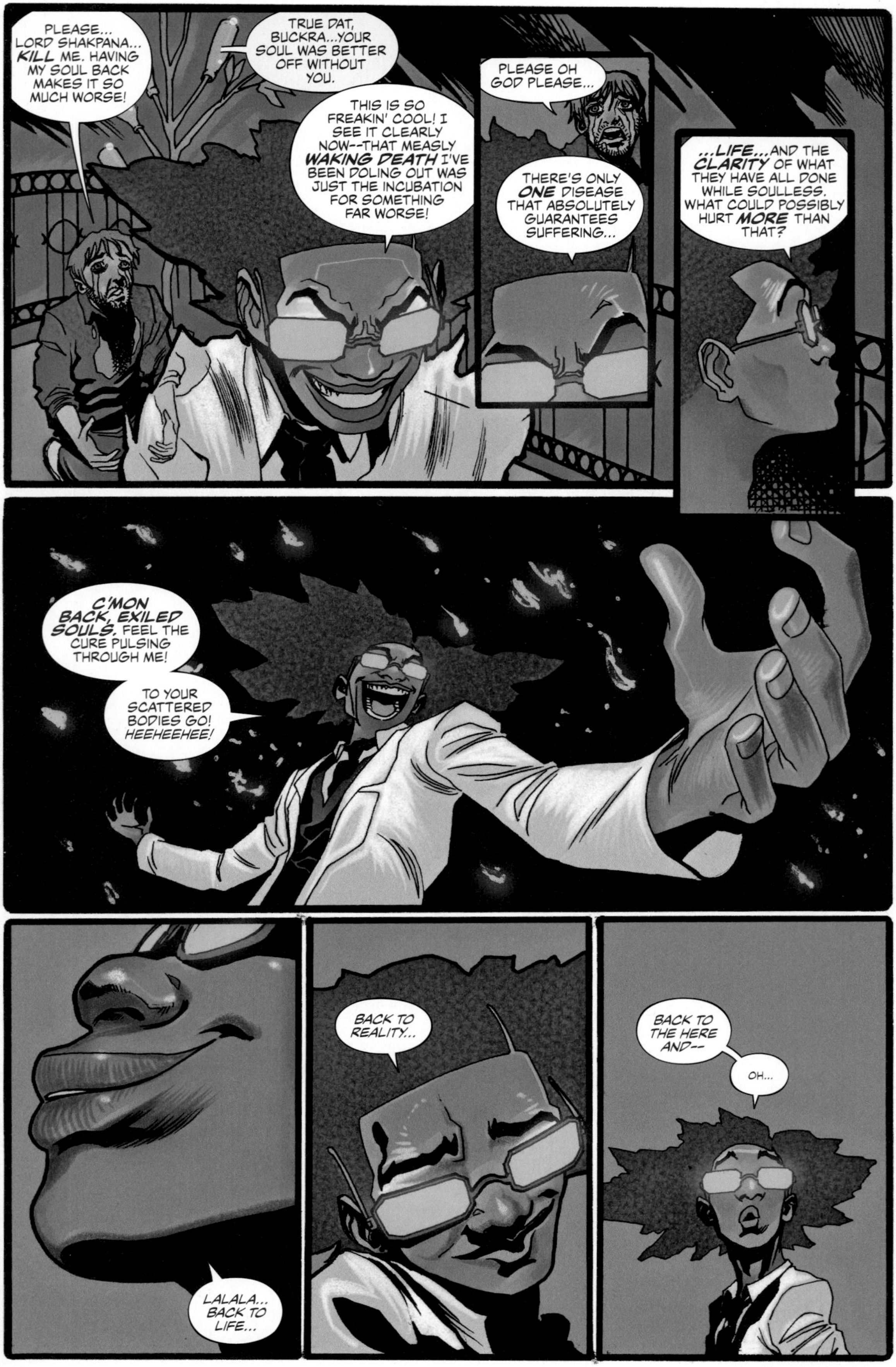
PLEASE... LORD SHAKPANA... KILL ME. HAVING MY SOUL BACK MAKES IT SO MUCH WORSE!
TRUE DAT, BUCKRA...YOUR SOUL WAS BETTER OFF WITHOUT YOU.
THIS IS SO FREAKIN' COOL! I SEE IT CLEARLY NOW--THAT MEASLY WAKING DEATH I'VE BEEN DOLING OUT WAS JUST THE INCUBATION FOR SOMETHING FAR WORSE!
PLEASE OH GOD PLEASE...
THERE'S ONLY ONE DISEASE THAT ABSOLUTELY GUARANTEES SUFFERING...
...LIFE...AND THE CLARITY OF WHAT THEY HAVE ALL DONE WHILE SOULLESS. WHAT COULD POSSIBLY HURT MORE THAN THAT?
C'MON BACK, EXILED SOULS. FEEL THE CURE PULSING THROUGH ME!
TO YOUR SCATTERED BODIES GO! HEEHEEHEE!
LALALA... BACK TO LIFE...
BACK TO REALITY...
BACK TO THE HERE AND--
OH...

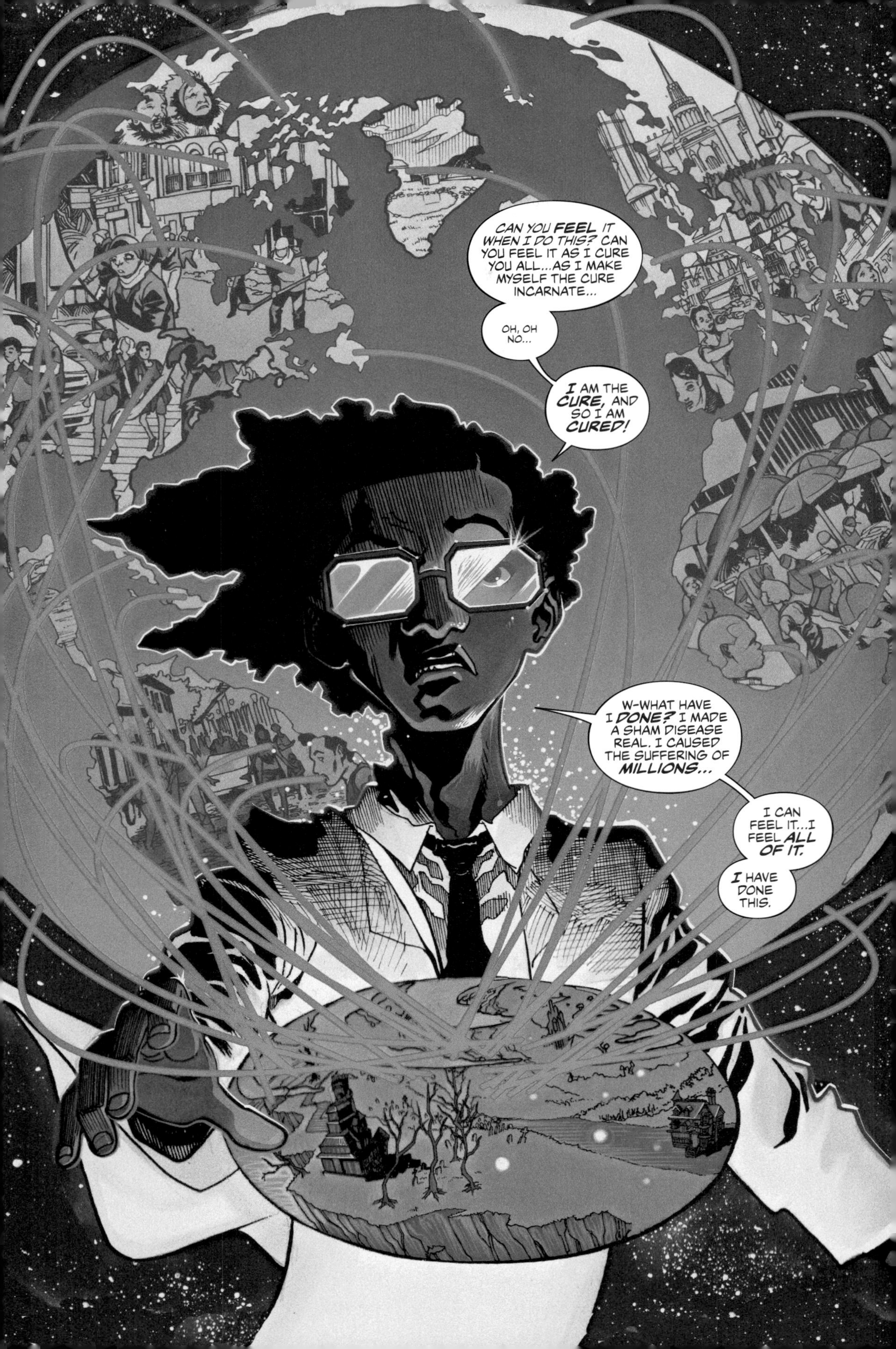
CAN YOU FEEL IT WHEN I DO THIS? CAN YOU FEEL IT AS I CURE YOU ALL...AS I MAKE MYSELF THE CURE INCARNATE...
OH, OH NO...
I AM THE CURE, AND SO I AM CURED!
W-WHAT HAVE I DONE? I MADE A SHAM DISEASE REAL. I CAUSED THE SUFFERING OF MILLIONS...
I CAN FEEL IT...I FEEL ALL OF IT.
I HAVE DONE THIS.

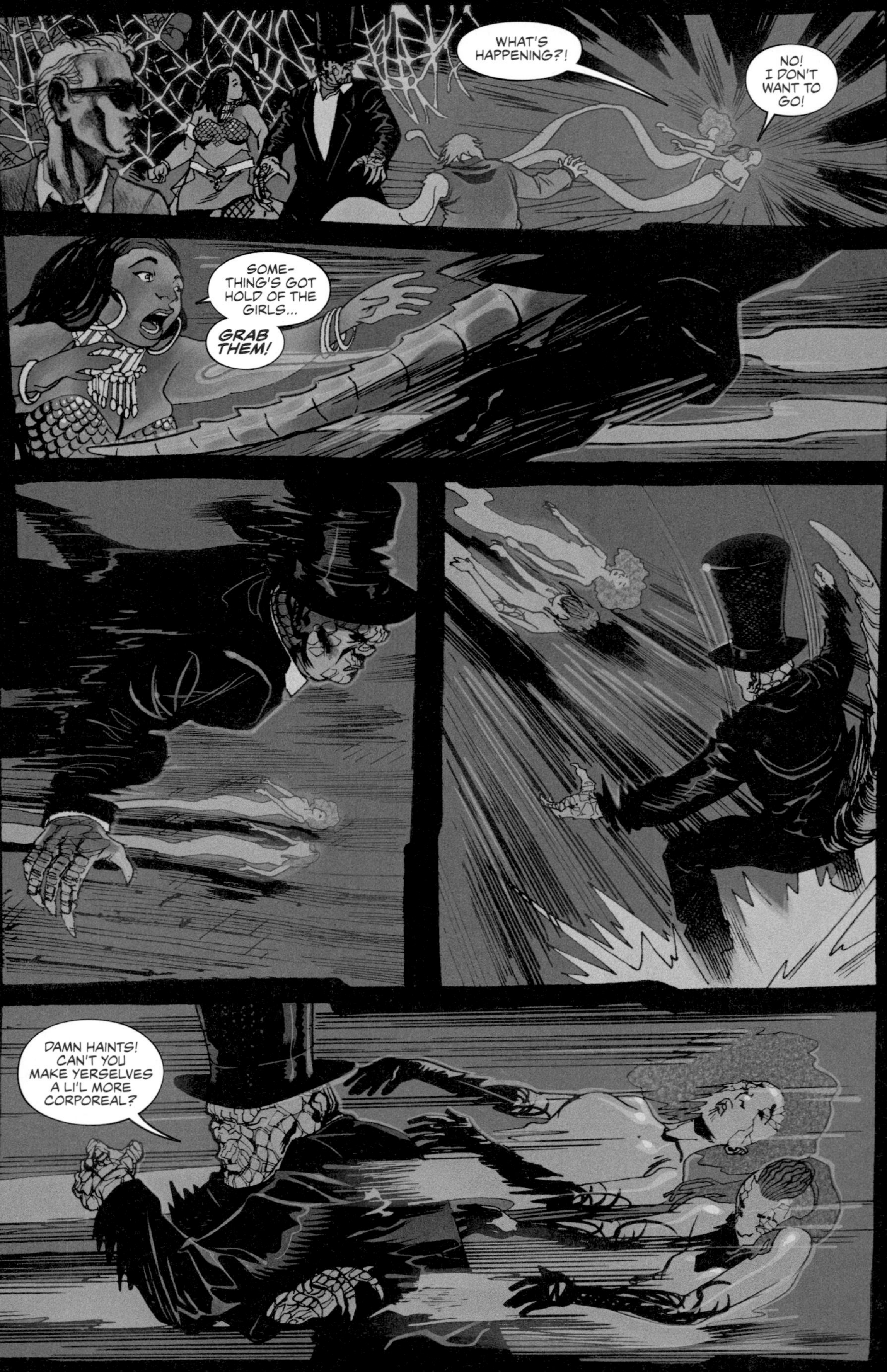
WHAT'S HAPPENING?!
NO! I DON'T WANT TO GO!
SOME-THING'S GOT HOLD OF THE GIRLS...
GRAB THEM!
DAMN HAINTS! CAN'T YOU MAKE YERSELVES A LI'L MORE CORPOREAL?

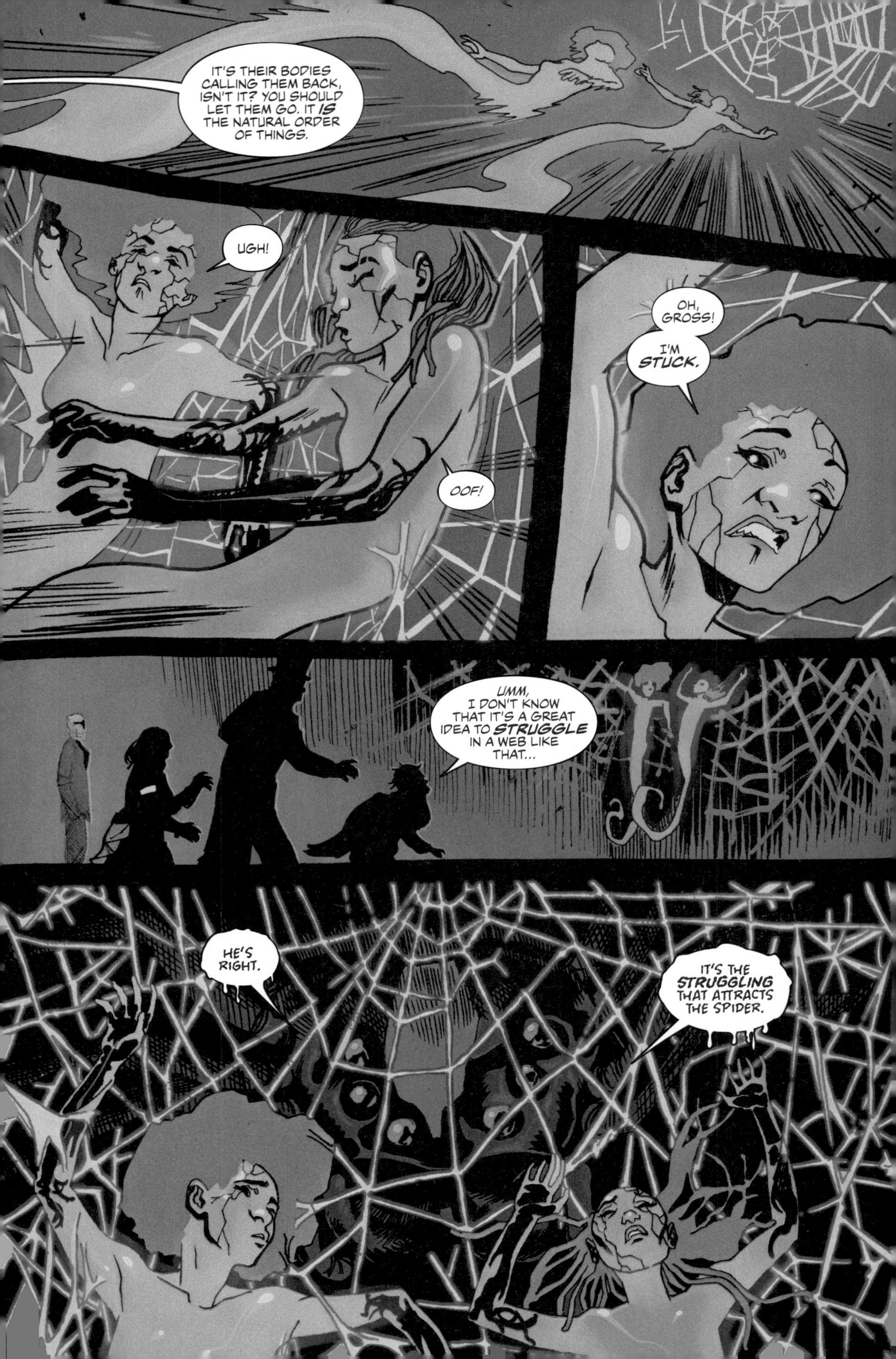
IT'S THEIR BODIES CALLING THEM BACK, ISN'T IT? YOU SHOULD LET THEM GO. IT IS THE NATURAL ORDER OF THINGS.
UGH!
OOF!
OH, GROSS!
I'M STUCK.
UMM, I DON'T KNOW THAT IT'S A GREAT IDEA TO STRUGGLE IN A WEB LIKE THAT...
HE'S RIGHT.
IT'S THE STRUGGLING THAT ATTRACTS THE SPIDER.

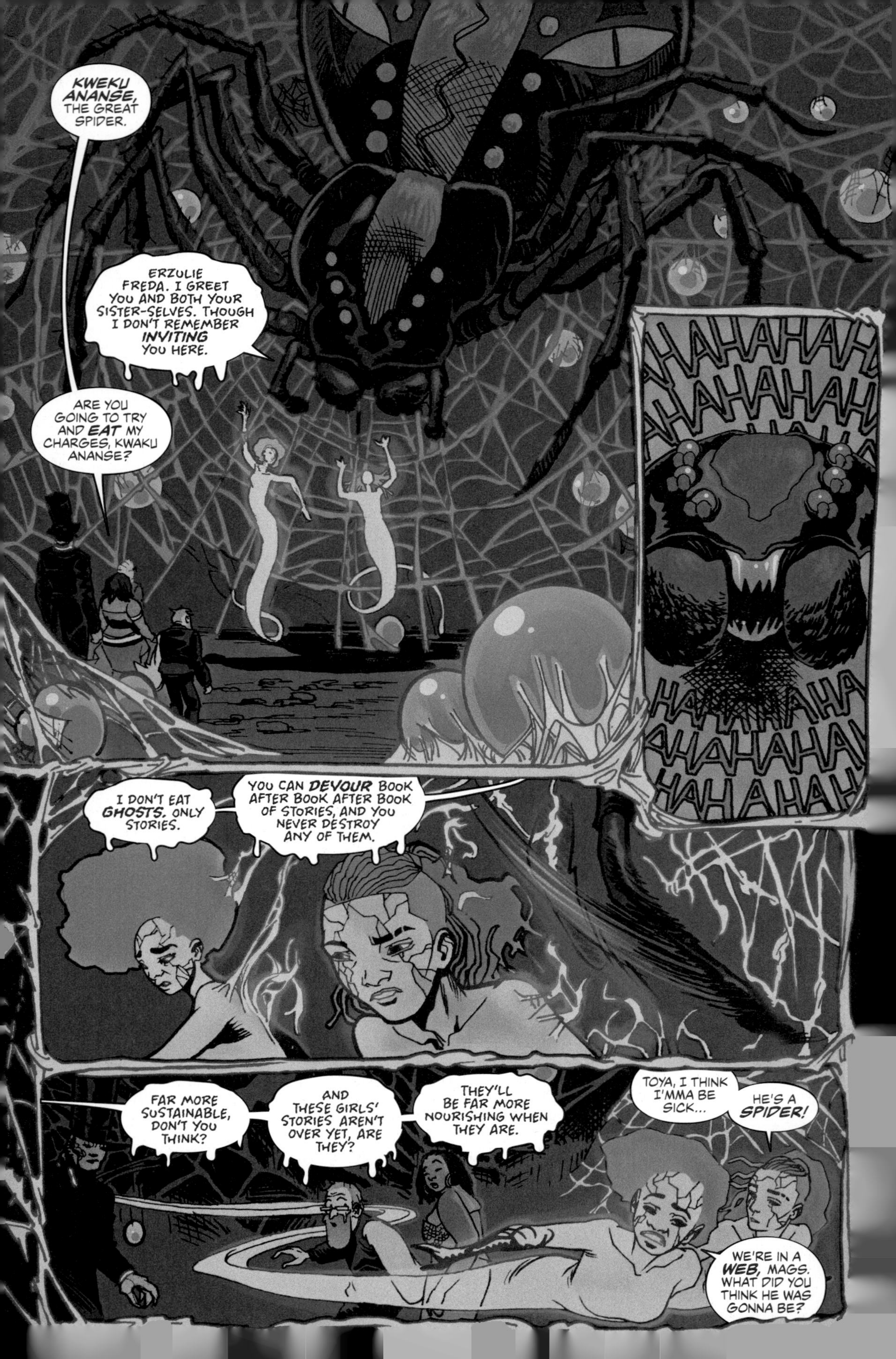
KWEKU ANANSE, THE GREAT SPIDER.
ERZULIE FREDA. I GREET YOU AND BOTH YOUR SISTER-SELVES. THOUGH I DON'T REMEMBER INVITING YOU HERE.
ARE YOU GOING TO TRY AND EAT MY CHARGES, KWAKU ANANSE?
HAHAHAHAHAHAHAHAH
HAHAHAHAHAHAHAHAHAHAH
I DON'T EAT GHOSTS. ONLY STORIES.
YOU CAN DEVOUR BOOK AFTER BOOK AFTER BOOK OF STORIES, AND YOU NEVER DESTROY ANY OF THEM.
FAR MORE SUSTAINABLE, DON'T YOU THINK?
AND THESE GIRLS' STORIES AREN'T OVER YET, ARE THEY?
THEY'LL BE FAR MORE NOURISHING WHEN THEY ARE.
TOYA, I THINK I'MMA BE SICK...
HE'S A SPIDER!
WE'RE IN A WEB, MAGS. WHAT DID YOU THINK HE WAS GONNA BE?

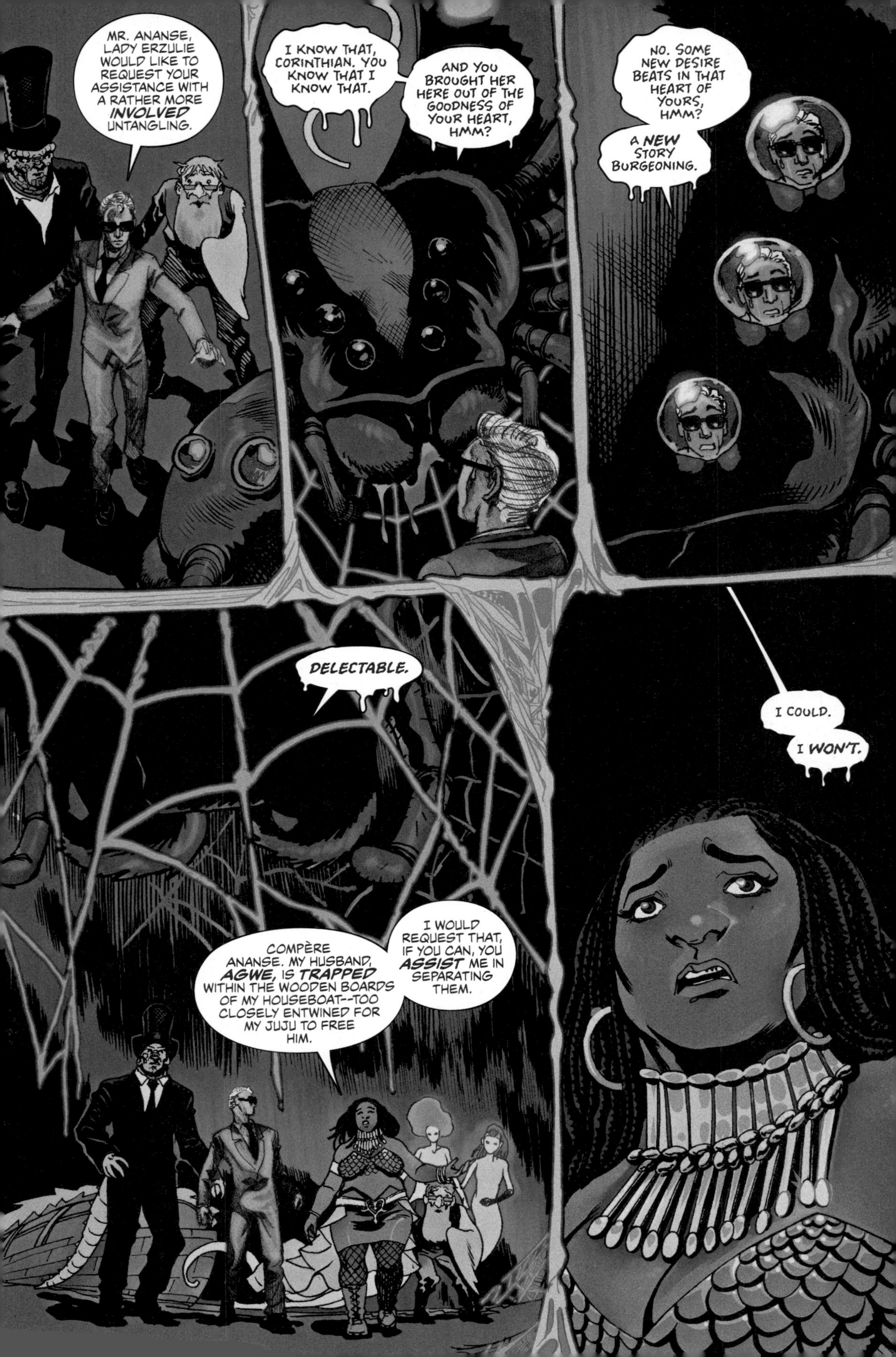
MR. ANANSE, LADY ERZULIE WOULD LIKE TO REQUEST YOUR ASSISTANCE WITH A RATHER MORE INVOLVED UNTANGLING.
I KNOW THAT, CORINTHIAN. YOU KNOW THAT I KNOW THAT.
AND YOU BROUGHT HER HERE OUT OF THE GOODNESS OF YOUR HEART, HMM?
NO. SOME NEW DESIRE BEATS IN THAT HEART OF YOURS, HMM?
A NEW STORY BURGEONING.
DELECTABLE.
COMPÈRE ANANSE. MY HUSBAND, AGWE, IS TRAPPED WITHIN THE WOODEN BOARDS OF MY HOUSEBOAT--TOO CLOSELY ENTWINED FOR MY JUJU TO FREE HIM.
I WOULD REQUEST THAT, IF YOU CAN, YOU ASSIST ME IN SEPARATING THEM.
I COULD.
I WON'T.

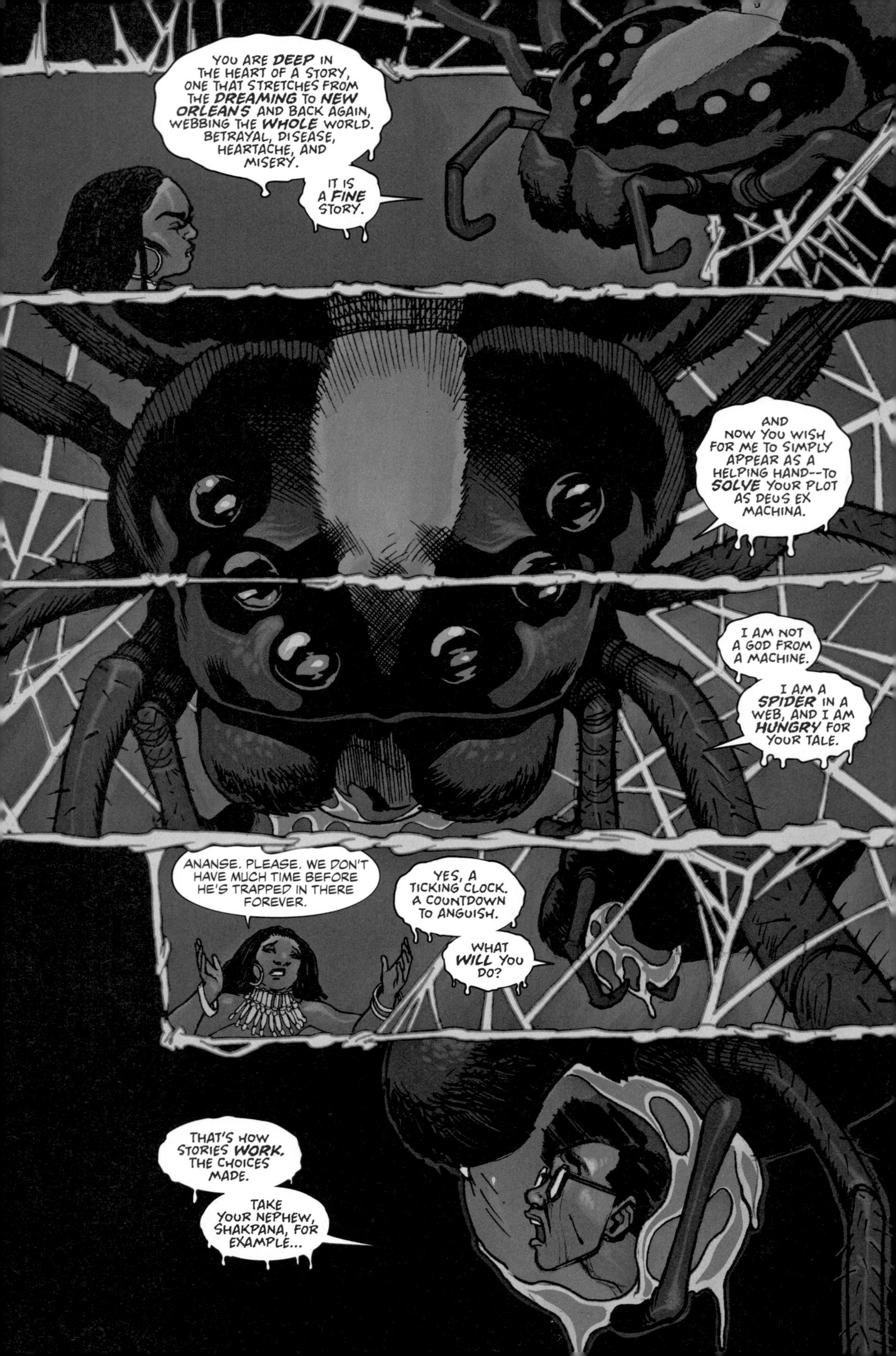
YOU ARE DEEP IN THE HEART OF A STORY, ONE THAT STRETCHES FROM THE DREAMING TO NEW ORLEANS AND BACK AGAIN, WEBBING THE WHOLE WORLD. BETRAYAL, DISEASE, HEARTACHE, AND MISERY.
IT IS A FINE STORY.
AND NOW YOU WISH FOR ME TO SIMPLY APPEAR AS A HELPING HAND--TO SOLVE YOUR PLOT AS DEUS EX MACHINA.
I AM NOT A GOD FROM A MACHINE.
I AM A SPIDER IN A WEB, AND I AM HUNGRY FOR YOUR TALE.
ANANSE. PLEASE. WE DON'T HAVE MUCH TIME BEFORE HE'S TRAPPED IN THERE FOREVER.
YES, A TICKING CLOCK. A COUNTDOWN TO ANGUISH.
WHAT WILL YOU DO?
THAT'S HOW STORIES WORK. THE CHOICES MADE.
TAKE YOUR NEPHEW, SHAKPANA, FOR EXAMPLE...

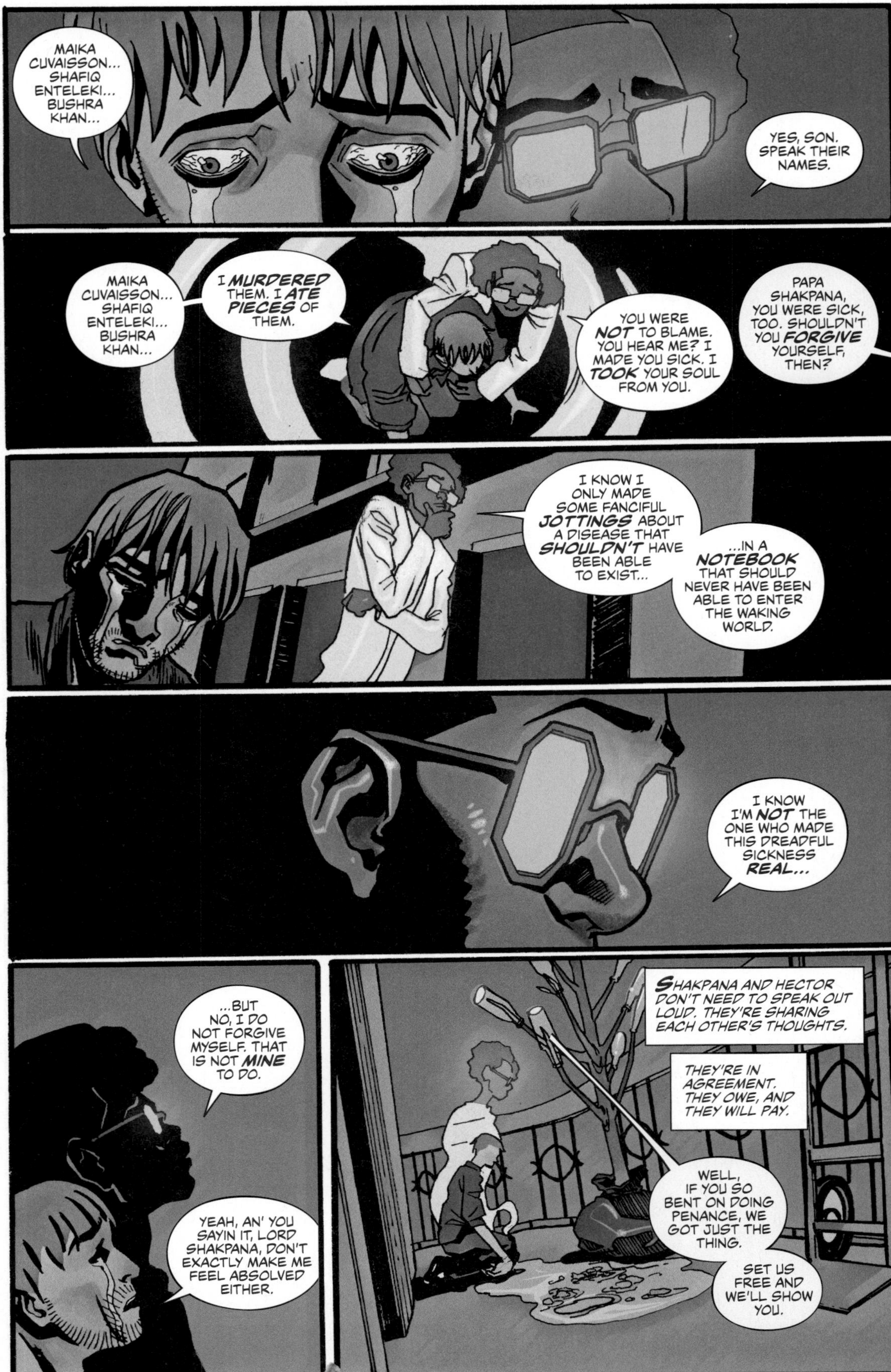
MAIKA CUVAISSON... SHAFIQ ENTELEKI... BUSHRA KHAN...
YES, SON. SPEAK THEIR NAMES.
MAIKA CUVAISSON... SHAFIQ ENTELEKI... BUSHRA KHAN...
I MURDERED THEM. I ATE PIECES OF THEM.
YOU WERE NOT TO BLAME. YOU HEAR ME? I MADE YOU SICK. I TOOK YOUR SOUL FROM YOU.
PAPA SHAKPANA, YOU WERE SICK, TOO. SHOULDN'T YOU FORGIVE YOURSELF, THEN?
I KNOW I ONLY MADE SOME FANCIFUL JOTTINGS ABOUT A DISEASE THAT SHOULDN'T HAVE BEEN ABLE TO EXIST...
...IN A NOTEBOOK THAT SHOULD NEVER HAVE BEEN ABLE TO ENTER THE WAKING WORLD.
I KNOW I'M NOT THE ONE WHO MADE THIS DREADFUL SICKNESS REAL...
...BUT NO, I DO NOT FORGIVE MYSELF. THAT IS NOT MINE TO DO.
YEAH, AN' YOU SAYIN IT, LORD SHAKPANA, DON'T EXACTLY MAKE ME FEEL ABSOLVED EITHER.
SHAKPANA AND HECTOR DON'T NEED TO SPEAK OUT LOUD. THEY'RE SHARING EACH OTHER'S THOUGHTS.
THEY'RE IN AGREEMENT. THEY OWE, AND THEY WILL PAY.
WELL, IF YOU SO BENT ON DOING PENANCE, WE GOT JUST THE THING.
SET US FREE AND WE'LL SHOW YOU.

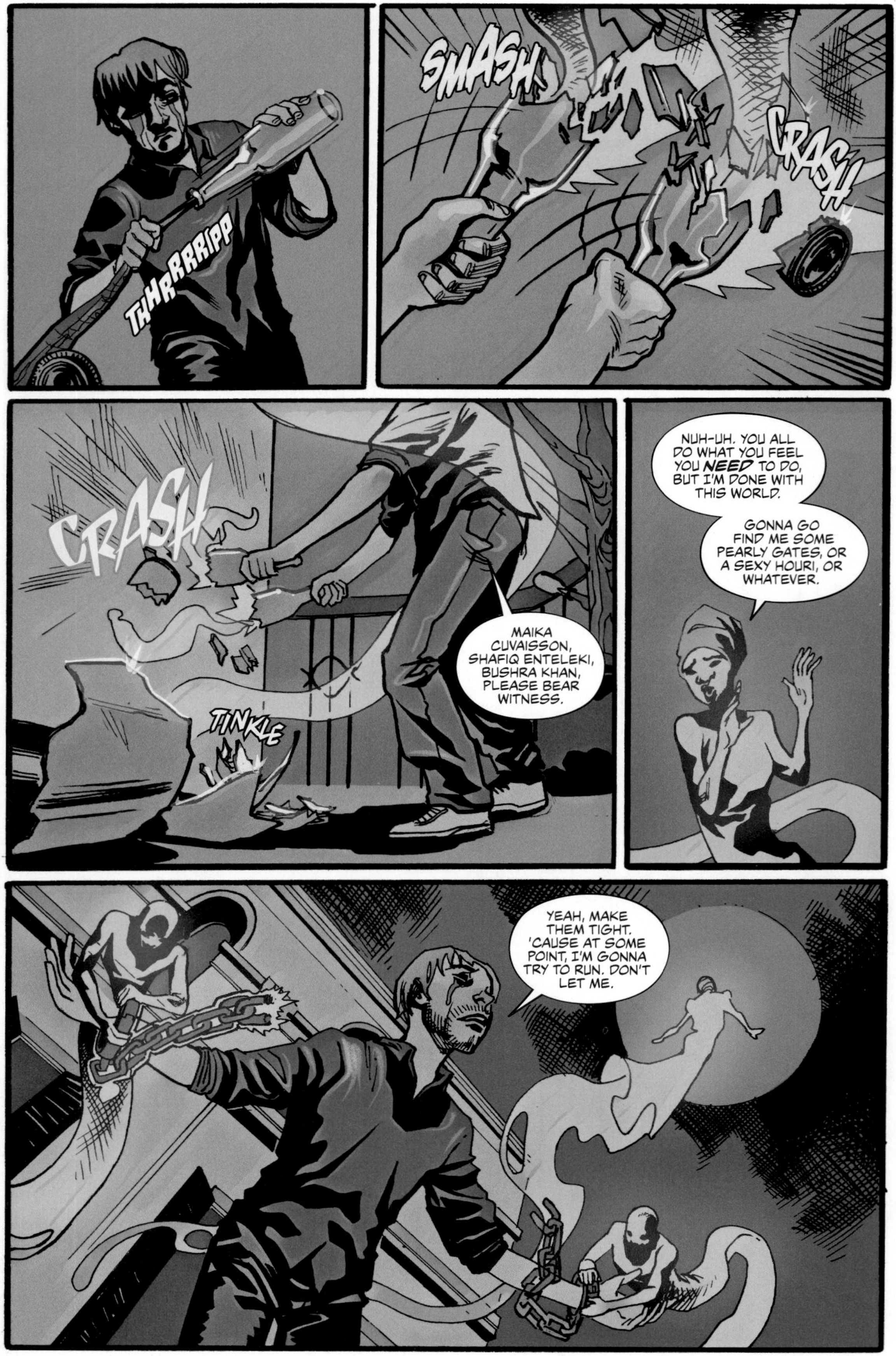
THRRRRIPP
SMASH
CRASH
CRASH
TINKLE
MAIKA CUVAISSON, SHAFIQ ENTELEKI, BUSHRA KHAN, PLEASE BEAR WITNESS.
NUH-UH. YOU ALL DO WHAT YOU FEEL YOU **NEED** TO DO, BUT I'M DONE WITH THIS WORLD.
GONNA GO FIND ME SOME PEARLY GATES, OR A SEXY HOURI, OR WHATEVER.
YEAH, MAKE THEM TIGHT. 'CAUSE AT SOME POINT, I'M GONNA TRY TO RUN. DON'T LET ME.

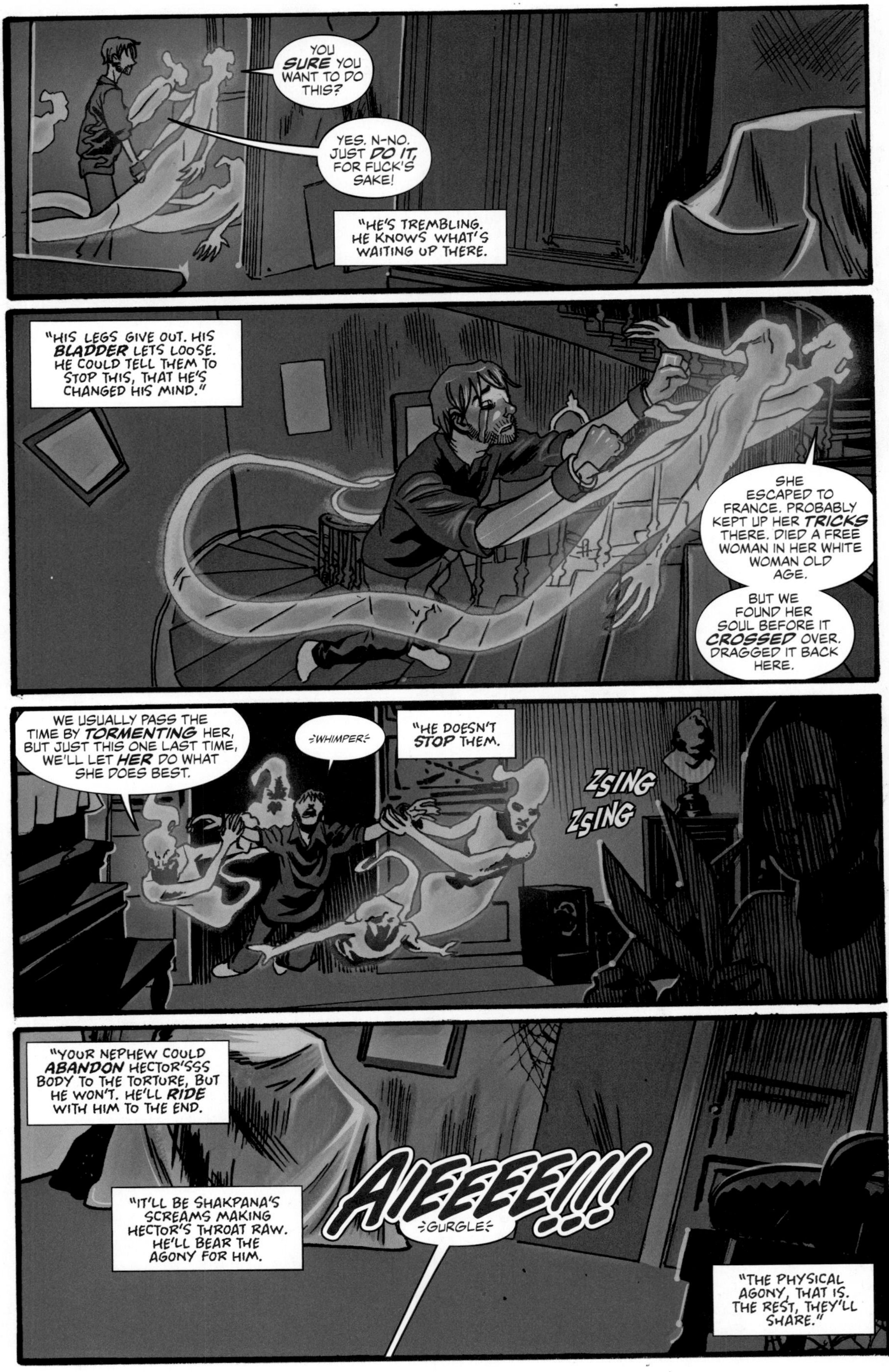
YOU SURE YOU WANT TO DO THIS?
YES. N-NO. JUST DO IT, FOR FUCK'S SAKE!
"HE'S TREMBLING. HE KNOWS WHAT'S WAITING UP THERE.
"HIS LEGS GIVE OUT. HIS BLADDER LETS LOOSE. HE COULD TELL THEM TO STOP THIS, THAT HE'S CHANGED HIS MIND."
SHE ESCAPED TO FRANCE. PROBABLY KEPT UP HER TRICKS THERE. DIED A FREE WOMAN IN HER WHITE WOMAN OLD AGE.
BUT WE FOUND HER SOUL BEFORE IT CROSSED OVER. DRAGGED IT BACK HERE.
WE USUALLY PASS THE TIME BY TORMENTING HER, BUT JUST THIS ONE LAST TIME, WE'LL LET HER DO WHAT SHE DOES BEST.
WHIMPER
"HE DOESN'T STOP THEM.
ZSING
ZSING
"YOUR NEPHEW COULD ABANDON HECTOR'SSS BODY TO THE TORTURE, BUT HE WON'T. HE'LL RIDE WITH HIM TO THE END.
"IT'LL BE SHAKPANA'S SCREAMS MAKING HECTOR'S THROAT RAW. HE'LL BEAR THE AGONY FOR HIM.
AIEEEE!!!
GURGLE
"THE PHYSICAL AGONY, THAT IS. THE REST, THEY'LL SHARE."

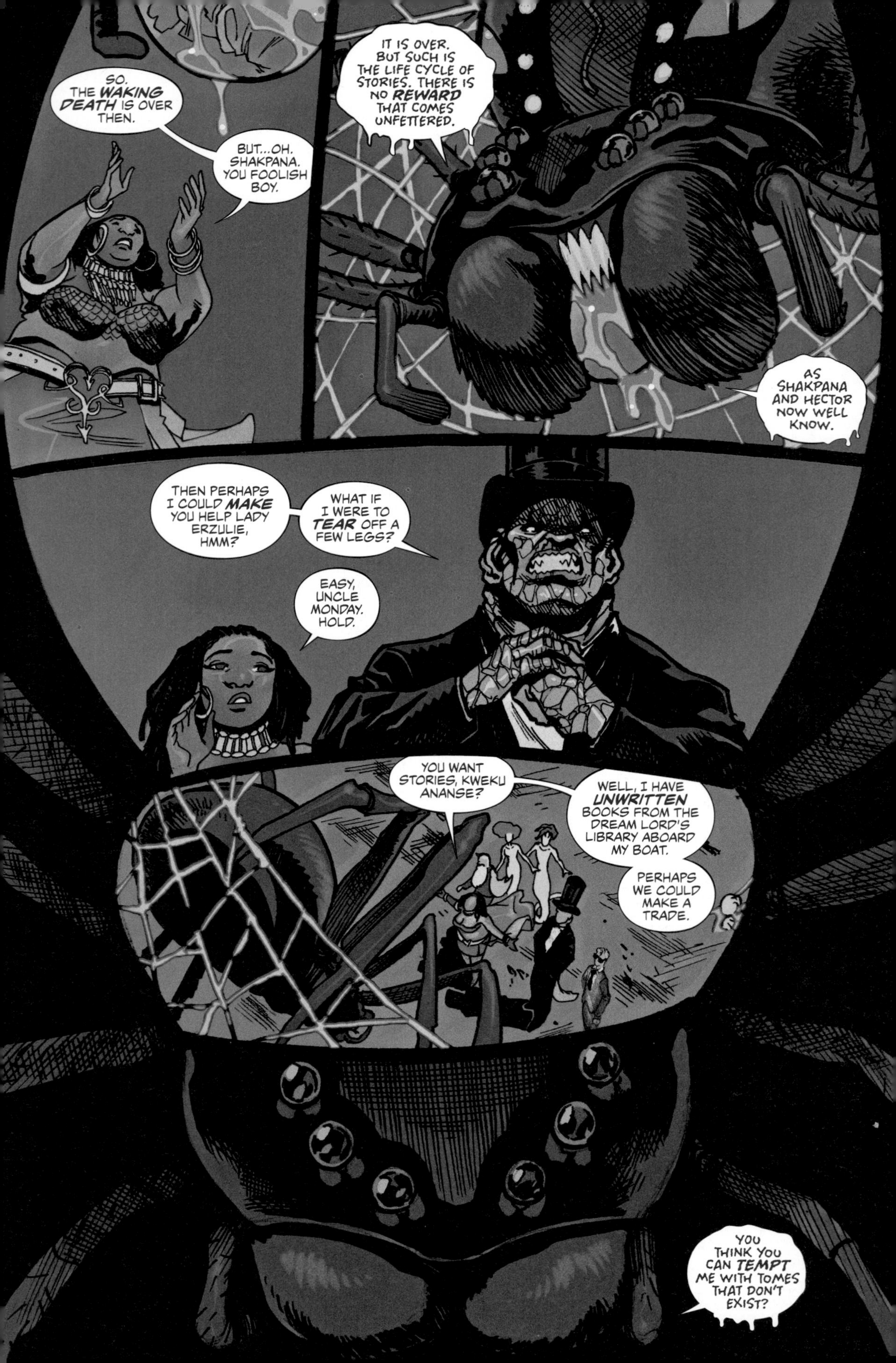
SO. THE WAKING DEATH IS OVER THEN.
BUT...OH. SHAKPANA. YOU FOOLISH BOY.
IT IS OVER. BUT SUCH IS THE LIFE CYCLE OF STORIES. THERE IS NO REWARD THAT COMES UNFETTERED.
AS SHAKPANA AND HECTOR NOW WELL KNOW.
THEN PERHAPS I COULD MAKE YOU HELP LADY ERZULIE, HMM?
WHAT IF I WERE TO TEAR OFF A FEW LEGS?
EASY, UNCLE MONDAY. HOLD.
YOU WANT STORIES, KWEKU ANANSE?
WELL, I HAVE UNWRITTEN BOOKS FROM THE DREAM LORD'S LIBRARY ABOARD MY BOAT.
PERHAPS WE COULD MAKE A TRADE.
YOU THINK YOU CAN TEMPT ME WITH TOMES THAT DON'T EXIST?

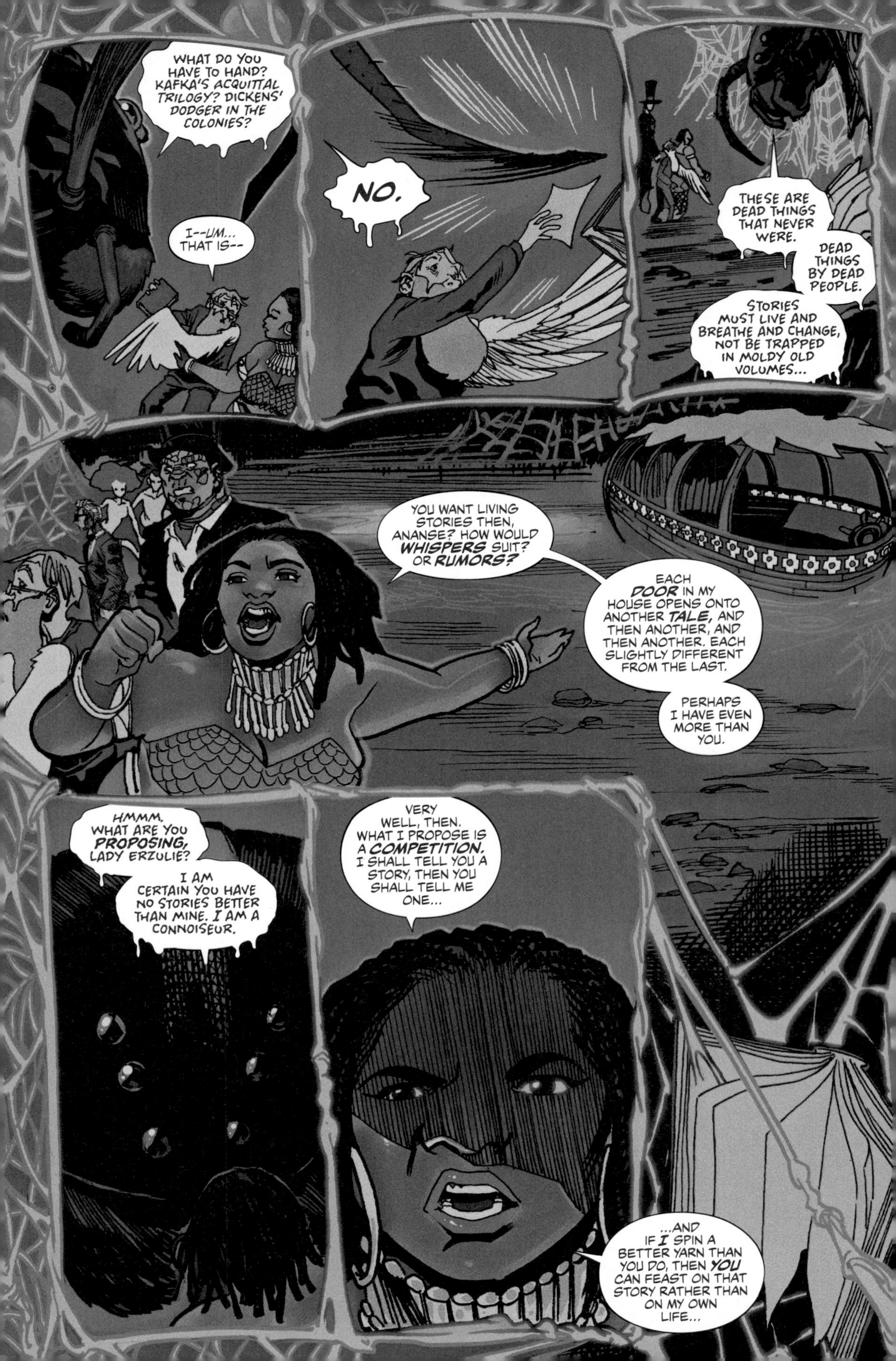
WHAT DO YOU HAVE TO HAND? KAFKA'S ACQUITTAL TRILOGY? DICKENS' DODGER IN THE COLONIES?
I--UM... THAT IS--
NO.
THESE ARE DEAD THINGS THAT NEVER WERE.
DEAD THINGS BY DEAD PEOPLE.
STORIES MUST LIVE AND BREATHE AND CHANGE, NOT BE TRAPPED IN MOLDY OLD VOLUMES...
YOU WANT LIVING STORIES THEN, ANANSE? HOW WOULD WHISPERS SUIT? OR RUMORS?
EACH DOOR IN MY HOUSE OPENS ONTO ANOTHER TALE, AND THEN ANOTHER, AND THEN ANOTHER. EACH SLIGHTLY DIFFERENT FROM THE LAST.
PERHAPS I HAVE EVEN MORE THAN YOU.
HMMM. WHAT ARE YOU PROPOSING, LADY ERZULIE?
I AM CERTAIN YOU HAVE NO STORIES BETTER THAN MINE. I AM A CONNOISEUR.
VERY WELL, THEN. WHAT I PROPOSE IS A COMPETITION. I SHALL TELL YOU A STORY, THEN YOU SHALL TELL ME ONE...
...AND IF I SPIN A BETTER YARN THAN YOU DO, THEN YOU CAN FEAST ON THAT STORY RATHER THAN ON MY OWN LIFE...

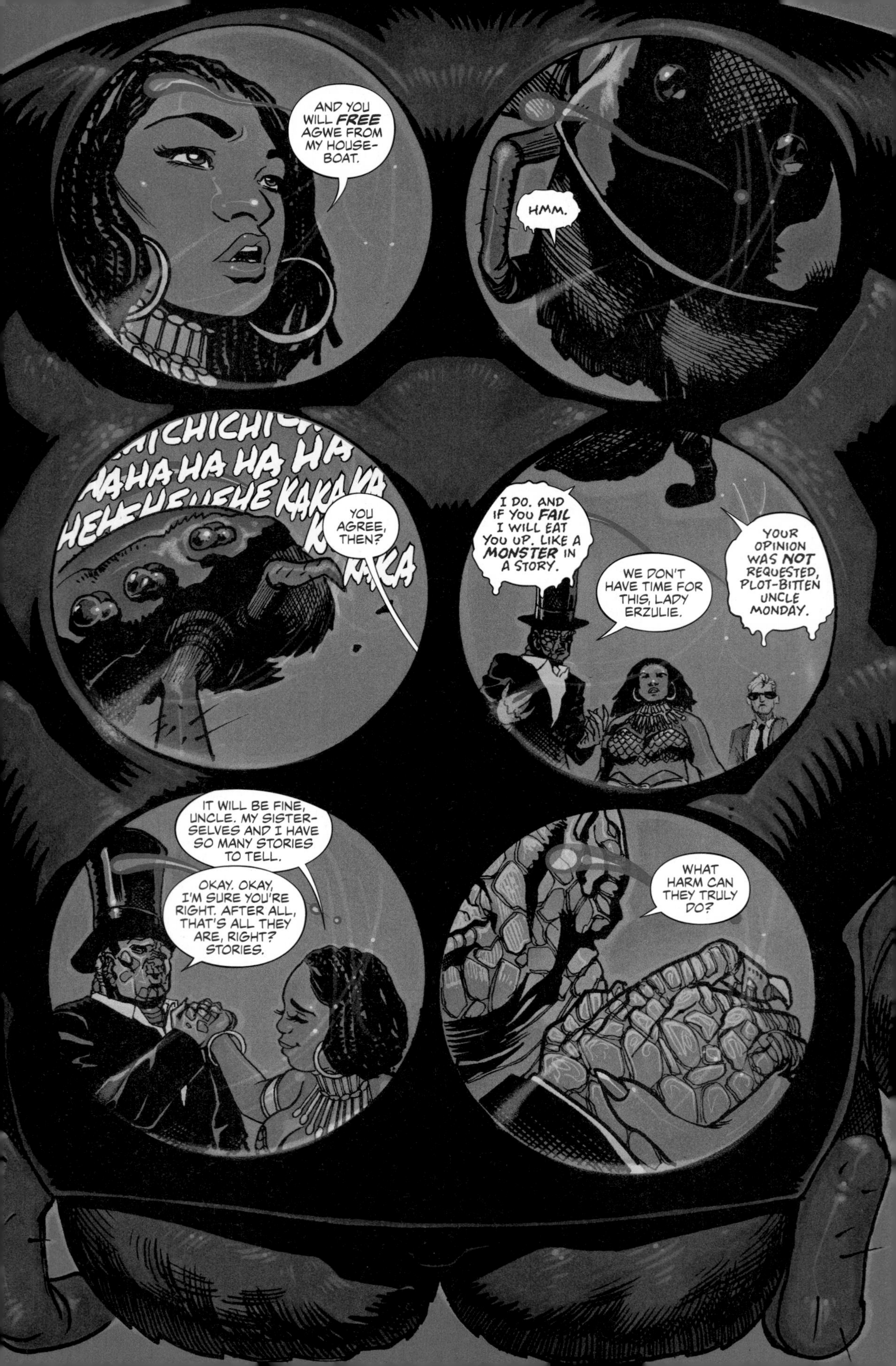
AND YOU WILL FREE AGWE FROM MY HOUSE-BOAT.
HMM.
HAHA HA HA HA
HEHEHEHEHE KAKAKA
KAKAKA
YOU AGREE, THEN?
I DO. AND IF YOU FAIL I WILL EAT YOU UP. LIKE A MONSTER IN A STORY.
WE DON'T HAVE TIME FOR THIS, LADY ERZULIE.
YOUR OPINION WAS NOT REQUESTED, PLOT-BITTEN UNCLE MONDAY.
IT WILL BE FINE, UNCLE. MY SISTER-SELVES AND I HAVE SO MANY STORIES TO TELL.
OKAY. OKAY, I'M SURE YOU'RE RIGHT. AFTER ALL, THAT'S ALL THEY ARE, RIGHT? STORIES.
WHAT HARM CAN THEY TRULY DO?

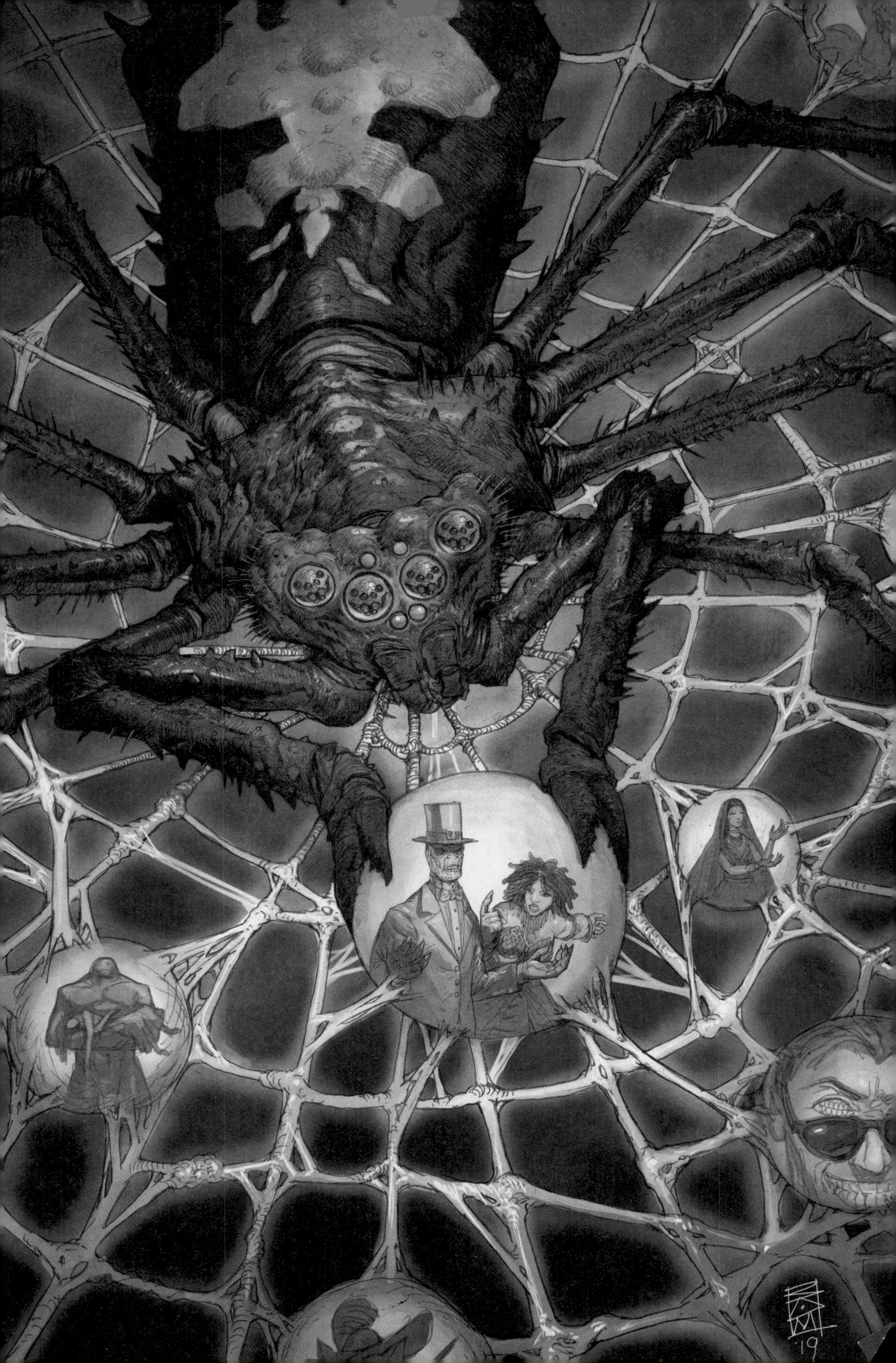

HOUSE OF WHISPERS

House Rules

WRITTEN BY
Nalo Hopkinson
and *Dan Watters*

ILLUSTRATED BY
Dominike "DOMO" Stanton

COLORS BY
John Rauch

LETTERS BY
AndWorld Design

COVER ART BY
Sean Andrew Murray

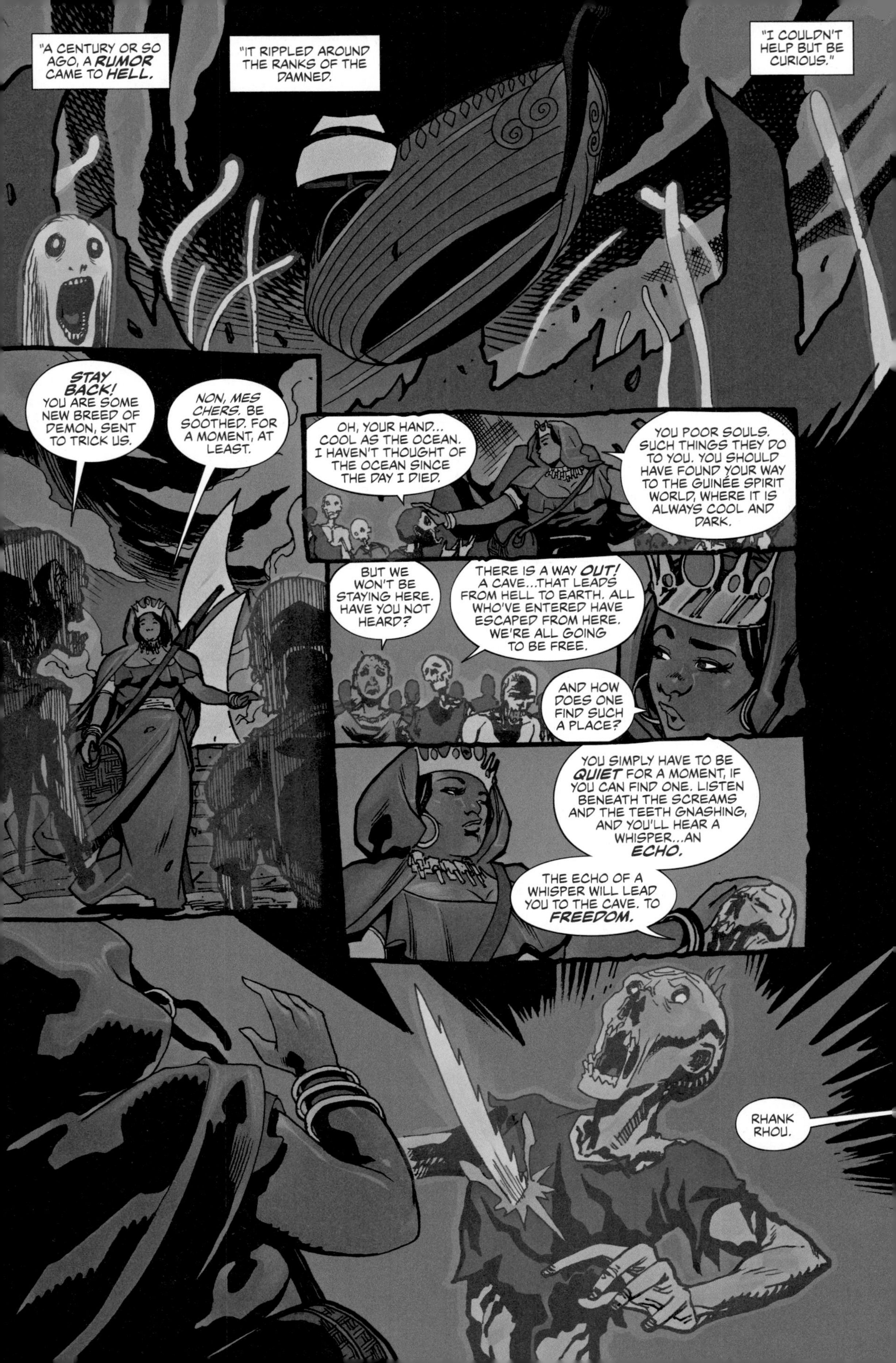
"A CENTURY OR SO AGO, A RUMOR CAME TO HELL.
"IT RIPPLED AROUND THE RANKS OF THE DAMNED.
"I COULDN'T HELP BUT BE CURIOUS."
STAY BACK! YOU ARE SOME NEW BREED OF DEMON, SENT TO TRICK US.
NON, MES CHERS. BE SOOTHED. FOR A MOMENT, AT LEAST.
OH, YOUR HAND... COOL AS THE OCEAN. I HAVEN'T THOUGHT OF THE OCEAN SINCE THE DAY I DIED.
YOU POOR SOULS. SUCH THINGS THEY DO TO YOU. YOU SHOULD HAVE FOUND YOUR WAY TO THE GUINÉE SPIRIT WORLD, WHERE IT IS ALWAYS COOL AND DARK.
BUT WE WON'T BE STAYING HERE. HAVE YOU NOT HEARD?
THERE IS A WAY OUT! A CAVE...THAT LEADS FROM HELL TO EARTH. ALL WHO'VE ENTERED HAVE ESCAPED FROM HERE. WE'RE ALL GOING TO BE FREE.
AND HOW DOES ONE FIND SUCH A PLACE?
YOU SIMPLY HAVE TO BE QUIET FOR A MOMENT, IF YOU CAN FIND ONE. LISTEN BENEATH THE SCREAMS AND THE TEETH GNASHING, AND YOU'LL HEAR A WHISPER...AN ECHO.
THE ECHO OF A WHISPER WILL LEAD YOU TO THE CAVE. TO FREEDOM.
RHANK RHOU.

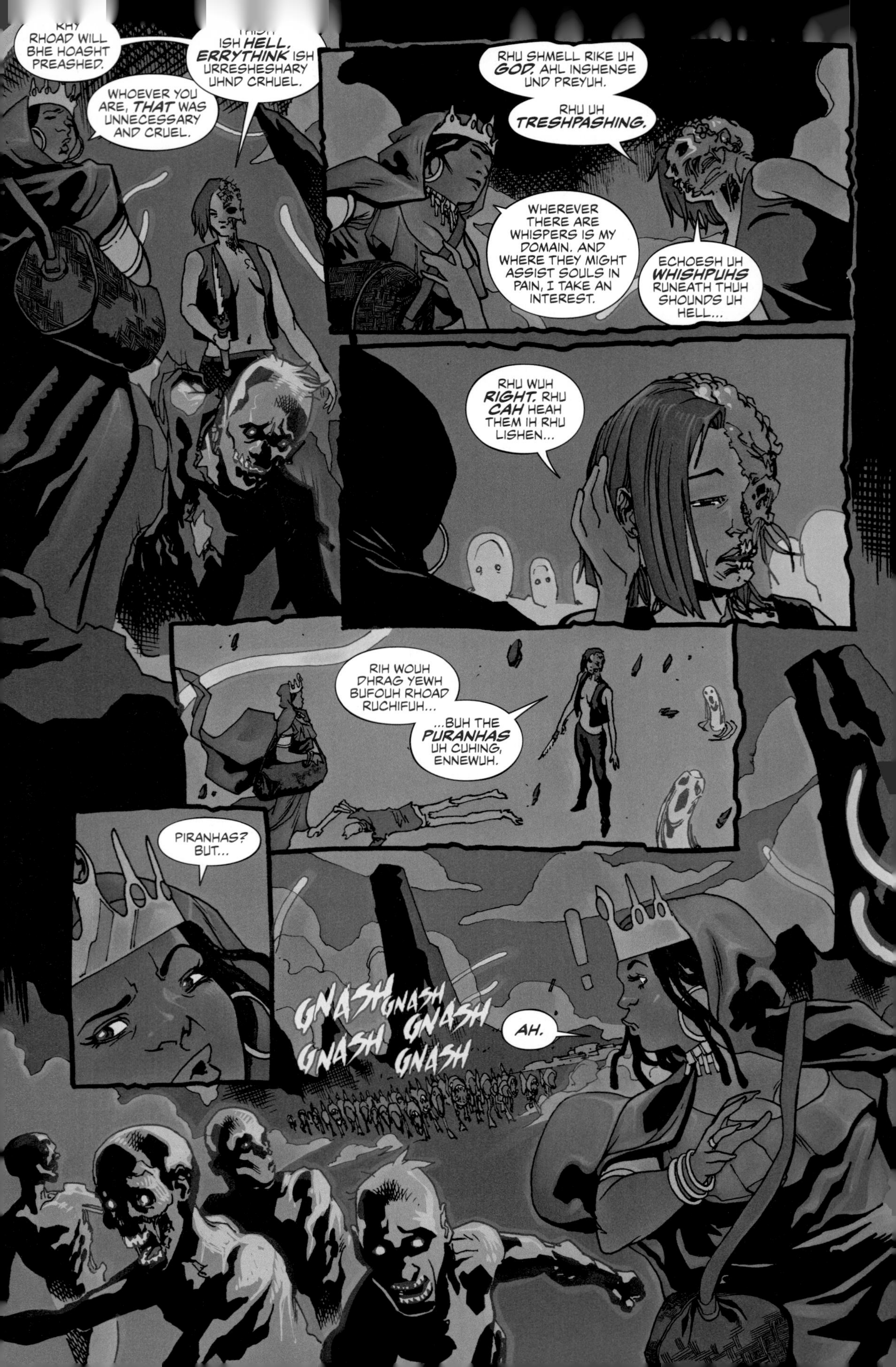

RHOAD WILL BHE HOASHT PREASHED.
ISH HELL. ERRYTHINK ISH URRESHESHARY UHND CRHUEL.
WHOEVER YOU ARE, THAT WAS UNNECESSARY AND CRUEL.
RHU SHMELL RIKE UH GOD. AHL INSHENSE UND PREYUH.
RHU UH TRESHPASHING.
WHEREVER THERE ARE WHISPERS IS MY DOMAIN. AND WHERE THEY MIGHT ASSIST SOULS IN PAIN, I TAKE AN INTEREST.
ECHOESH UH WHISHPUHS RUNEATH THUH SHOUNDS UH HELL...
RHU WUH RIGHT. RHU CAH HEAH THEM IH RHU LISHEN...
RIH WOUH DHRAG YEWH BUFOUH RHOAD RUCHIFUH...
...BUH THE PURANHAS UH CUHING, ENNEWUH.
PIRANHAS? BUT...
GNASH GNASH GNASH GNASH GNASH GNASH
AH.

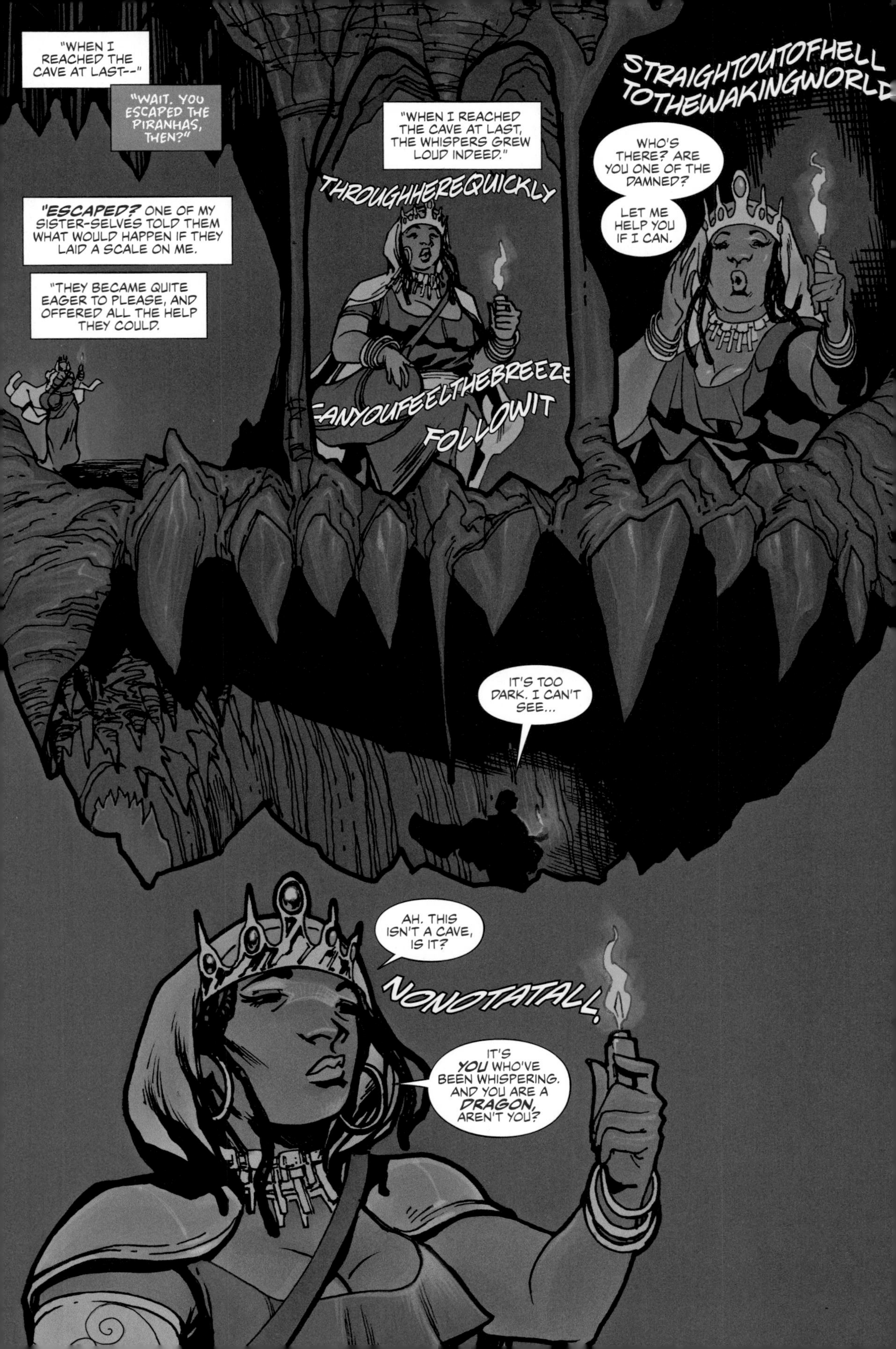
"WHEN I REACHED THE CAVE AT LAST--"
"WAIT. YOU ESCAPED THE PIRANHAS, THEN?"
"ESCAPED? ONE OF MY SISTER-SELVES TOLD THEM WHAT WOULD HAPPEN IF THEY LAID A SCALE ON ME.
"THEY BECAME QUITE EAGER TO PLEASE, AND OFFERED ALL THE HELP THEY COULD.
"WHEN I REACHED THE CAVE AT LAST, THE WHISPERS GREW LOUD INDEED."
THROUGHHEREQUICKLY
CANYOUFEELTHEBREEZE
FOLLOWIT
STRAIGHTOUTOFHELL TOTHEWAKINGWORLD
WHO'S THERE? ARE YOU ONE OF THE DAMNED?
LET ME HELP YOU IF I CAN.
IT'S TOO DARK. I CAN'T SEE...
AH. THIS ISN'T A CAVE, IS IT?
NONOTATALL
IT'S YOU WHO'VE BEEN WHISPERING. AND YOU ARE A DRAGON, AREN'T YOU?

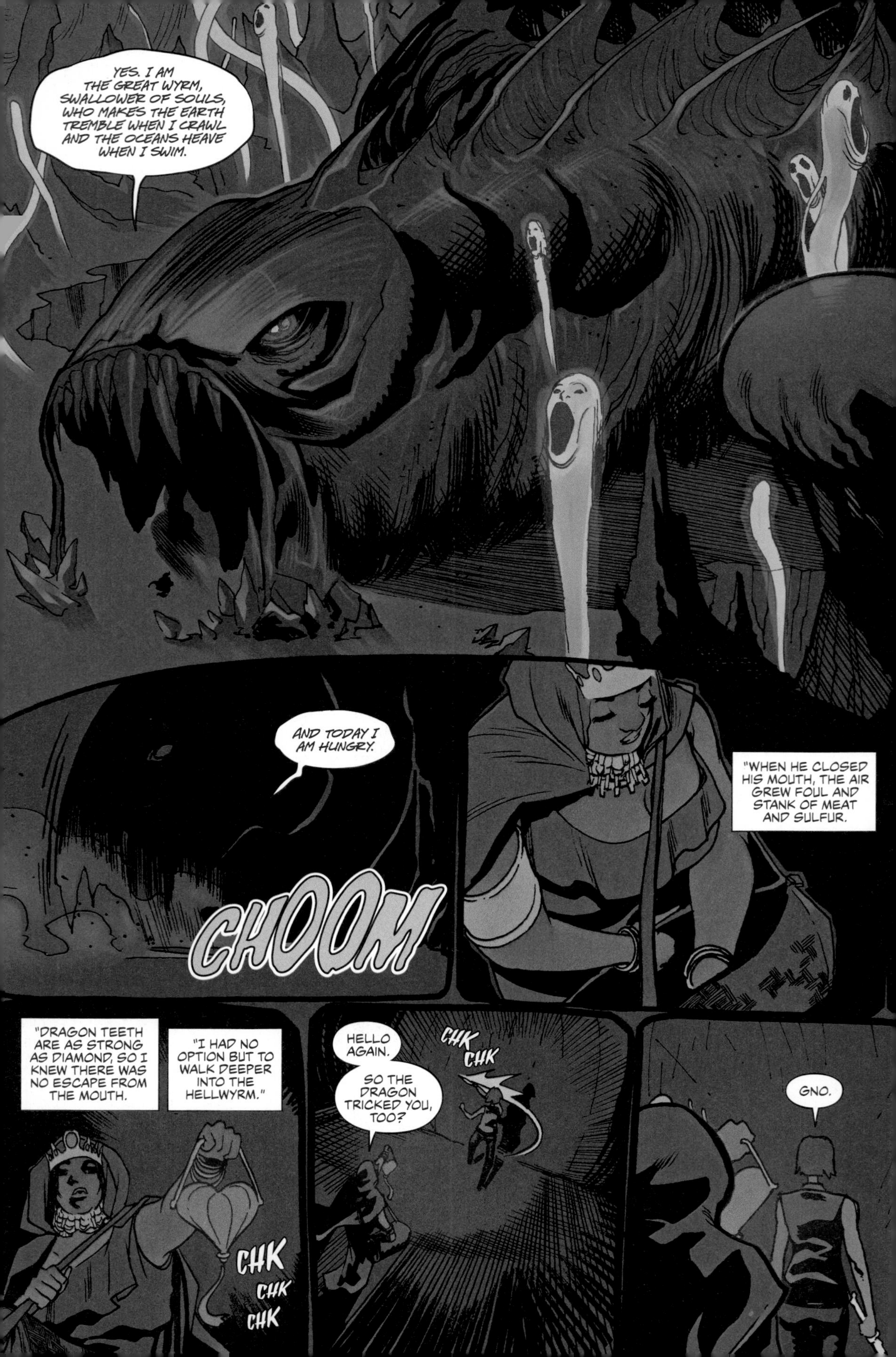
YES. I AM THE GREAT WYRM, SWALLOWER OF SOULS, WHO MAKES THE EARTH TREMBLE WHEN I CRAWL AND THE OCEANS HEAVE WHEN I SWIM.
AND TODAY I AM HUNGRY.
CHOOM
"WHEN HE CLOSED HIS MOUTH, THE AIR GREW FOUL AND STANK OF MEAT AND SULFUR.
"DRAGON TEETH ARE AS STRONG AS DIAMOND, SO I KNEW THERE WAS NO ESCAPE FROM THE MOUTH.
"I HAD NO OPTION BUT TO WALK DEEPER INTO THE HELLWYRM."
CHK CHK CHK
HELLO AGAIN.
SO THE DRAGON TRICKED YOU, TOO?
CHK CHK
GNO.

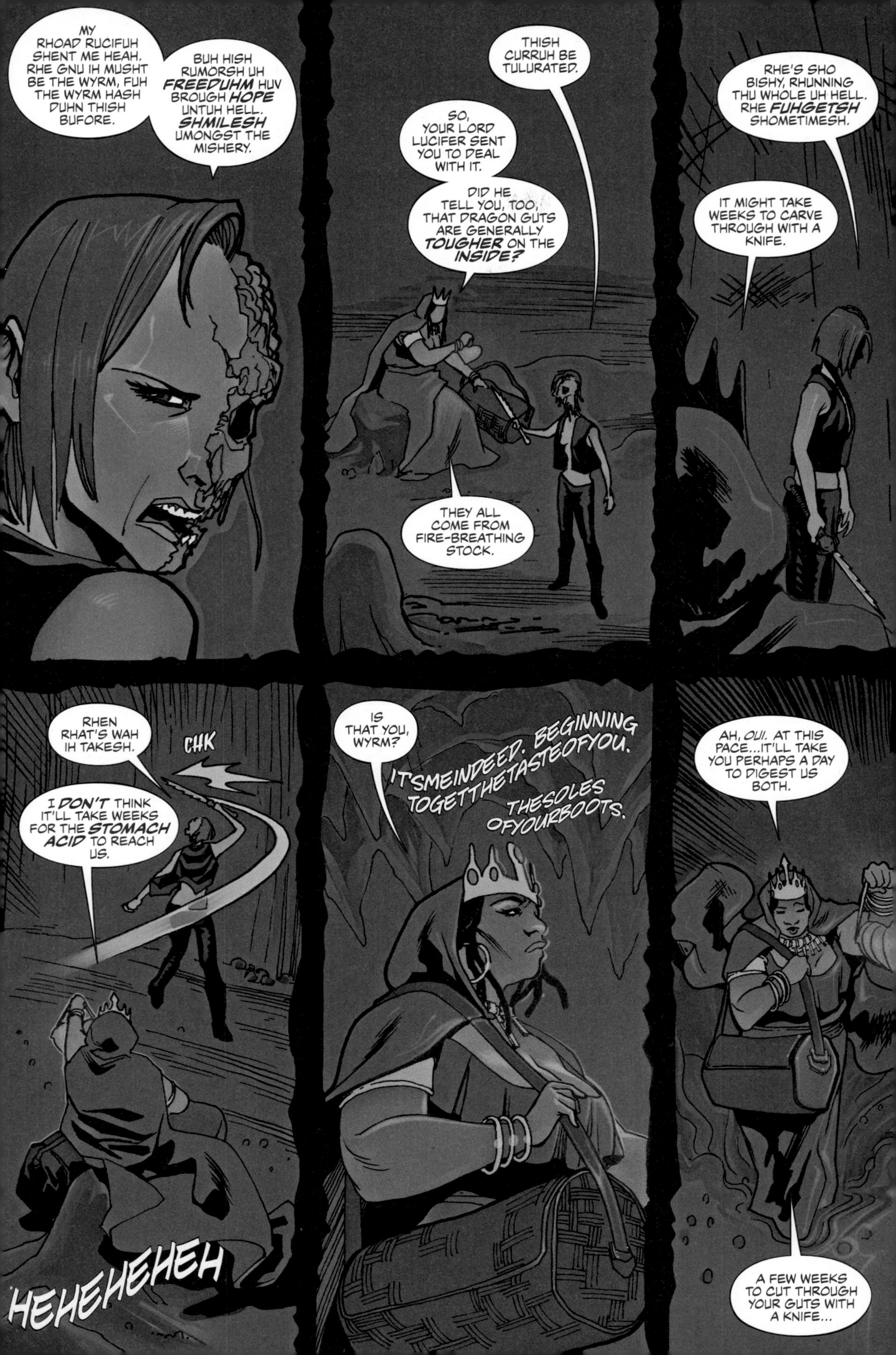
MY RHOAD RUCIFUH SHENT ME HEAH. RHE GNU IH MUSHT BE THE WYRM, FUH THE WYRM HASH DUHN THISH BUFORE.
BUH HISH RUMORSH UH FREEDUHM HUV BROUGH HOPE UNTUH HELL. SHMILESH UMONGST THE MISHERY.
THISH CURRUH BE TULURATED.
SO, YOUR LORD LUCIFER SENT YOU TO DEAL WITH IT.
DID HE TELL YOU, TOO, THAT DRAGON GUTS ARE GENERALLY TOUGHER ON THE INSIDE?
THEY ALL COME FROM FIRE-BREATHING STOCK.
RHE'S SHO BISHY, RHUNNING THU WHOLE UH HELL. RHE FUHGETSH SHOMETIMESH.
IT MIGHT TAKE WEEKS TO CARVE THROUGH WITH A KNIFE.
RHEN RHAT'S WAH IH TAKESH.
CHK
I DON'T THINK IT'LL TAKE WEEKS FOR THE STOMACH ACID TO REACH US.
HEHEHEHEH
IS THAT YOU, WYRM?
IT'SMEINDEED. BEGINNING TOGETTHETASTEOFYOU.
THESOLES OFYOURBOOTS.
AH, OUI. AT THIS PACE...IT'LL TAKE YOU PERHAPS A DAY TO DIGEST US BOTH.
A FEW WEEKS TO CUT THROUGH YOUR GUTS WITH A KNIFE...

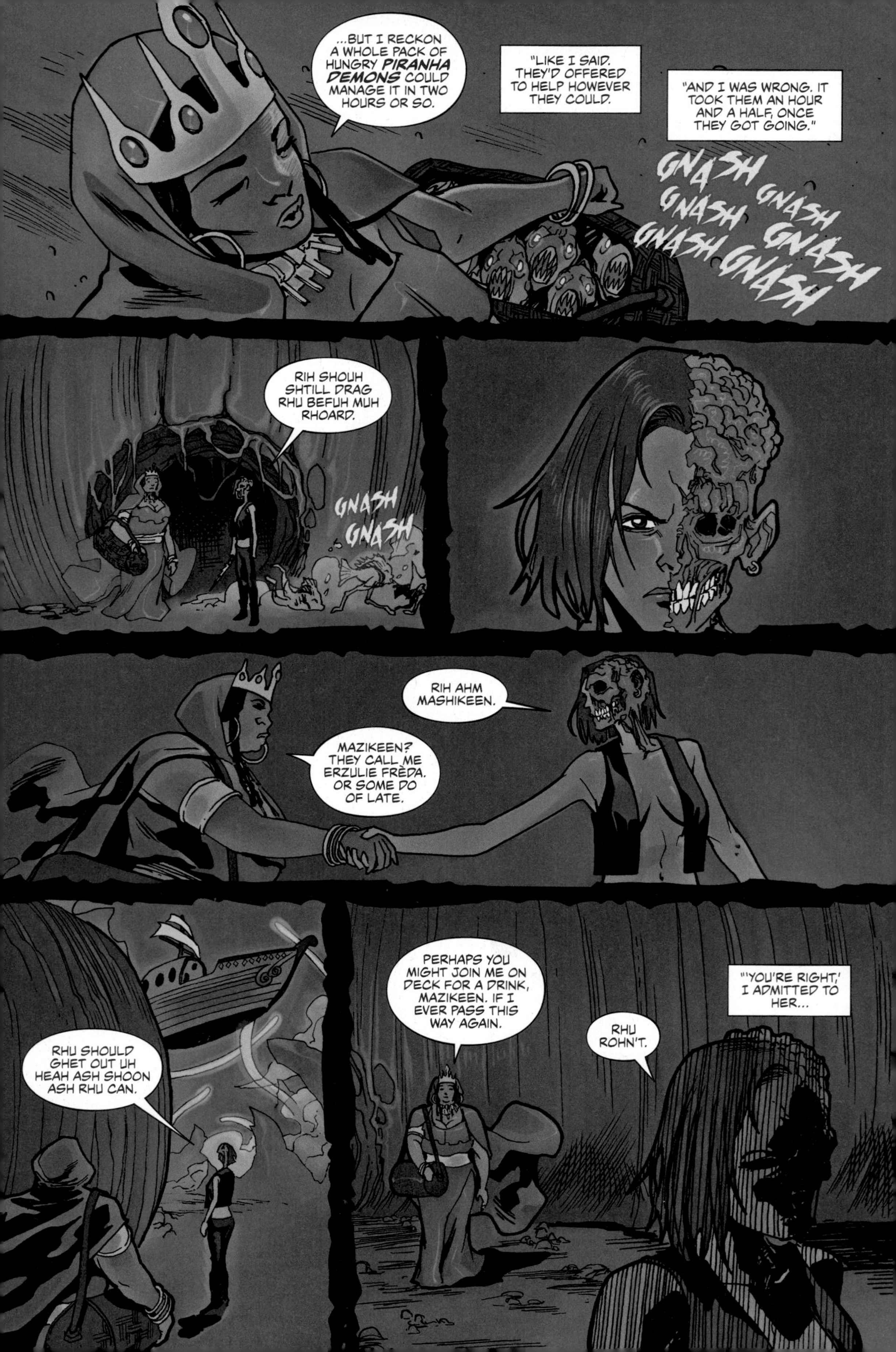

...BUT I RECKON A WHOLE PACK OF HUNGRY **PIRANHA DEMONS** COULD MANAGE IT IN TWO HOURS OR SO.
"LIKE I SAID. THEY'D OFFERED TO HELP HOWEVER THEY COULD.
"AND I WAS WRONG. IT TOOK THEM AN HOUR AND A HALF, ONCE THEY GOT GOING."
GNASH GNASH GNASH GNASH GNASH GNASH
RIH SHOUH SHTILL DRAG RHU BEFUH MUH RHOARD.
GNASH GNASH
RIH AHM MASHIKEEN.
MAZIKEEN? THEY CALL ME ERZULIE FRÈDA. OR SOME DO OF LATE.
RHU SHOULD GHET OUT UH HEAH ASH SHOON ASH RHU CAN.
PERHAPS YOU MIGHT JOIN ME ON DECK FOR A DRINK, MAZIKEEN. IF I EVER PASS THIS WAY AGAIN.
RHU ROHN'T.
"'YOU'RE RIGHT,' I ADMITTED TO HER...

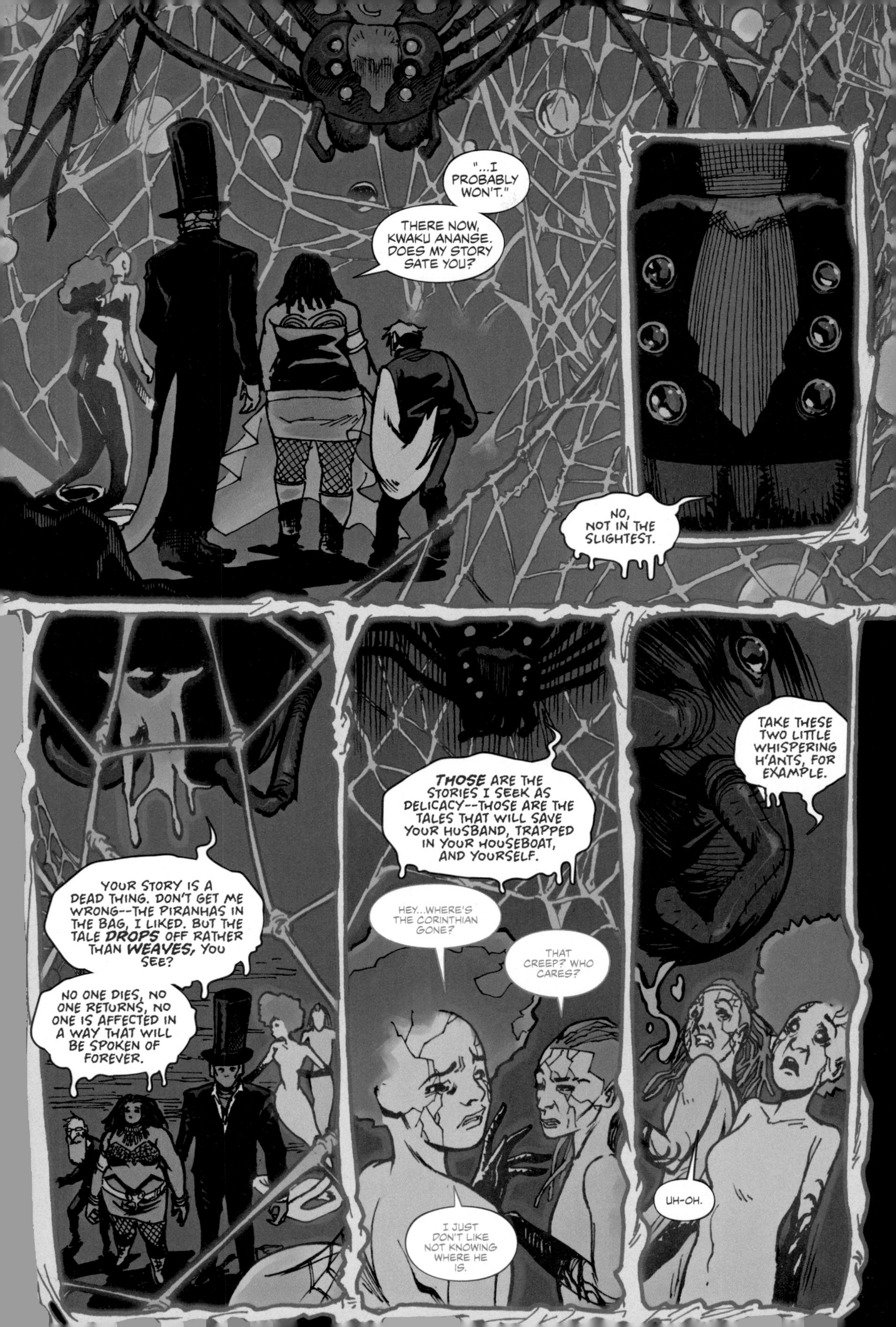
"...I PROBABLY WON'T."
THERE NOW, KWAKU ANANSE. DOES MY STORY SATE YOU?
NO, NOT IN THE SLIGHTEST.
YOUR STORY IS A DEAD THING. DON'T GET ME WRONG--THE PIRANHAS IN THE BAG, I LIKED. BUT THE TALE DROPS OFF RATHER THAN WEAVES, YOU SEE?
NO ONE DIES, NO ONE RETURNS, NO ONE IS AFFECTED IN A WAY THAT WILL BE SPOKEN OF FOREVER.
THOSE ARE THE STORIES I SEEK AS DELICACY--THOSE ARE THE TALES THAT WILL SAVE YOUR HUSBAND, TRAPPED IN YOUR HOUSEBOAT, AND YOURSELF.
HEY...WHERE'S THE CORINTHIAN GONE?
THAT CREEP? WHO CARES?
I JUST DON'T LIKE NOT KNOWING WHERE HE IS.
TAKE THESE TWO LITTLE WHISPERING H'ANTS, FOR EXAMPLE.
UH-OH.

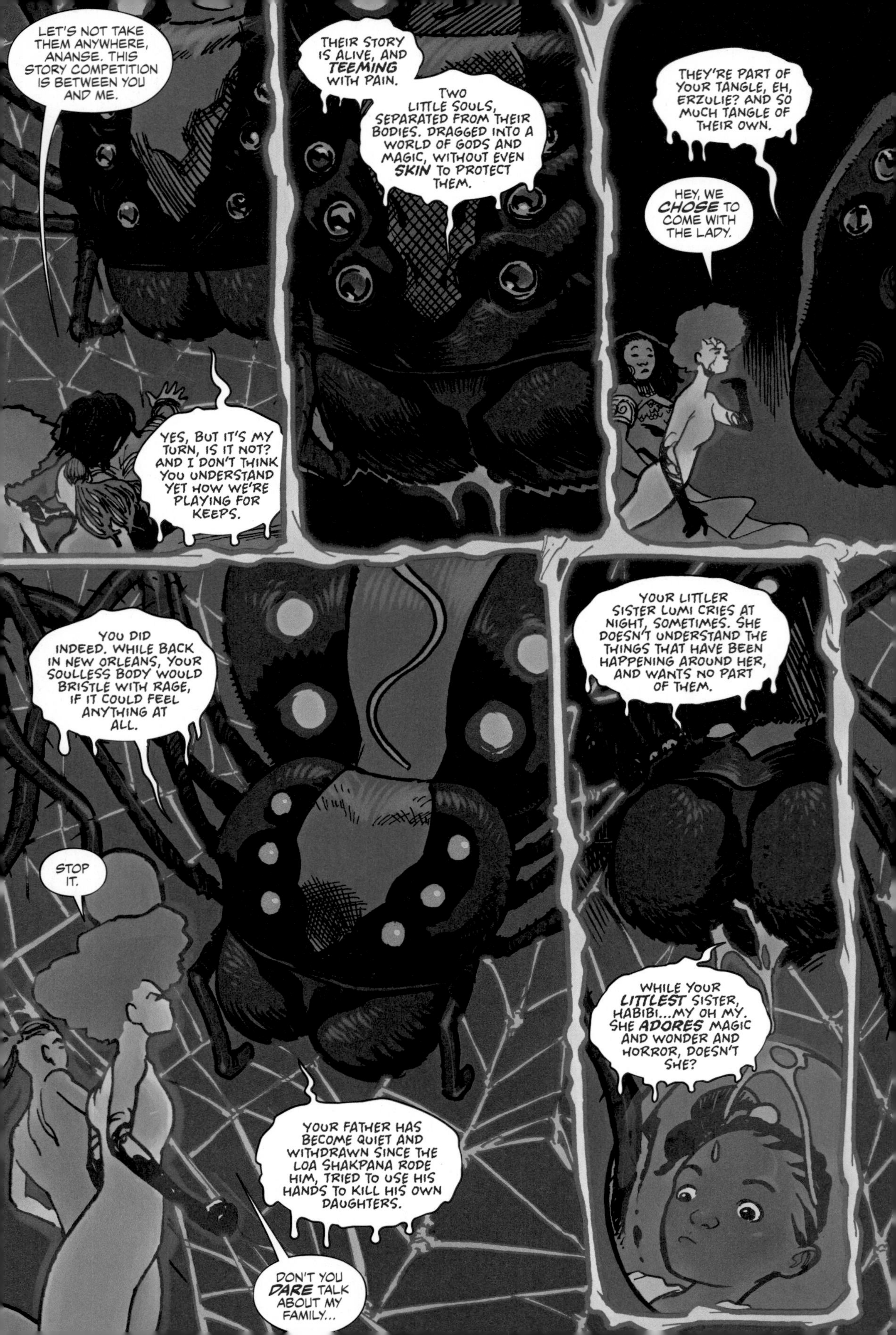
LET'S NOT TAKE THEM ANYWHERE, ANANSE. THIS STORY COMPETITION IS BETWEEN YOU AND ME.
YES, BUT IT'S MY TURN, IS IT NOT? AND I DON'T THINK YOU UNDERSTAND YET HOW WE'RE PLAYING FOR KEEPS.
THEIR STORY IS ALIVE, AND TEEMING WITH PAIN.
TWO LITTLE SOULS, SEPARATED FROM THEIR BODIES. DRAGGED INTO A WORLD OF GODS AND MAGIC, WITHOUT EVEN SKIN TO PROTECT THEM.
THEY'RE PART OF YOUR TANGLE, EH, ERZULIE? AND SO MUCH TANGLE OF THEIR OWN.
HEY, WE CHOSE TO COME WITH THE LADY.
YOU DID INDEED. WHILE BACK IN NEW ORLEANS, YOUR SOULLESS BODY WOULD BRISTLE WITH RAGE, IF IT COULD FEEL ANYTHING AT ALL.
STOP IT.
YOUR FATHER HAS BECOME QUIET AND WITHDRAWN SINCE THE LOA SHAKPANA RODE HIM, TRIED TO USE HIS HANDS TO KILL HIS OWN DAUGHTERS.
DON'T YOU DARE TALK ABOUT MY FAMILY...
YOUR LITTLER SISTER LUMI CRIES AT NIGHT, SOMETIMES. SHE DOESN'T UNDERSTAND THE THINGS THAT HAVE BEEN HAPPENING AROUND HER, AND WANTS NO PART OF THEM.
WHILE YOUR LITTLEST SISTER, HABIBI...MY OH MY. SHE ADORES MAGIC AND WONDER AND HORROR, DOESN'T SHE?

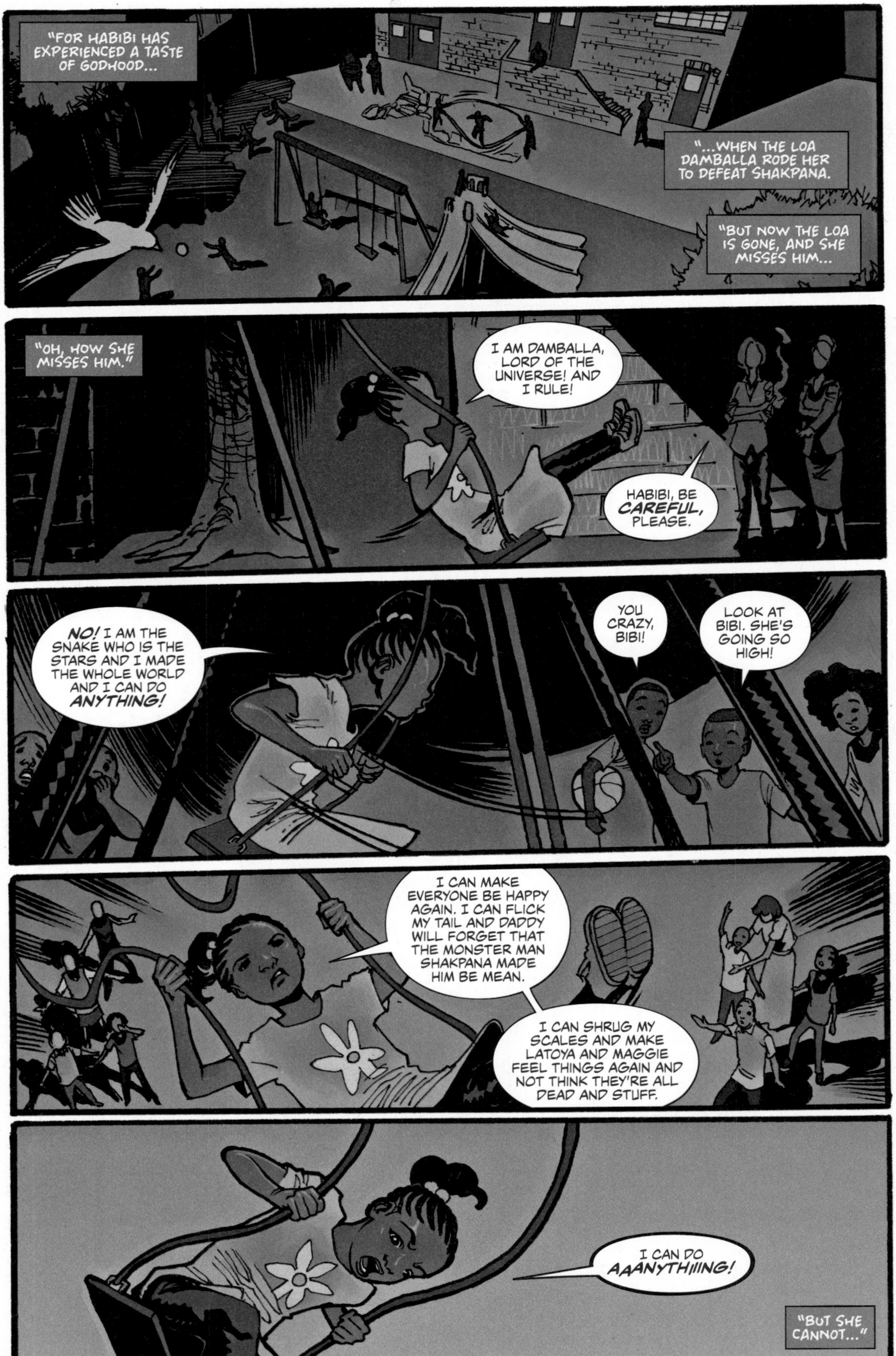
"FOR HABIBI HAS EXPERIENCED A TASTE OF GODHOOD...
"...WHEN THE LOA DAMBALLA RODE HER TO DEFEAT SHAKPANA.
"BUT NOW THE LOA IS GONE, AND SHE MISSES HIM...
"OH, HOW SHE MISSES HIM."
I AM DAMBALLA, LORD OF THE UNIVERSE! AND I RULE!
HABIBI, BE CAREFUL, PLEASE.
NO! I AM THE SNAKE WHO IS THE STARS AND I MADE THE WHOLE WORLD AND I CAN DO ANYTHING!
YOU CRAZY, BIBI!
LOOK AT BIBI. SHE'S GOING SO HIGH!
I CAN MAKE EVERYONE BE HAPPY AGAIN. I CAN FLICK MY TAIL AND DADDY WILL FORGET THAT THE MONSTER MAN SHAKPANA MADE HIM BE MEAN.
I CAN SHRUG MY SCALES AND MAKE LATOYA AND MAGGIE FEEL THINGS AGAIN AND NOT THINK THEY'RE ALL DEAD AND STUFF.
I CAN DO AAANYTHIIING!
"BUT SHE CANNOT..."

"FOR SHE IS NOT DAMBALLA, GREAT MASTER AND SERPENT SPIRIT."

"ANANSE, YOU'VE MADE YOUR POINT."

"SHE IS A TEN-YEAR-OLD GIRL WHO IS SAD ABOUT HER FAMILY, AND WISHES SHE COULD SAVE THEM."

"ANANSE, THIS ISN'T FAIR."

"SHE IS NOT DAMBALLA, WHO SHAPED THE HILLS AND VALLEYS WITH HIS SEVEN THOUSAND COILS..."

"ANANSE!"

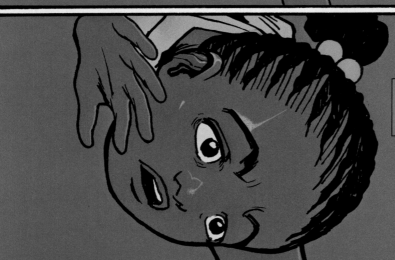

"SHE IS A CHILD WATCHING THE ASPHALT RUSH UP TO MEET HER AS SHE TUMBLES HEADFIRST. SHE HASN'T EVEN TIME TO YELL OUT.

"SHE WONDERS IF THERE WILL BE A LOT OF BLOOD, AND IF THERE IS, IF SHE'LL BE CONSCIOUS LONG ENOUGH TO SEE IT..."

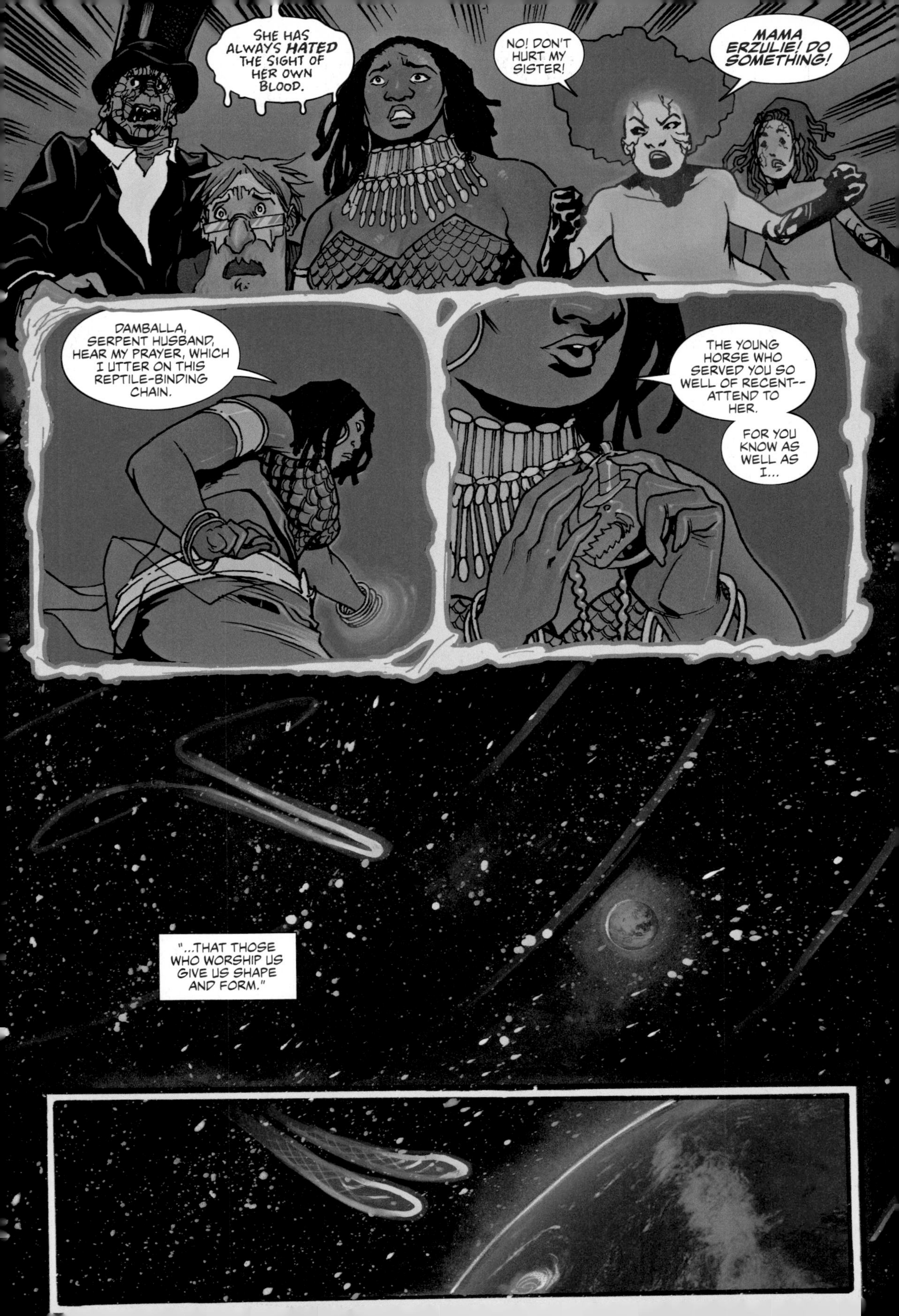
SHE HAS ALWAYS HATED THE SIGHT OF HER OWN BLOOD.
NO! DON'T HURT MY SISTER!
MAMA ERZULIE! DO SOMETHING!
DAMBALLA, SERPENT HUSBAND, HEAR MY PRAYER, WHICH I UTTER ON THIS REPTILE-BINDING CHAIN.
THE YOUNG HORSE WHO SERVED YOU SO WELL OF RECENT-- ATTEND TO HER.
FOR YOU KNOW AS WELL AS I...
"...THAT THOSE WHO WORSHIP US GIVE US SHAPE AND FORM."

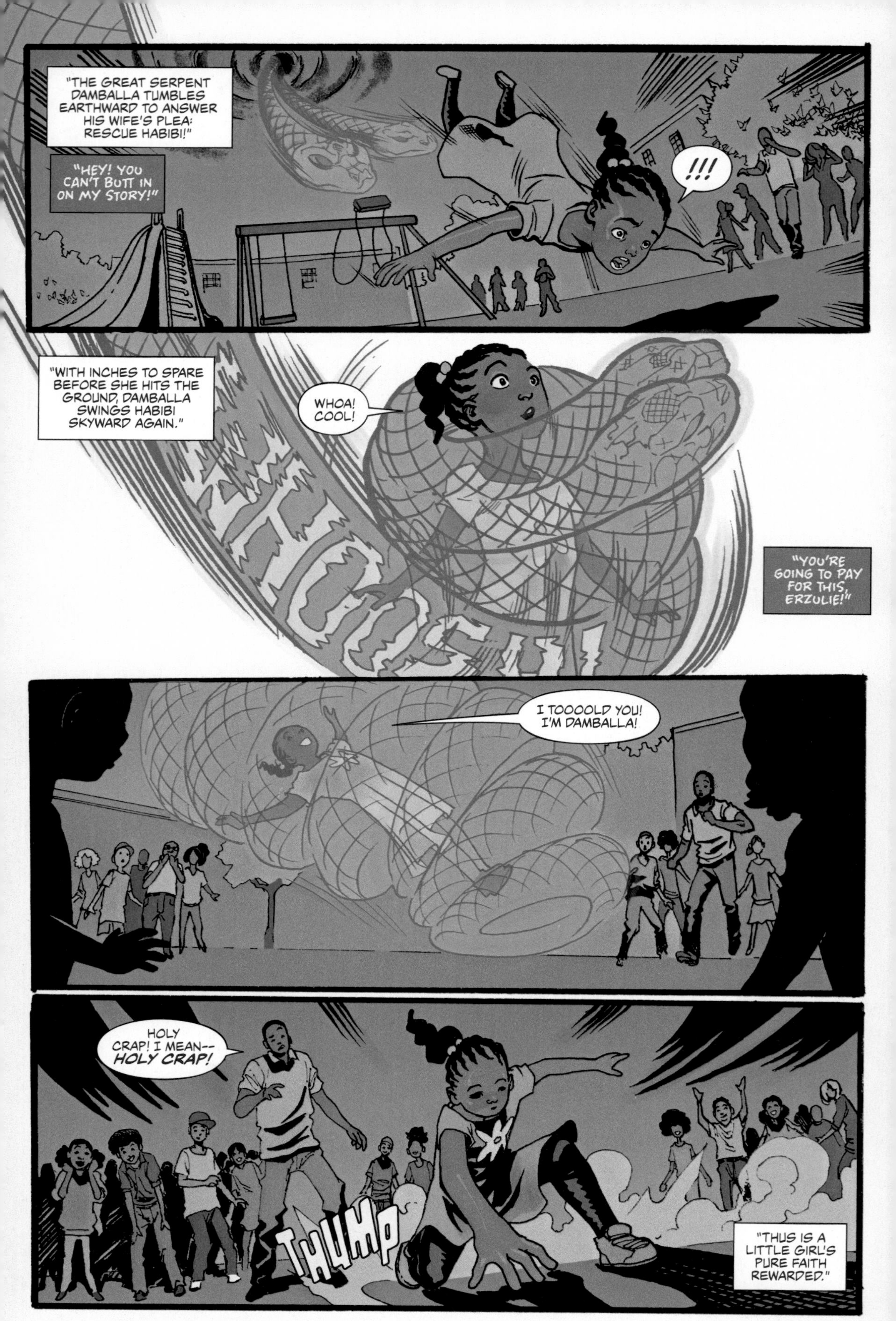

"THE GREAT SERPENT DAMBALLA TUMBLES EARTHWARD TO ANSWER HIS WIFE'S PLEA: RESCUE HABIBI!"
"HEY! YOU CAN'T BUTT IN ON MY STORY!"
!!!
"WITH INCHES TO SPARE BEFORE SHE HITS THE GROUND, DAMBALLA SWINGS HABIBI SKYWARD AGAIN."
WHOA! COOL!
"YOU'RE GOING TO PAY FOR THIS, ERZULIE!"
I TOOOOLD YOU! I'M DAMBALLA!
HOLY CRAP! I MEAN-- HOLY CRAP!
THUMP
"THUS IS A LITTLE GIRL'S PURE FAITH REWARDED."

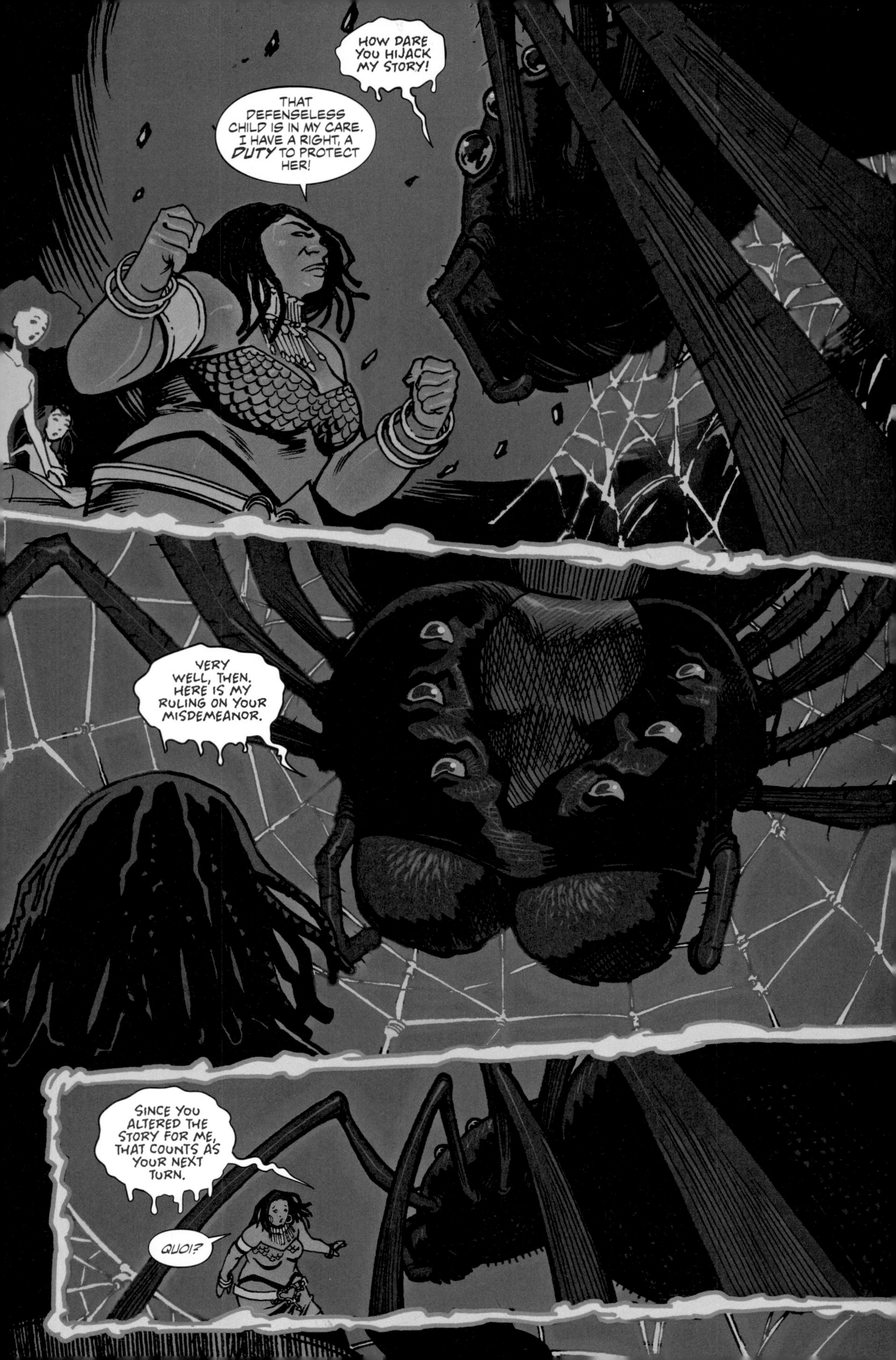
HOW DARE YOU HIJACK MY STORY!
THAT DEFENSELESS CHILD IS IN MY CARE. I HAVE A RIGHT, A *DUTY* TO PROTECT HER!
VERY WELL, THEN. HERE IS MY RULING ON YOUR MISDEMEANOR.
SINCE YOU ALTERED THE STORY FOR ME, THAT COUNTS AS YOUR NEXT TURN.
QUOI?

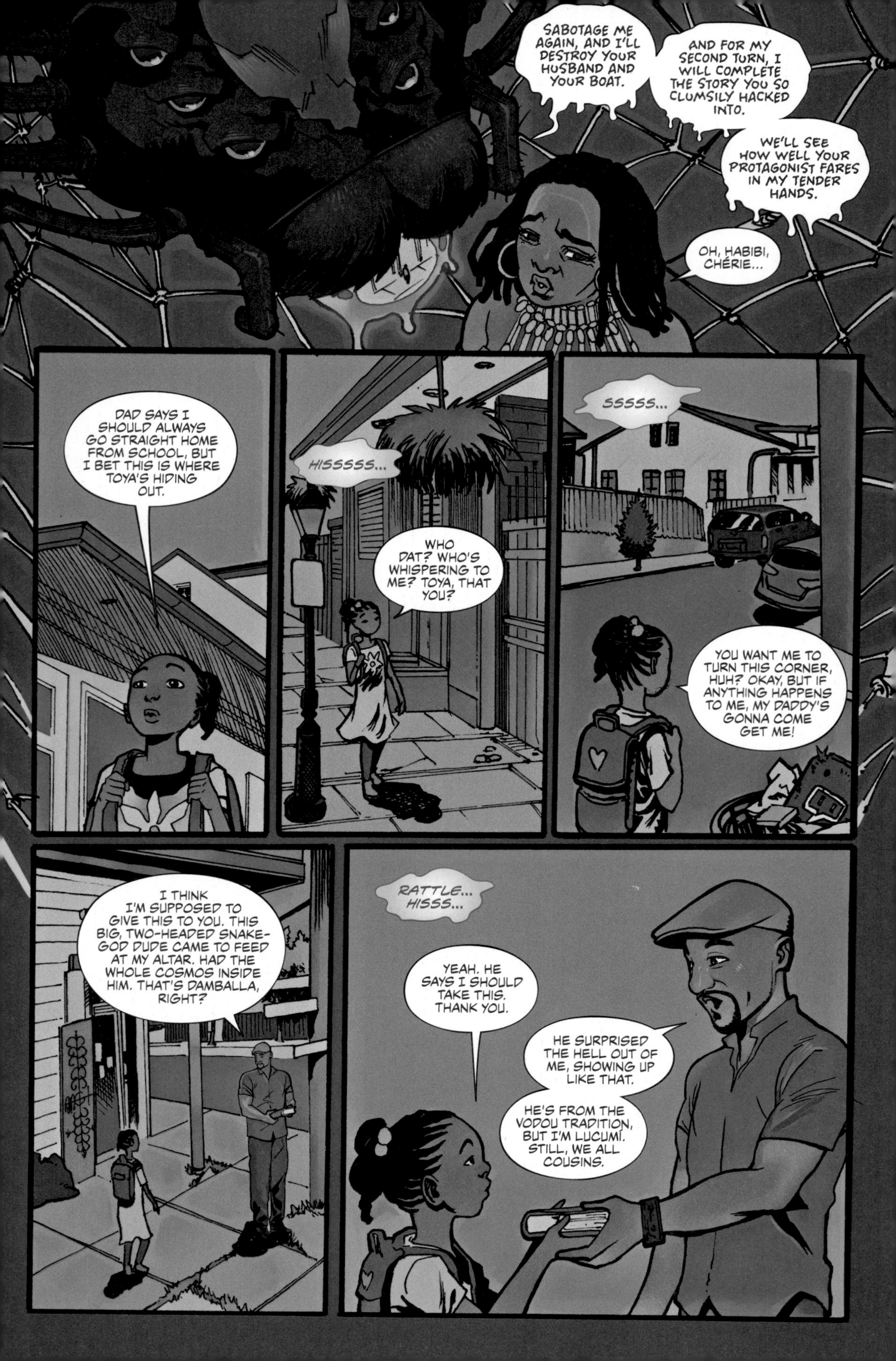
SABOTAGE ME AGAIN, AND I'LL DESTROY YOUR HUSBAND AND YOUR BOAT.
AND FOR MY SECOND TURN, I WILL COMPLETE THE STORY YOU SO CLUMSILY HACKED INTO.
WE'LL SEE HOW WELL YOUR PROTAGONIST FARES IN MY TENDER HANDS.
OH, HABIBI, CHÉRIE...
DAD SAYS I SHOULD ALWAYS GO STRAIGHT HOME FROM SCHOOL, BUT I BET THIS IS WHERE TOYA'S HIDING OUT.
HISSSSS...
WHO DAT? WHO'S WHISPERING TO ME? TOYA, THAT YOU?
SSSSS...
YOU WANT ME TO TURN THIS CORNER, HUH? OKAY, BUT IF ANYTHING HAPPENS TO ME, MY DADDY'S GONNA COME GET ME!
I THINK I'M SUPPOSED TO GIVE THIS TO YOU. THIS BIG, TWO-HEADED SNAKE-GOD DUDE CAME TO FEED AT MY ALTAR. HAD THE WHOLE COSMOS INSIDE HIM. THAT'S DAMBALLA, RIGHT?
RATTLE... HISSS...
YEAH. HE SAYS I SHOULD TAKE THIS. THANK YOU.
HE SURPRISED THE HELL OUT OF ME, SHOWING UP LIKE THAT.
HE'S FROM THE VODOU TRADITION, BUT I'M LUCUMÍ. STILL, WE ALL COUSINS.

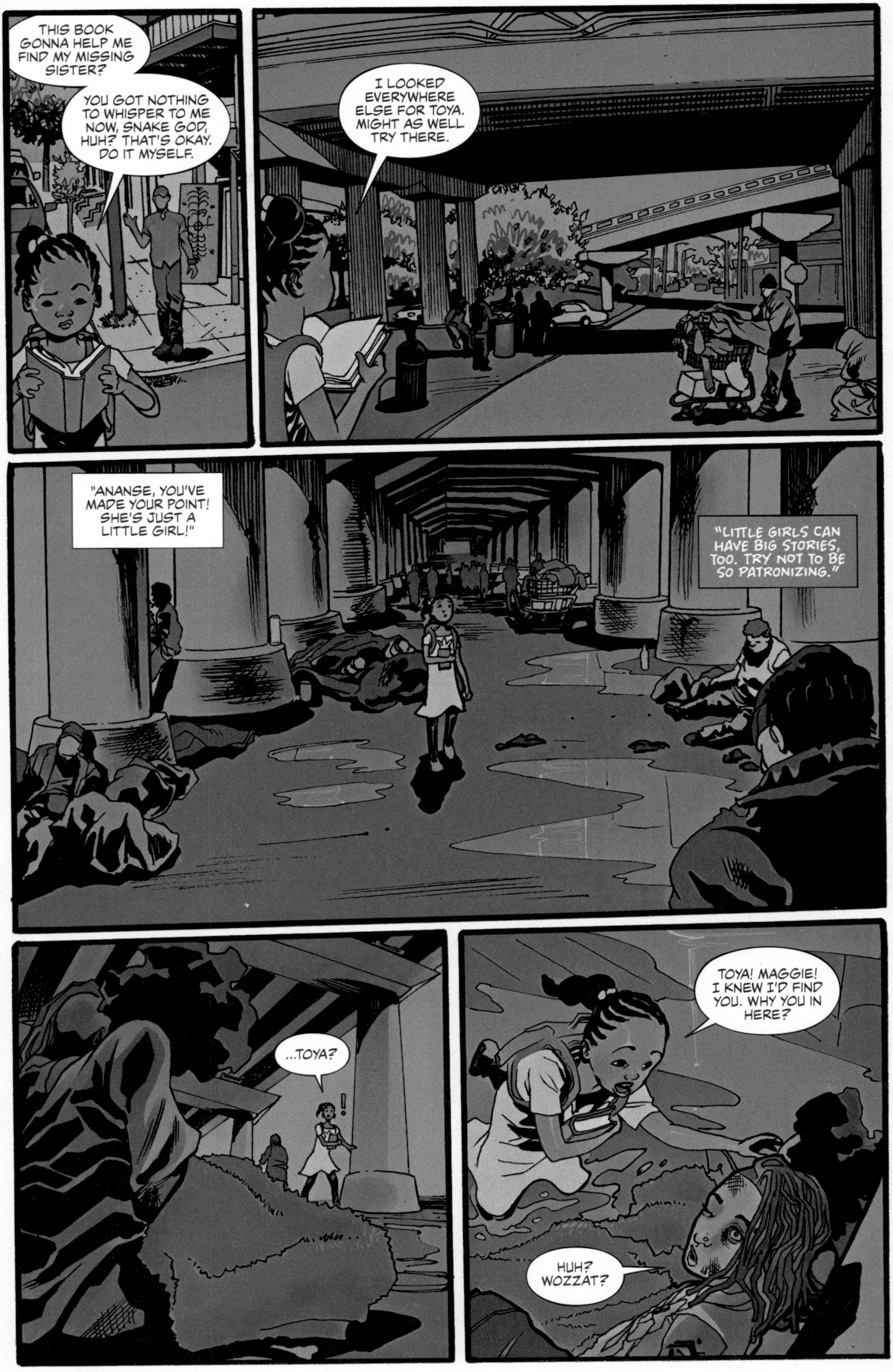
THIS BOOK GONNA HELP ME FIND MY MISSING SISTER?
YOU GOT NOTHING TO WHISPER TO ME NOW, SNAKE GOD, HUH? THAT'S OKAY. DO IT MYSELF.
I LOOKED EVERYWHERE ELSE FOR TOYA. MIGHT AS WELL TRY THERE.
"ANANSE, YOU'VE MADE YOUR POINT! SHE'S JUST A LITTLE GIRL!"
"LITTLE GIRLS CAN HAVE BIG STORIES, TOO. TRY NOT TO BE SO PATRONIZING."
...TOYA?
!
TOYA! MAGGIE! I KNEW I'D FIND YOU. WHY YOU IN HERE?
HUH? WOZZAT?

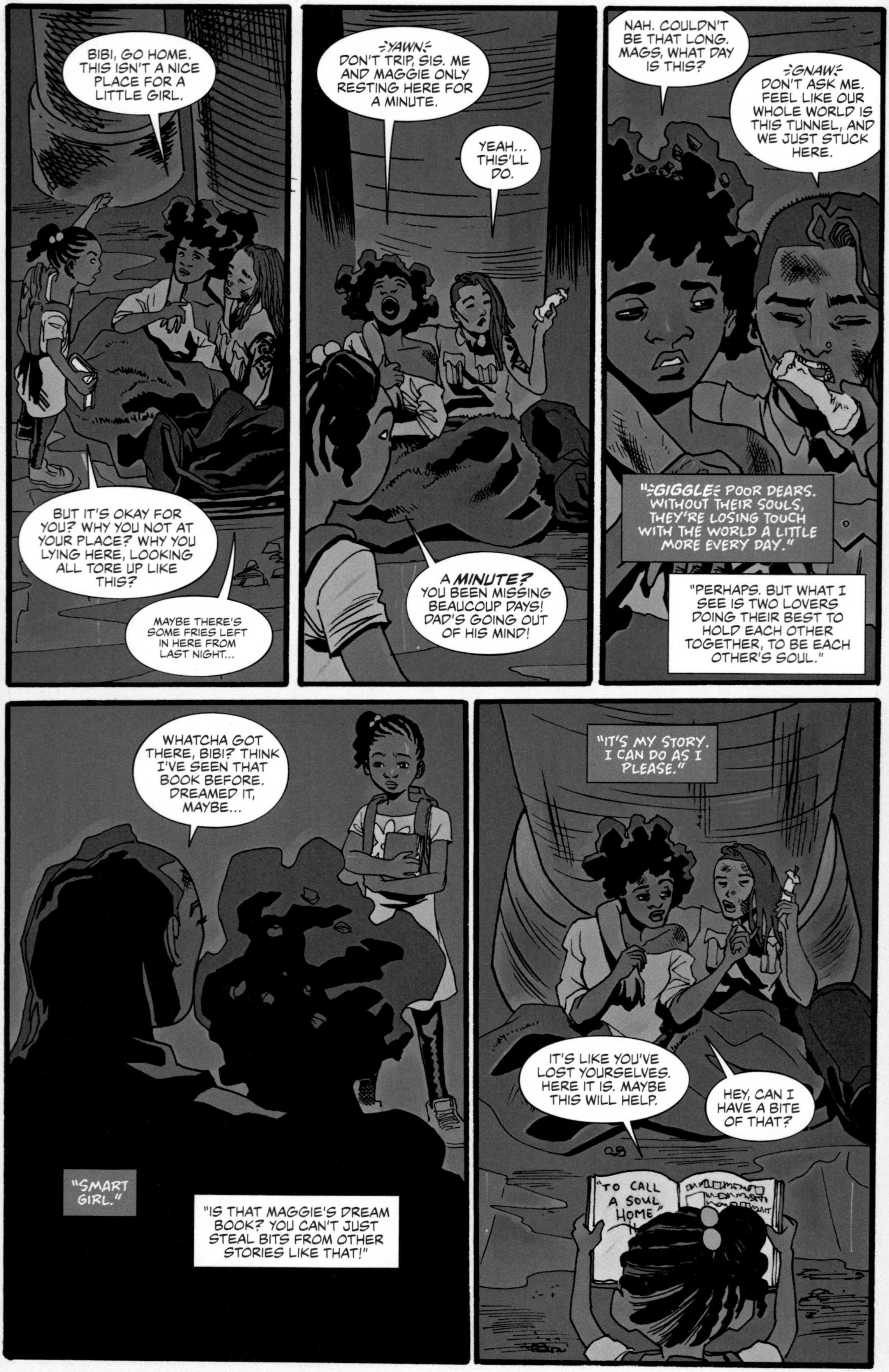
BIBI, GO HOME. THIS ISN'T A NICE PLACE FOR A LITTLE GIRL.
BUT IT'S OKAY FOR YOU? WHY YOU NOT AT YOUR PLACE? WHY YOU LYING HERE, LOOKING ALL TORE UP LIKE THIS?
MAYBE THERE'S SOME FRIES LEFT IN HERE FROM LAST NIGHT...
YAWN
DON'T TRIP, SIS. ME AND MAGGIE ONLY RESTING HERE FOR A MINUTE.
YEAH... THIS'LL DO.
A MINUTE? YOU BEEN MISSING BEAUCOUP DAYS! DAD'S GOING OUT OF HIS MIND!
NAH. COULDN'T BE THAT LONG. MAGS, WHAT DAY IS THIS?
GNAW
DON'T ASK ME. FEEL LIKE OUR WHOLE WORLD IS THIS TUNNEL, AND WE JUST STUCK HERE.
"GIGGLE POOR DEARS. WITHOUT THEIR SOULS, THEY'RE LOSING TOUCH WITH THE WORLD A LITTLE MORE EVERY DAY."
"PERHAPS. BUT WHAT I SEE IS TWO LOVERS DOING THEIR BEST TO HOLD EACH OTHER TOGETHER, TO BE EACH OTHER'S SOUL."
WHATCHA GOT THERE, BIBI? THINK I'VE SEEN THAT BOOK BEFORE. DREAMED IT, MAYBE...
"SMART GIRL."
"IS THAT MAGGIE'S DREAM BOOK? YOU CAN'T JUST STEAL BITS FROM OTHER STORIES LIKE THAT!"
"IT'S MY STORY. I CAN DO AS I PLEASE."
IT'S LIKE YOU'VE LOST YOURSELVES. HERE IT IS. MAYBE THIS WILL HELP.
HEY, CAN I HAVE A BITE OF THAT?
"TO CALL A SOUL HOME"

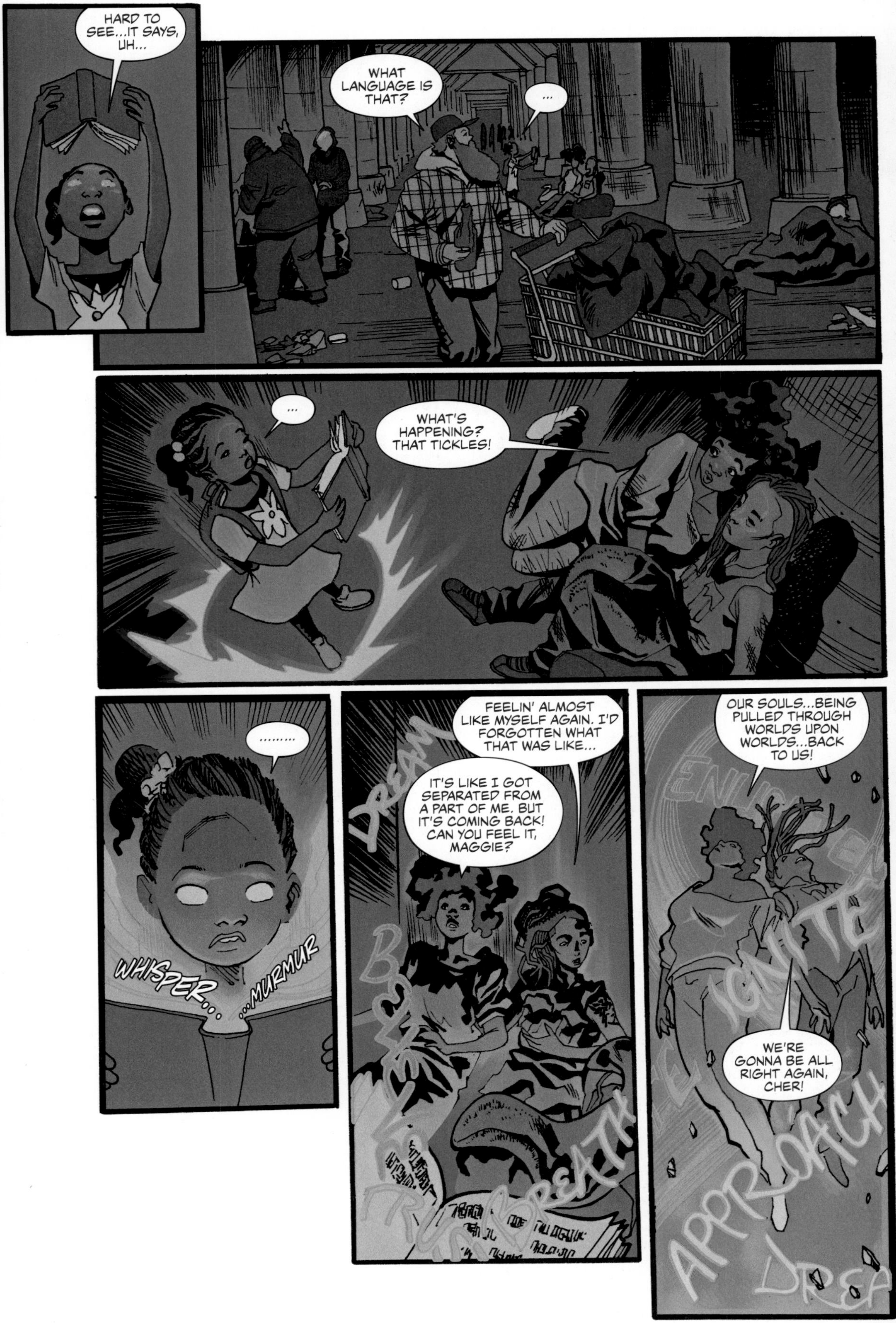
HARD TO SEE...IT SAYS, UH...
WHAT LANGUAGE IS THAT?
...
...
WHAT'S HAPPENING? THAT TICKLES!
....
WHISPER...
...MURMUR
FEELIN' ALMOST LIKE MYSELF AGAIN. I'D FORGOTTEN WHAT THAT WAS LIKE...
IT'S LIKE I GOT SEPARATED FROM A PART OF ME. BUT IT'S COMING BACK! CAN YOU FEEL IT, MAGGIE?
DREAM
BREATH
OUR SOULS...BEING PULLED THROUGH WORLDS UPON WORLDS...BACK TO US!
IGNITE
WE'RE GONNA BE ALL RIGHT AGAIN, CHER!
APPROACH

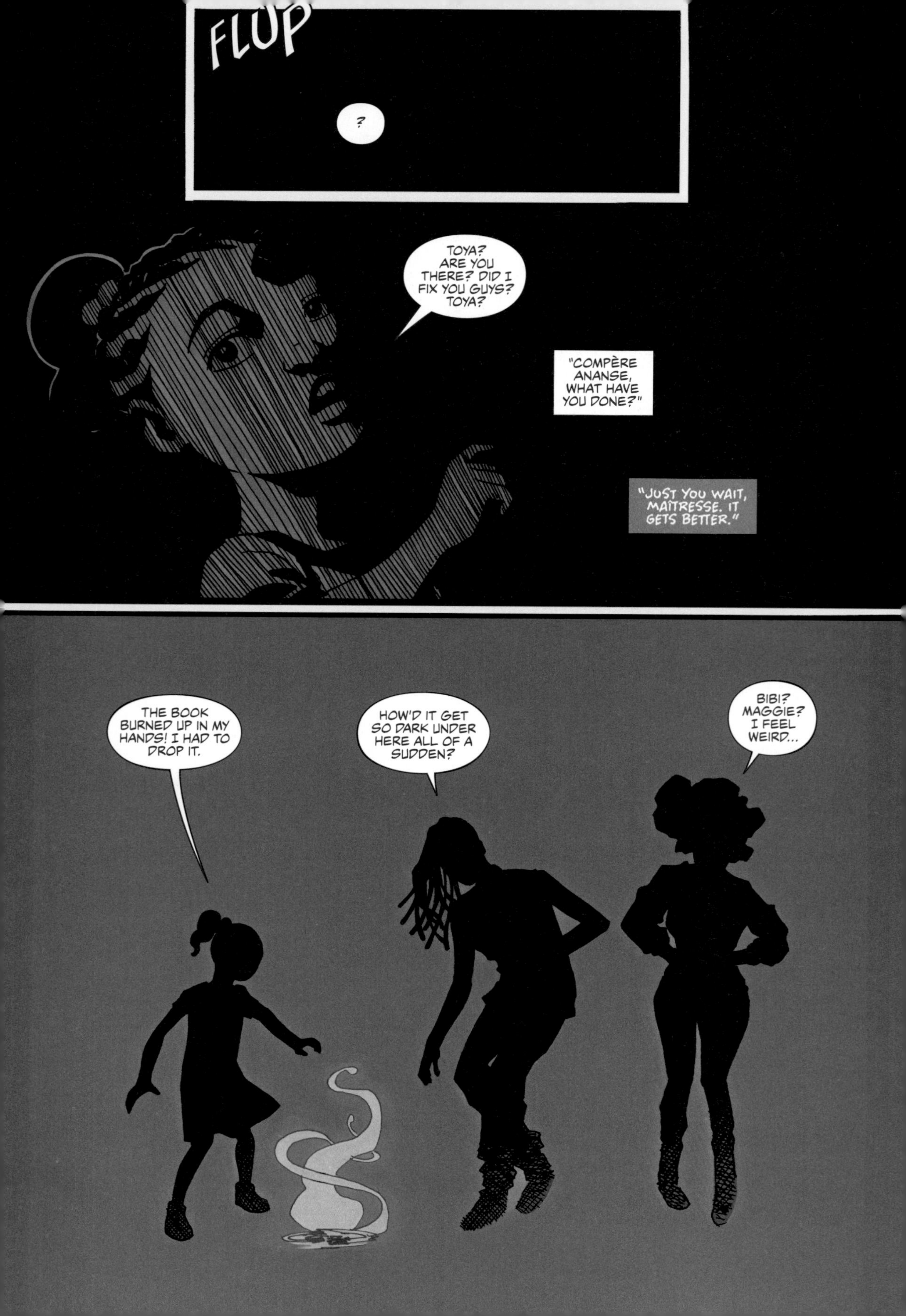
FLUP
?
TOYA? ARE YOU THERE? DID I FIX YOU GUYS? TOYA?
"COMPÈRE ANANSE, WHAT HAVE YOU DONE?"
"JUST YOU WAIT, MAÎTRESSE. IT GETS BETTER."
THE BOOK BURNED UP IN MY HANDS! I HAD TO DROP IT.
HOW'D IT GET SO DARK UNDER HERE ALL OF A SUDDEN?
BIBI? MAGGIE? I FEEL WEIRD...

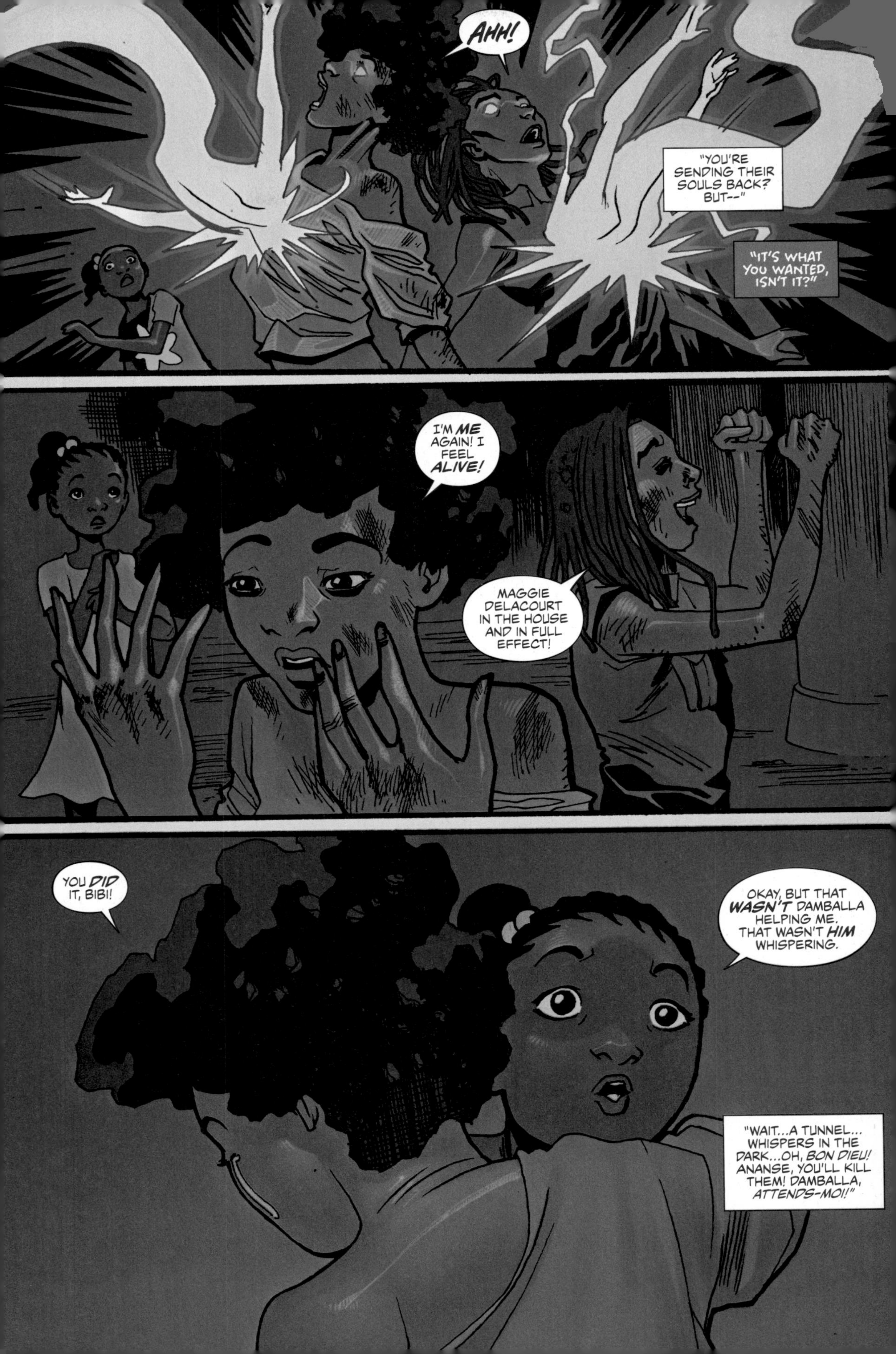
AHH!
"YOU'RE SENDING THEIR SOULS BACK? BUT--"
"IT'S WHAT YOU WANTED, ISN'T IT?"
I'M ME AGAIN! I FEEL ALIVE!
MAGGIE DELACOURT IN THE HOUSE AND IN FULL EFFECT!
YOU DID IT, BIBI!
OKAY, BUT THAT WASN'T DAMBALLA HELPING ME. THAT WASN'T HIM WHISPERING.
"WAIT...A TUNNEL... WHISPERS IN THE DARK...OH, BON DIEU! ANANSE, YOU'LL KILL THEM! DAMBALLA, ATTENDS-MOI!"

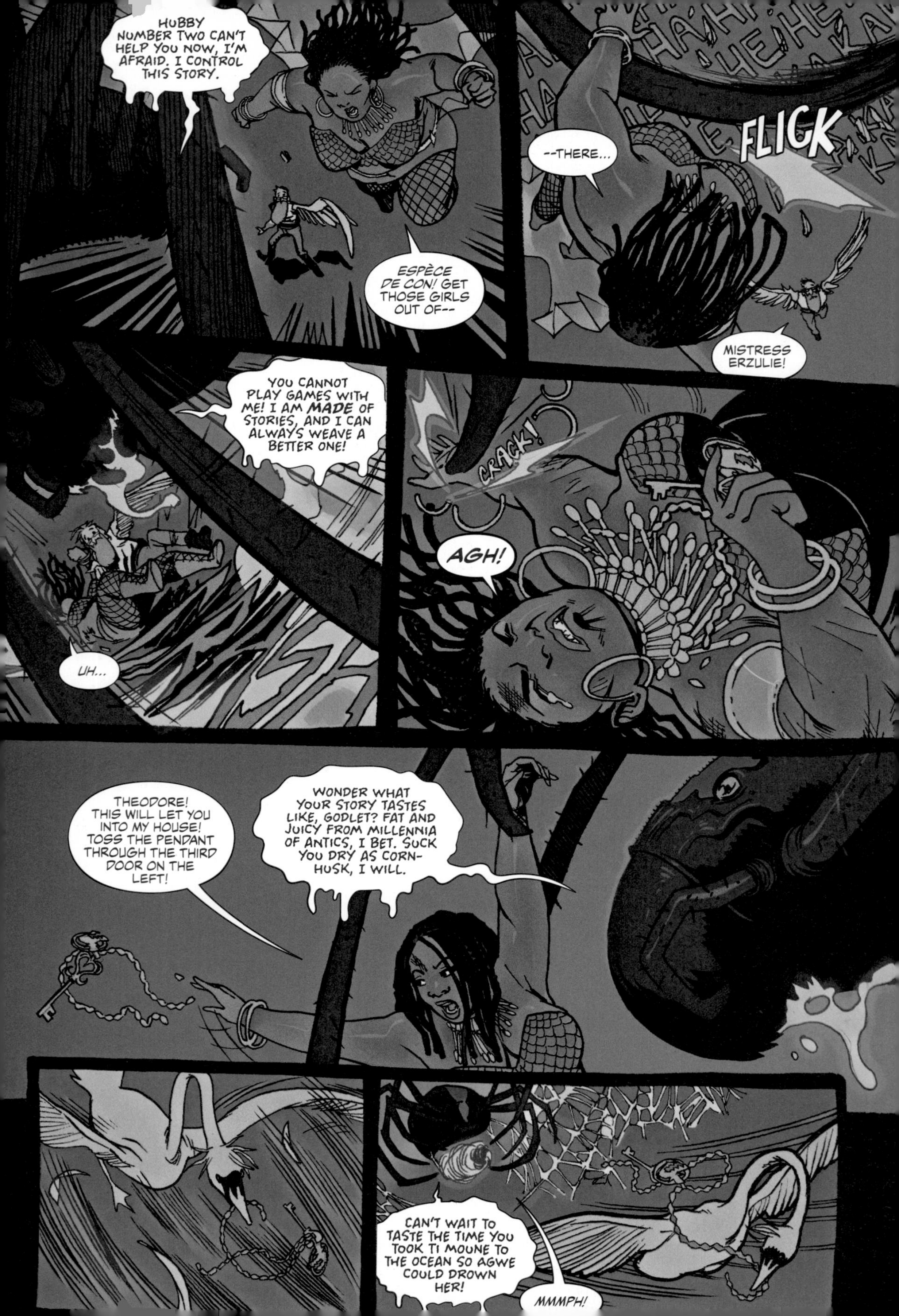
HUBBY NUMBER TWO CAN'T HELP YOU NOW, I'M AFRAID. I CONTROL THIS STORY.
ESPÈCE DE CON! GET THOSE GIRLS OUT OF--
--THERE...
FLICK
MISTRESS ERZULIE!
YOU CANNOT PLAY GAMES WITH ME! I AM MADE OF STORIES, AND I CAN ALWAYS WEAVE A BETTER ONE!
UH...
CRACK!
AGH!
THEODORE! THIS WILL LET YOU INTO MY HOUSE! TOSS THE PENDANT THROUGH THE THIRD DOOR ON THE LEFT!
WONDER WHAT YOUR STORY TASTES LIKE, GODLET? FAT AND JUICY FROM MILLENNIA OF ANTICS, I BET. SUCK YOU DRY AS CORN-HUSK, I WILL.
CAN'T WAIT TO TASTE THE TIME YOU TOOK TI MOUNE TO THE OCEAN SO AGWE COULD DROWN HER!
MMMPH!

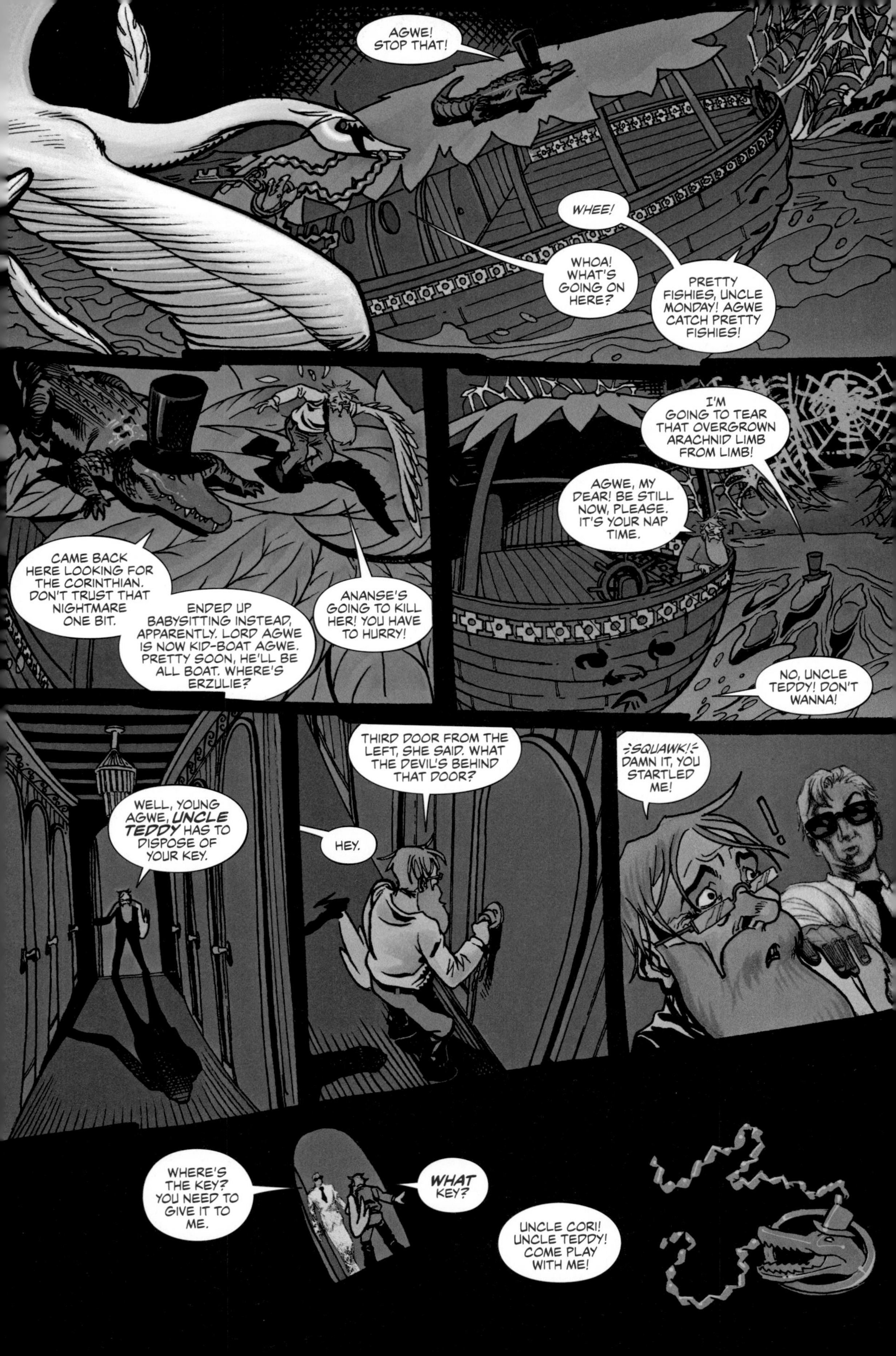
AGWE! STOP THAT!
WHEE!
WHOA! WHAT'S GOING ON HERE?
PRETTY FISHIES, UNCLE MONDAY! AGWE CATCH PRETTY FISHIES!
CAME BACK HERE LOOKING FOR THE CORINTHIAN. DON'T TRUST THAT NIGHTMARE ONE BIT.
ENDED UP BABYSITTING INSTEAD, APPARENTLY. LORD AGWE IS NOW KID-BOAT AGWE. PRETTY SOON, HE'LL BE ALL BOAT. WHERE'S ERZULIE?
ANANSE'S GOING TO KILL HER! YOU HAVE TO HURRY!
I'M GOING TO TEAR THAT OVERGROWN ARACHNID LIMB FROM LIMB!
AGWE, MY DEAR! BE STILL NOW, PLEASE. IT'S YOUR NAP TIME.
NO, UNCLE TEDDY! DON'T WANNA!
WELL, YOUNG AGWE, UNCLE TEDDY HAS TO DISPOSE OF YOUR KEY.
THIRD DOOR FROM THE LEFT, SHE SAID. WHAT THE DEVIL'S BEHIND THAT DOOR?
HEY.
SQUAWK! DAMN IT, YOU STARTLED ME!
WHERE'S THE KEY? YOU NEED TO GIVE IT TO ME.
WHAT KEY?
UNCLE CORI! UNCLE TEDDY! COME PLAY WITH ME!

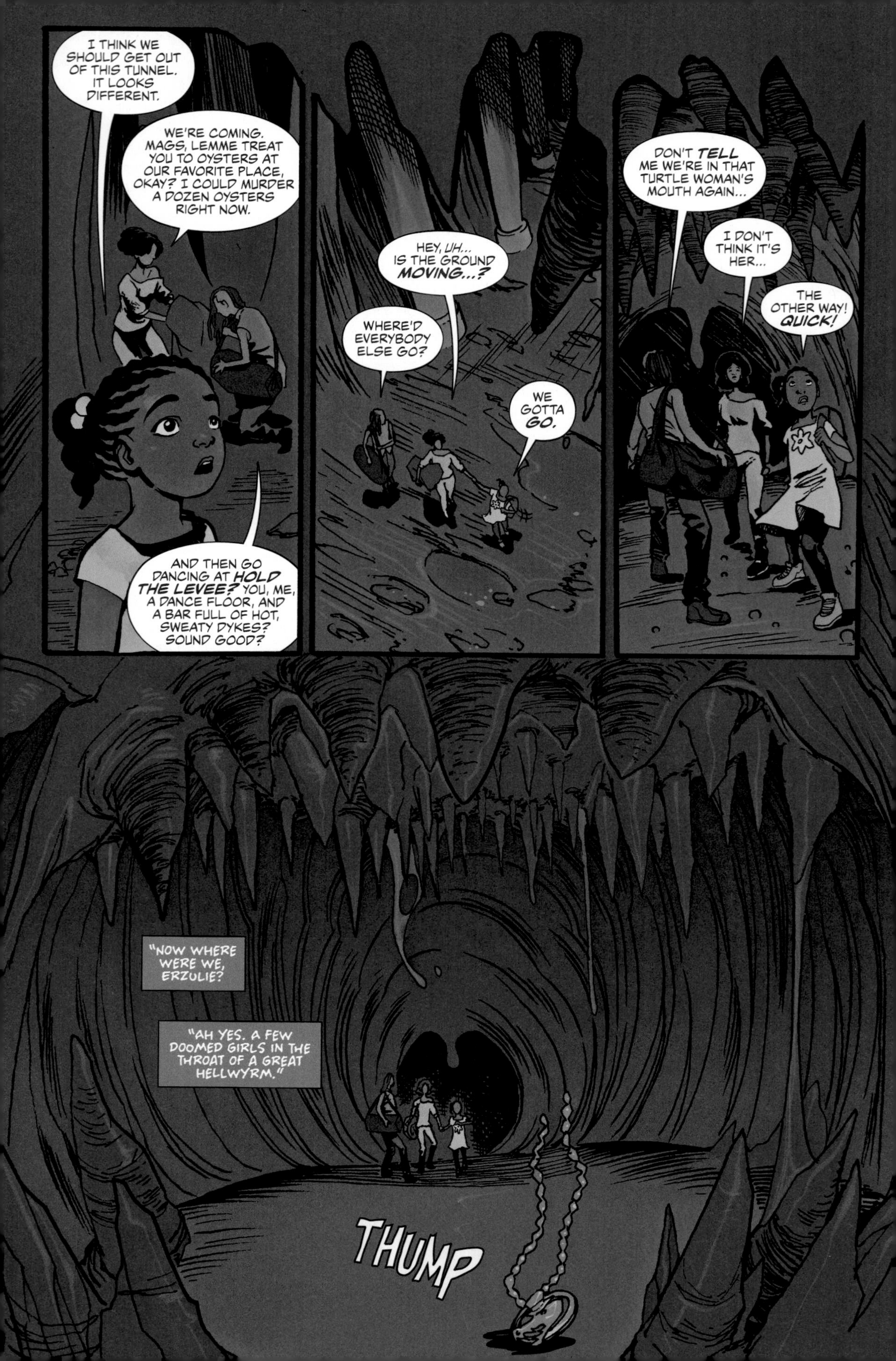

I THINK WE SHOULD GET OUT OF THIS TUNNEL. IT LOOKS DIFFERENT.
WE'RE COMING. MAGS, LEMME TREAT YOU TO OYSTERS AT OUR FAVORITE PLACE, OKAY? I COULD MURDER A DOZEN OYSTERS RIGHT NOW.
AND THEN GO DANCING AT HOLD THE LEVEE? YOU, ME, A DANCE FLOOR, AND A BAR FULL OF HOT, SWEATY DYKES? SOUND GOOD?
HEY, UH... IS THE GROUND MOVING...?
WHERE'D EVERYBODY ELSE GO?
WE GOTTA GO.
DON'T TELL ME WE'RE IN THAT TURTLE WOMAN'S MOUTH AGAIN...
I DON'T THINK IT'S HER...
THE OTHER WAY! QUICK!
"NOW WHERE WERE WE, ERZULIE?
"AH YES. A FEW DOOMED GIRLS IN THE THROAT OF A GREAT HELLWYRM."
THUMP

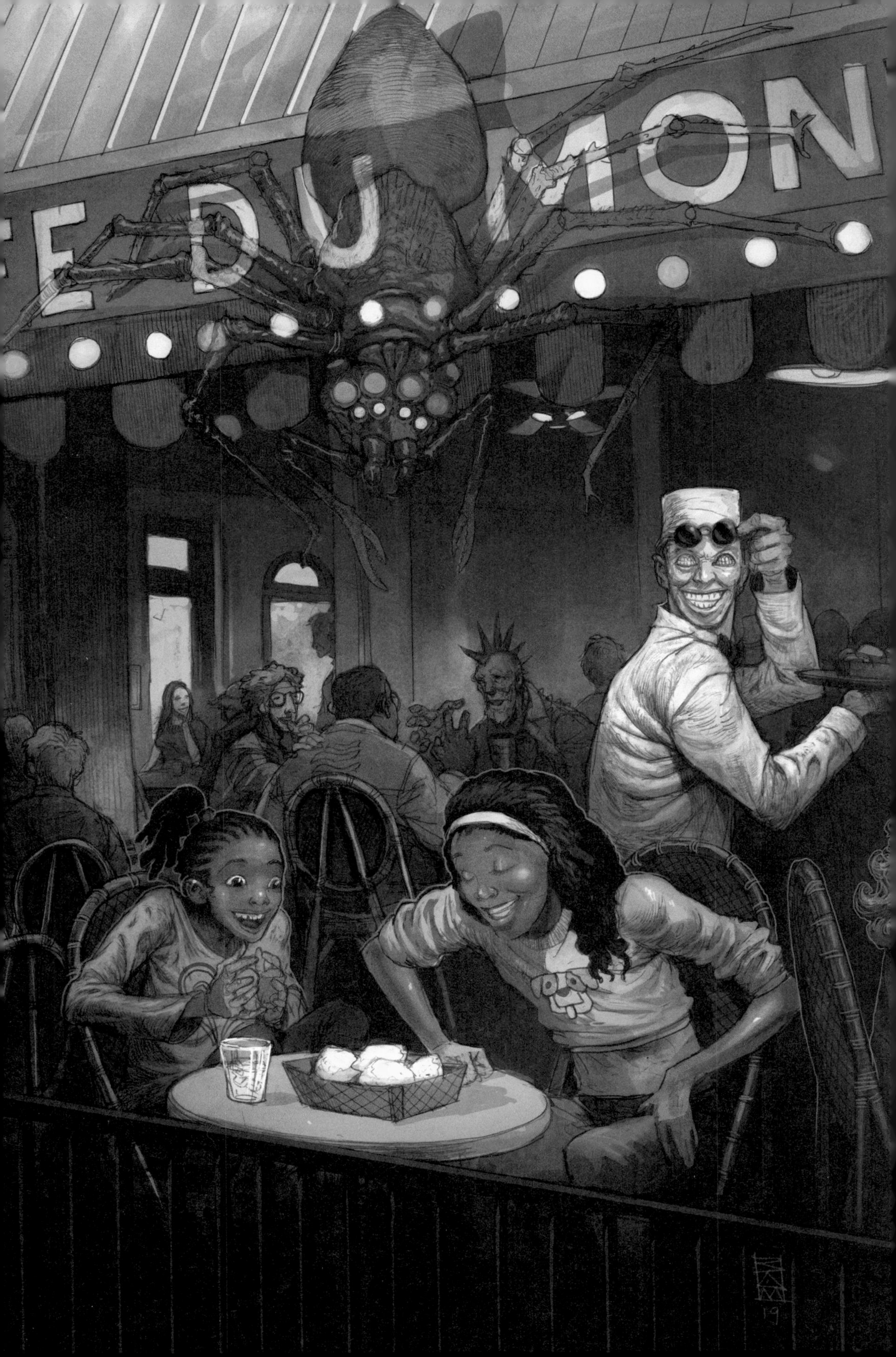
E DU MON

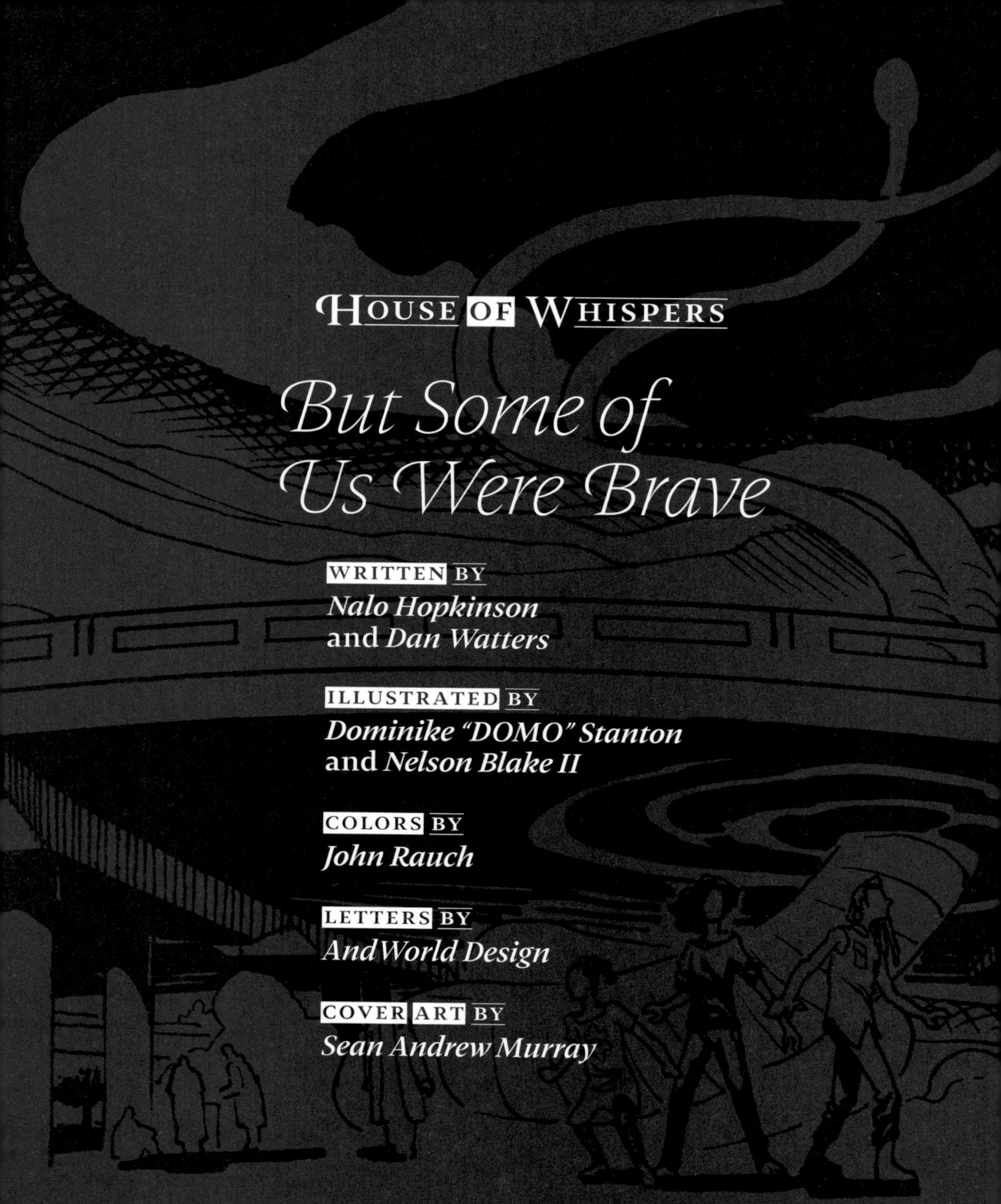

House of Whispers

But Some of Us Were Brave

WRITTEN BY
Nalo Hopkinson
and *Dan Watters*

ILLUSTRATED BY
Dominike "DOMO" Stanton
and *Nelson Blake II*

COLORS BY
John Rauch

LETTERS BY
AndWorld Design

COVER ART BY
Sean Andrew Murray

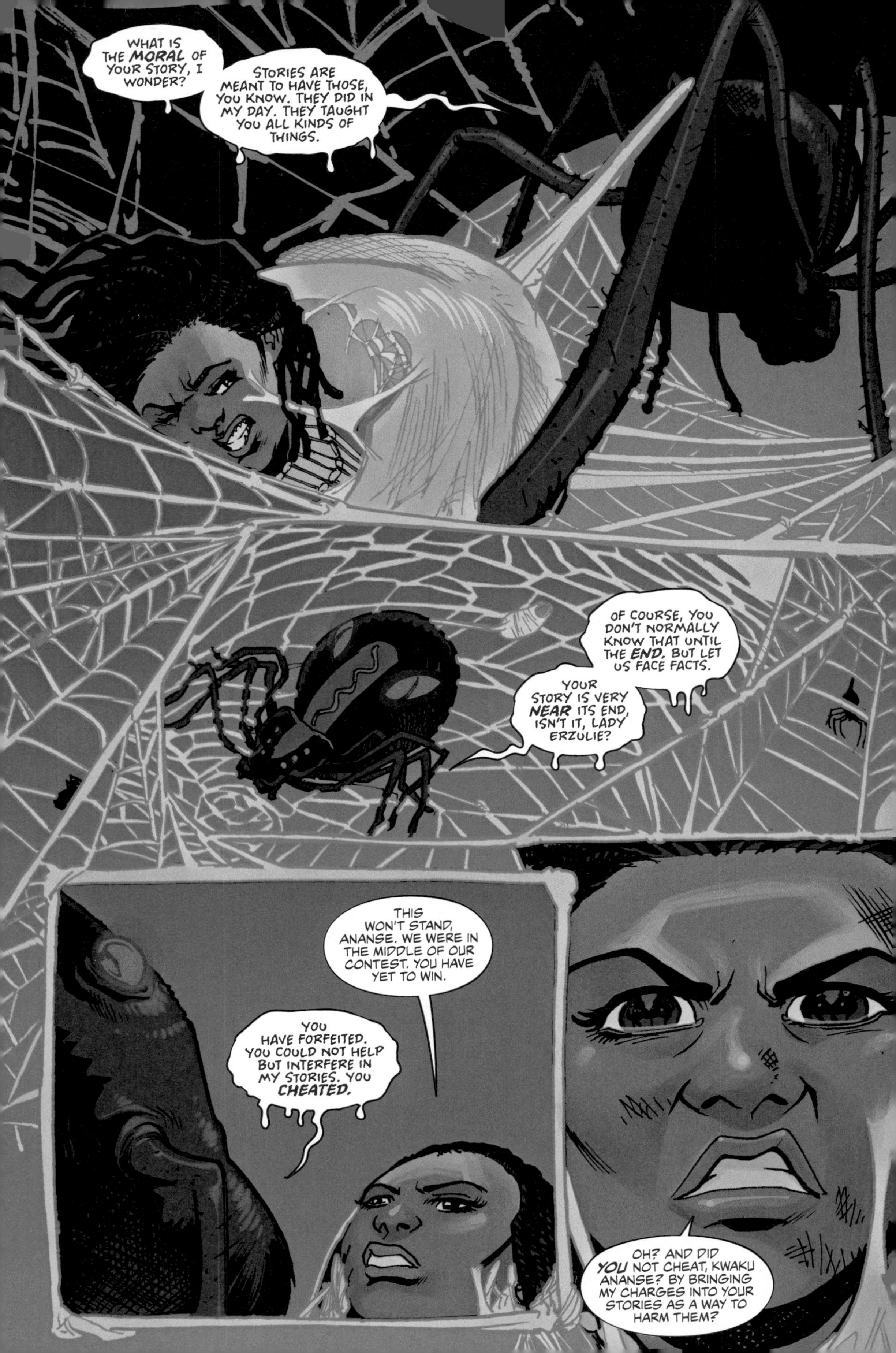
WHAT IS THE MORAL OF YOUR STORY, I WONDER?
STORIES ARE MEANT TO HAVE THOSE, YOU KNOW. THEY DID IN MY DAY. THEY TAUGHT YOU ALL KINDS OF THINGS.
OF COURSE, YOU DON'T NORMALLY KNOW THAT UNTIL THE END. BUT LET US FACE FACTS.
YOUR STORY IS VERY NEAR ITS END, ISN'T IT, LADY ERZULIE?
THIS WON'T STAND, ANANSE. WE WERE IN THE MIDDLE OF OUR CONTEST. YOU HAVE YET TO WIN.
YOU HAVE FORFEITED. YOU COULD NOT HELP BUT INTERFERE IN MY STORIES. YOU CHEATED.
OH? AND DID YOU NOT CHEAT, KWAKU ANANSE? BY BRINGING MY CHARGES INTO YOUR STORIES AS A WAY TO HARM THEM?

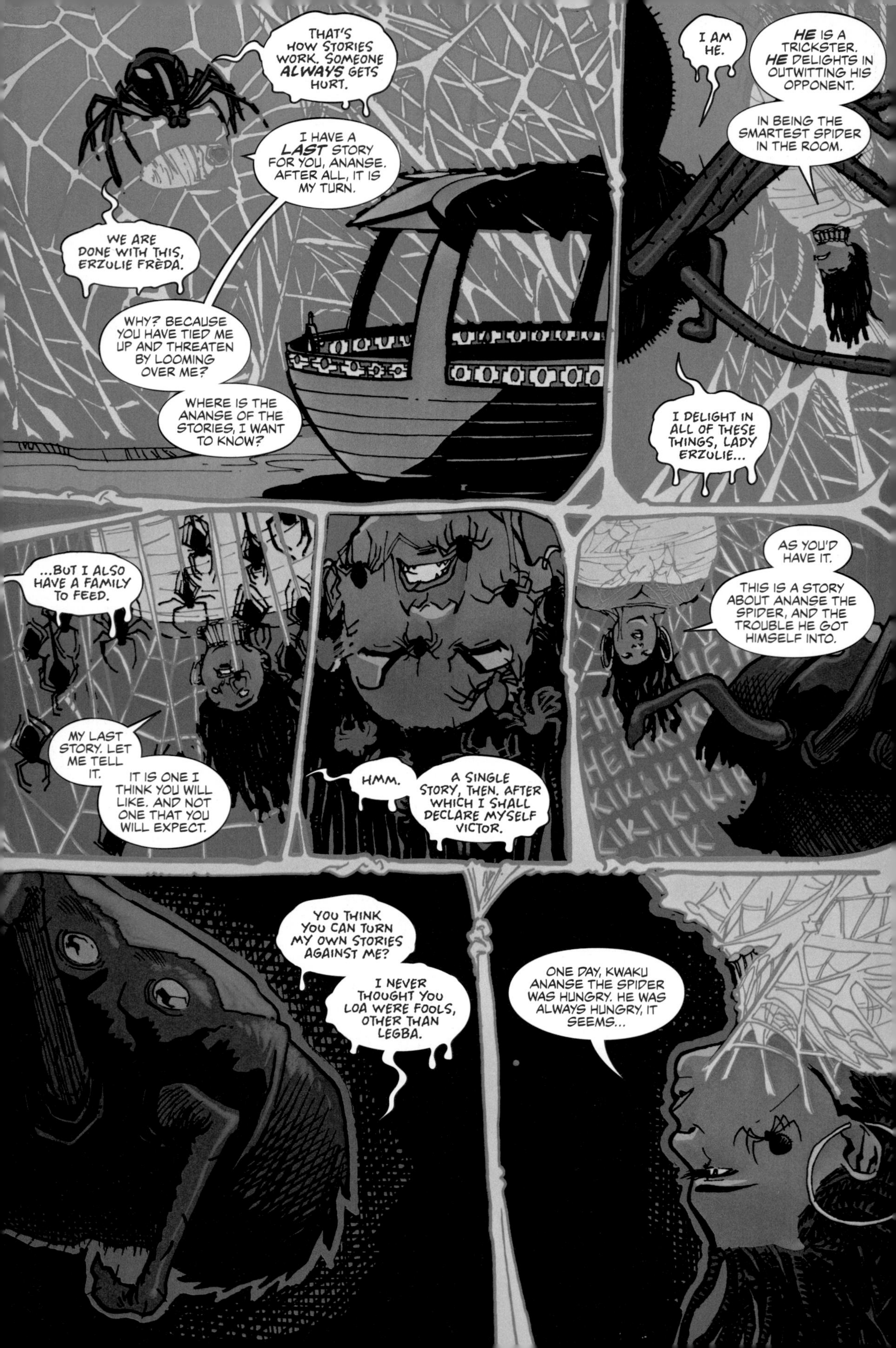
THAT'S HOW STORIES WORK. SOMEONE ALWAYS GETS HURT.
I HAVE A LAST STORY FOR YOU, ANANSE. AFTER ALL, IT IS MY TURN.
WE ARE DONE WITH THIS, ERZULIE FRÈDA.
WHY? BECAUSE YOU HAVE TIED ME UP AND THREATEN BY LOOMING OVER ME?
WHERE IS THE ANANSE OF THE STORIES, I WANT TO KNOW?
I AM HE.
HE IS A TRICKSTER. HE DELIGHTS IN OUTWITTING HIS OPPONENT.
IN BEING THE SMARTEST SPIDER IN THE ROOM.
I DELIGHT IN ALL OF THESE THINGS, LADY ERZULIE...
...BUT I ALSO HAVE A FAMILY TO FEED.
MY LAST STORY. LET ME TELL IT.
IT IS ONE I THINK YOU WILL LIKE. AND NOT ONE THAT YOU WILL EXPECT.
HMM.
A SINGLE STORY, THEN. AFTER WHICH I SHALL DECLARE MYSELF VICTOR.
AS YOU'D HAVE IT.
THIS IS A STORY ABOUT ANANSE THE SPIDER, AND THE TROUBLE HE GOT HIMSELF INTO.
HEHEHE KIKIKIKI
YOU THINK YOU CAN TURN MY OWN STORIES AGAINST ME?
I NEVER THOUGHT YOU LOA WERE FOOLS, OTHER THAN LEGBA.
ONE DAY, KWAKU ANANSE THE SPIDER WAS HUNGRY. HE WAS ALWAYS HUNGRY, IT SEEMS...

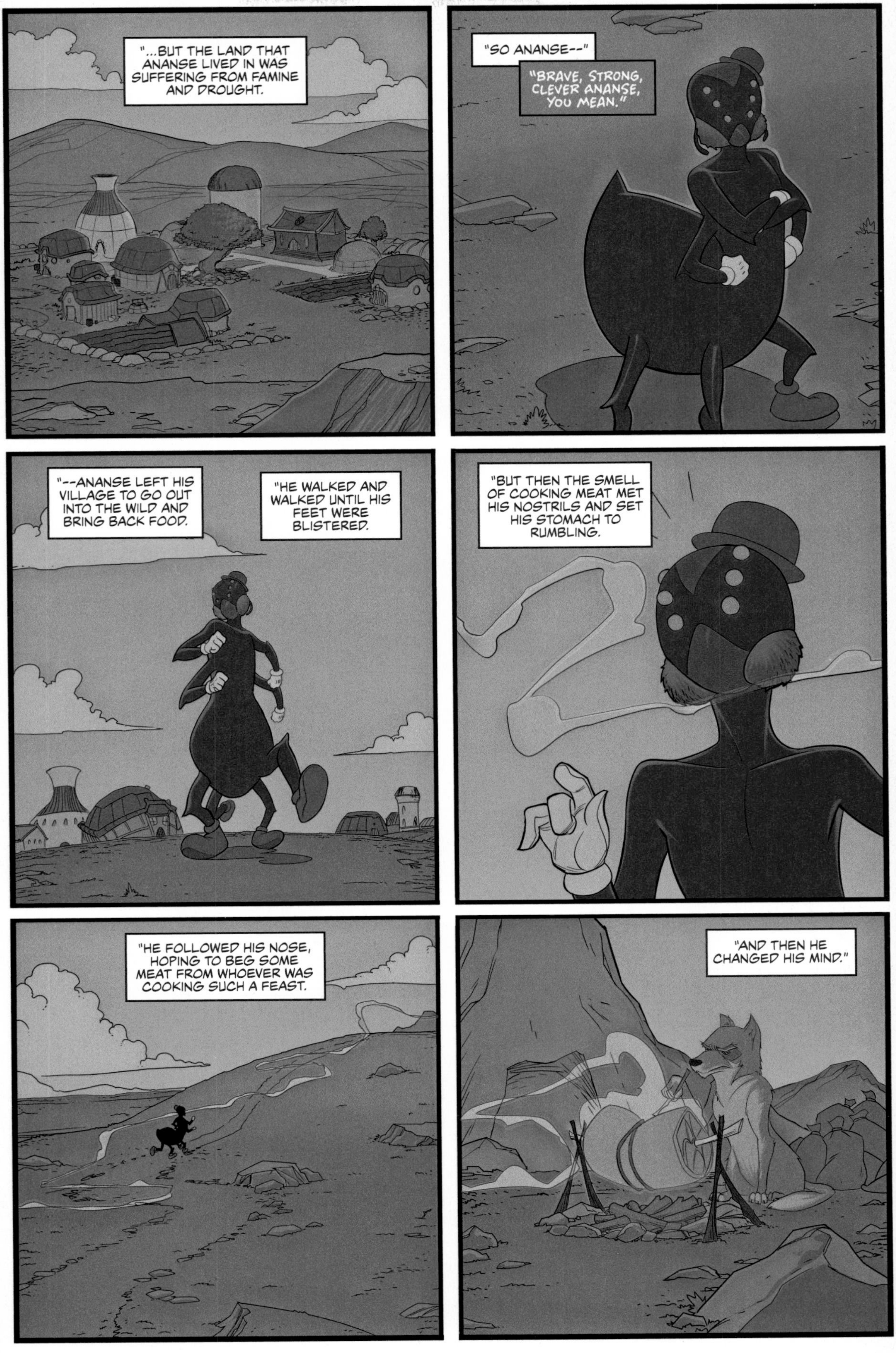
"...BUT THE LAND THAT ANANSE LIVED IN WAS SUFFERING FROM FAMINE AND DROUGHT.
"SO ANANSE--"
"BRAVE, STRONG, CLEVER ANANSE, YOU MEAN."
"--ANANSE LEFT HIS VILLAGE TO GO OUT INTO THE WILD AND BRING BACK FOOD.
"HE WALKED AND WALKED UNTIL HIS FEET WERE BLISTERED.
"BUT THEN THE SMELL OF COOKING MEAT MET HIS NOSTRILS AND SET HIS STOMACH TO RUMBLING.
"HE FOLLOWED HIS NOSE, HOPING TO BEG SOME MEAT FROM WHOEVER WAS COOKING SUCH A FEAST.
"AND THEN HE CHANGED HIS MIND."

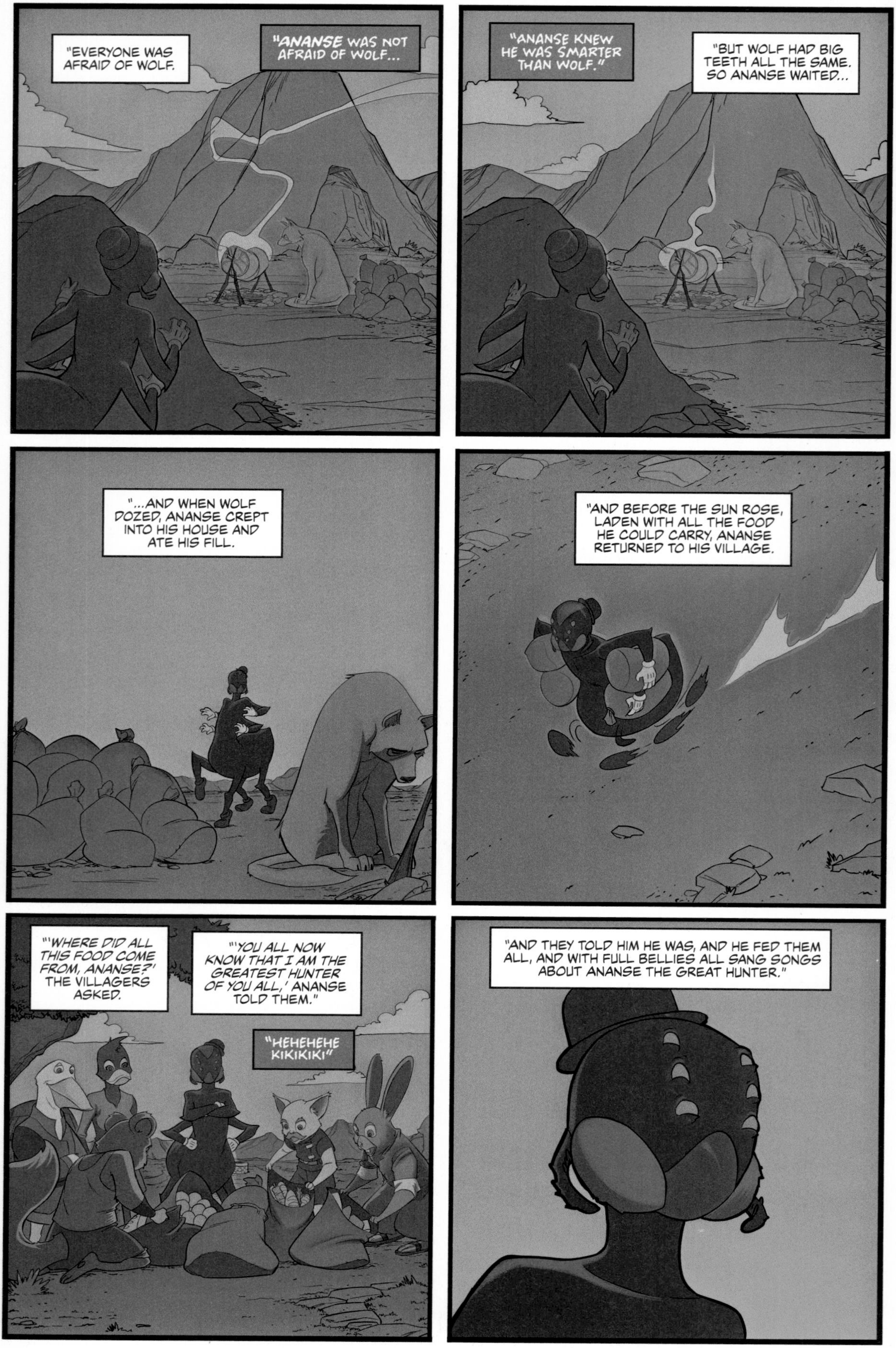
"EVERYONE WAS AFRAID OF WOLF.
"ANANSE WAS NOT AFRAID OF WOLF...
"ANANSE KNEW HE WAS SMARTER THAN WOLF."
"BUT WOLF HAD BIG TEETH ALL THE SAME. SO ANANSE WAITED...
"...AND WHEN WOLF DOZED, ANANSE CREPT INTO HIS HOUSE AND ATE HIS FILL.
"AND BEFORE THE SUN ROSE, LADEN WITH ALL THE FOOD HE COULD CARRY, ANANSE RETURNED TO HIS VILLAGE.
"'WHERE DID ALL THIS FOOD COME FROM, ANANSE?' THE VILLAGERS ASKED.
"'YOU ALL NOW KNOW THAT I AM THE GREATEST HUNTER OF YOU ALL,' ANANSE TOLD THEM."
"HEHEHEHE KIKIKIKI"
"AND THEY TOLD HIM HE WAS, AND HE FED THEM ALL, AND WITH FULL BELLIES ALL SANG SONGS ABOUT ANANSE THE GREAT HUNTER."

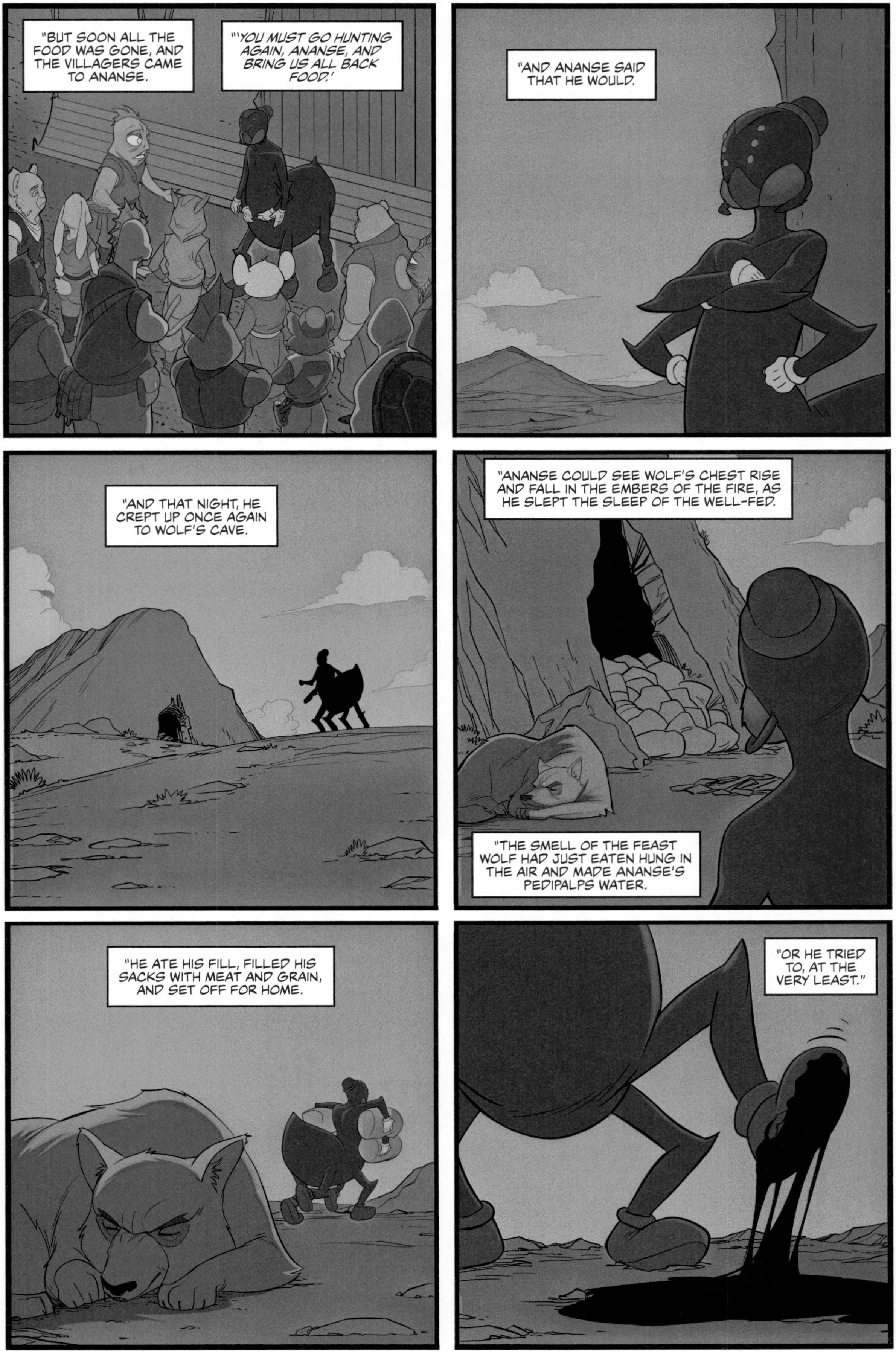
"BUT SOON ALL THE FOOD WAS GONE, AND THE VILLAGERS CAME TO ANANSE.
"'YOU MUST GO HUNTING AGAIN, ANANSE, AND BRING US ALL BACK FOOD.'
"AND ANANSE SAID THAT HE WOULD.
"AND THAT NIGHT, HE CREPT UP ONCE AGAIN TO WOLF'S CAVE.
"ANANSE COULD SEE WOLF'S CHEST RISE AND FALL IN THE EMBERS OF THE FIRE, AS HE SLEPT THE SLEEP OF THE WELL-FED.
"THE SMELL OF THE FEAST WOLF HAD JUST EATEN HUNG IN THE AIR AND MADE ANANSE'S PEDIPALPS WATER.
"HE ATE HIS FILL, FILLED HIS SACKS WITH MEAT AND GRAIN, AND SET OFF FOR HOME.
"OR HE TRIED TO, AT THE VERY LEAST."

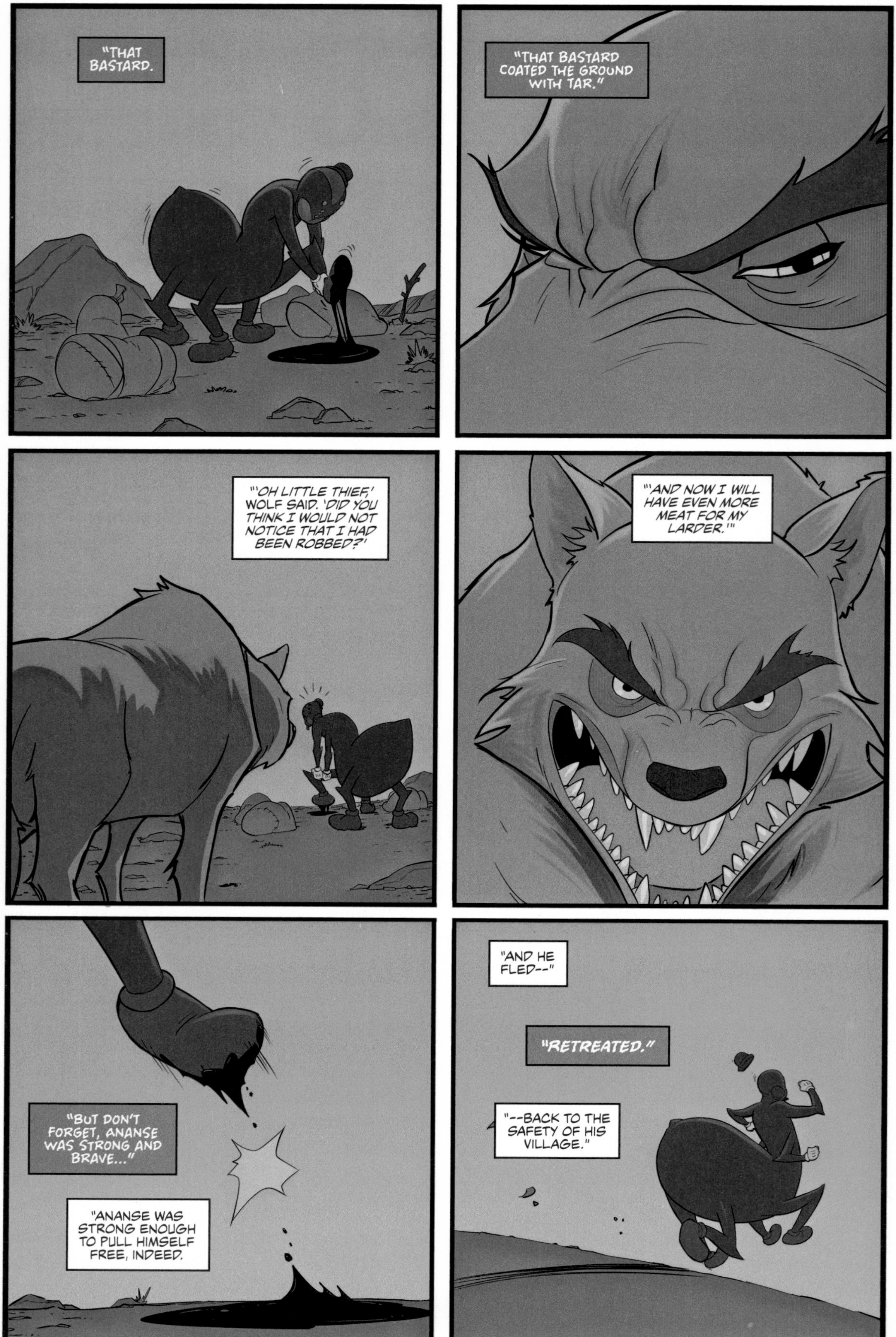
"THAT BASTARD.
"THAT BASTARD COATED THE GROUND WITH TAR."
"'OH LITTLE THIEF,' WOLF SAID. 'DID YOU THINK I WOULD NOT NOTICE THAT I HAD BEEN ROBBED?'
"'AND NOW I WILL HAVE EVEN MORE MEAT FOR MY LARDER.'"
"BUT DON'T FORGET, ANANSE WAS STRONG AND BRAVE..."
"ANANSE WAS STRONG ENOUGH TO PULL HIMSELF FREE, INDEED.
"AND HE FLED--"
"RETREATED."
"--BACK TO THE SAFETY OF HIS VILLAGE."

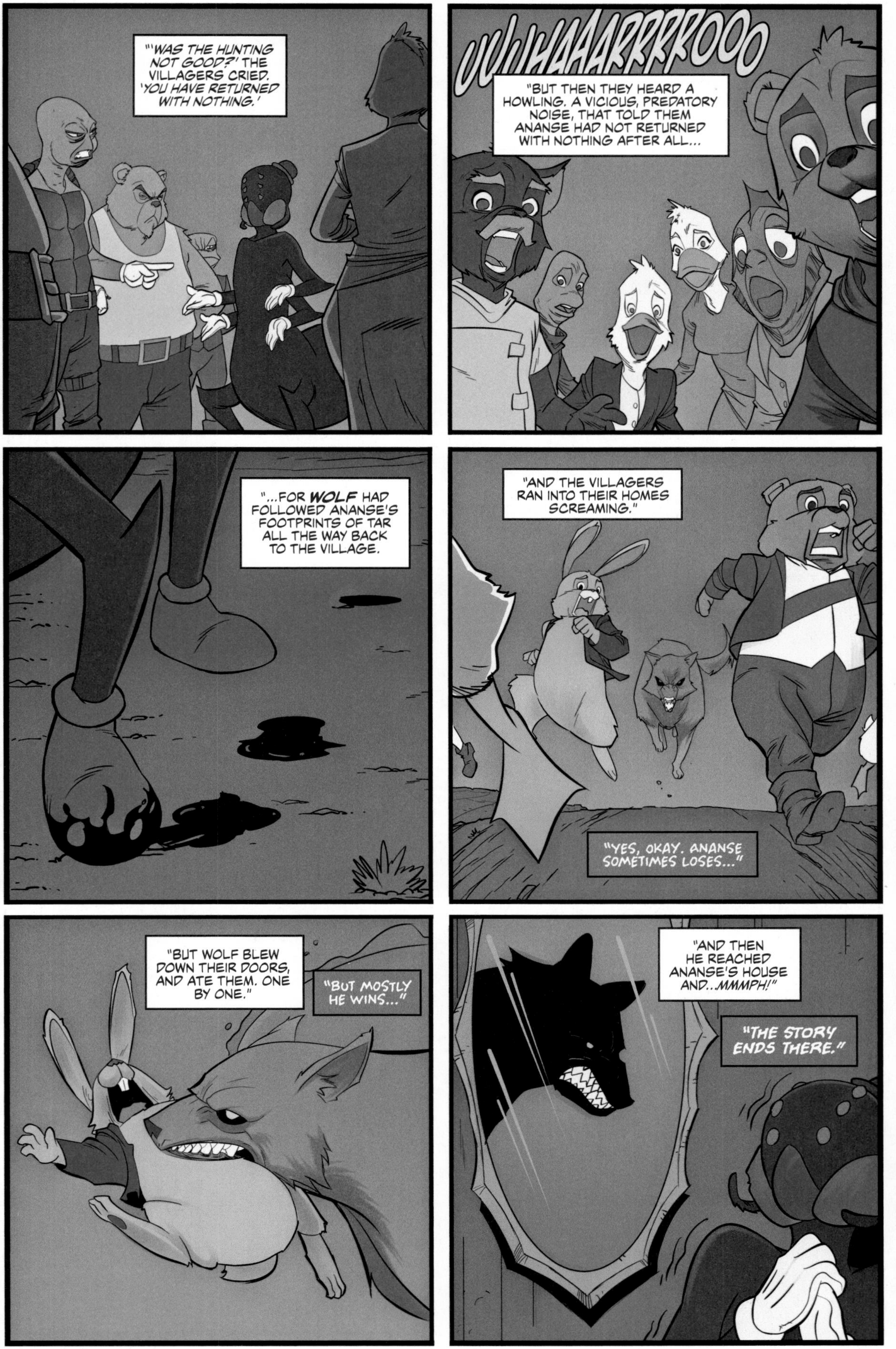
"'WAS THE HUNTING NOT GOOD?' THE VILLAGERS CRIED. 'YOU HAVE RETURNED WITH NOTHING.'
UUUHAAARRRRROOO
"BUT THEN THEY HEARD A HOWLING. A VICIOUS, PREDATORY NOISE, THAT TOLD THEM ANANSE HAD NOT RETURNED WITH NOTHING AFTER ALL...
"...FOR WOLF HAD FOLLOWED ANANSE'S FOOTPRINTS OF TAR ALL THE WAY BACK TO THE VILLAGE.
"AND THE VILLAGERS RAN INTO THEIR HOMES SCREAMING."
"YES, OKAY. ANANSE SOMETIMES LOSES..."
"BUT WOLF BLEW DOWN THEIR DOORS, AND ATE THEM. ONE BY ONE."
"BUT MOSTLY HE WINS..."
"AND THEN HE REACHED ANANSE'S HOUSE AND...MMMPH!"
"THE STORY ENDS THERE."

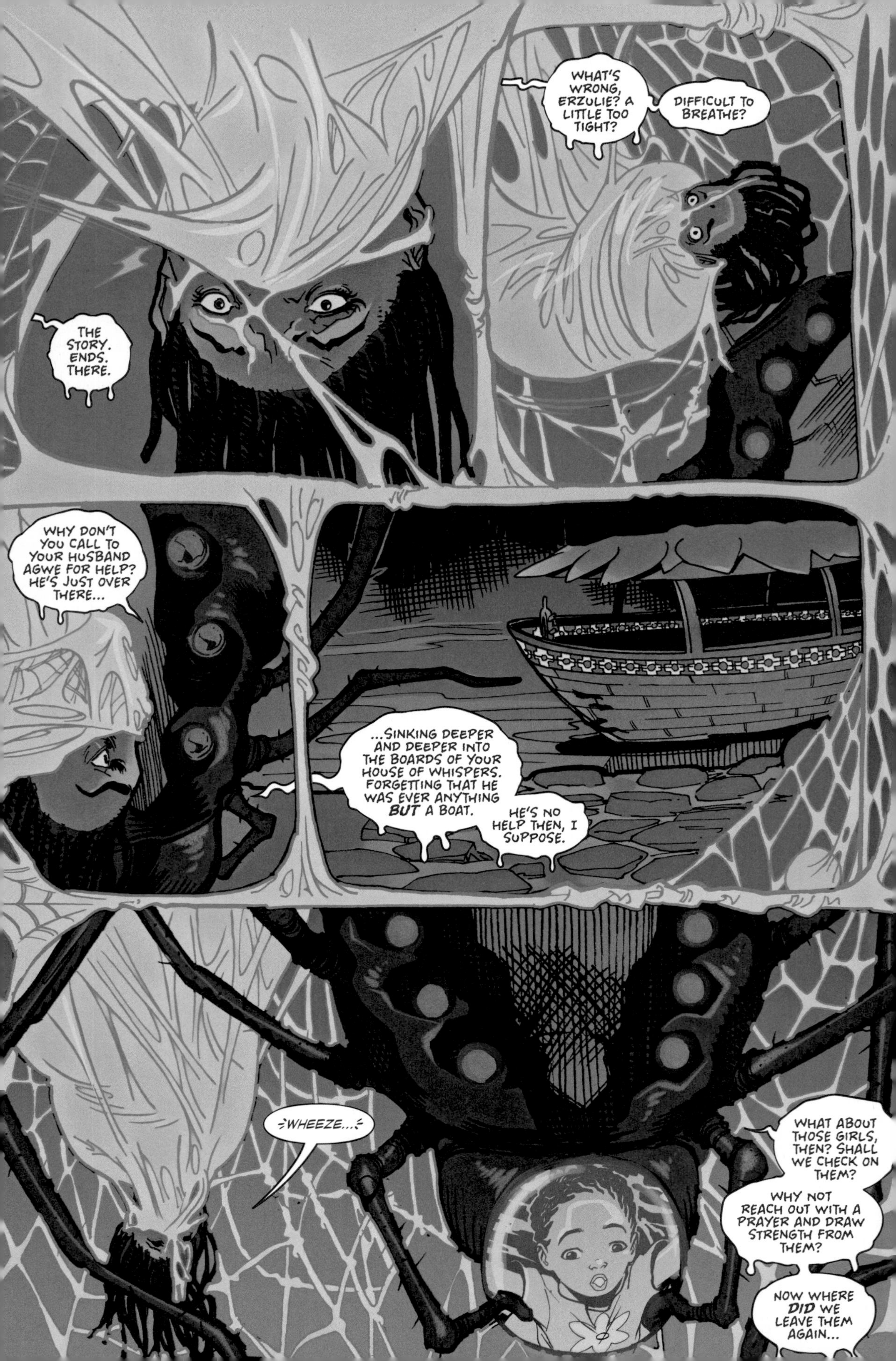
WHAT'S WRONG, ERZULIE? A LITTLE TOO TIGHT?
DIFFICULT TO BREATHE?
THE STORY. ENDS. THERE.
WHY DON'T YOU CALL TO YOUR HUSBAND AGWE FOR HELP? HE'S JUST OVER THERE...
...SINKING DEEPER AND DEEPER INTO THE BOARDS OF YOUR HOUSE OF WHISPERS. FORGETTING THAT HE WAS EVER ANYTHING BUT A BOAT.
HE'S NO HELP THEN, I SUPPOSE.
WHEEZE...
WHAT ABOUT THOSE GIRLS, THEN? SHALL WE CHECK ON THEM?
WHY NOT REACH OUT WITH A PRAYER AND DRAW STRENGTH FROM THEM?
NOW WHERE DID WE LEAVE THEM AGAIN...

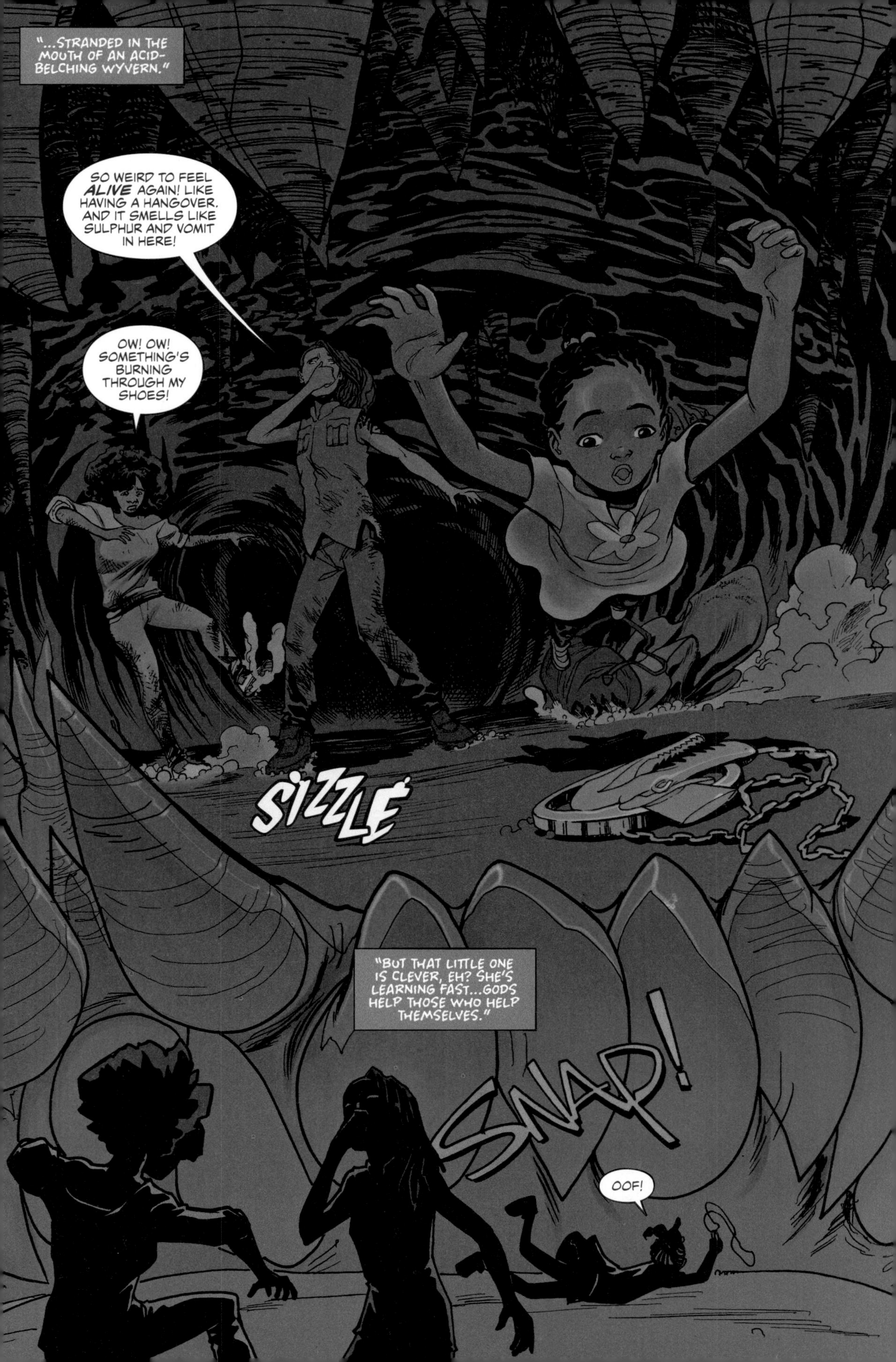
"...STRANDED IN THE MOUTH OF AN ACID-BELCHING WYVERN."
SO WEIRD TO FEEL ALIVE AGAIN! LIKE HAVING A HANGOVER. AND IT SMELLS LIKE SULPHUR AND VOMIT IN HERE!
OW! OW! SOMETHING'S BURNING THROUGH MY SHOES!
SIZZLE
"BUT THAT LITTLE ONE IS CLEVER, EH? SHE'S LEARNING FAST...GODS HELP THOSE WHO HELP THEMSELVES."
SNAP!
OOF!

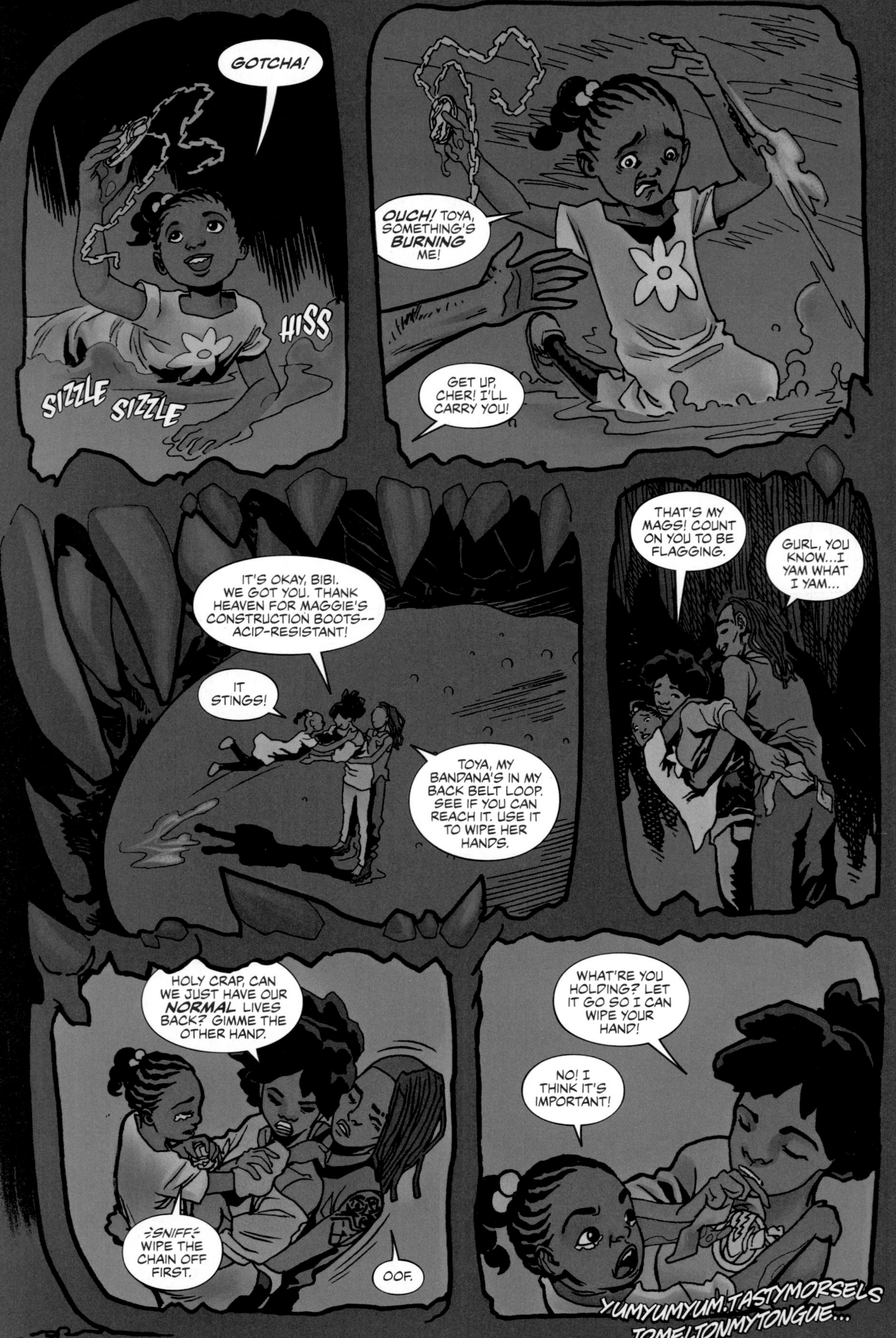
GOTCHA!
HISS
SIZZLE SIZZLE
OUCH! TOYA, SOMETHING'S BURNING ME!
GET UP, CHER! I'LL CARRY YOU!
IT'S OKAY, BIBI. WE GOT YOU. THANK HEAVEN FOR MAGGIE'S CONSTRUCTION BOOTS--ACID-RESISTANT!
IT STINGS!
TOYA, MY BANDANA'S IN MY BACK BELT LOOP. SEE IF YOU CAN REACH IT. USE IT TO WIPE HER HANDS.
THAT'S MY MAGS! COUNT ON YOU TO BE FLAGGING.
GURL, YOU KNOW...I YAM WHAT I YAM...
HOLY CRAP, CAN WE JUST HAVE OUR NORMAL LIVES BACK? GIMME THE OTHER HAND.
SNIFF WIPE THE CHAIN OFF FIRST.
OOF.
WHAT'RE YOU HOLDING? LET IT GO SO I CAN WIPE YOUR HAND!
NO! I THINK IT'S IMPORTANT!
YUMYUMYUM.TASTYMORSELS TOMELTONMYTONGUE...

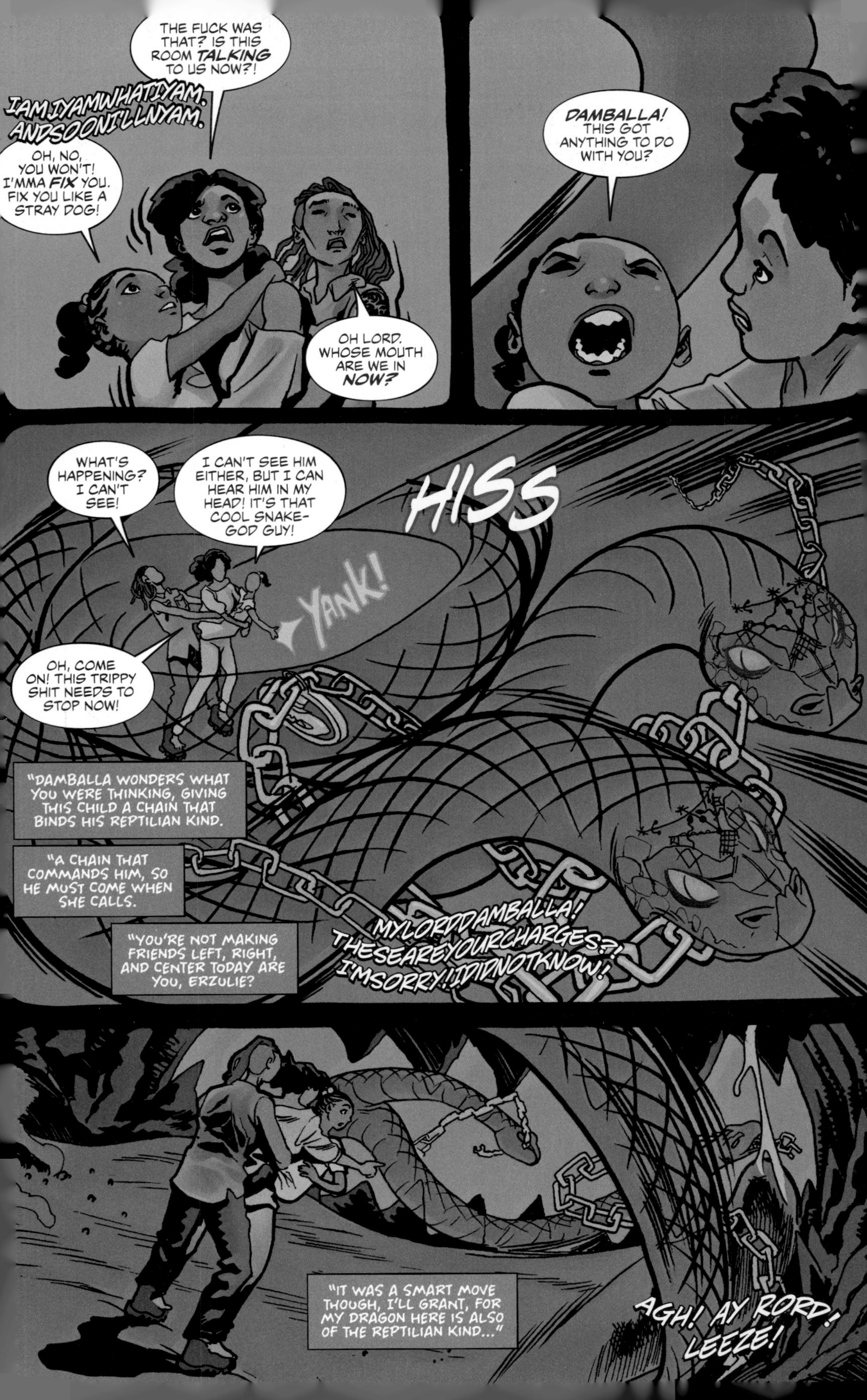
THE FUCK WAS THAT? IS THIS ROOM TALKING TO US NOW?!
IAMIYAMWHATIYAM. ANDSOONI'LLNYAM.
OH, NO, YOU WON'T! I'MMA FIX YOU. FIX YOU LIKE A STRAY DOG!
OH LORD. WHOSE MOUTH ARE WE IN NOW?
DAMBALLA! THIS GOT ANYTHING TO DO WITH YOU?
WHAT'S HAPPENING? I CAN'T SEE!
I CAN'T SEE HIM EITHER, BUT I CAN HEAR HIM IN MY HEAD! IT'S THAT COOL SNAKE-GOD GUY!
HISS
YANK!
OH, COME ON! THIS TRIPPY SHIT NEEDS TO STOP NOW!
"DAMBALLA WONDERS WHAT YOU WERE THINKING, GIVING THIS CHILD A CHAIN THAT BINDS HIS REPTILIAN KIND.
"A CHAIN THAT COMMANDS HIM, SO HE MUST COME WHEN SHE CALLS.
"YOU'RE NOT MAKING FRIENDS LEFT, RIGHT, AND CENTER TODAY ARE YOU, ERZULIE?
MYLORDDAMBALLA! THESEAREYOURCHARGES?! I'MSORRY! IDIDNOTKNOW!
"IT WAS A SMART MOVE THOUGH, I'LL GRANT, FOR MY DRAGON HERE IS ALSO OF THE REPTILIAN KIND..."
AGH! AY RORD! LEEZE!

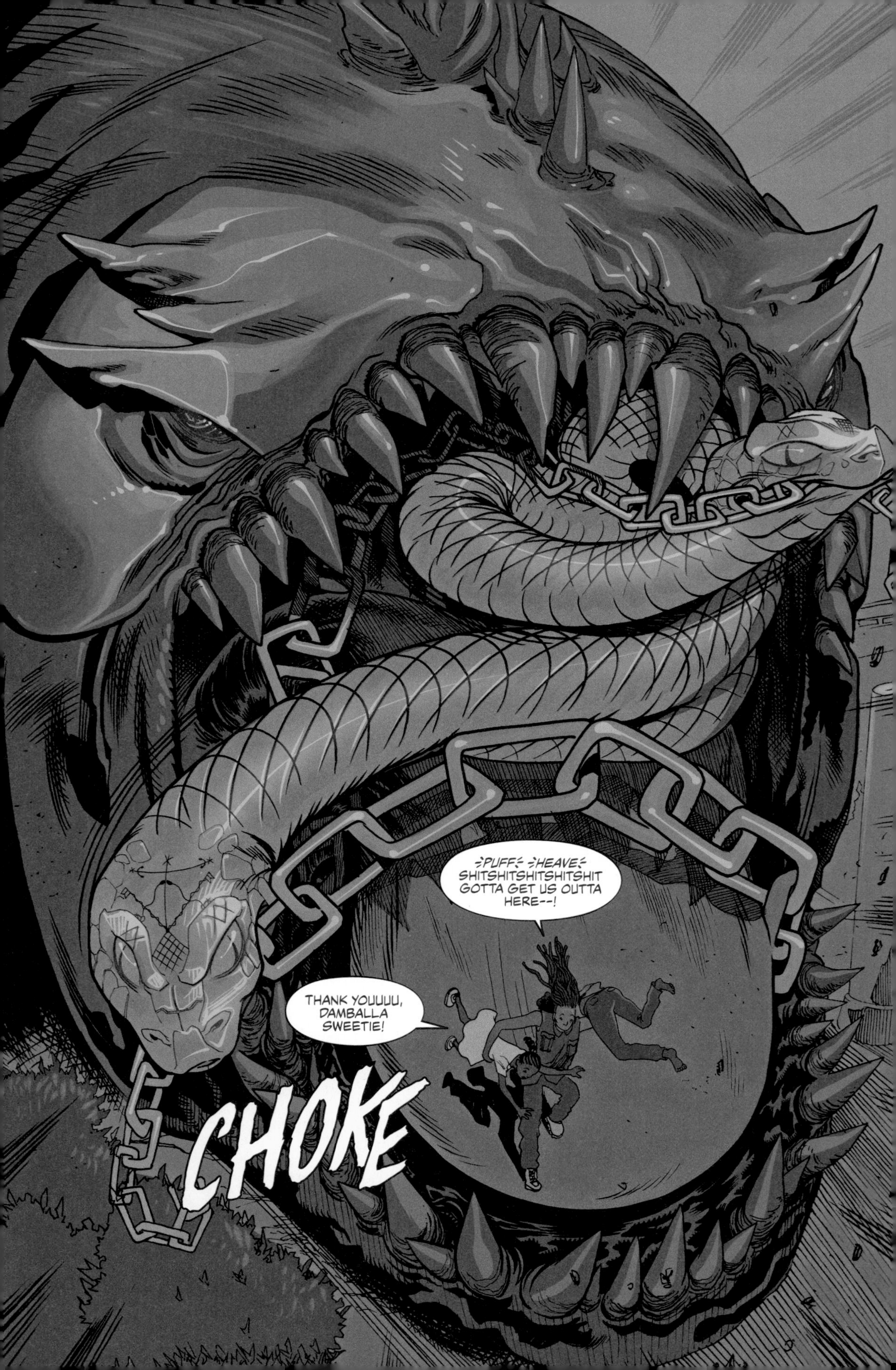

=PUFF= =HEAVE= SHITSHITSHITSHITSHIT GOTTA GET US OUTTA HERE--!
THANK YOUUUU, DAMBALLA SWEETIE!
CHOKE

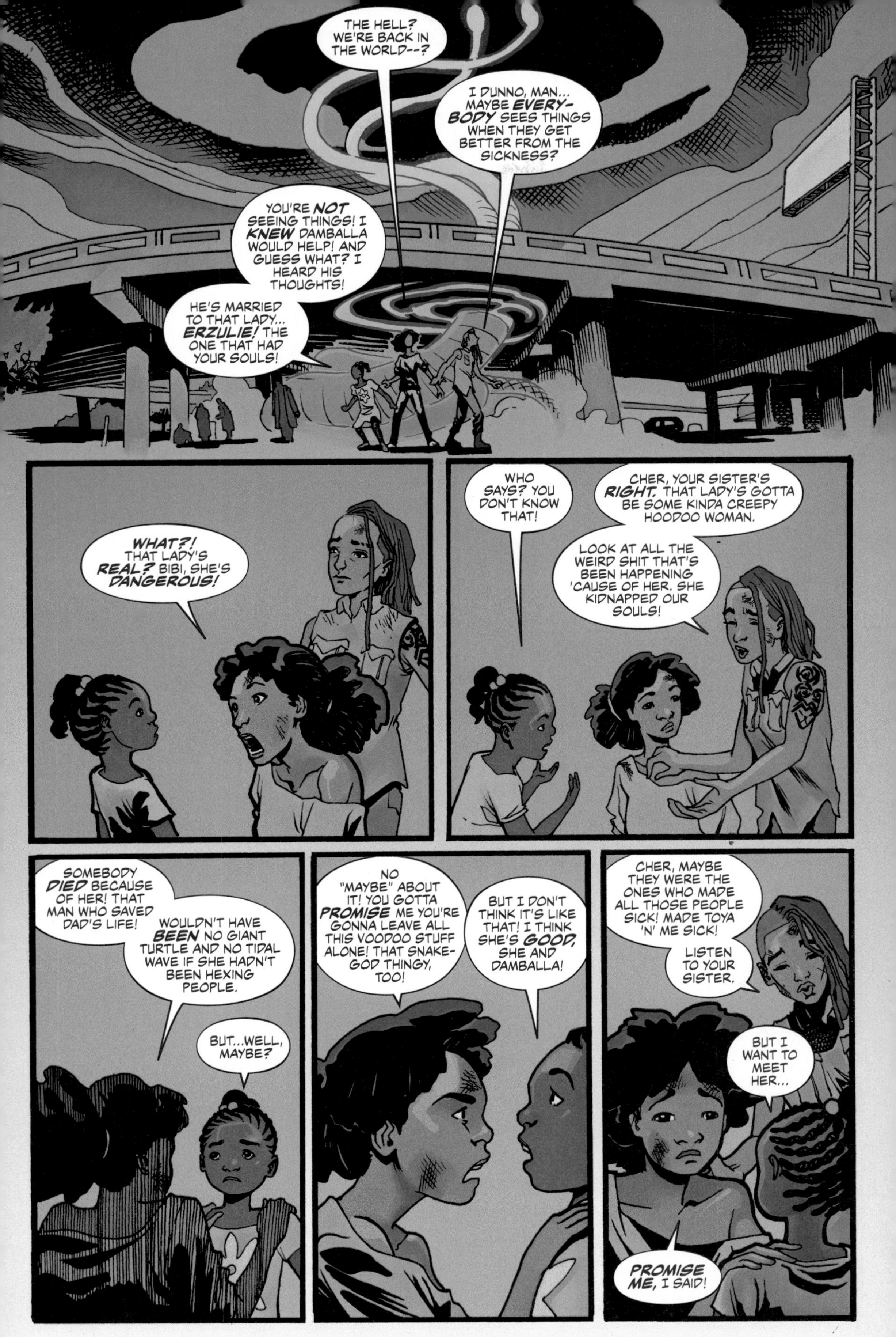
THE HELL? WE'RE BACK IN THE WORLD--?
I DUNNO, MAN... MAYBE EVERY-BODY SEES THINGS WHEN THEY GET BETTER FROM THE SICKNESS?
YOU'RE NOT SEEING THINGS! I KNEW DAMBALLA WOULD HELP! AND GUESS WHAT? I HEARD HIS THOUGHTS!
HE'S MARRIED TO THAT LADY... ERZULIE! THE ONE THAT HAD YOUR SOULS!
WHAT?! THAT LADY'S REAL? BIBI, SHE'S DANGEROUS!
WHO SAYS? YOU DON'T KNOW THAT!
CHER, YOUR SISTER'S RIGHT. THAT LADY'S GOTTA BE SOME KINDA CREEPY HOODOO WOMAN.
LOOK AT ALL THE WEIRD SHIT THAT'S BEEN HAPPENING 'CAUSE OF HER. SHE KIDNAPPED OUR SOULS!
SOMEBODY DIED BECAUSE OF HER! THAT MAN WHO SAVED DAD'S LIFE!
WOULDN'T HAVE BEEN NO GIANT TURTLE AND NO TIDAL WAVE IF SHE HADN'T BEEN HEXING PEOPLE.
BUT...WELL, MAYBE?
NO "MAYBE" ABOUT IT! YOU GOTTA PROMISE ME YOU'RE GONNA LEAVE ALL THIS VOODOO STUFF ALONE! THAT SNAKE-GOD THINGY, TOO!
BUT I DON'T THINK IT'S LIKE THAT! I THINK SHE'S GOOD, SHE AND DAMBALLA!
CHER, MAYBE THEY WERE THE ONES WHO MADE ALL THOSE PEOPLE SICK! MADE TOYA 'N' ME SICK!
LISTEN TO YOUR SISTER.
BUT I WANT TO MEET HER...
PROMISE ME, I SAID!

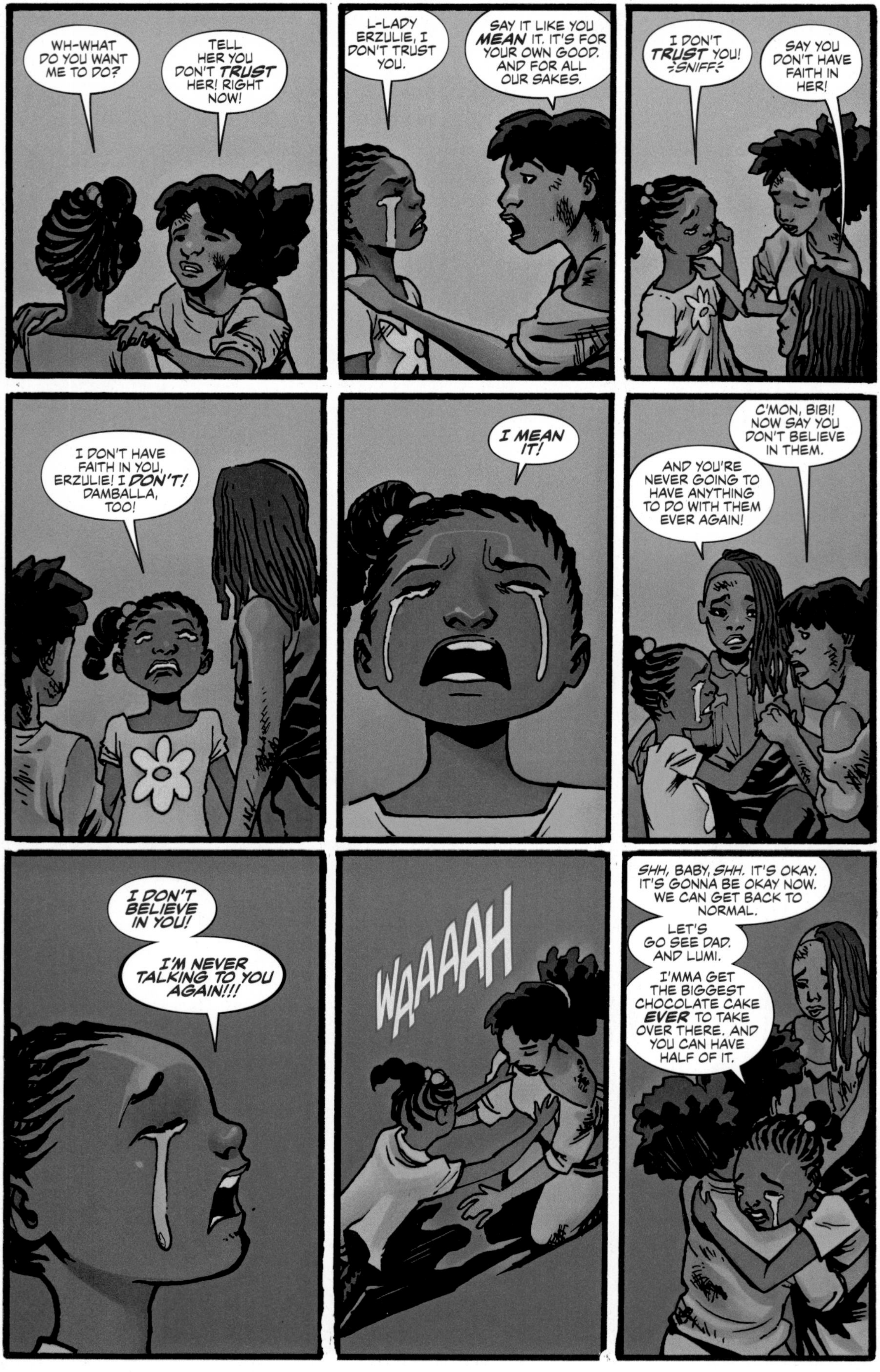
WH-WHAT DO YOU WANT ME TO DO?
TELL HER YOU DON'T TRUST HER! RIGHT NOW!
L-LADY ERZULIE, I DON'T TRUST YOU.
SAY IT LIKE YOU MEAN IT. IT'S FOR YOUR OWN GOOD. AND FOR ALL OUR SAKES.
I DON'T TRUST YOU! SNIFF
SAY YOU DON'T HAVE FAITH IN HER!
I DON'T HAVE FAITH IN YOU, ERZULIE! I DON'T! DAMBALLA, TOO!
I MEAN IT!
C'MON, BIBI! NOW SAY YOU DON'T BELIEVE IN THEM.
AND YOU'RE NEVER GOING TO HAVE ANYTHING TO DO WITH THEM EVER AGAIN!
I DON'T BELIEVE IN YOU!
I'M NEVER TALKING TO YOU AGAIN!!!
WAAAAH
SHH, BABY, SHH. IT'S OKAY. IT'S GONNA BE OKAY NOW. WE CAN GET BACK TO NORMAL.
LET'S GO SEE DAD. AND LUMI.
I'MMA GET THE BIGGEST CHOCOLATE CAKE EVER TO TAKE OVER THERE. AND YOU CAN HAVE HALF OF IT.

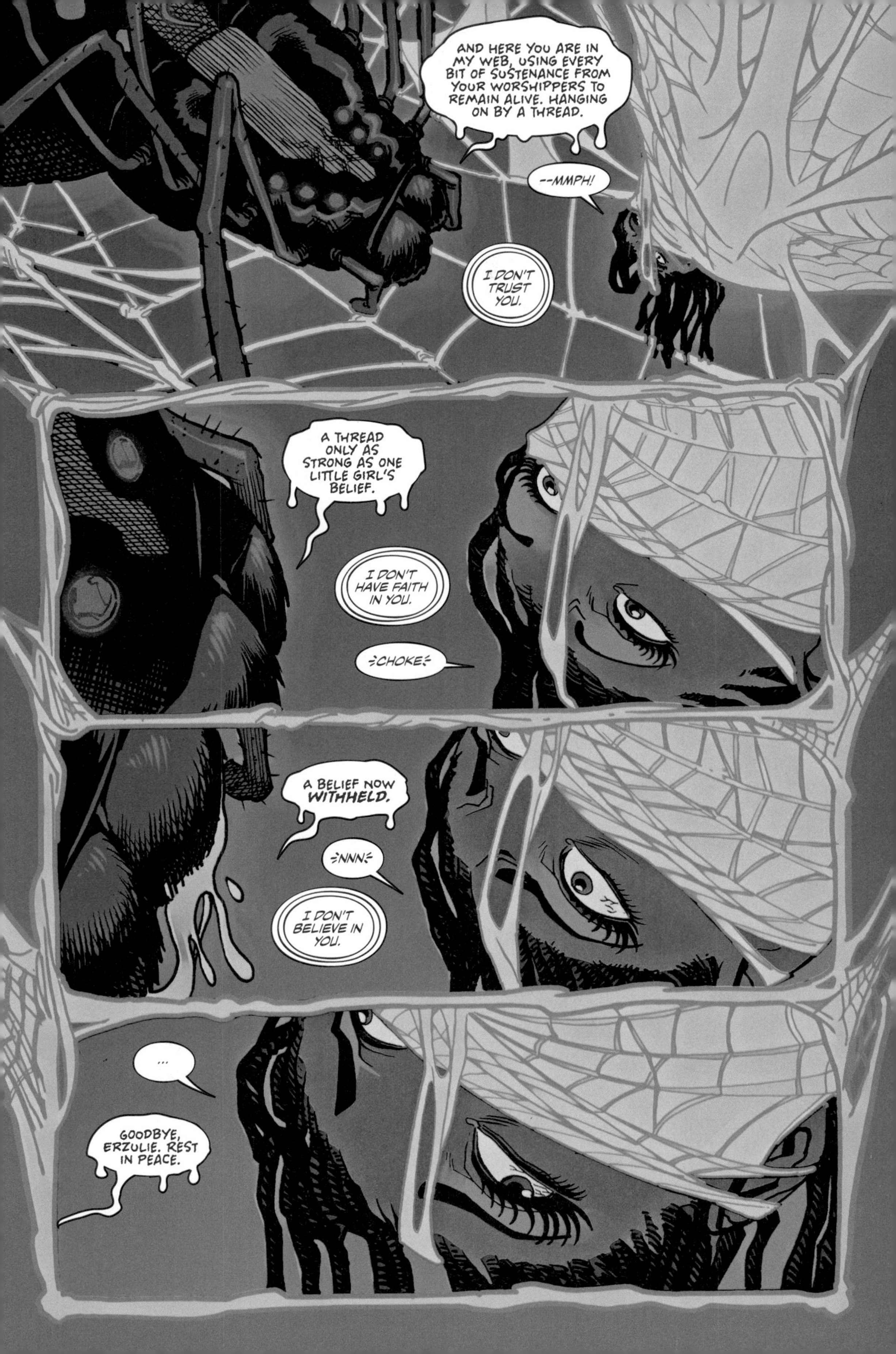
AND HERE YOU ARE IN MY WEB, USING EVERY BIT OF SUSTENANCE FROM YOUR WORSHIPPERS TO REMAIN ALIVE. HANGING ON BY A THREAD.
--MMPH!
I DON'T TRUST YOU.
A THREAD ONLY AS STRONG AS ONE LITTLE GIRL'S BELIEF.
I DON'T HAVE FAITH IN YOU.
CHOKE
A BELIEF NOW WITHHELD.
NNN
I DON'T BELIEVE IN YOU.
...
GOODBYE, ERZULIE. REST IN PEACE.

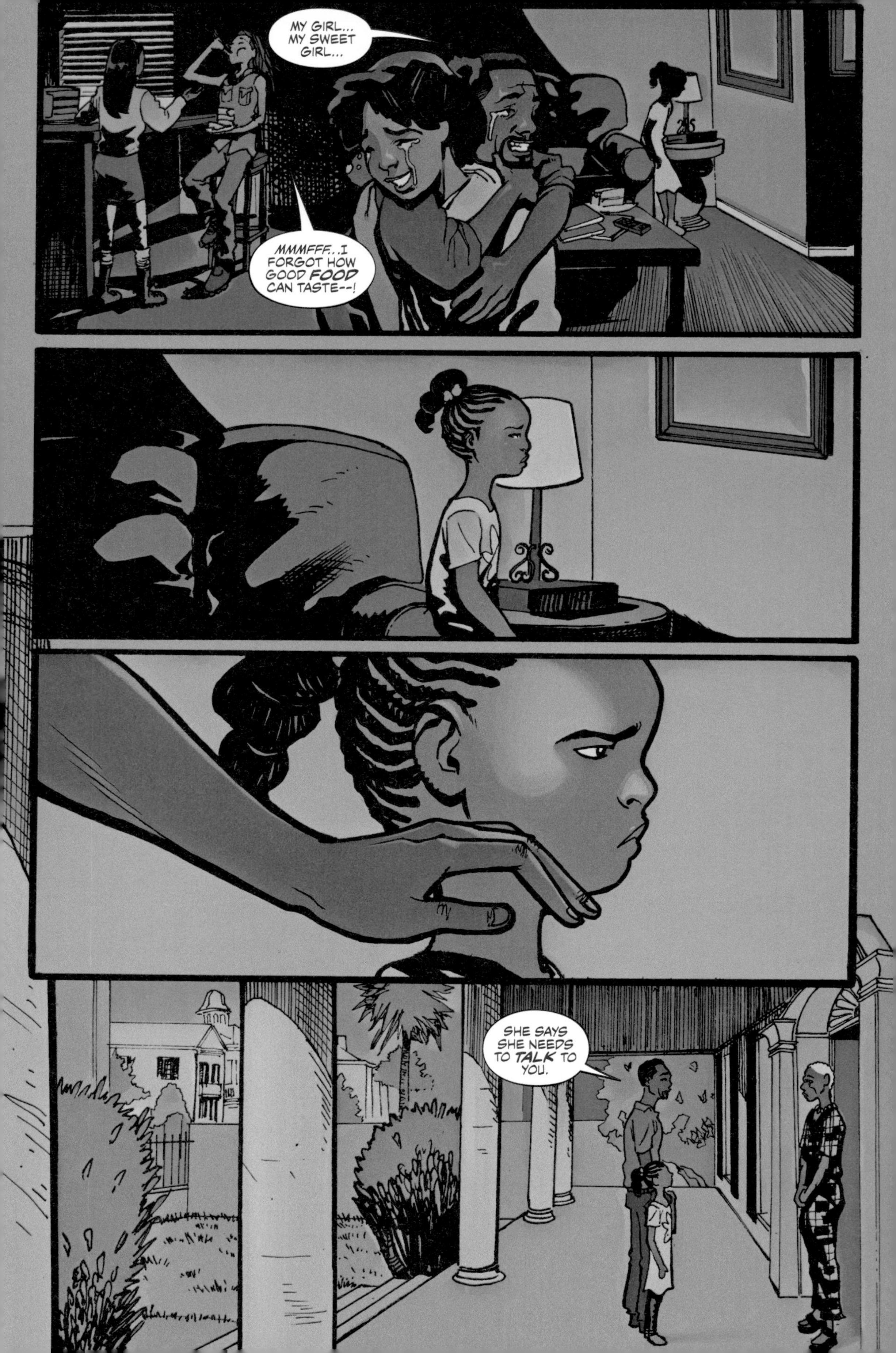
MY GIRL... MY SWEET GIRL...
MMMFFF..I FORGOT HOW GOOD FOOD CAN TASTE--!
SHE SAYS SHE NEEDS TO TALK TO YOU.

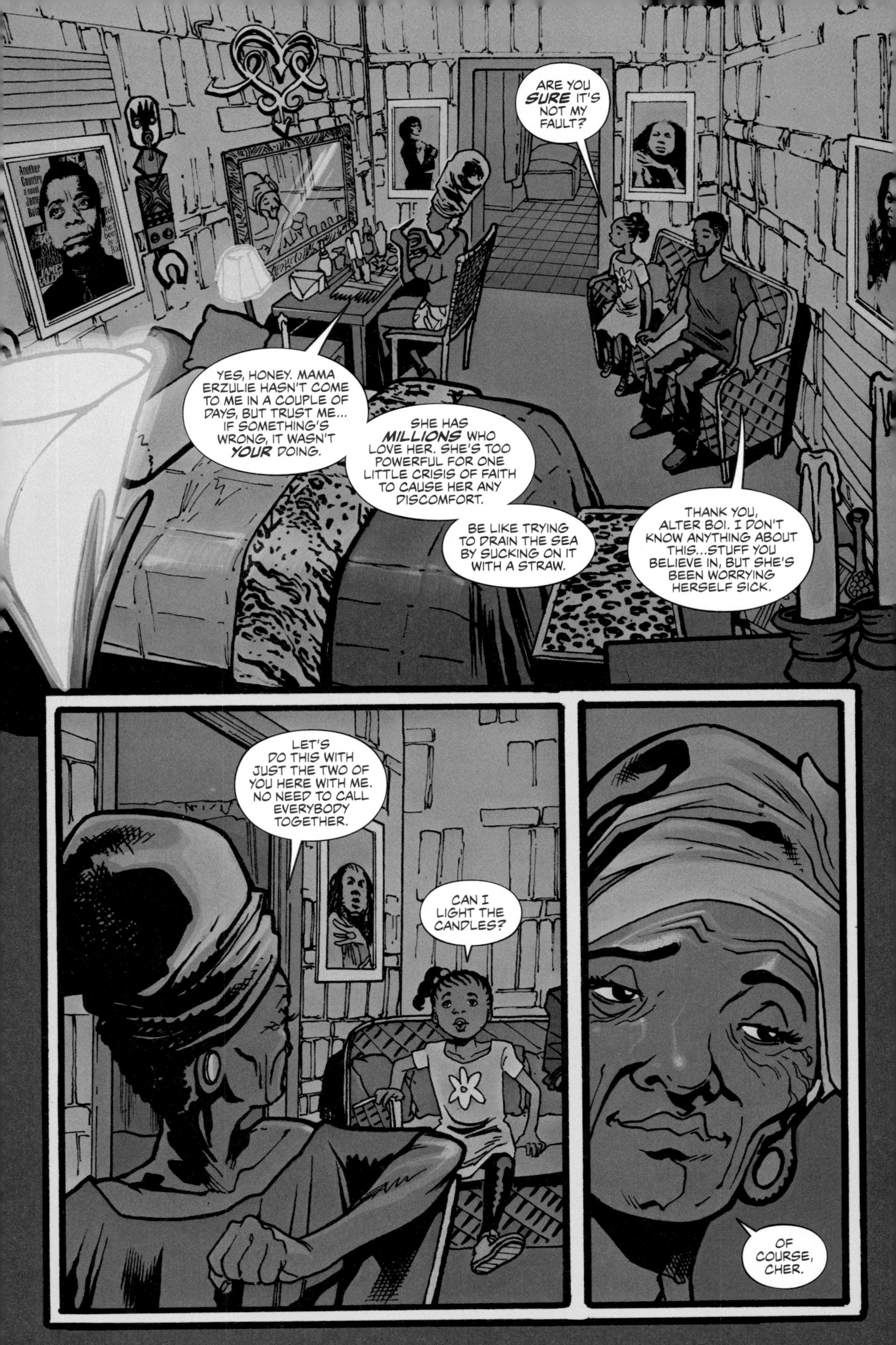
Another Country
a novel
ARE YOU *SURE* IT'S NOT MY FAULT?
YES, HONEY. MAMA ERZULIE HASN'T COME TO ME IN A COUPLE OF DAYS, BUT TRUST ME... IF SOMETHING'S WRONG, IT WASN'T *YOUR* DOING.
SHE HAS *MILLIONS* WHO LOVE HER. SHE'S TOO POWERFUL FOR ONE LITTLE CRISIS OF FAITH TO CAUSE HER ANY DISCOMFORT.
BE LIKE TRYING TO DRAIN THE SEA BY SUCKING ON IT WITH A STRAW.
THANK YOU, ALTER BOI. I DON'T KNOW ANYTHING ABOUT THIS...STUFF YOU BELIEVE IN, BUT SHE'S BEEN WORRYING HERSELF SICK.
LET'S DO THIS WITH JUST THE TWO OF YOU HERE WITH ME. NO NEED TO CALL EVERYBODY TOGETHER.
CAN I LIGHT THE CANDLES?
OF COURSE, CHER.

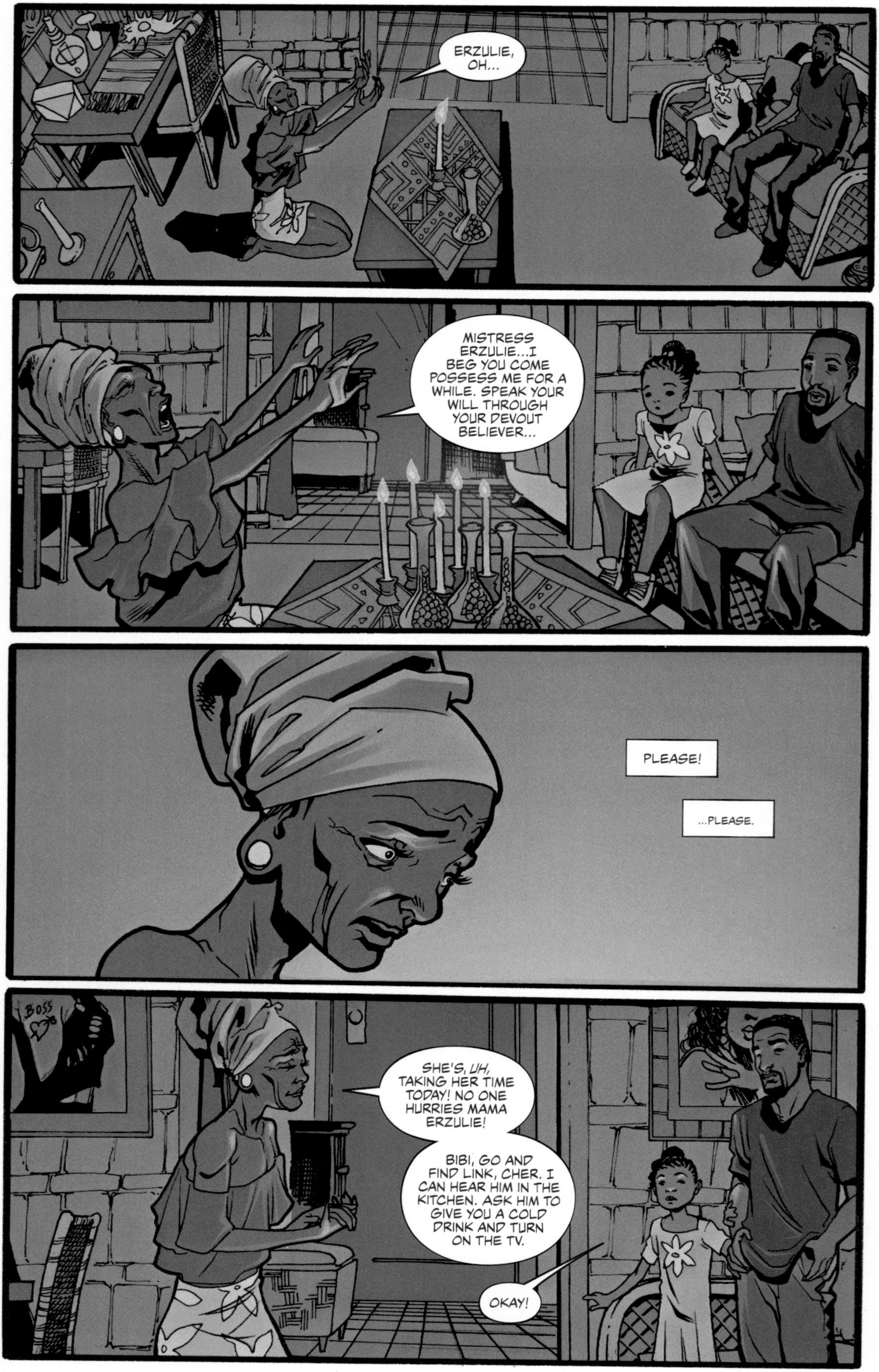
ERZULIE, OH...
MISTRESS ERZULIE...I BEG YOU COME POSSESS ME FOR A WHILE. SPEAK YOUR WILL THROUGH YOUR DEVOUT BELIEVER...
PLEASE!
...PLEASE.
BOSS
SHE'S, *UH*, TAKING HER TIME TODAY! NO ONE HURRIES MAMA ERZULIE!
BIBI, GO AND FIND LINK, CHER. I CAN HEAR HIM IN THE KITCHEN. ASK HIM TO GIVE YOU A COLD DRINK AND TURN ON THE TV.
OKAY!

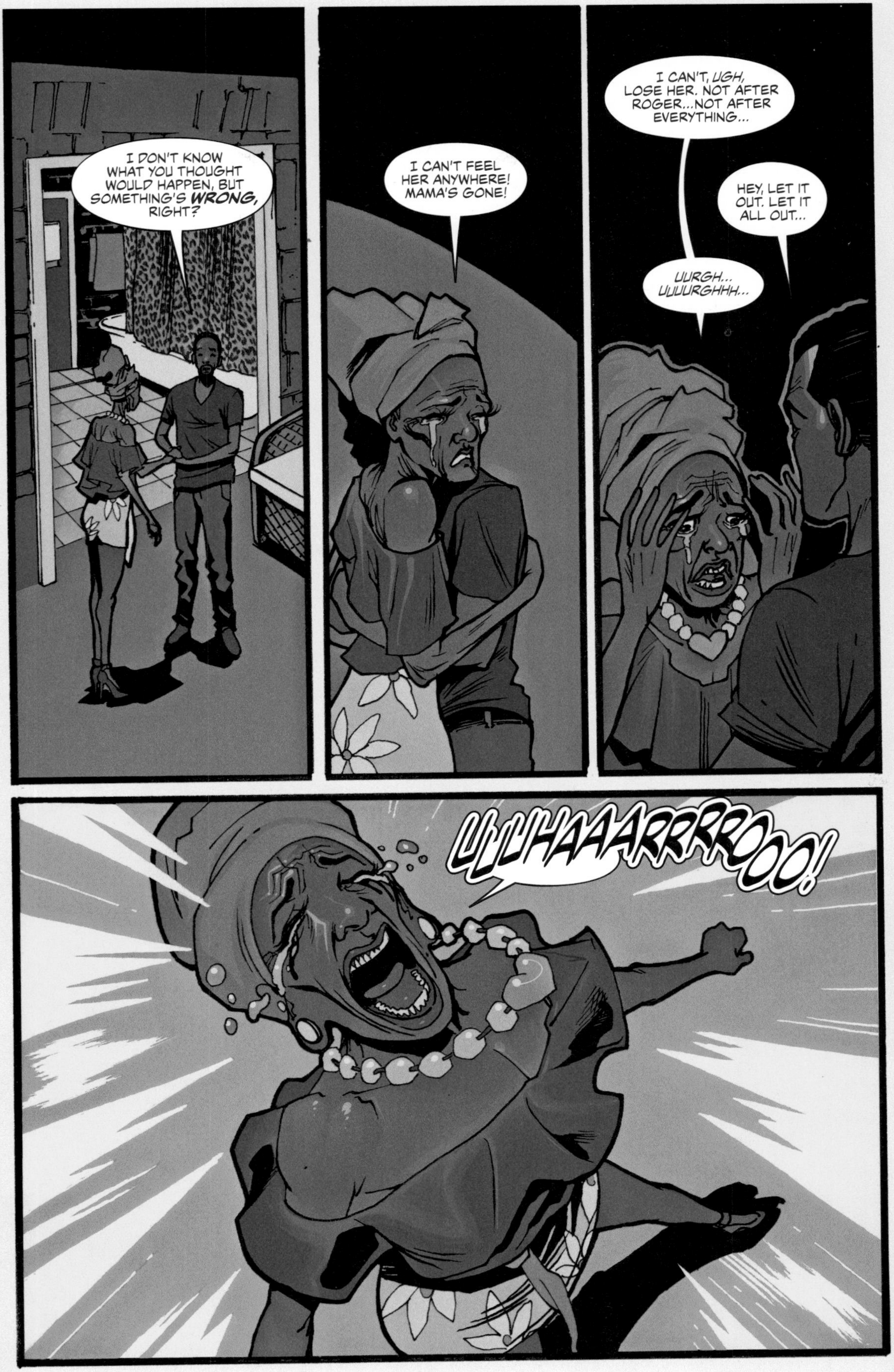
I DON'T KNOW WHAT YOU THOUGHT WOULD HAPPEN, BUT SOMETHING'S **WRONG,** RIGHT?
I CAN'T FEEL HER ANYWHERE! MAMA'S GONE!
I CAN'T, *UGH,* LOSE HER. NOT AFTER ROGER...NOT AFTER EVERYTHING...
HEY, LET IT OUT. LET IT ALL OUT...
UURGH... UUUURGHHH...
UUUHAAARRRROOO!

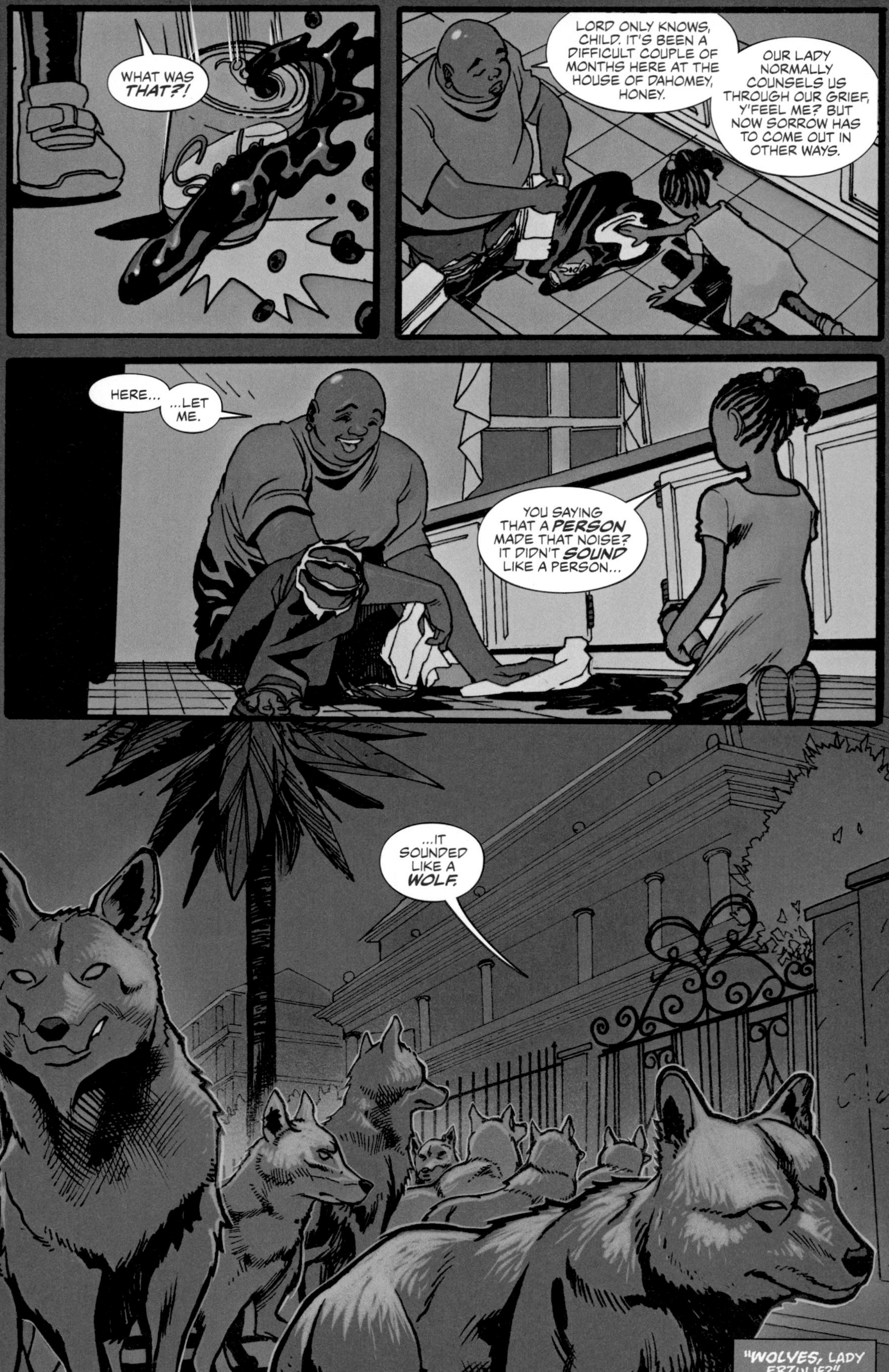
WHAT WAS THAT?!
LORD ONLY KNOWS, CHILD. IT'S BEEN A DIFFICULT COUPLE OF MONTHS HERE AT THE HOUSE OF DAHOMEY, HONEY.
OUR LADY NORMALLY COUNSELS US THROUGH OUR GRIEF, Y'FEEL ME? BUT NOW SORROW HAS TO COME OUT IN OTHER WAYS.
HERE...
...LET ME.
YOU SAYING THAT A PERSON MADE THAT NOISE? IT DIDN'T SOUND LIKE A PERSON...
...IT SOUNDED LIKE A WOLF.
"WOLVES, LADY ERZULIE?"

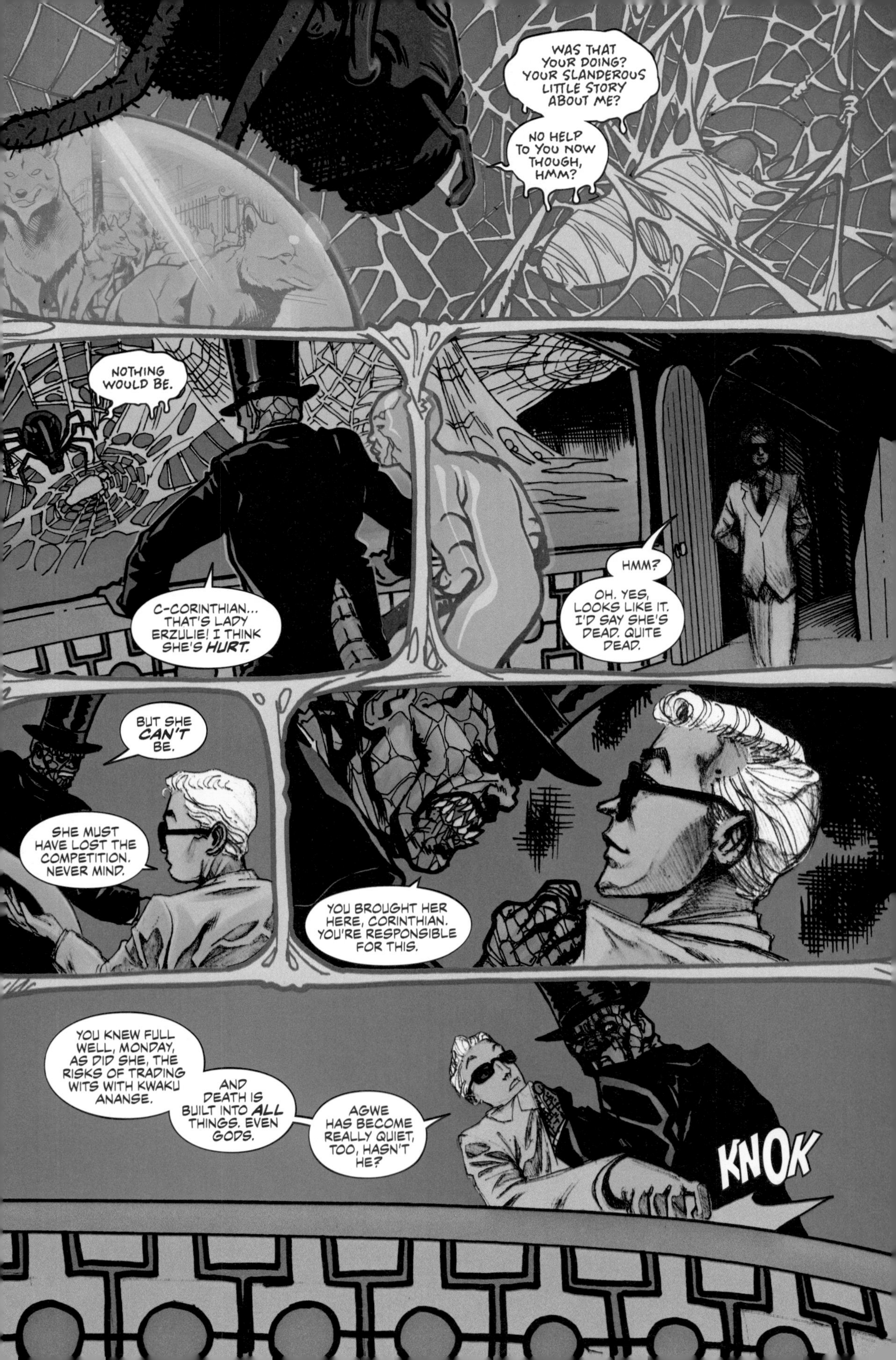

WAS THAT YOUR DOING? YOUR SLANDEROUS LITTLE STORY ABOUT ME?
NO HELP TO YOU NOW THOUGH, HMM?
NOTHING WOULD BE.
C-CORINTHIAN... THAT'S LADY ERZULIE! I THINK SHE'S *HURT.*
HMM?
OH. YES, LOOKS LIKE IT. I'D SAY SHE'S DEAD. QUITE DEAD.
BUT SHE *CAN'T* BE.
SHE MUST HAVE LOST THE COMPETITION. NEVER MIND.
YOU BROUGHT HER HERE, CORINTHIAN. YOU'RE RESPONSIBLE FOR THIS.
YOU KNEW FULL WELL, MONDAY, AS DID SHE, THE RISKS OF TRADING WITS WITH KWAKU ANANSE.
AND DEATH IS BUILT INTO *ALL* THINGS. EVEN GODS.
AGWE HAS BECOME REALLY QUIET, TOO, HASN'T HE?
KNOK

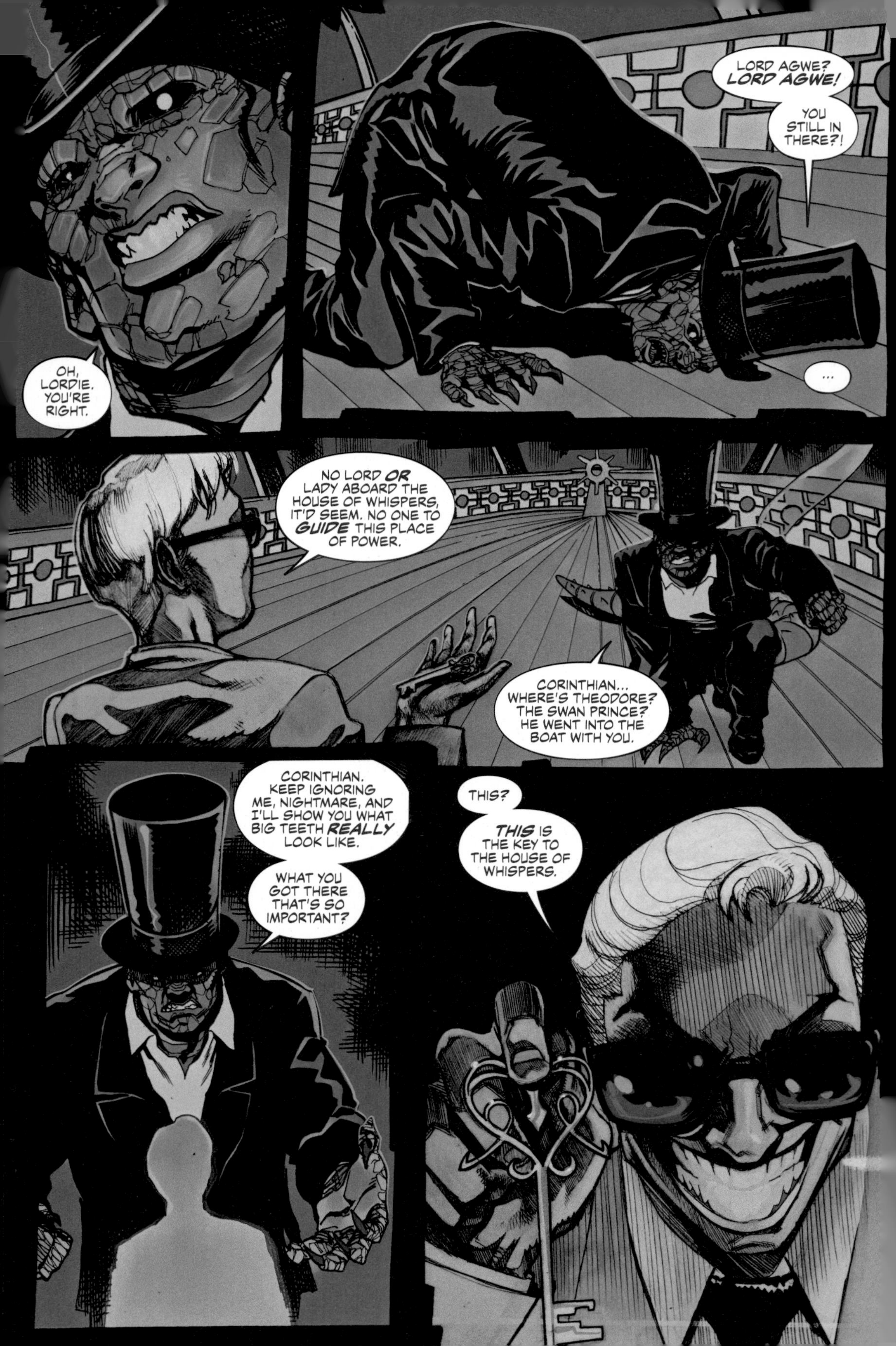
OH, LORDIE. YOU'RE RIGHT.
LORD AGWE? LORD AGWE!
YOU STILL IN THERE?!
...
NO LORD OR LADY ABOARD THE HOUSE OF WHISPERS, IT'D SEEM. NO ONE TO GUIDE THIS PLACE OF POWER.
CORINTHIAN... WHERE'S THEODORE? THE SWAN PRINCE? HE WENT INTO THE BOAT WITH YOU.
CORINTHIAN. KEEP IGNORING ME, NIGHTMARE, AND I'LL SHOW YOU WHAT BIG TEETH REALLY LOOK LIKE.
WHAT YOU GOT THERE THAT'S SO IMPORTANT?
THIS?
THIS IS THE KEY TO THE HOUSE OF WHISPERS.

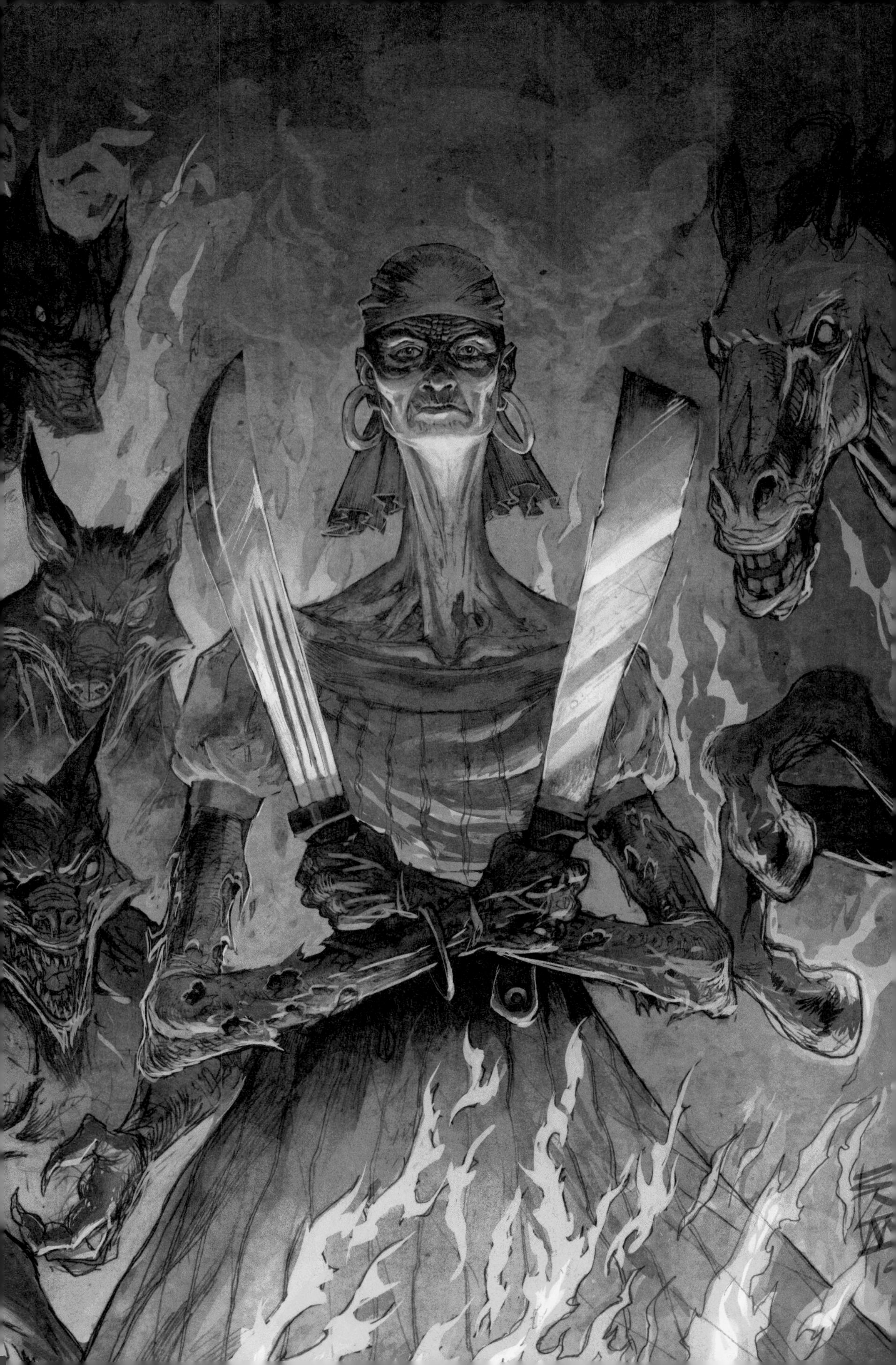

HOUSE OF WHISPERS

For I Know What I Do Must Be Wrong

WRITTEN BY
Nalo Hopkinson
and *Dan Watters*

ILLUSTRATED BY
Dominike "DOMO" Stanton

COLORS BY
Zac Atkinson

LETTERS BY
AndWorld Design

COVER ART BY
Sean Andrew Murray

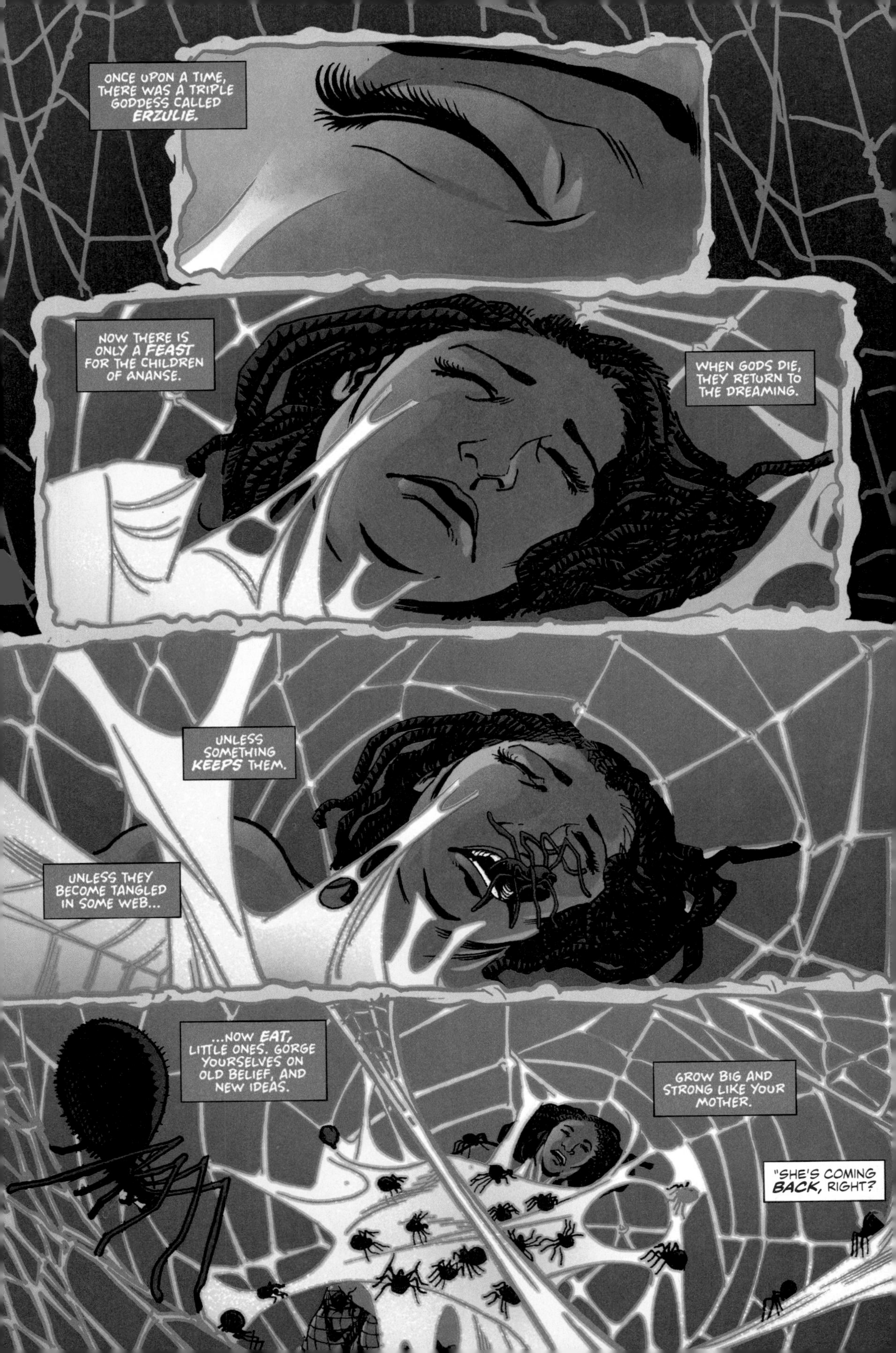
ONCE UPON A TIME, THERE WAS A TRIPLE GODDESS CALLED ERZULIE.
NOW THERE IS ONLY A FEAST FOR THE CHILDREN OF ANANSE.
WHEN GODS DIE, THEY RETURN TO THE DREAMING.
UNLESS SOMETHING KEEPS THEM.
UNLESS THEY BECOME TANGLED IN SOME WEB...
...NOW EAT, LITTLE ONES. GORGE YOURSELVES ON OLD BELIEF, AND NEW IDEAS.
GROW BIG AND STRONG LIKE YOUR MOTHER.
"SHE'S COMING BACK, RIGHT?

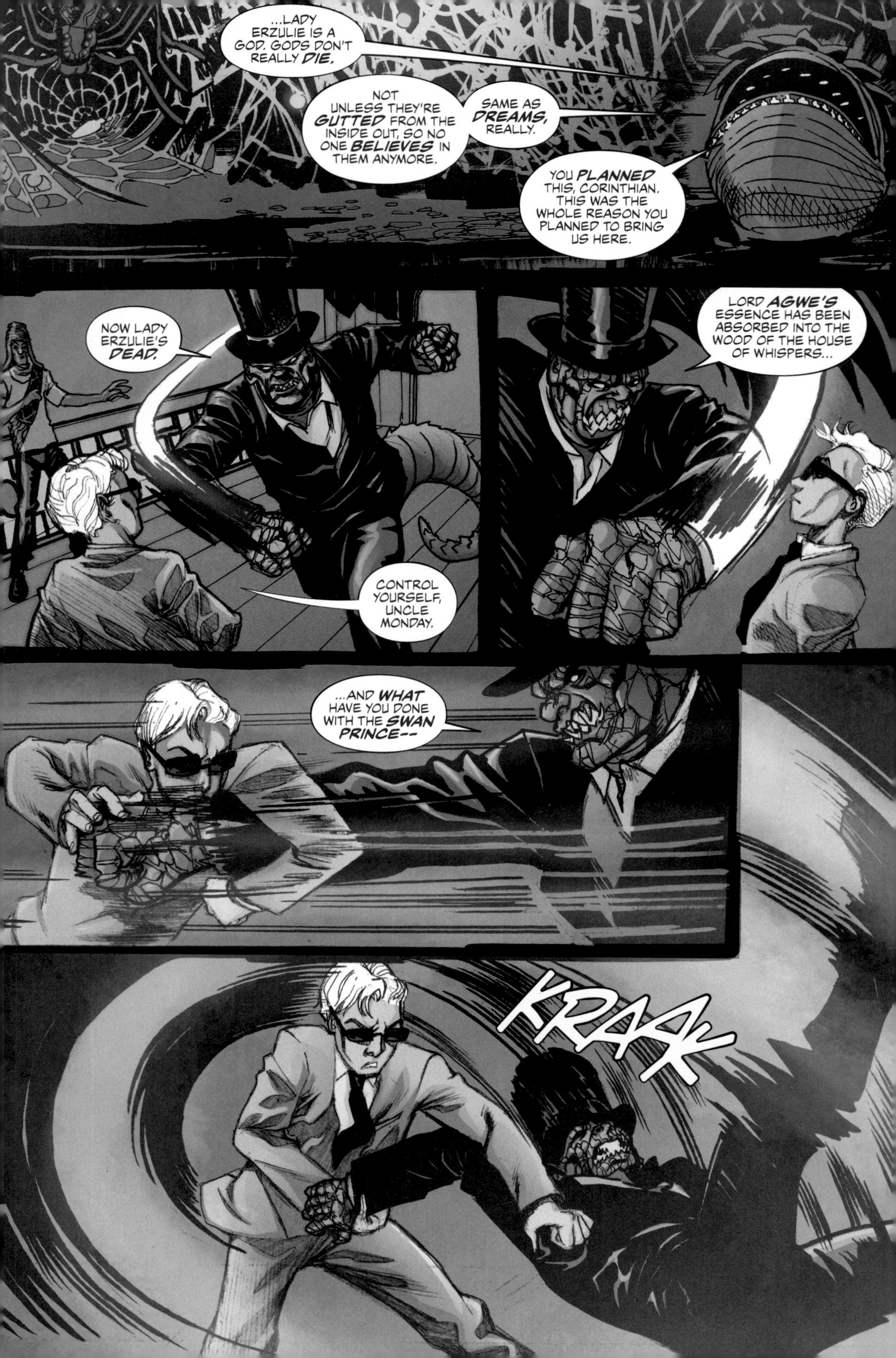
...LADY ERZULIE IS A GOD. GODS DON'T REALLY DIE.
NOT UNLESS THEY'RE GUTTED FROM THE INSIDE OUT, SO NO ONE BELIEVES IN THEM ANYMORE.
SAME AS DREAMS, REALLY.
YOU PLANNED THIS, CORINTHIAN. THIS WAS THE WHOLE REASON YOU PLANNED TO BRING US HERE.
NOW LADY ERZULIE'S DEAD.
CONTROL YOURSELF, UNCLE MONDAY.
LORD AGWE'S ESSENCE HAS BEEN ABSORBED INTO THE WOOD OF THE HOUSE OF WHISPERS...
...AND WHAT HAVE YOU DONE WITH THE SWAN PRINCE--
KRAAK

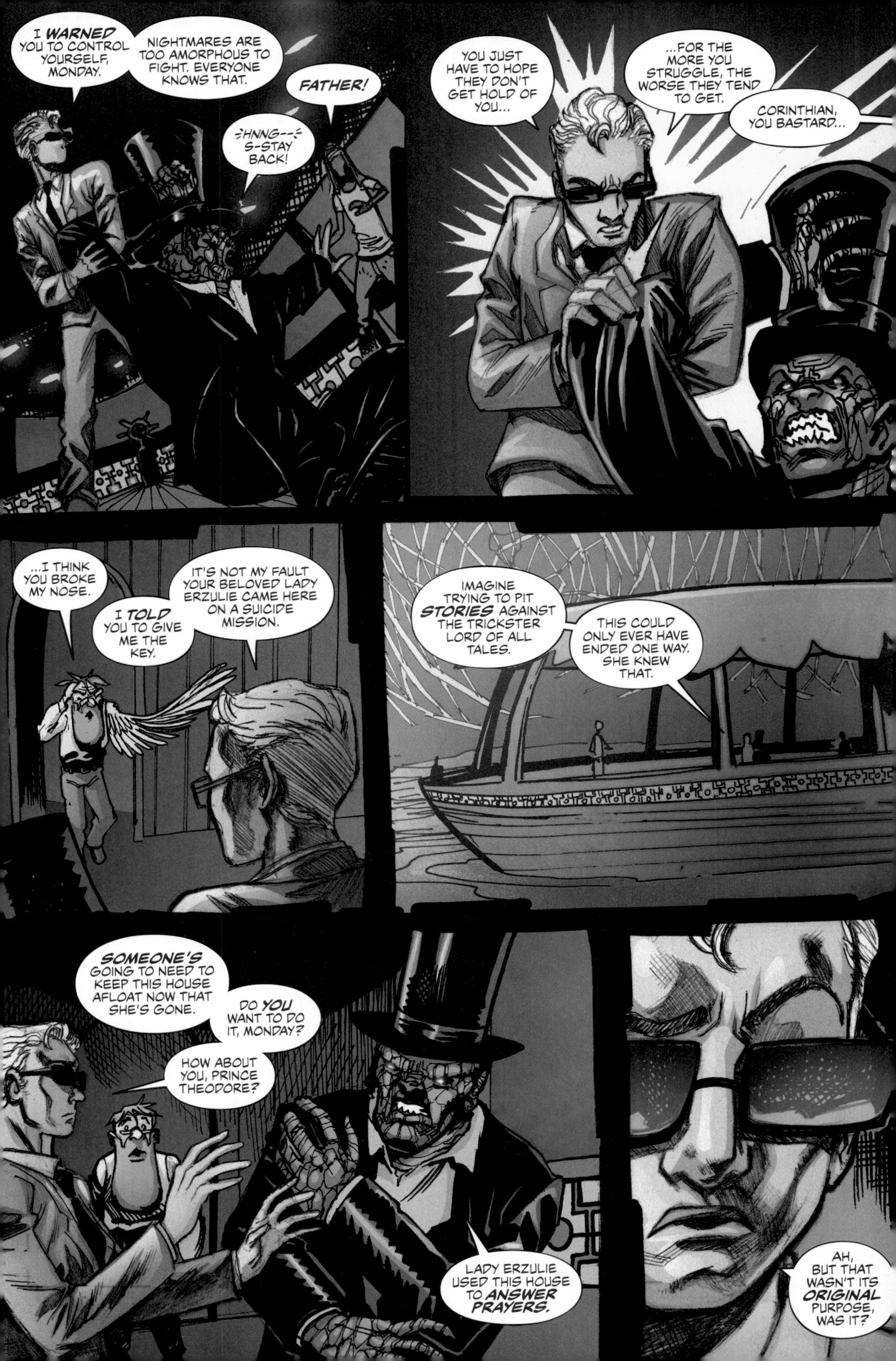
I WARNED YOU TO CONTROL YOURSELF, MONDAY.
NIGHTMARES ARE TOO AMORPHOUS TO FIGHT. EVERYONE KNOWS THAT.
FATHER!
HNNG-- S-STAY BACK!
YOU JUST HAVE TO HOPE THEY DON'T GET HOLD OF YOU...
...FOR THE MORE YOU STRUGGLE, THE WORSE THEY TEND TO GET.
CORINTHIAN, YOU BASTARD...
...I THINK YOU BROKE MY NOSE.
I TOLD YOU TO GIVE ME THE KEY.
IT'S NOT MY FAULT YOUR BELOVED LADY ERZULIE CAME HERE ON A SUICIDE MISSION.
IMAGINE TRYING TO PIT STORIES AGAINST THE TRICKSTER LORD OF ALL TALES.
THIS COULD ONLY EVER HAVE ENDED ONE WAY. SHE KNEW THAT.
SOMEONE'S GOING TO NEED TO KEEP THIS HOUSE AFLOAT NOW THAT SHE'S GONE.
DO YOU WANT TO DO IT, MONDAY?
HOW ABOUT YOU, PRINCE THEODORE?
LADY ERZULIE USED THIS HOUSE TO ANSWER PRAYERS.
AH, BUT THAT WASN'T ITS ORIGINAL PURPOSE, WAS IT?

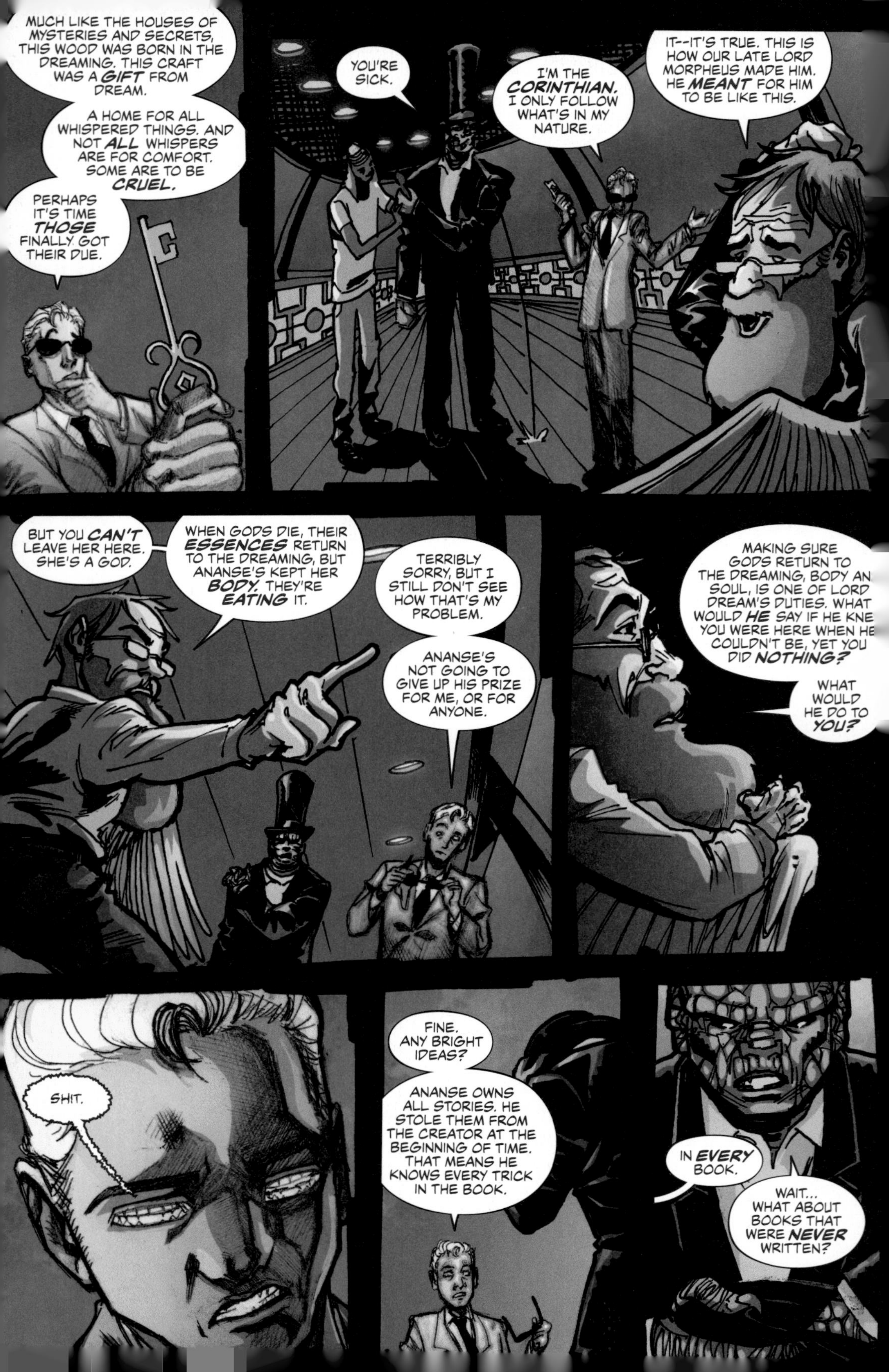
MUCH LIKE THE HOUSES OF MYSTERIES AND SECRETS, THIS WOOD WAS BORN IN THE DREAMING. THIS CRAFT WAS A GIFT FROM DREAM.
A HOME FOR ALL WHISPERED THINGS. AND NOT ALL WHISPERS ARE FOR COMFORT. SOME ARE TO BE CRUEL.
PERHAPS IT'S TIME THOSE FINALLY GOT THEIR DUE.
YOU'RE SICK.
I'M THE CORINTHIAN. I ONLY FOLLOW WHAT'S IN MY NATURE.
IT--IT'S TRUE. THIS IS HOW OUR LATE LORD MORPHEUS MADE HIM. HE MEANT FOR HIM TO BE LIKE THIS.
BUT YOU CAN'T LEAVE HER HERE. SHE'S A GOD.
WHEN GODS DIE, THEIR ESSENCES RETURN TO THE DREAMING, BUT ANANSE'S KEPT HER BODY. THEY'RE EATING IT.
TERRIBLY SORRY, BUT I STILL DON'T SEE HOW THAT'S MY PROBLEM.
ANANSE'S NOT GOING TO GIVE UP HIS PRIZE FOR ME, OR FOR ANYONE.
MAKING SURE GODS RETURN TO THE DREAMING, BODY AN SOUL, IS ONE OF LORD DREAM'S DUTIES. WHAT WOULD HE SAY IF HE KNE YOU WERE HERE WHEN HE COULDN'T BE, YET YOU DID NOTHING?
WHAT WOULD HE DO TO YOU?
SHIT.
FINE. ANY BRIGHT IDEAS?
ANANSE OWNS ALL STORIES. HE STOLE THEM FROM THE CREATOR AT THE BEGINNING OF TIME. THAT MEANS HE KNOWS EVERY TRICK IN THE BOOK.
IN EVERY BOOK.
WAIT... WHAT ABOUT BOOKS THAT WERE NEVER WRITTEN?

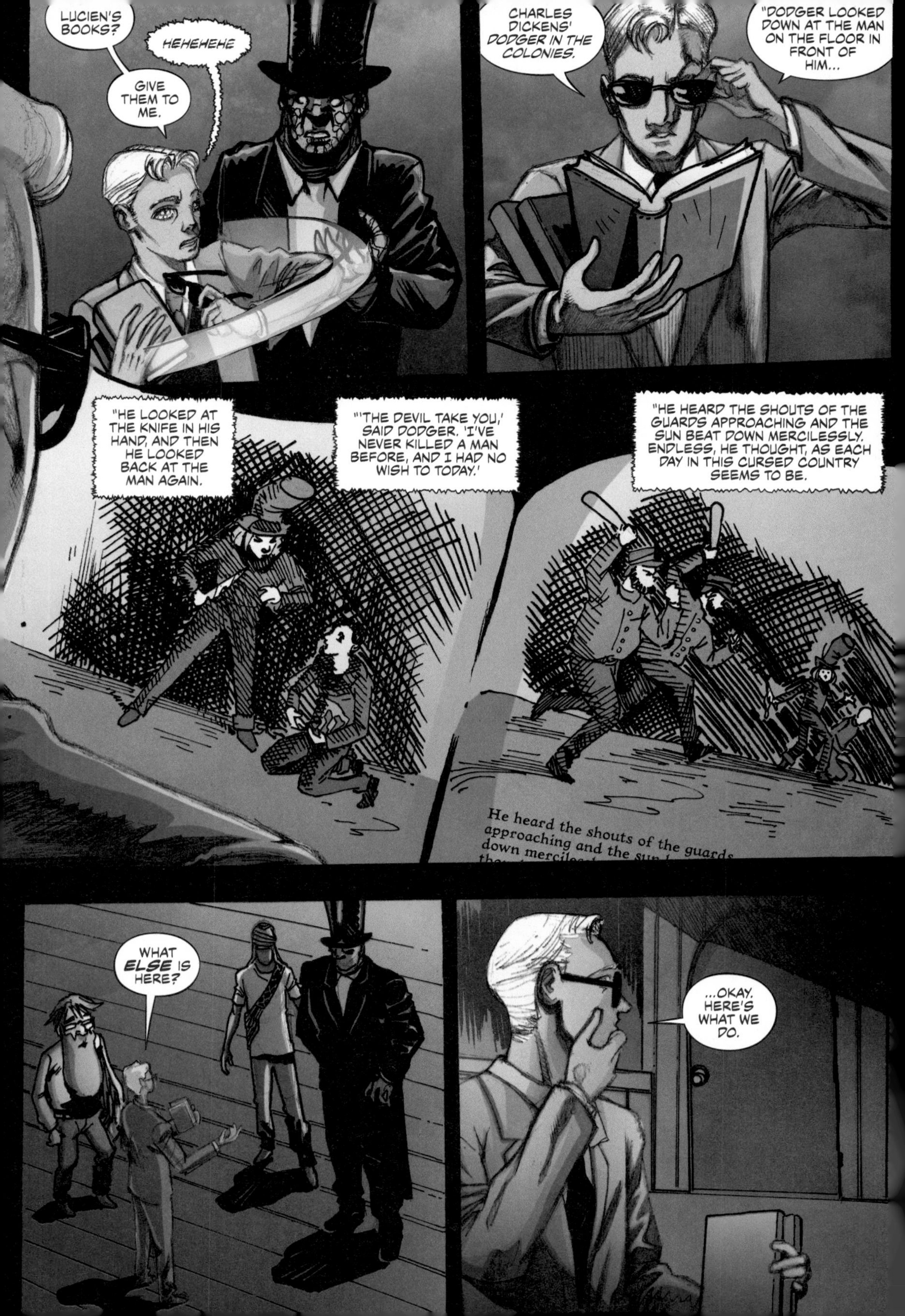
LUCIEN'S BOOKS?
HEHEHEHE
GIVE THEM TO ME.
CHARLES DICKENS' DODGER IN THE COLONIES.
"DODGER LOOKED DOWN AT THE MAN ON THE FLOOR IN FRONT OF HIM...
"HE LOOKED AT THE KNIFE IN HIS HAND, AND THEN HE LOOKED BACK AT THE MAN AGAIN.
"'THE DEVIL TAKE YOU,' SAID DODGER. 'I'VE NEVER KILLED A MAN BEFORE, AND I HAD NO WISH TO TODAY.'
"HE HEARD THE SHOUTS OF THE GUARDS APPROACHING AND THE SUN BEAT DOWN MERCILESSLY. ENDLESS, HE THOUGHT, AS EACH DAY IN THIS CURSED COUNTRY SEEMS TO BE.
He heard the shouts of the guards approaching and the sun
WHAT ELSE IS HERE?
...OKAY. HERE'S WHAT WE DO.

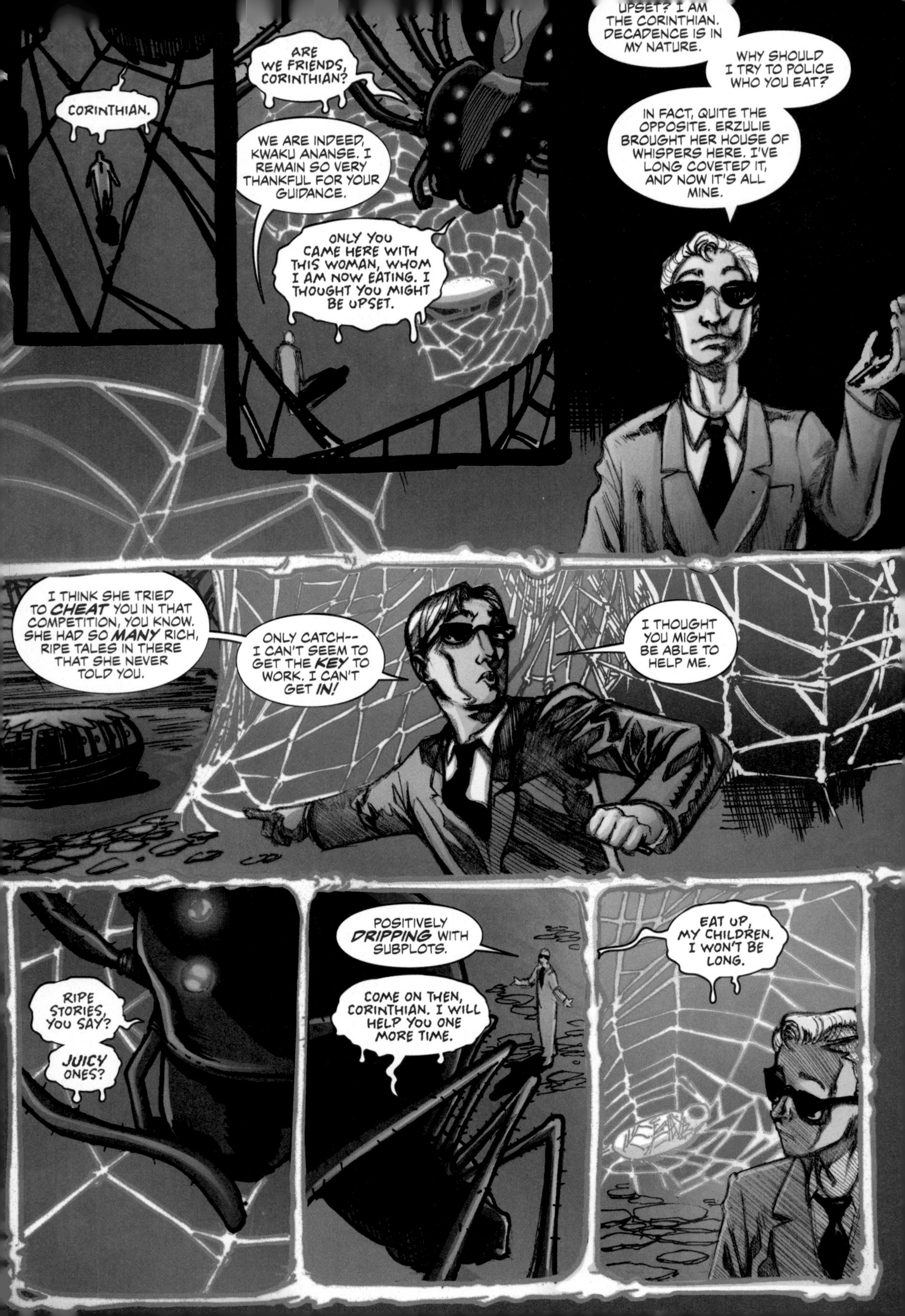
CORINTHIAN.
ARE WE FRIENDS, CORINTHIAN?
WE ARE INDEED, KWAKU ANANSE. I REMAIN SO VERY THANKFUL FOR YOUR GUIDANCE.
ONLY YOU CAME HERE WITH THIS WOMAN, WHOM I AM NOW EATING. I THOUGHT YOU MIGHT BE UPSET.
UPSET? I AM THE CORINTHIAN. DECADENCE IS IN MY NATURE.
WHY SHOULD I TRY TO POLICE WHO YOU EAT?
IN FACT, QUITE THE OPPOSITE. ERZULIE BROUGHT HER HOUSE OF WHISPERS HERE. I'VE LONG COVETED IT, AND NOW IT'S ALL MINE.
I THINK SHE TRIED TO **CHEAT** YOU IN THAT COMPETITION, YOU KNOW. SHE HAD SO **MANY** RICH, RIPE TALES IN THERE THAT SHE NEVER TOLD YOU.
ONLY CATCH-- I CAN'T SEEM TO GET THE **KEY** TO WORK. I CAN'T GET **IN!**
I THOUGHT YOU MIGHT BE ABLE TO HELP ME.
RIPE STORIES, YOU SAY?
JUICY ONES?
POSITIVELY **DRIPPING** WITH SUBPLOTS.
COME ON THEN, CORINTHIAN. I WILL HELP YOU ONE MORE TIME.
EAT UP, MY CHILDREN. I WON'T BE LONG.

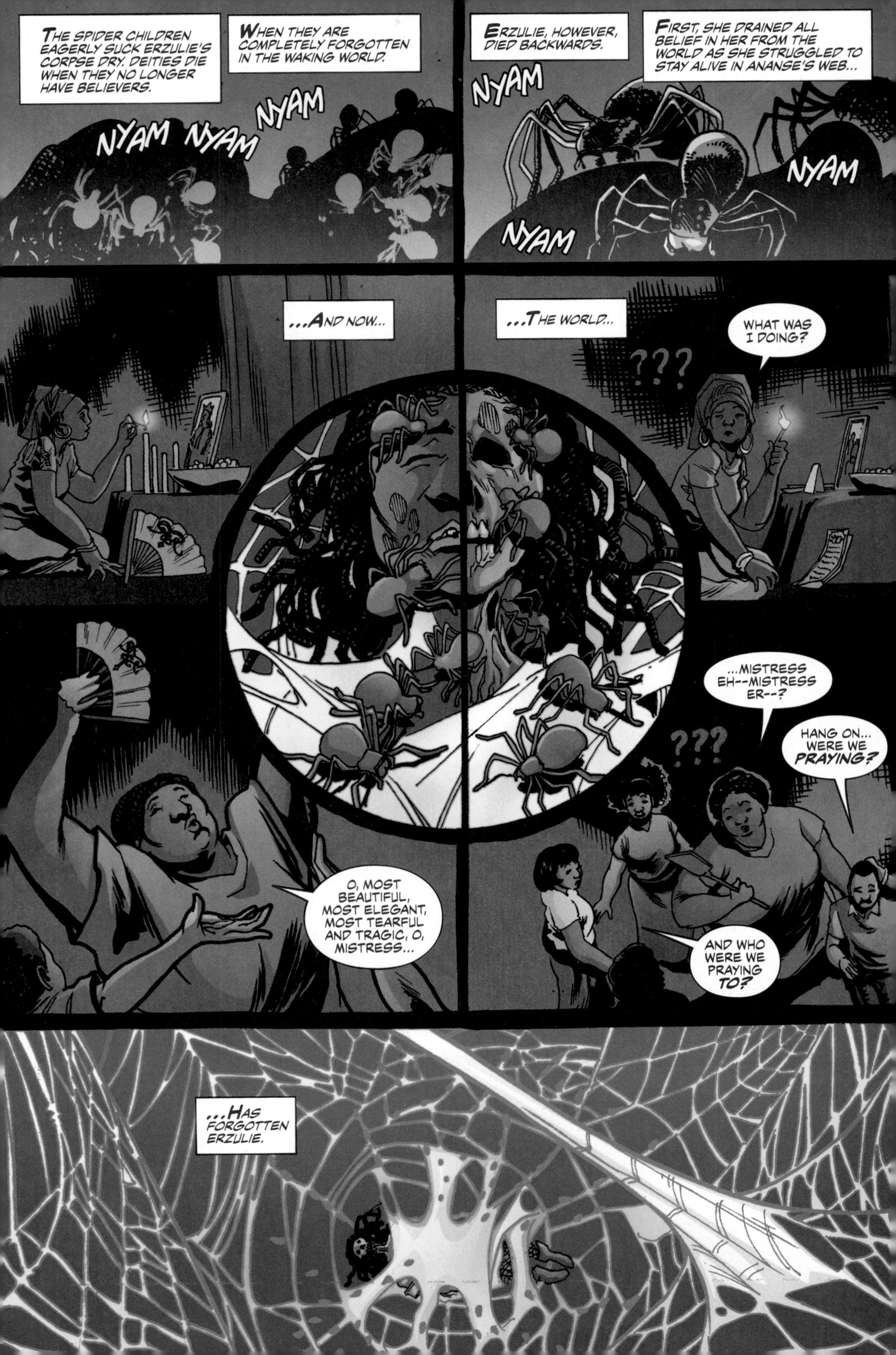
THE SPIDER CHILDREN EAGERLY SUCK ERZULIE'S CORPSE DRY. DEITIES DIE WHEN THEY NO LONGER HAVE BELIEVERS.
WHEN THEY ARE COMPLETELY FORGOTTEN IN THE WAKING WORLD.
NYAM NYAM NYAM
ERZULIE, HOWEVER, DIED BACKWARDS.
FIRST, SHE DRAINED ALL BELIEF IN HER FROM THE WORLD AS SHE STRUGGLED TO STAY ALIVE IN ANANSE'S WEB...
NYAM
NYAM
NYAM
...AND NOW...
...THE WORLD...
???
WHAT WAS I DOING?
O, MOST BEAUTIFUL, MOST ELEGANT, MOST TEARFUL AND TRAGIC, O, MISTRESS...
???
...MISTRESS EH--MISTRESS ER--?
HANG ON... WERE WE PRAYING?
AND WHO WERE WE PRAYING TO?
...HAS FORGOTTEN ERZULIE.

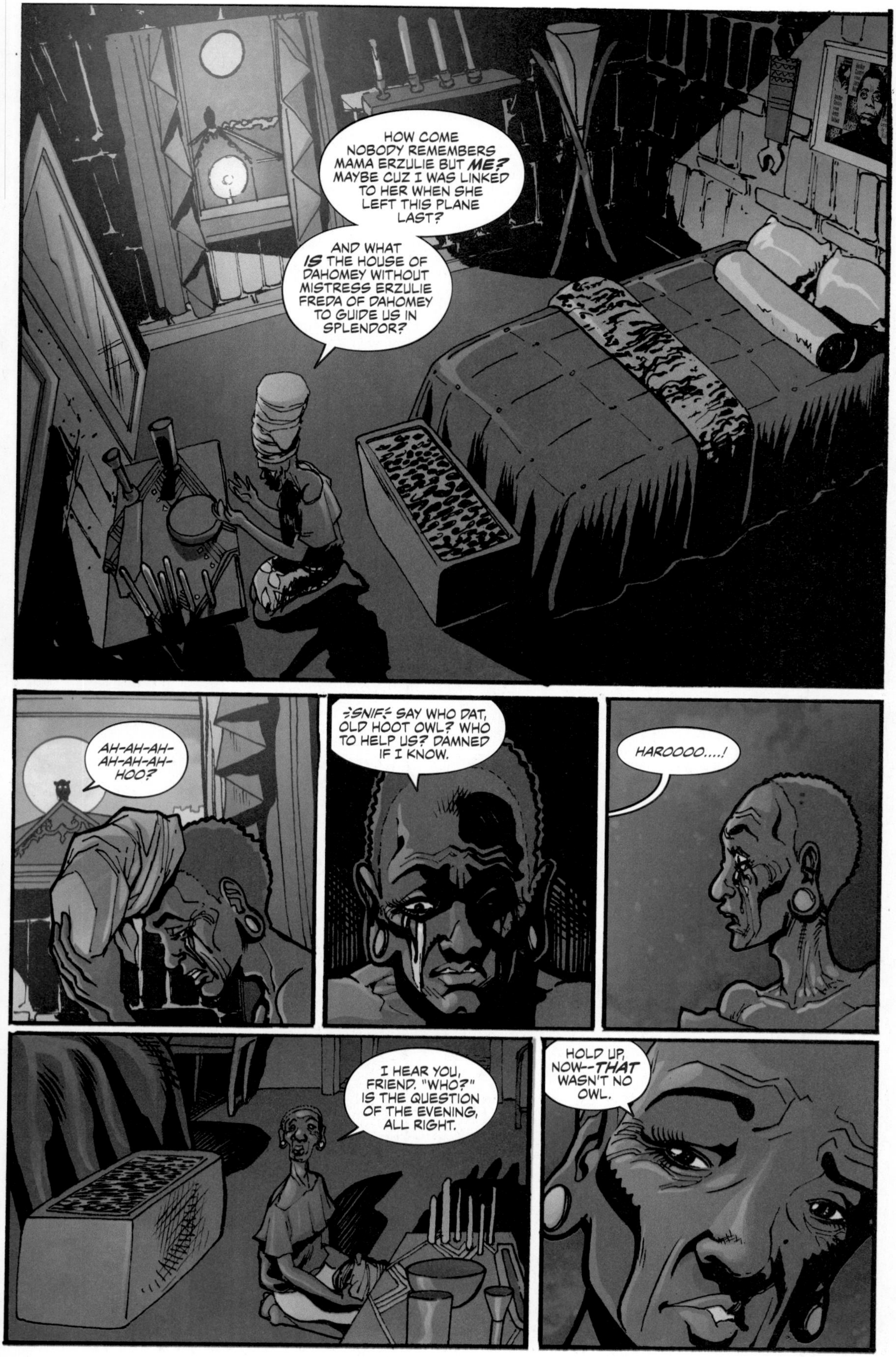
HOW COME NOBODY REMEMBERS MAMA ERZULIE BUT ME? MAYBE CUZ I WAS LINKED TO HER WHEN SHE LEFT THIS PLANE LAST?
AND WHAT IS THE HOUSE OF DAHOMEY WITHOUT MISTRESS ERZULIE FREDA OF DAHOMEY TO GUIDE US IN SPLENDOR?
AH-AH-AH-AH-AH-AH-HOO?
-SNIF- SAY WHO DAT, OLD HOOT OWL? WHO TO HELP US? DAMNED IF I KNOW.
HAROOOO....!
I HEAR YOU, FRIEND. "WHO?" IS THE QUESTION OF THE EVENING, ALL RIGHT.
HOLD UP, NOW--THAT WASN'T NO OWL.

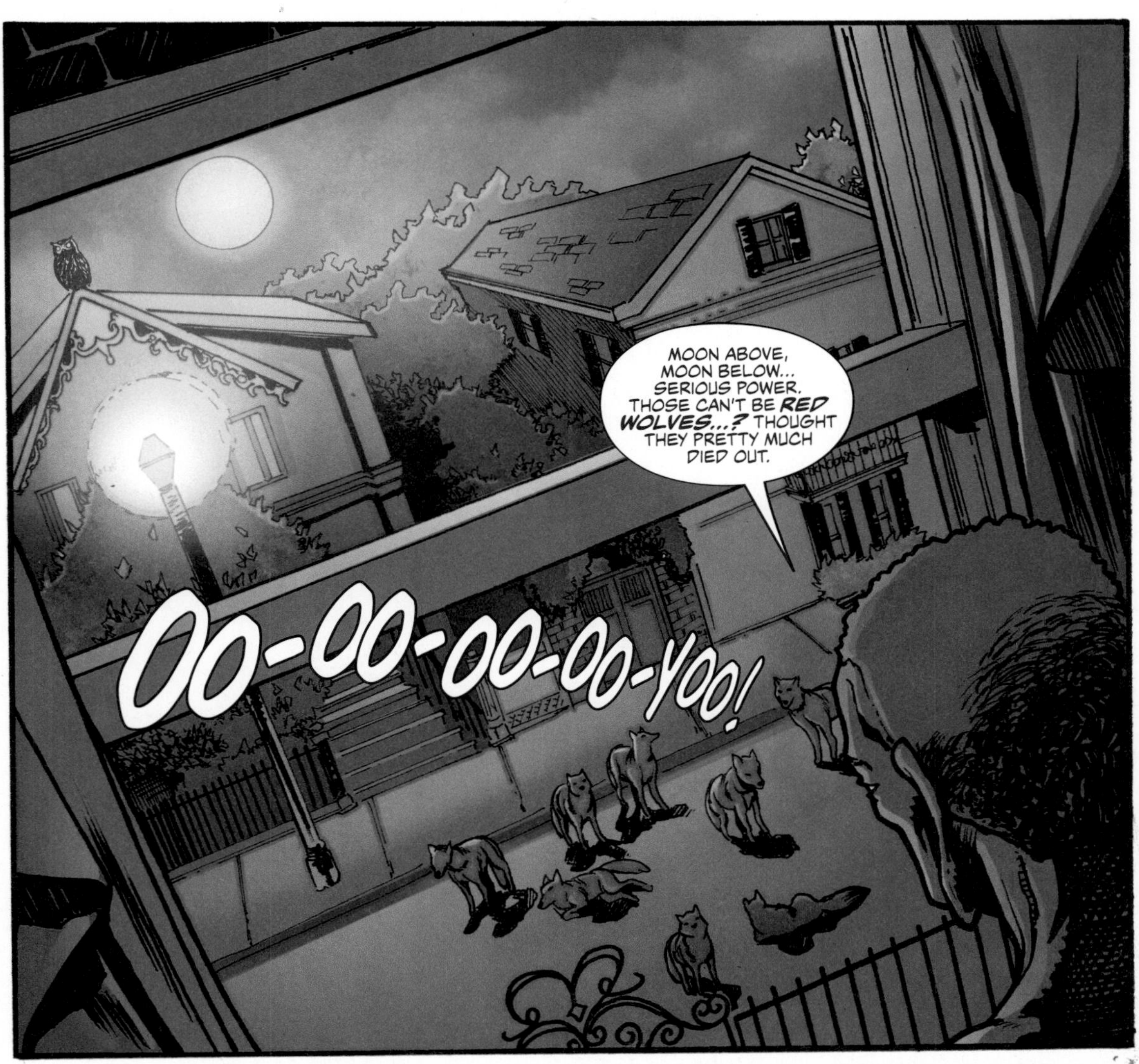
MOON ABOVE, MOON BELOW... SERIOUS POWER. THOSE CAN'T BE RED WOLVES...? THOUGHT THEY PRETTY MUCH DIED OUT.
OO-OO-OO-OO-OO-YOO!

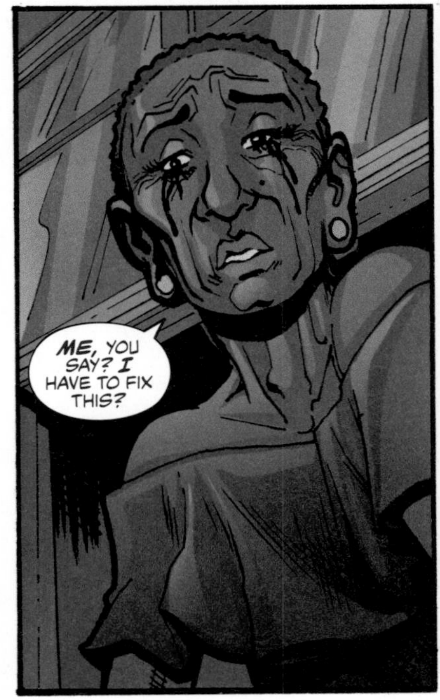
ME, YOU SAY? I HAVE TO FIX THIS?

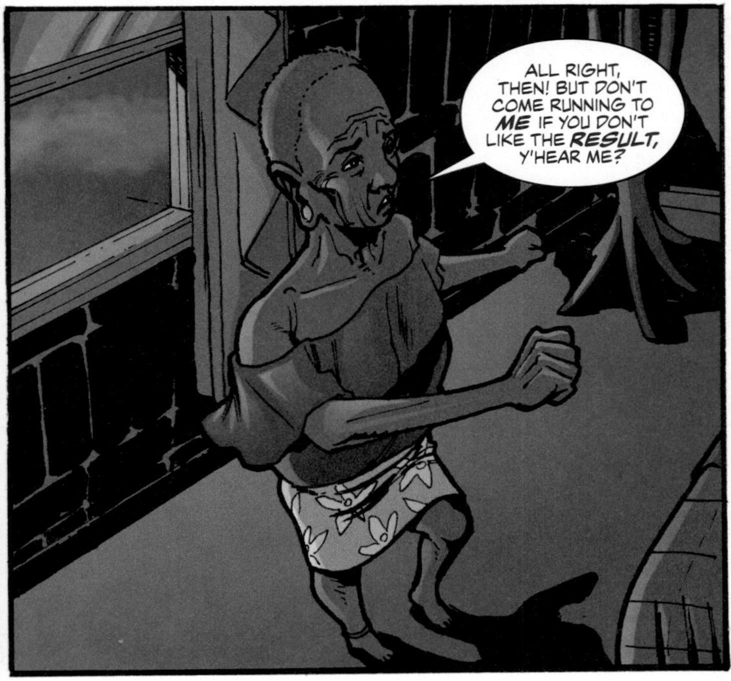
ALL RIGHT, THEN! BUT DON'T COME RUNNING TO ME IF YOU DON'T LIKE THE RESULT, Y'HEAR ME?

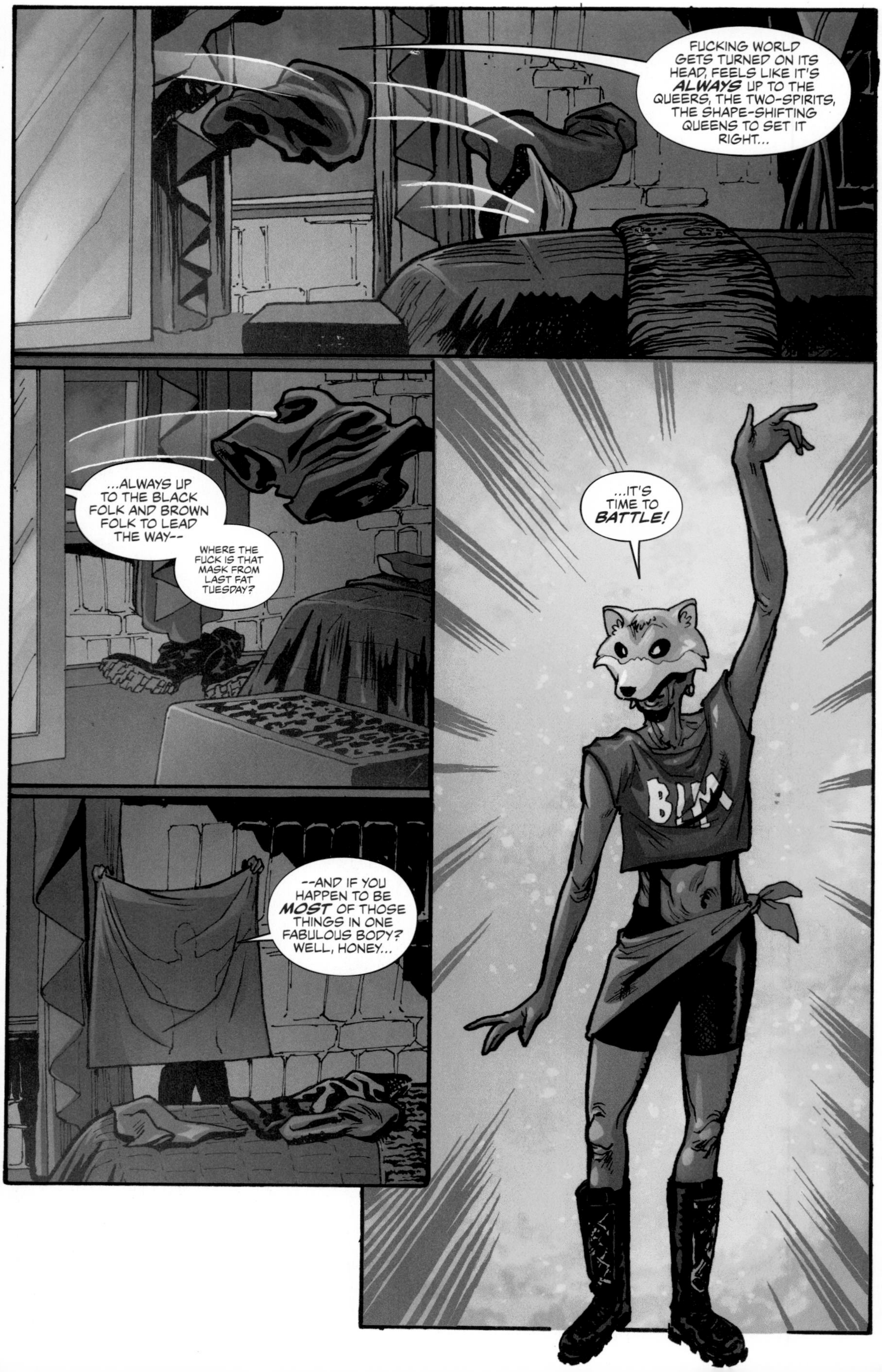
FUCKING WORLD GETS TURNED ON ITS HEAD, FEELS LIKE IT'S ALWAYS UP TO THE QUEERS, THE TWO-SPIRITS, THE SHAPE-SHIFTING QUEENS TO SET IT RIGHT...
...ALWAYS UP TO THE BLACK FOLK AND BROWN FOLK TO LEAD THE WAY--
WHERE THE FUCK IS THAT MASK FROM LAST FAT TUESDAY?
--AND IF YOU HAPPEN TO BE MOST OF THOSE THINGS IN ONE FABULOUS BODY? WELL, HONEY...
...IT'S TIME TO BATTLE!
BLM

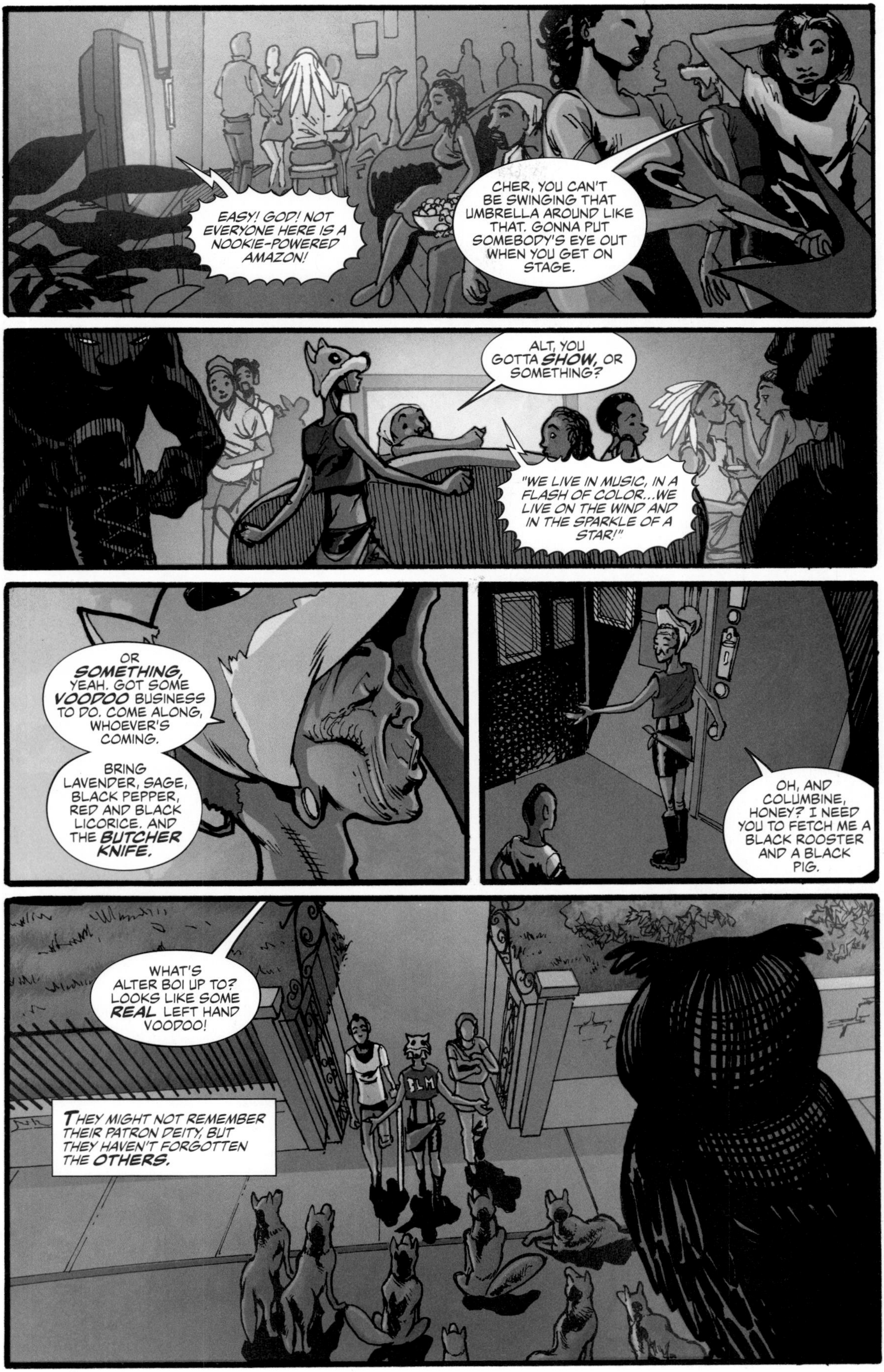
EASY! GOD! NOT EVERYONE HERE IS A NOOKIE-POWERED AMAZON!
CHER, YOU CAN'T BE SWINGING THAT UMBRELLA AROUND LIKE THAT. GONNA PUT SOMEBODY'S EYE OUT WHEN YOU GET ON STAGE.
ALT, YOU GOTTA SHOW, OR SOMETHING?
"WE LIVE IN MUSIC, IN A FLASH OF COLOR...WE LIVE ON THE WIND AND IN THE SPARKLE OF A STAR!"
OR SOMETHING, YEAH. GOT SOME VOODOO BUSINESS TO DO. COME ALONG, WHOEVER'S COMING.
BRING LAVENDER, SAGE, BLACK PEPPER, RED AND BLACK LICORICE. AND THE BUTCHER KNIFE.
OH, AND COLUMBINE, HONEY? I NEED YOU TO FETCH ME A BLACK ROOSTER AND A BLACK PIG.
WHAT'S ALTER BOI UP TO? LOOKS LIKE SOME REAL LEFT HAND VOODOO!
BLM
THEY MIGHT NOT REMEMBER THEIR PATRON DEITY, BUT THEY HAVEN'T FORGOTTEN THE OTHERS.

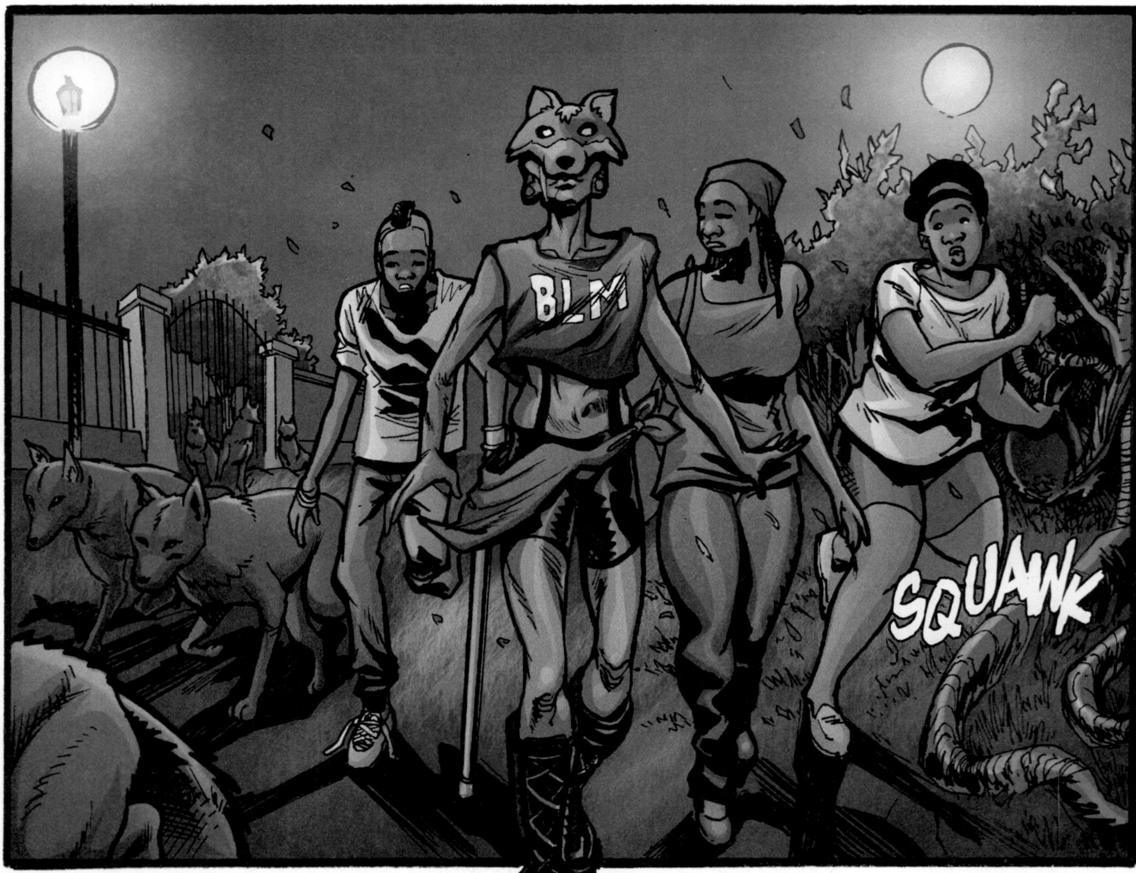
SQUAWK

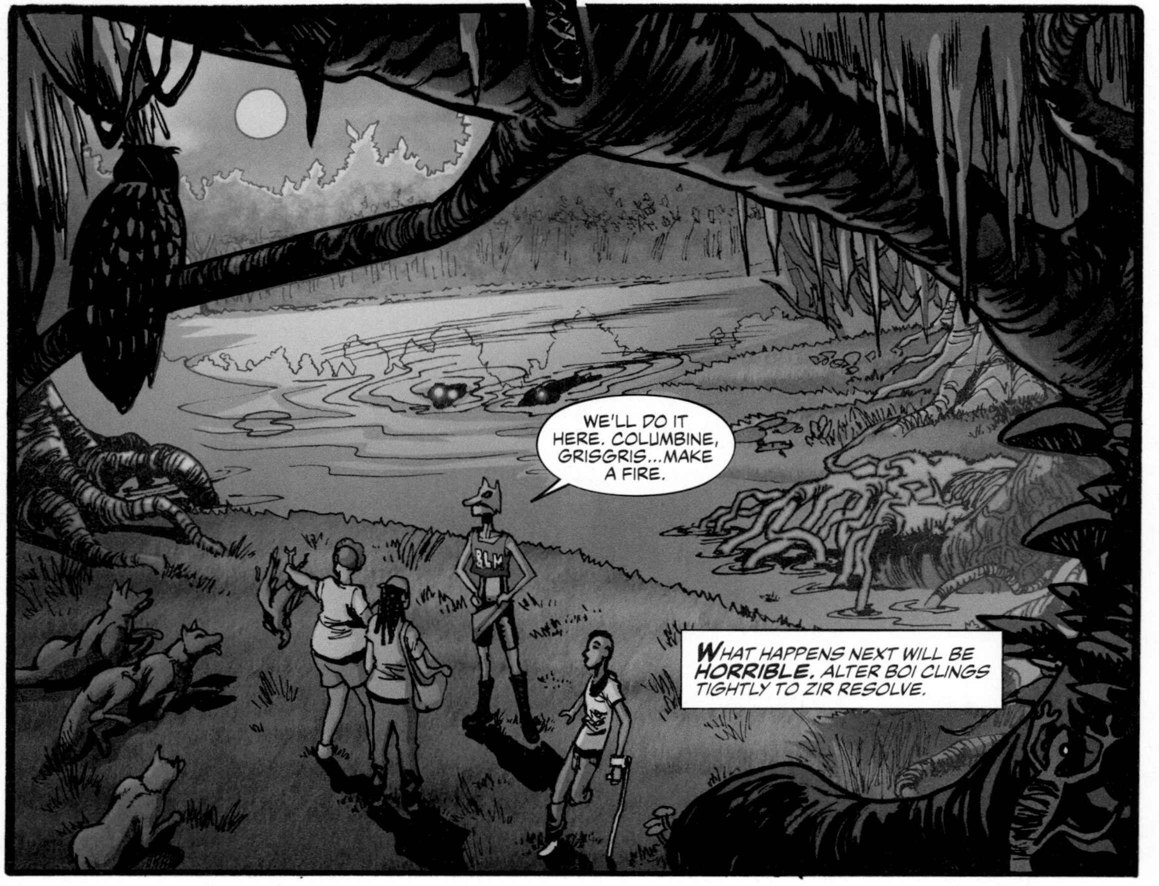
WE'LL DO IT HERE. COLUMBINE, GRISGRIS...MAKE A FIRE.
WHAT HAPPENS NEXT WILL BE HORRIBLE. ALTER BOI CLINGS TIGHTLY TO ZIR RESOLVE.

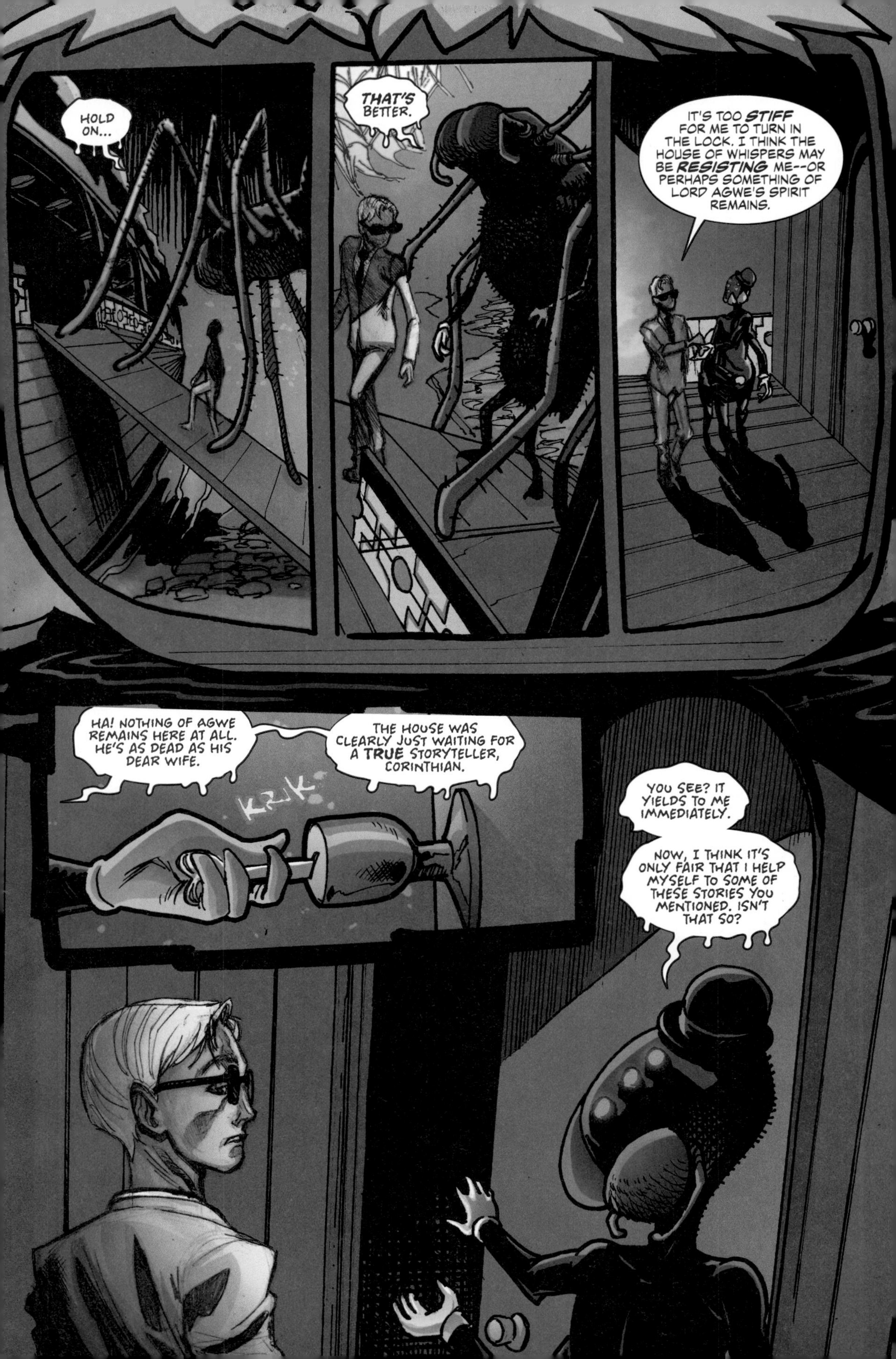
HOLD ON...
THAT'S BETTER.
IT'S TOO STIFF FOR ME TO TURN IN THE LOCK. I THINK THE HOUSE OF WHISPERS MAY BE RESISTING ME--OR PERHAPS SOMETHING OF LORD AGWE'S SPIRIT REMAINS.
HA! NOTHING OF AGWE REMAINS HERE AT ALL. HE'S AS DEAD AS HIS DEAR WIFE.
THE HOUSE WAS CLEARLY JUST WAITING FOR A TRUE STORYTELLER, CORINTHIAN.
KRIK
YOU SEE? IT YIELDS TO ME IMMEDIATELY.
NOW, I THINK IT'S ONLY FAIR THAT I HELP MYSELF TO SOME OF THESE STORIES YOU MENTIONED. ISN'T THAT SO?

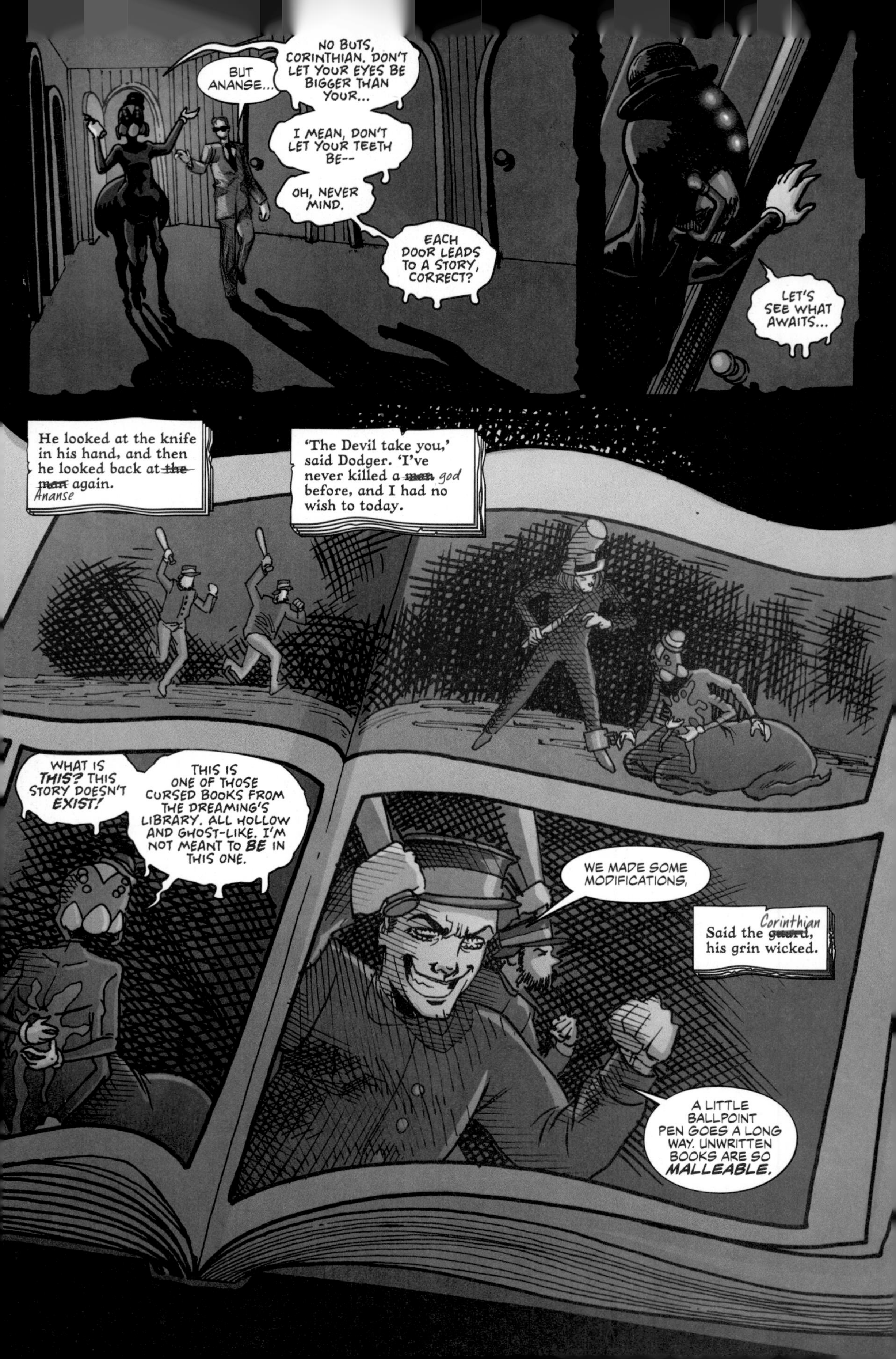
BUT ANANSE...
NO BUTS, CORINTHIAN. DON'T LET YOUR EYES BE BIGGER THAN YOUR...
I MEAN, DON'T LET YOUR TEETH BE--
OH, NEVER MIND.
EACH DOOR LEADS TO A STORY, CORRECT?
LET'S SEE WHAT AWAITS...
He looked at the knife in his hand, and then he looked back at ~~the man~~ Ananse again.
'The Devil take you,' said Dodger. 'I've never killed a ~~man~~ god before, and I had no wish to today.
WHAT IS THIS? THIS STORY DOESN'T EXIST!
THIS IS ONE OF THOSE CURSED BOOKS FROM THE DREAMING'S LIBRARY. ALL HOLLOW AND GHOST-LIKE. I'M NOT MEANT TO BE IN THIS ONE.
WE MADE SOME MODIFICATIONS,
Said the ~~guard~~ Corinthian, his grin wicked.
A LITTLE BALLPOINT PEN GOES A LONG WAY. UNWRITTEN BOOKS ARE SO MALLEABLE.

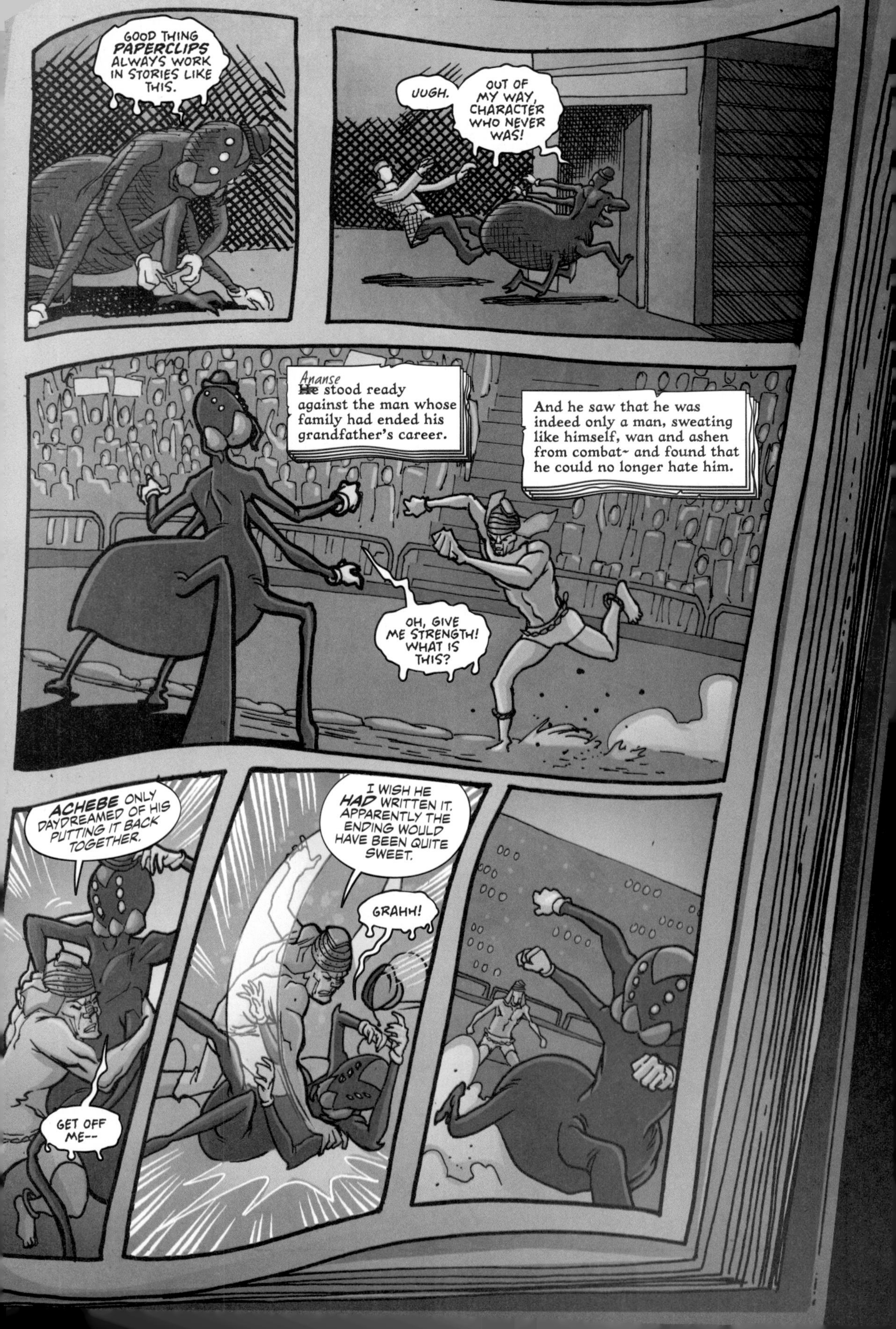
GOOD THING PAPERCLIPS ALWAYS WORK IN STORIES LIKE THIS.
UUGH.
OUT OF MY WAY, CHARACTER WHO NEVER WAS!
Ananse He stood ready against the man whose family had ended his grandfather's career.
And he saw that he was indeed only a man, sweating like himself, wan and ashen from combat~ and found that he could no longer hate him.
OH, GIVE ME STRENGTH! WHAT IS THIS?
ACHEBE ONLY DAYDREAMED OF HIS PUTTING IT BACK TOGETHER.
GET OFF ME--
I WISH HE HAD WRITTEN IT. APPARENTLY THE ENDING WOULD HAVE BEEN QUITE SWEET.
GRAHH!

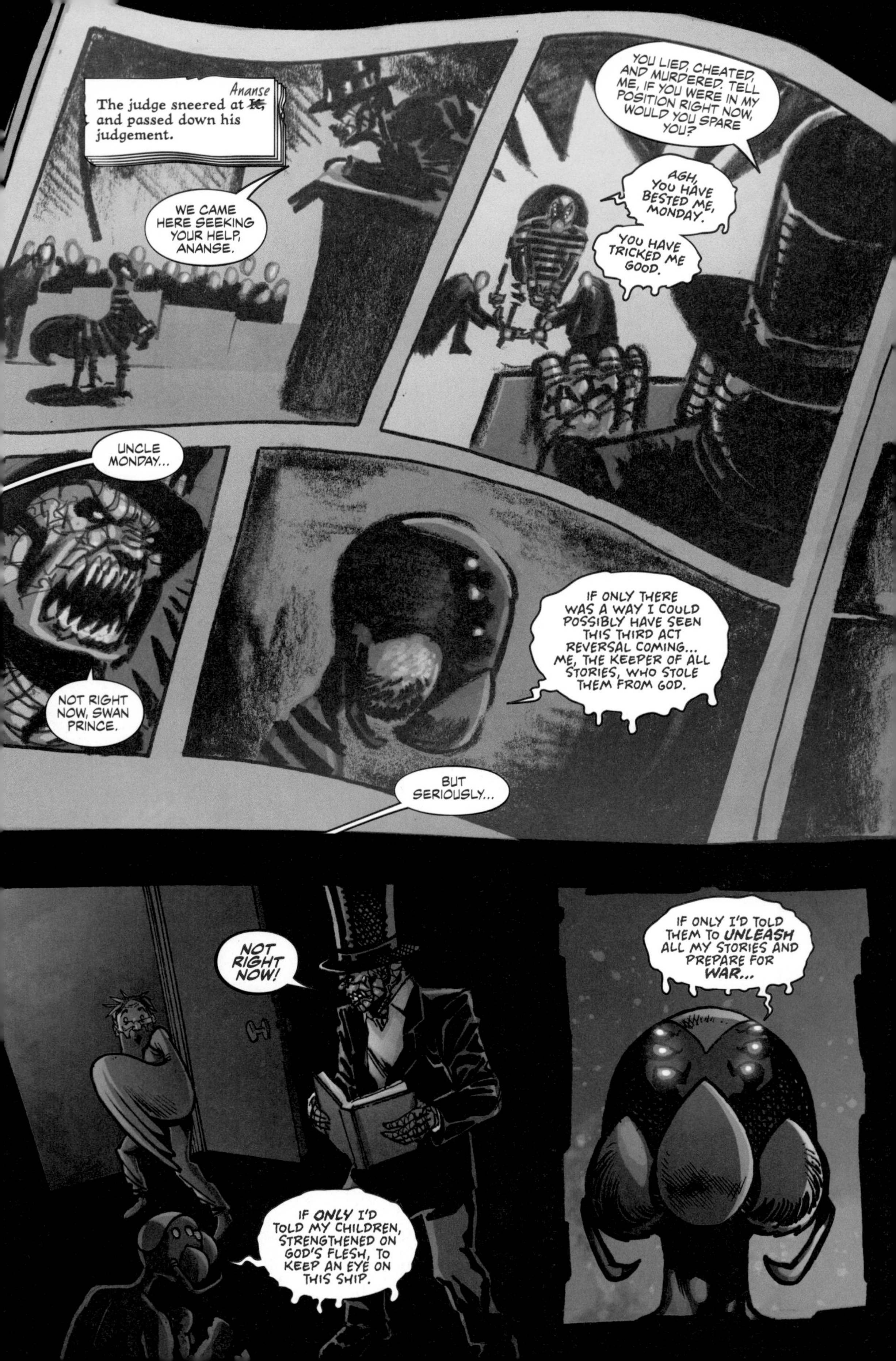

Ananse
The judge sneered at Ie, and passed down his judgement.
WE CAME HERE SEEKING YOUR HELP, ANANSE.
YOU LIED, CHEATED, AND MURDERED. TELL ME, IF YOU WERE IN MY POSITION RIGHT NOW, WOULD YOU SPARE YOU?
AGH, YOU HAVE BESTED ME, MONDAY.
YOU HAVE TRICKED ME GOOD.
UNCLE MONDAY...
NOT RIGHT NOW, SWAN PRINCE.
IF ONLY THERE WAS A WAY I COULD POSSIBLY HAVE SEEN THIS THIRD ACT REVERSAL COMING... ME, THE KEEPER OF ALL STORIES, WHO STOLE THEM FROM GOD.
BUT SERIOUSLY...
NOT RIGHT NOW!
IF ONLY I'D TOLD MY CHILDREN, STRENGTHENED ON GOD'S FLESH, TO KEEP AN EYE ON THIS SHIP.
IF ONLY I'D TOLD THEM TO UNLEASH ALL MY STORIES AND PREPARE FOR WAR...

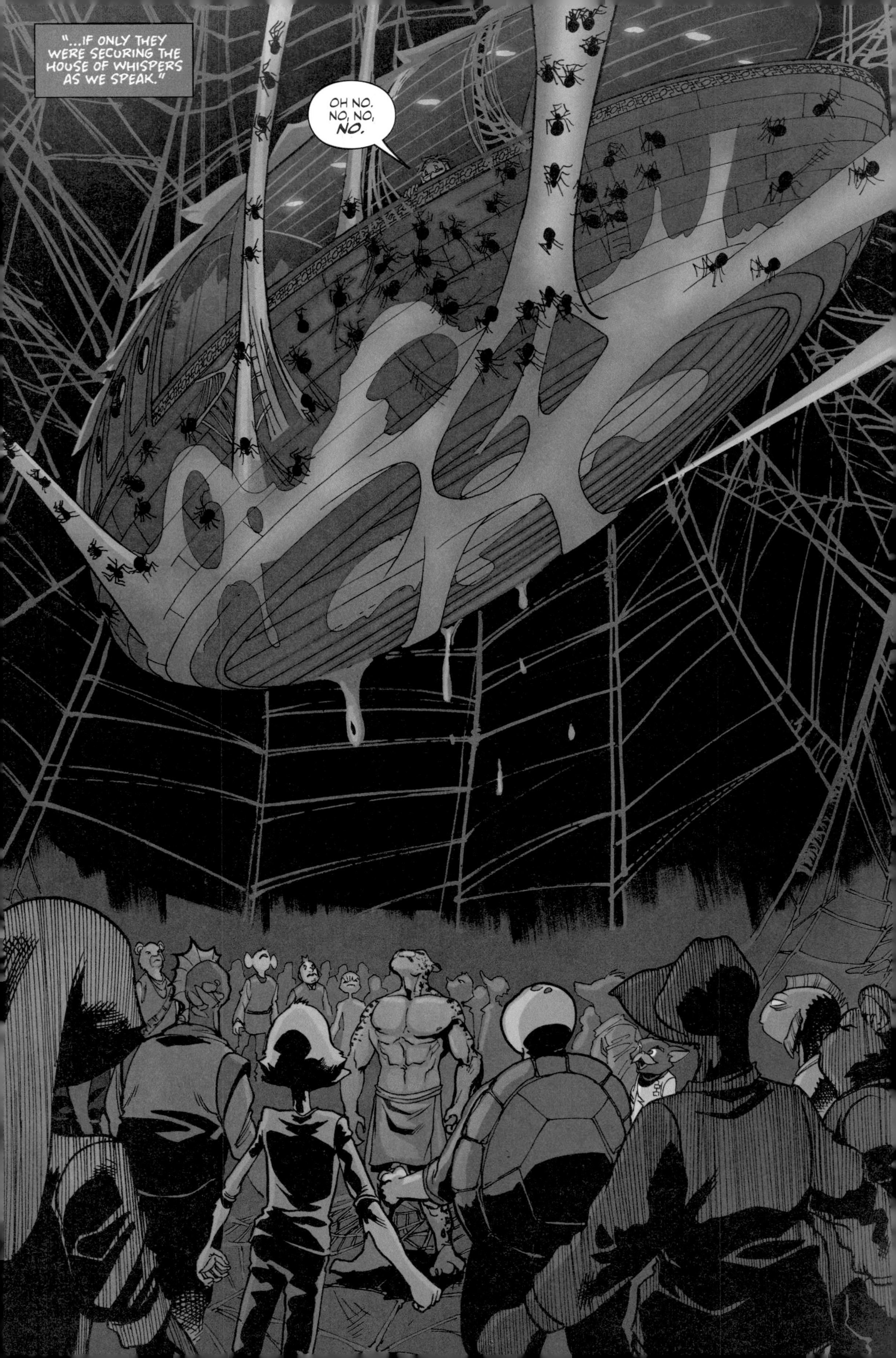
"...IF ONLY THEY WERE SECURING THE HOUSE OF WHISPERS AS WE SPEAK."
OH NO. NO, NO, NO.

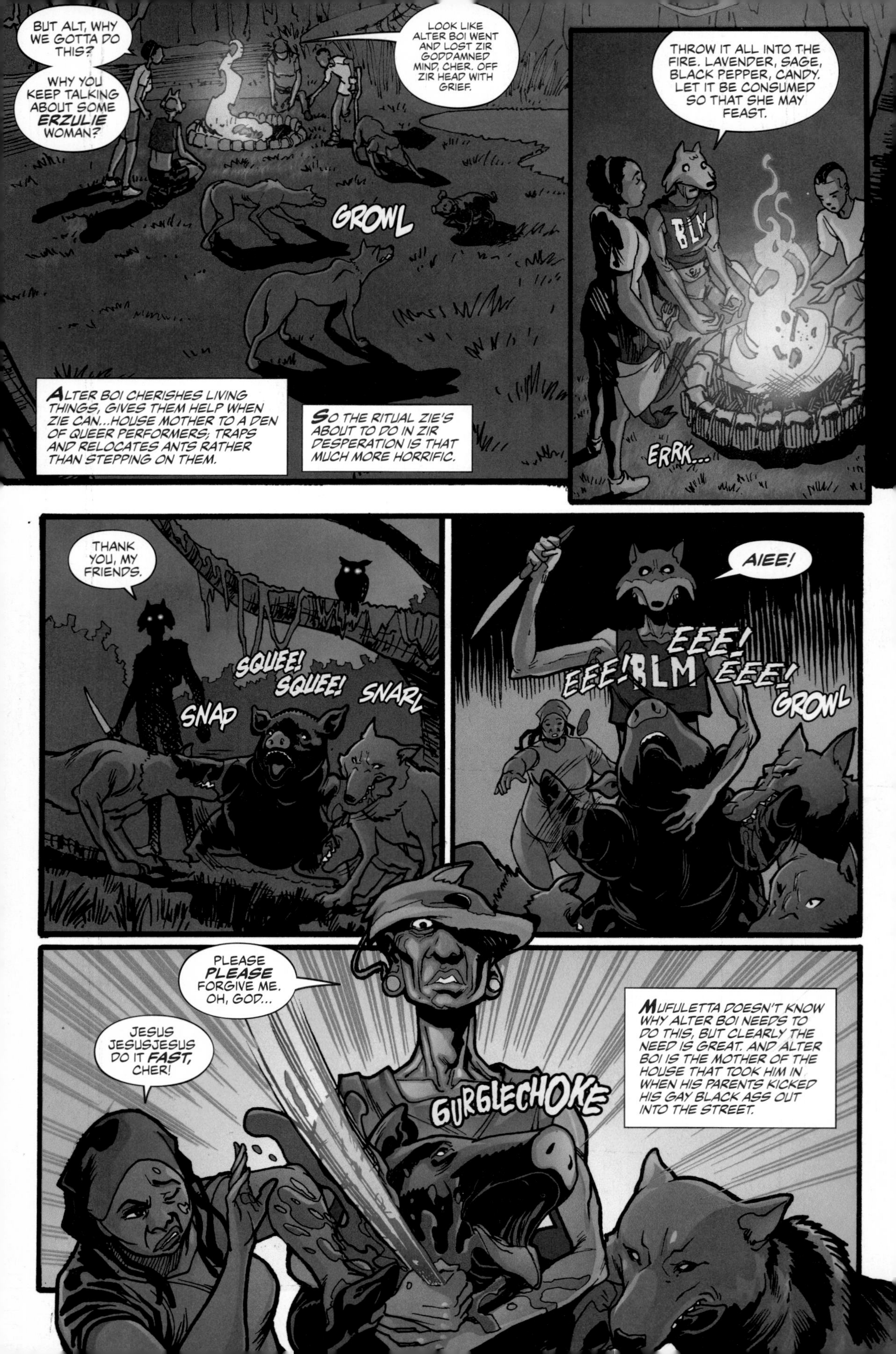
BUT ALT, WHY WE GOTTA DO THIS?
WHY YOU KEEP TALKING ABOUT SOME ERZULIE WOMAN?
LOOK LIKE ALTER BOI WENT AND LOST ZIR GODDAMNED MIND, CHER. OFF ZIR HEAD WITH GRIEF.
GROWL
ALTER BOI CHERISHES LIVING THINGS, GIVES THEM HELP WHEN ZIE CAN...HOUSE MOTHER TO A DEN OF QUEER PERFORMERS; TRAPS AND RELOCATES ANTS RATHER THAN STEPPING ON THEM.
SO THE RITUAL ZIE'S ABOUT TO DO IN ZIR DESPERATION IS THAT MUCH MORE HORRIFIC.
THROW IT ALL INTO THE FIRE. LAVENDER, SAGE, BLACK PEPPER, CANDY. LET IT BE CONSUMED SO THAT SHE MAY FEAST.
BLM
ERRK...
THANK YOU, MY FRIENDS.
SQUEE! SQUEE!
SNARL
SNAP
AIEE!
EEE! EEE! EEE!
BLM
GROWL
PLEASE PLEASE FORGIVE ME. OH, GOD...
JESUS JESUSJESUS DO IT FAST, CHER!
GURGLECHOKE
MUFULETTA DOESN'T KNOW WHY ALTER BOI NEEDS TO DO THIS, BUT CLEARLY THE NEED IS GREAT. AND ALTER BOI IS THE MOTHER OF THE HOUSE THAT TOOK HIM IN WHEN HIS PARENTS KICKED HIS GAY BLACK ASS OUT INTO THE STREET.

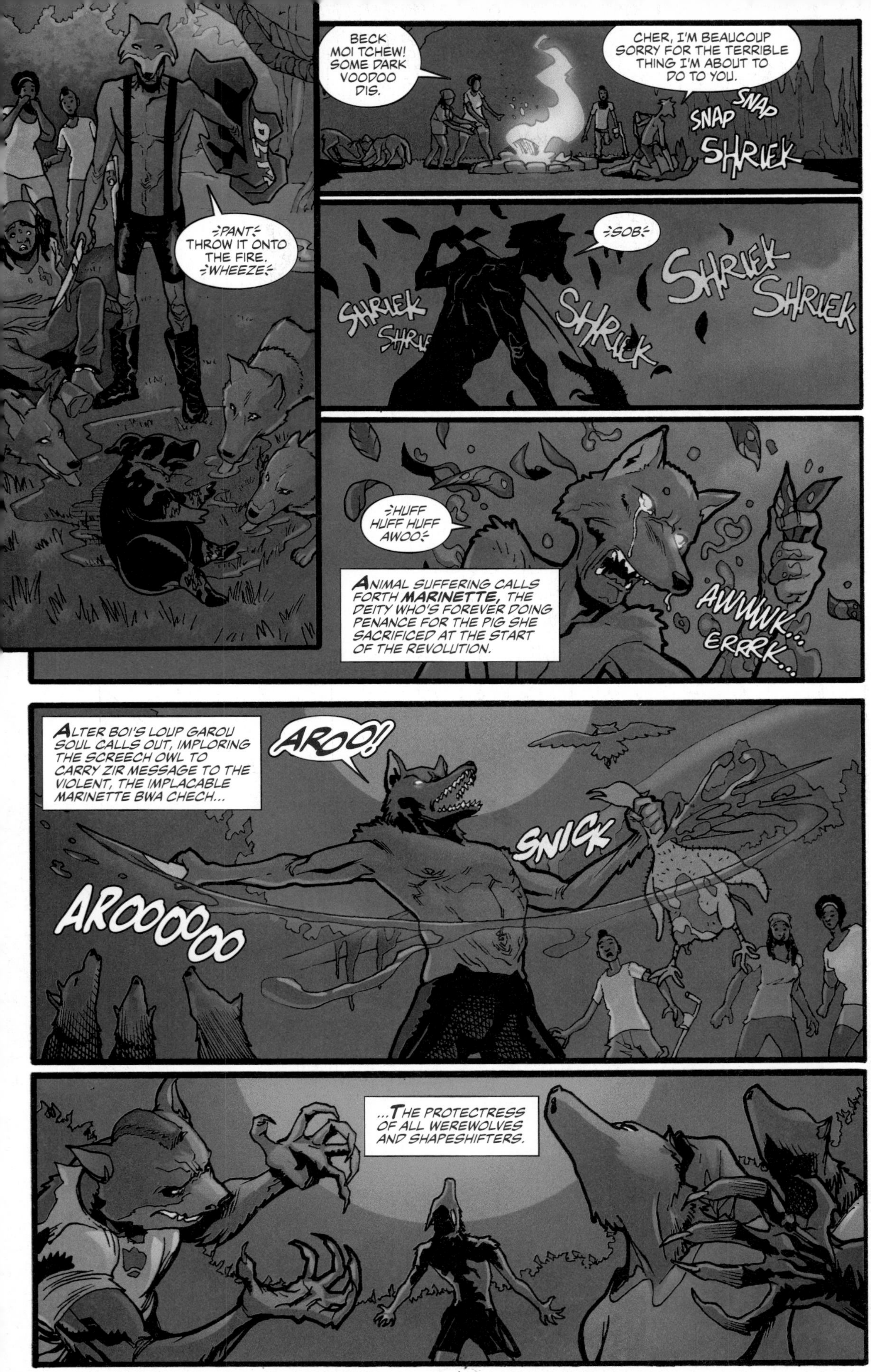
~PANT~
THROW IT ONTO THE FIRE.
~WHEEZE~
BECK MOI TCHEW! SOME DARK VOODOO DIS.
CHER, I'M BEAUCOUP SORRY FOR THE TERRIBLE THING I'M ABOUT TO DO TO YOU.
SNAP
SNAP
SHRIEK
~SOB~
SHRIEK
SHRIEK
SHRIEK
SHRIEK
SHRIEK
~HUFF HUFF HUFF AWOO~
ANIMAL SUFFERING CALLS FORTH MARINETTE, THE DEITY WHO'S FOREVER DOING PENANCE FOR THE PIG SHE SACRIFICED AT THE START OF THE REVOLUTION.
AWWWK...
ERRRK...
ALTER BOI'S LOUP GAROU SOUL CALLS OUT, IMPLORING THE SCREECH OWL TO CARRY ZIR MESSAGE TO THE VIOLENT, THE IMPLACABLE MARINETTE BWA CHECH...
AROO!
SNICK
AROOOOOO
...THE PROTECTRESS OF ALL WEREWOLVES AND SHAPESHIFTERS.

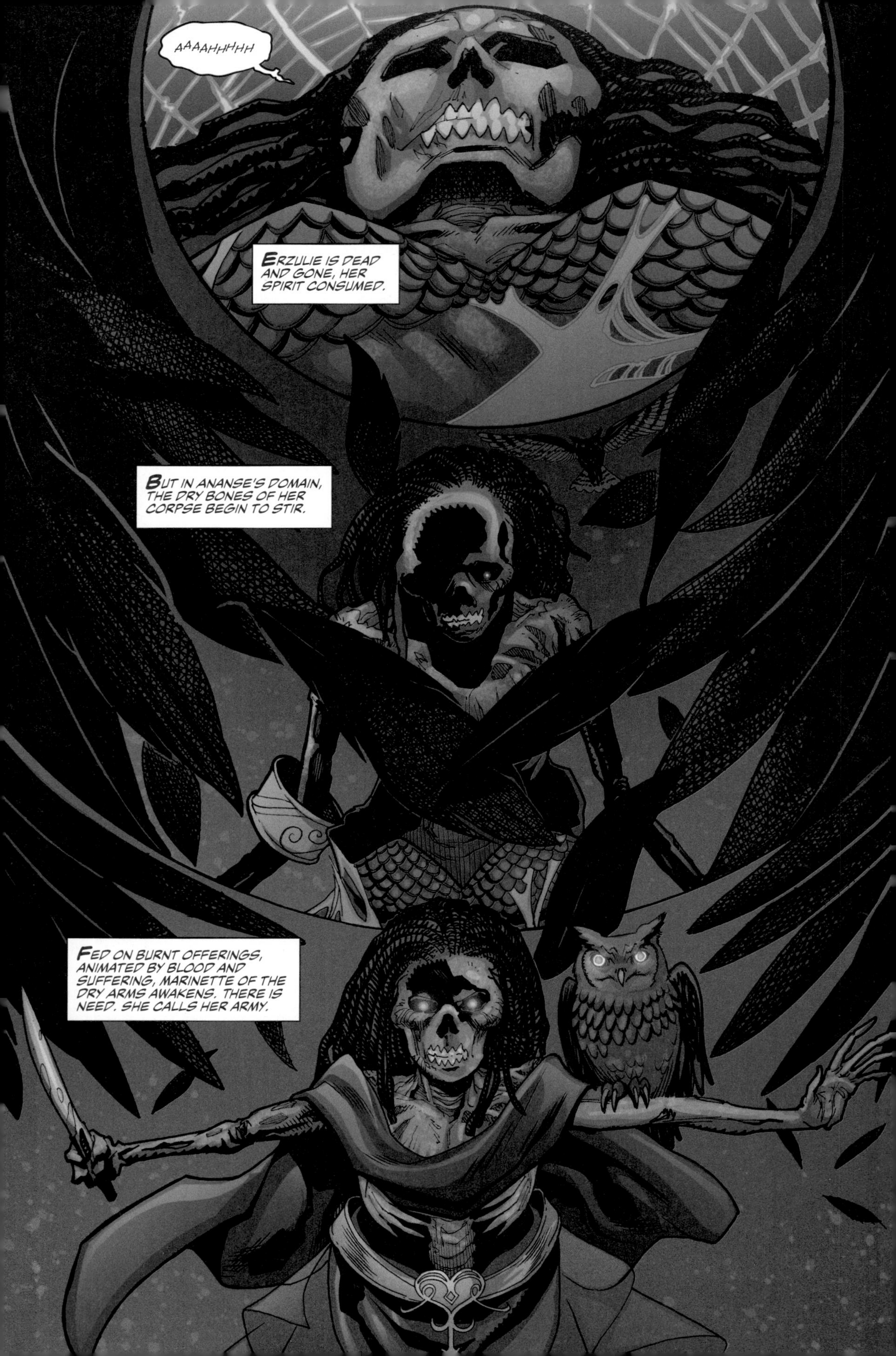
AAAAHHHHH
ERZULIE IS DEAD AND GONE, HER SPIRIT CONSUMED.
BUT IN ANANSE'S DOMAIN, THE DRY BONES OF HER CORPSE BEGIN TO STIR.
FED ON BURNT OFFERINGS, ANIMATED BY BLOOD AND SUFFERING, MARINETTE OF THE DRY ARMS AWAKENS. THERE IS NEED. SHE CALLS HER ARMY.

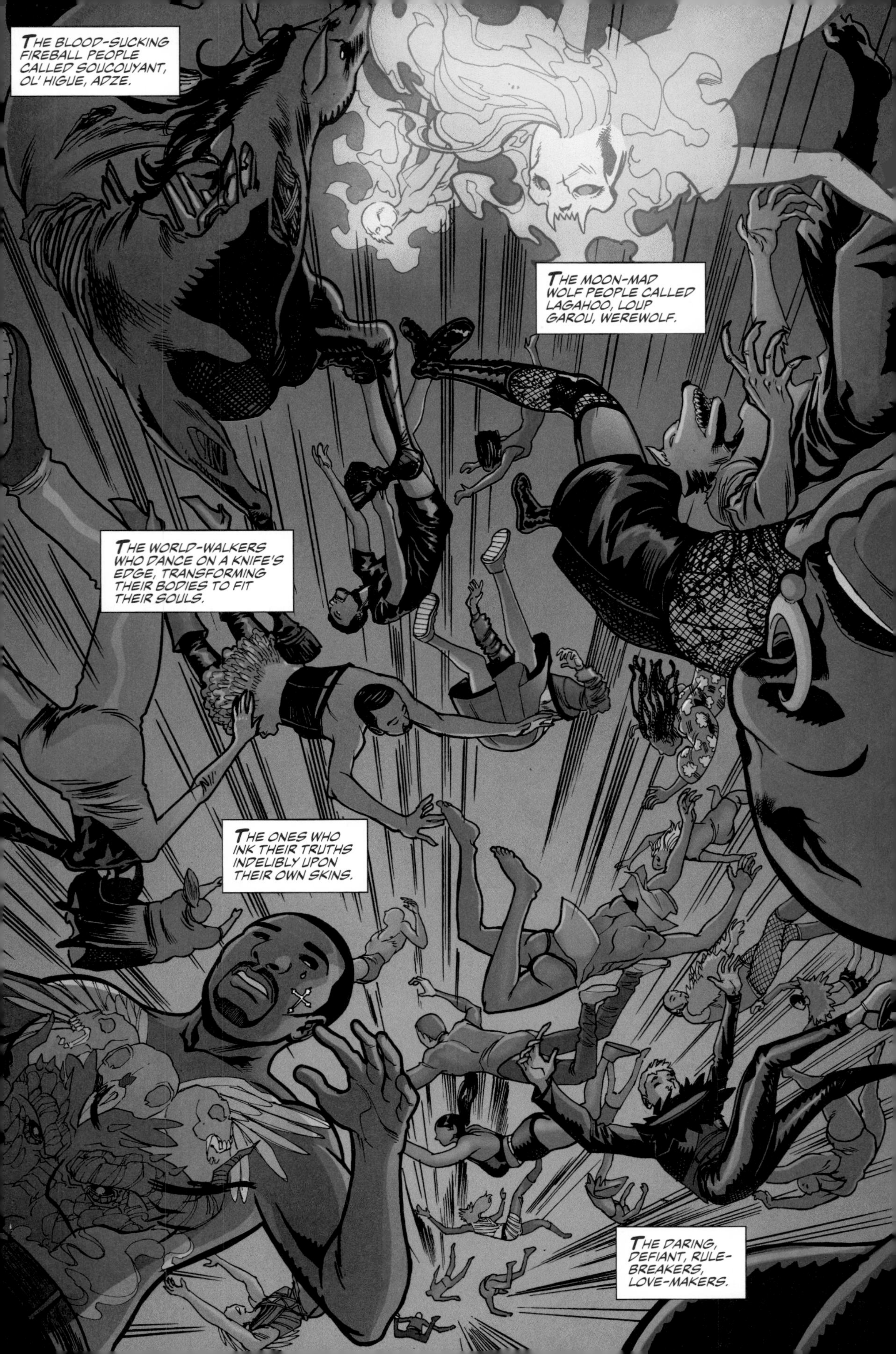
THE BLOOD-SUCKING FIREBALL PEOPLE CALLED SOUCOUYANT, OL' HIGUE, ADZE.
THE MOON-MAD WOLF PEOPLE CALLED LAGAHOO, LOUP GAROU, WEREWOLF.
THE WORLD-WALKERS WHO DANCE ON A KNIFE'S EDGE, TRANSFORMING THEIR BODIES TO FIT THEIR SOULS.
THE ONES WHO INK THEIR TRUTHS INDELIBLY UPON THEIR OWN SKINS.
THE DARING, DEFIANT, RULE-BREAKERS, LOVE-MAKERS.

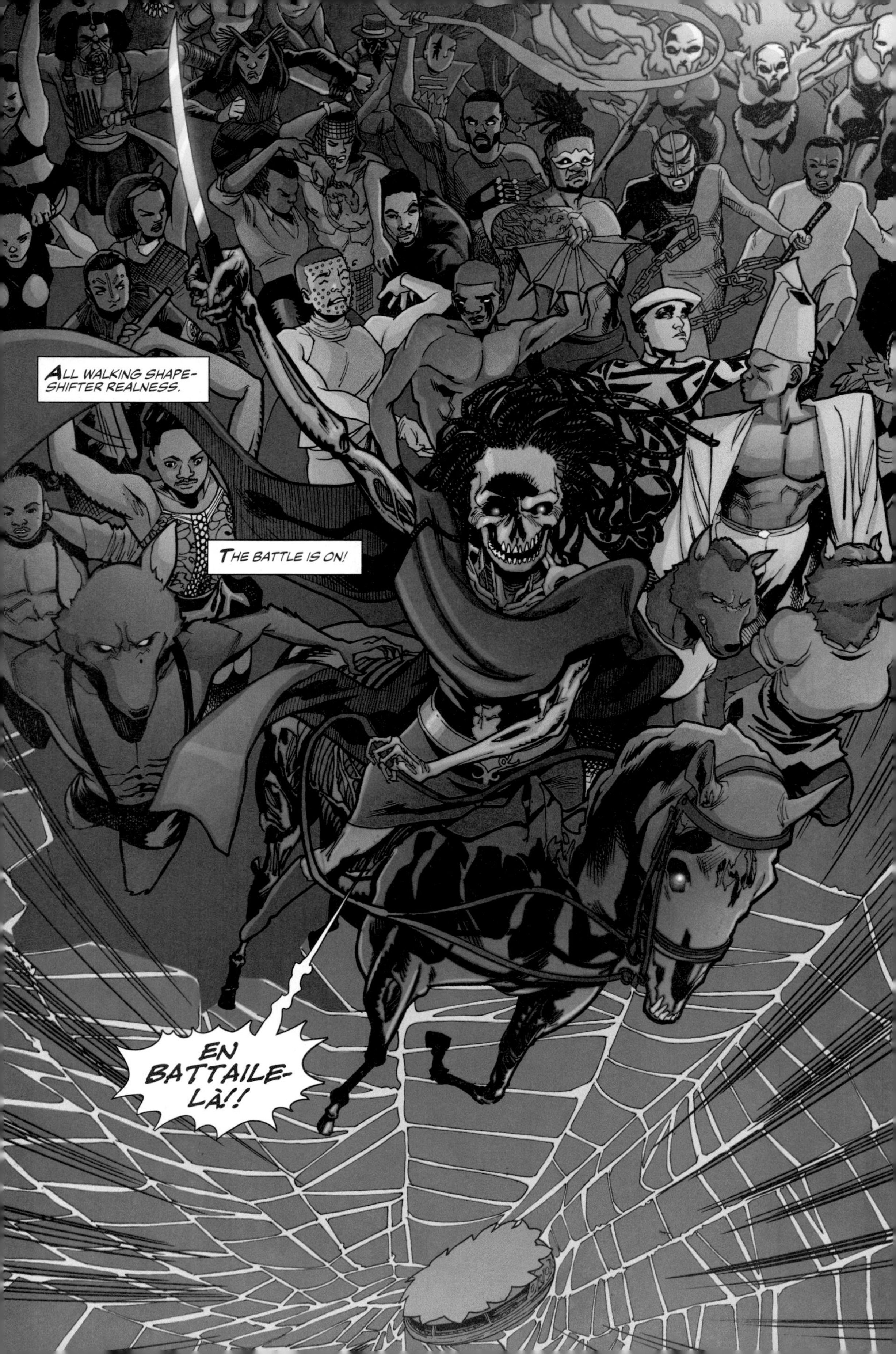
ALL WALKING SHAPE-SHIFTER REALNESS.
THE BATTLE IS ON!
EN BATTAILE-LÀ!!

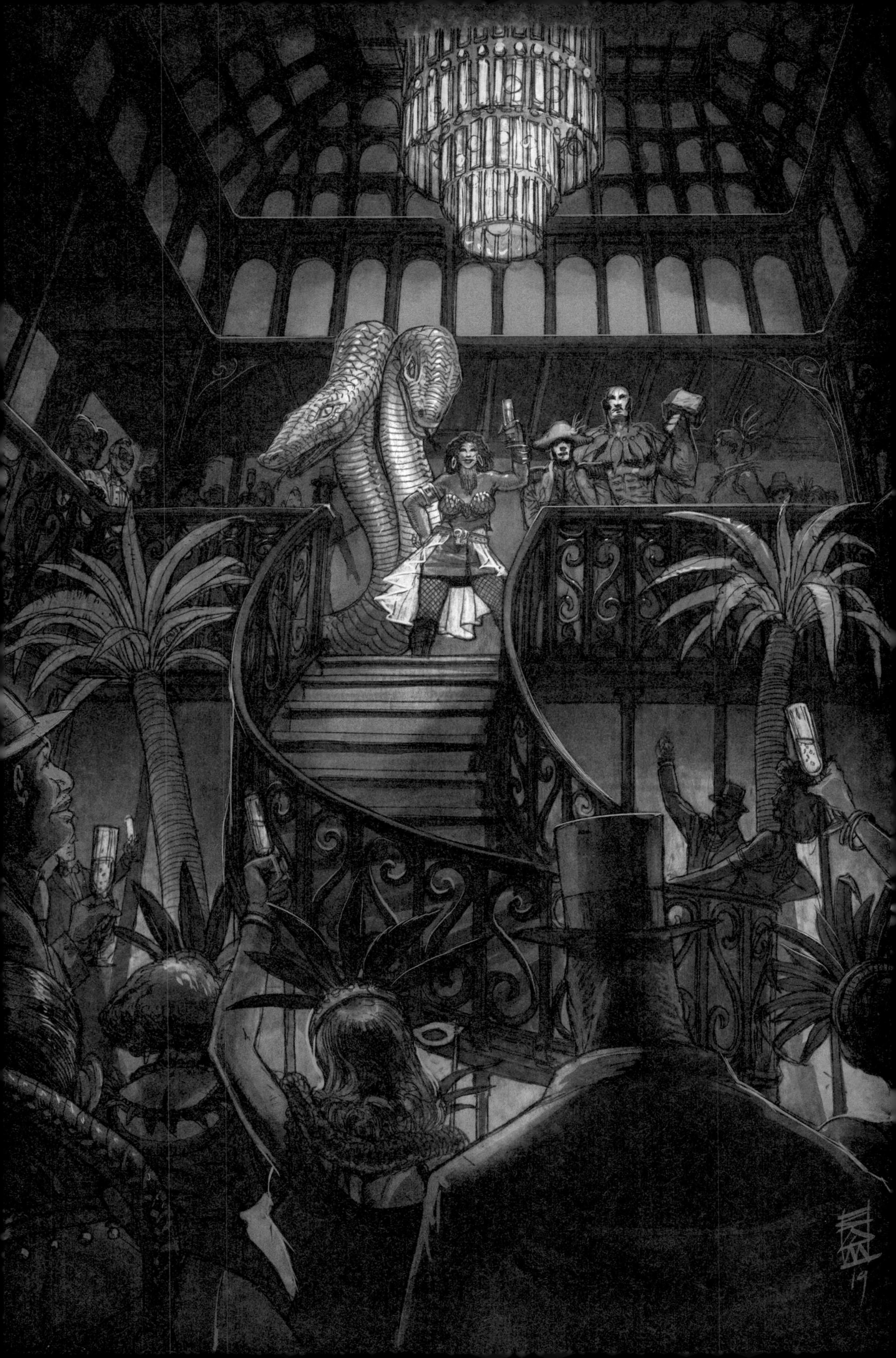

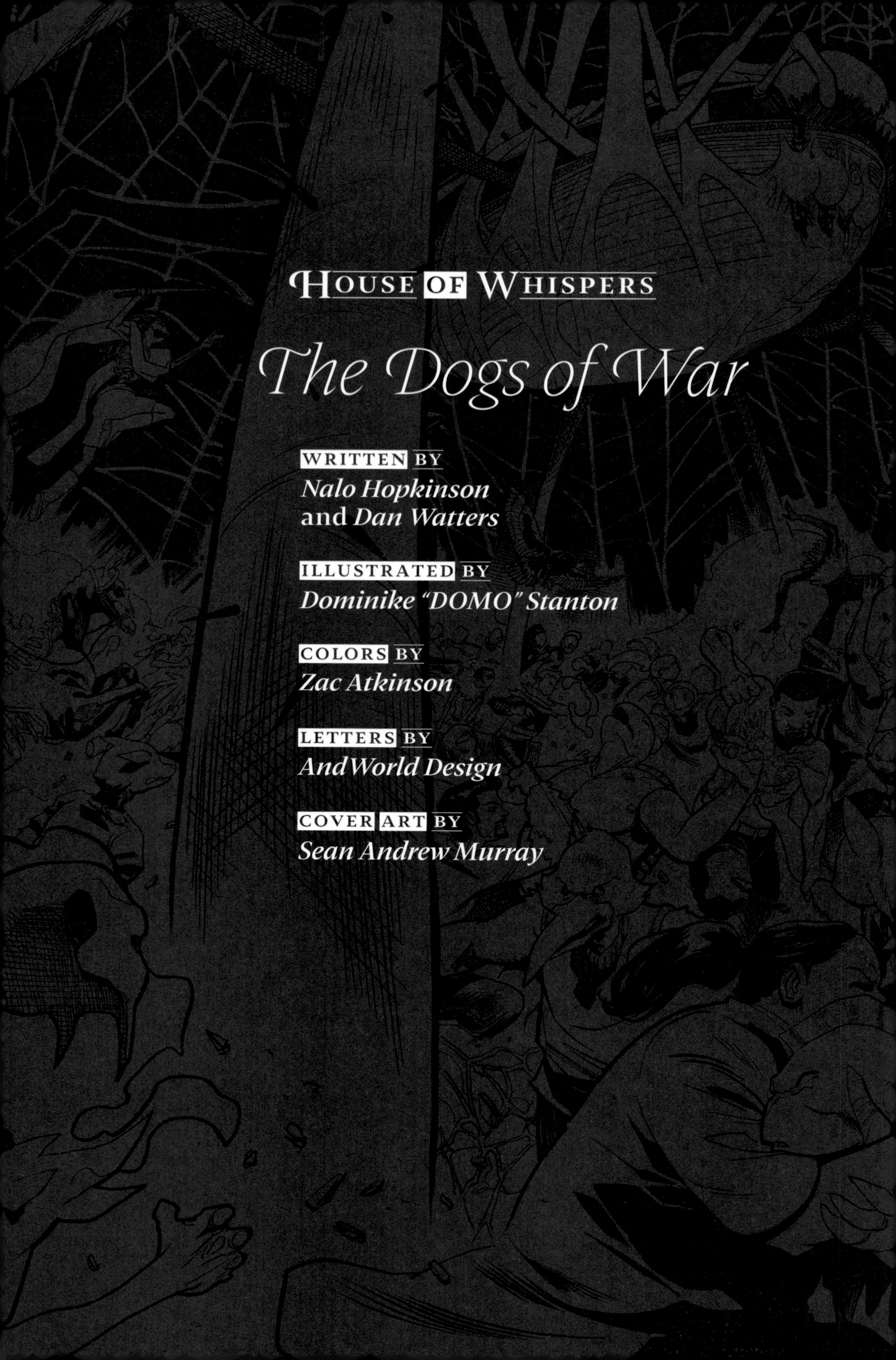

HOUSE OF WHISPERS

The Dogs of War

WRITTEN BY
Nalo Hopkinson
and *Dan Watters*

ILLUSTRATED BY
Dominike "DOMO" Stanton

COLORS BY
Zac Atkinson

LETTERS BY
AndWorld Design

COVER ART BY
Sean Andrew Murray

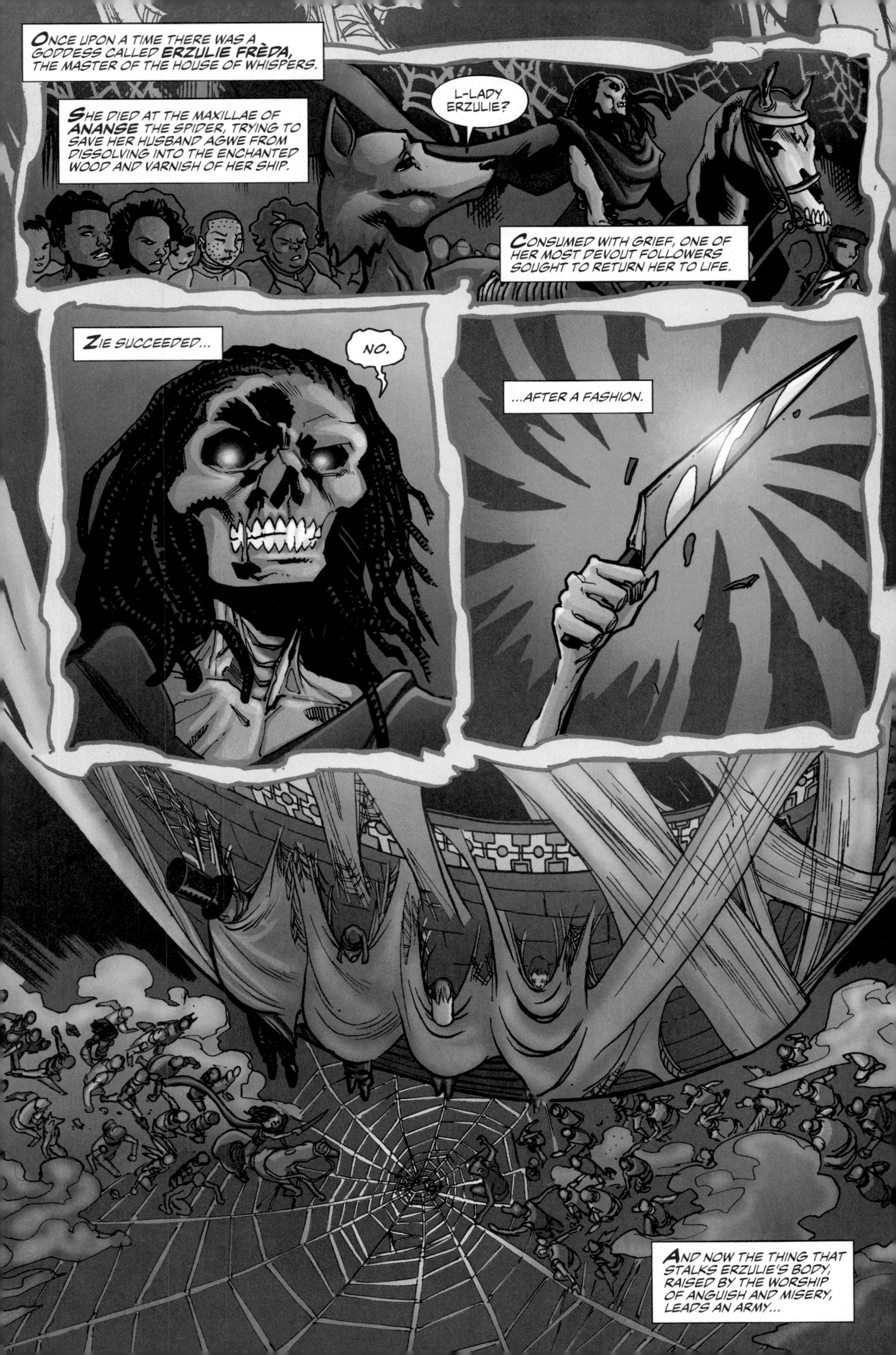
ONCE UPON A TIME THERE WAS A GODDESS CALLED ERZULIE FRÈDA, THE MASTER OF THE HOUSE OF WHISPERS.
SHE DIED AT THE MAXILLAE OF ANANSE THE SPIDER, TRYING TO SAVE HER HUSBAND AGWE FROM DISSOLVING INTO THE ENCHANTED WOOD AND VARNISH OF HER SHIP.
L-LADY ERZULIE?
CONSUMED WITH GRIEF, ONE OF HER MOST DEVOUT FOLLOWERS SOUGHT TO RETURN HER TO LIFE.
ZIE SUCCEEDED...
NO.
...AFTER A FASHION.
AND NOW THE THING THAT STALKS ERZULIE'S BODY, RAISED BY THE WORSHIP OF ANGUISH AND MISERY, LEADS AN ARMY...

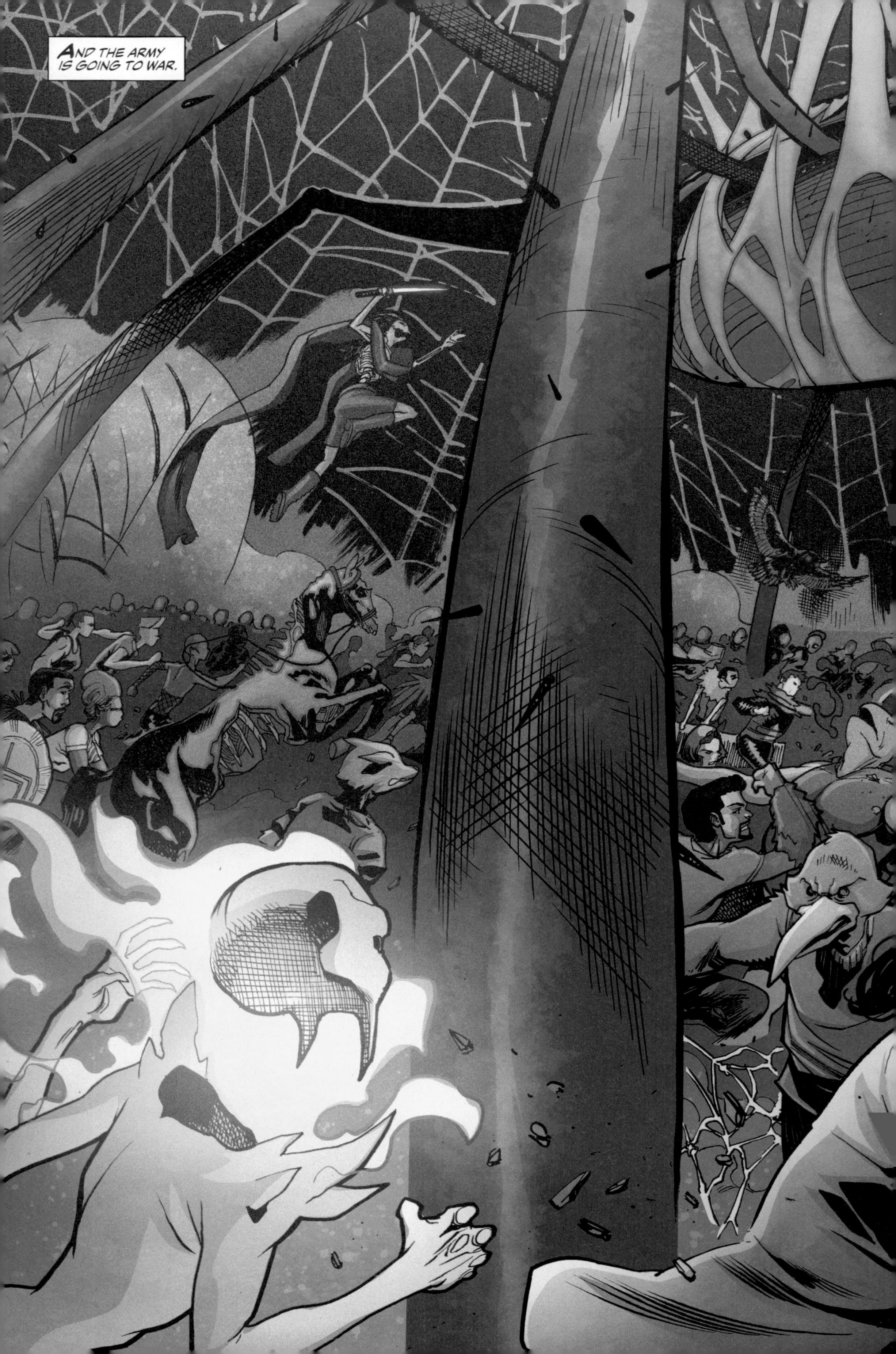
AND THE ARMY
IS GOING TO WAR.

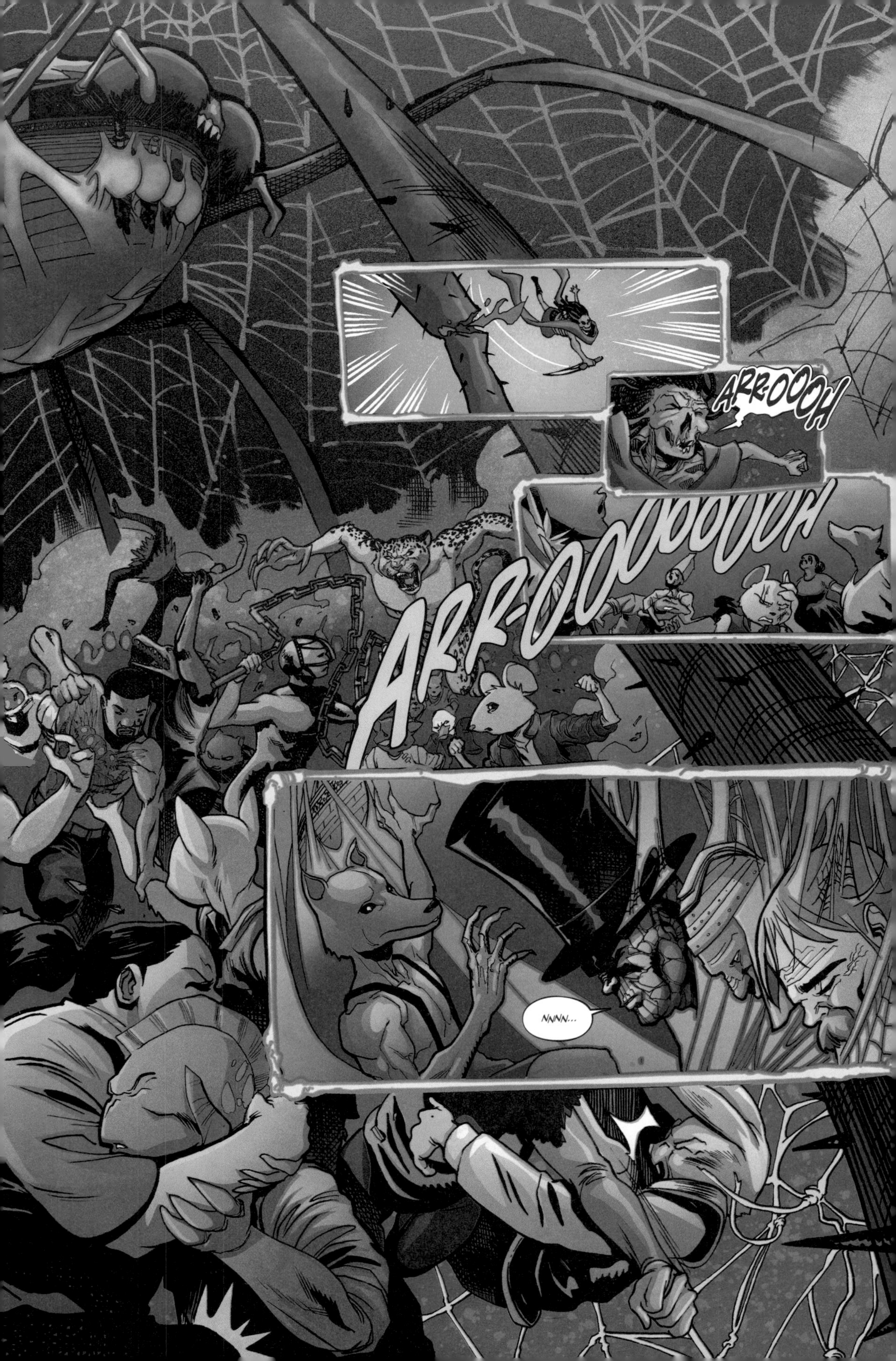

ARR-OOOH
ARR-OOOOOOOOOH
NNNN...

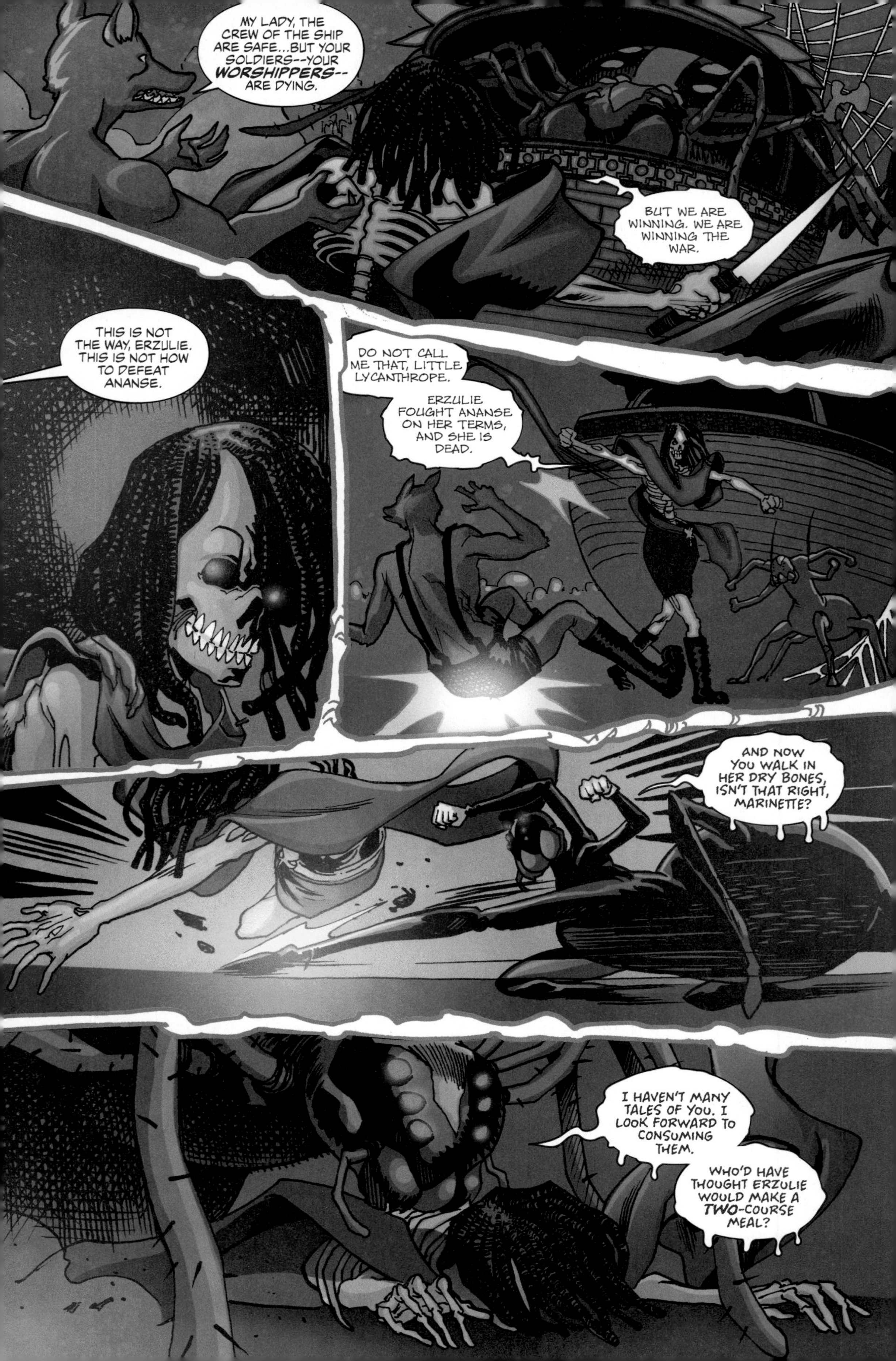

MY LADY, THE CREW OF THE SHIP ARE SAFE...BUT YOUR SOLDIERS--YOUR WORSHIPPERS--ARE DYING.
BUT WE ARE WINNING. WE ARE WINNING THE WAR.
THIS IS NOT THE WAY, ERZULIE. THIS IS NOT HOW TO DEFEAT ANANSE.
DO NOT CALL ME THAT, LITTLE LYCANTHROPE.
ERZULIE FOUGHT ANANSE ON HER TERMS, AND SHE IS DEAD.
AND NOW YOU WALK IN HER DRY BONES, ISN'T THAT RIGHT, MARINETTE?
I HAVEN'T MANY TALES OF YOU. I LOOK FORWARD TO CONSUMING THEM.
WHO'D HAVE THOUGHT ERZULIE WOULD MAKE A TWO-COURSE MEAL?

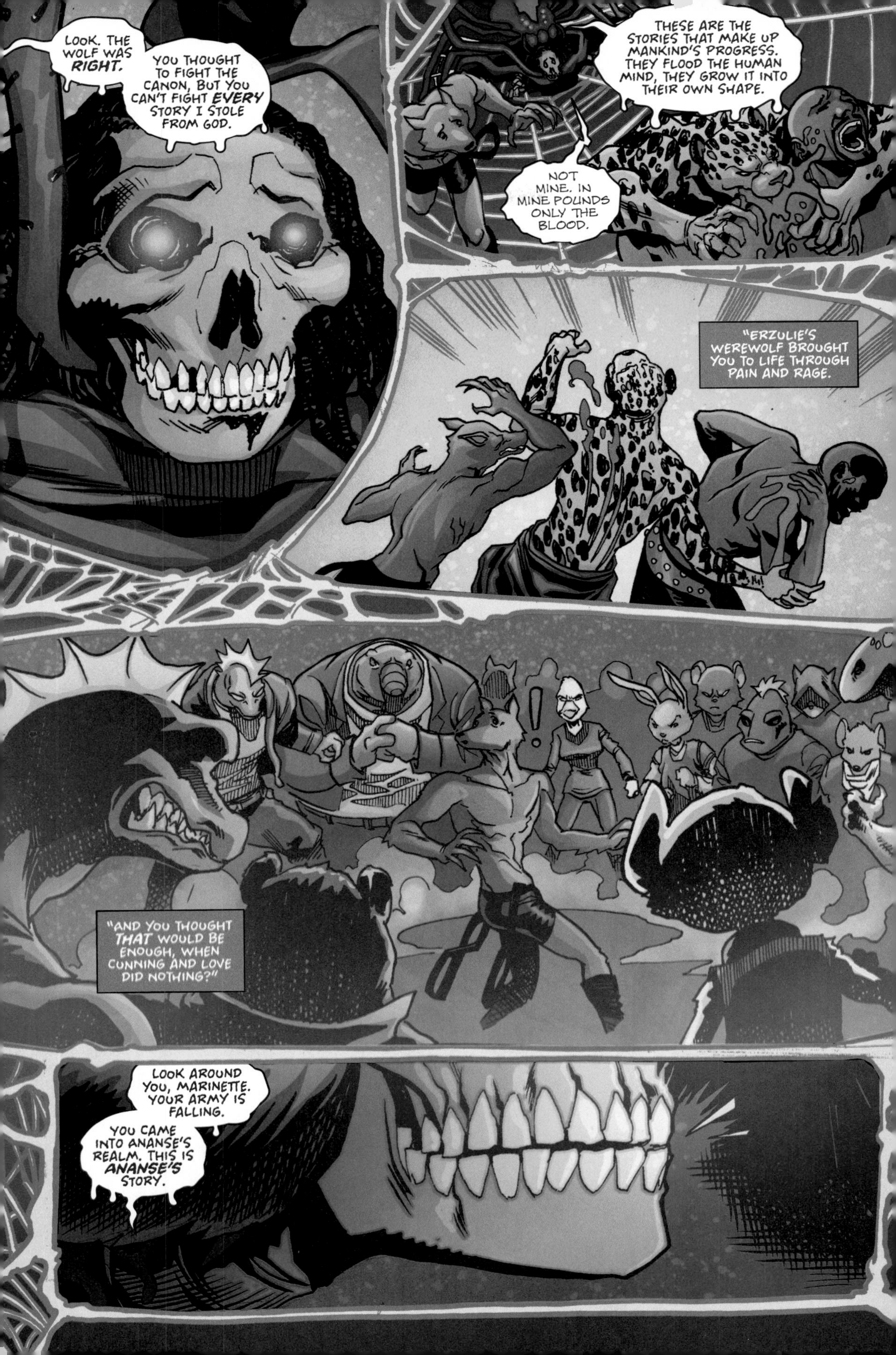

LOOK. THE WOLF WAS RIGHT.
YOU THOUGHT TO FIGHT THE CANON, BUT YOU CAN'T FIGHT EVERY STORY I STOLE FROM GOD.
THESE ARE THE STORIES THAT MAKE UP MANKIND'S PROGRESS. THEY FLOOD THE HUMAN MIND, THEY GROW IT INTO THEIR OWN SHAPE.
NOT MINE. IN MINE POUNDS ONLY THE BLOOD.
"ERZULIE'S WEREWOLF BROUGHT YOU TO LIFE THROUGH PAIN AND RAGE.
"AND YOU THOUGHT THAT WOULD BE ENOUGH, WHEN CUNNING AND LOVE DID NOTHING?"
LOOK AROUND YOU, MARINETTE. YOUR ARMY IS FALLING.
YOU CAME INTO ANANSE'S REALM. THIS IS ANANSE'S STORY.

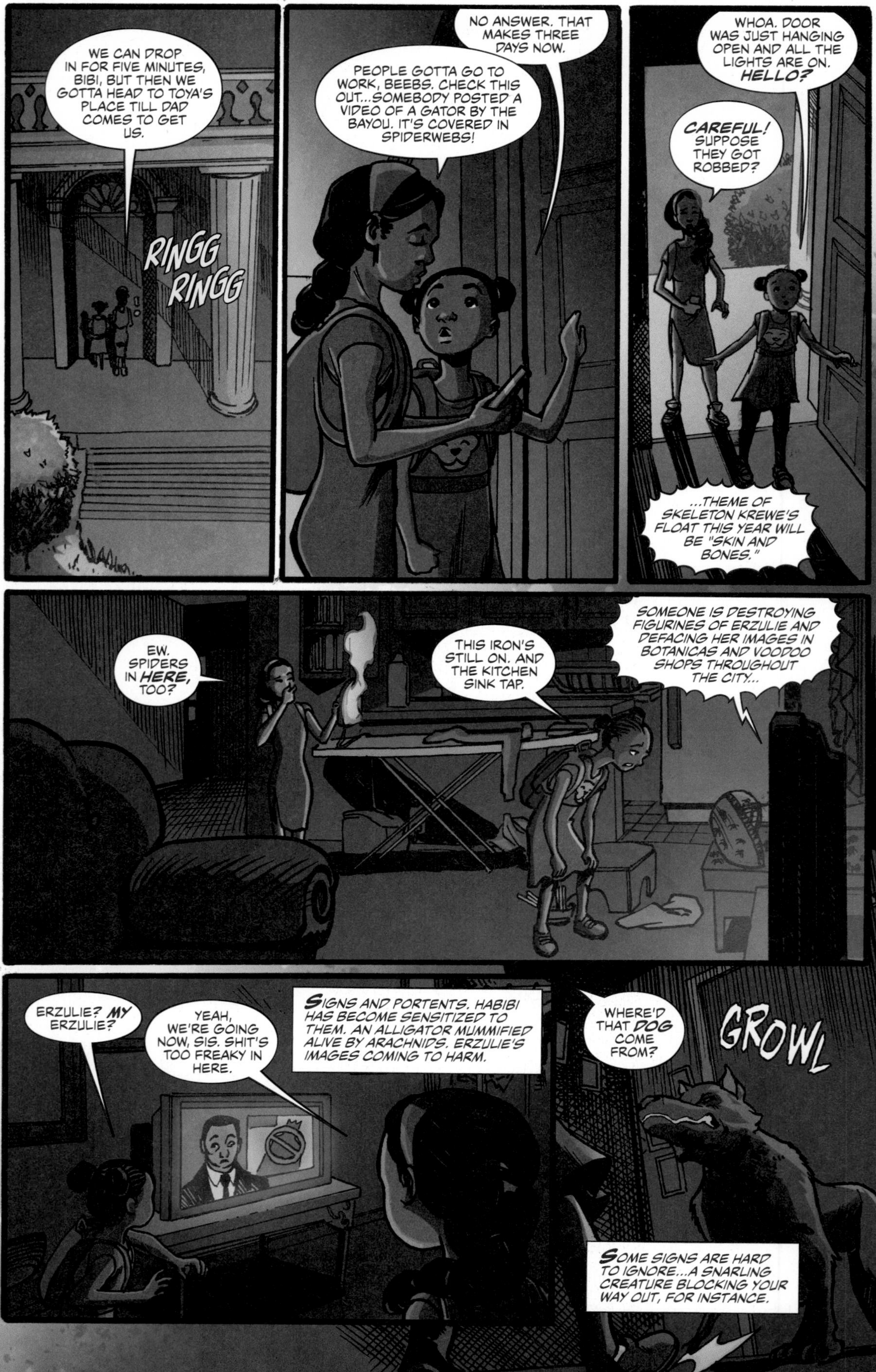

WE CAN DROP IN FOR FIVE MINUTES, BIBI, BUT THEN WE GOTTA HEAD TO TOYA'S PLACE TILL DAD COMES TO GET US.
RINGG RINGG
NO ANSWER. THAT MAKES THREE DAYS NOW.
PEOPLE GOTTA GO TO WORK, BEEBS. CHECK THIS OUT...SOMEBODY POSTED A VIDEO OF A GATOR BY THE BAYOU. IT'S COVERED IN SPIDERWEBS!
WHOA. DOOR WAS JUST HANGING OPEN AND ALL THE LIGHTS ARE ON. HELLO?
CAREFUL! SUPPOSE THEY GOT ROBBED?
...THEME OF SKELETON KREWE'S FLOAT THIS YEAR WILL BE "SKIN AND BONES."
EW. SPIDERS IN HERE, TOO?
THIS IRON'S STILL ON. AND THE KITCHEN SINK TAP.
SOMEONE IS DESTROYING FIGURINES OF ERZULIE AND DEFACING HER IMAGES IN BOTANICAS AND VOODOO SHOPS THROUGHOUT THE CITY...
ERZULIE? MY ERZULIE?
YEAH, WE'RE GOING NOW, SIS. SHIT'S TOO FREAKY IN HERE.
SIGNS AND PORTENTS. HABIBI HAS BECOME SENSITIZED TO THEM. AN ALLIGATOR MUMMIFIED ALIVE BY ARACHNIDS. ERZULIE'S IMAGES COMING TO HARM.
WHERE'D THAT DOG COME FROM?
GROWL
SOME SIGNS ARE HARD TO IGNORE...A SNARLING CREATURE BLOCKING YOUR WAY OUT, FOR INSTANCE.

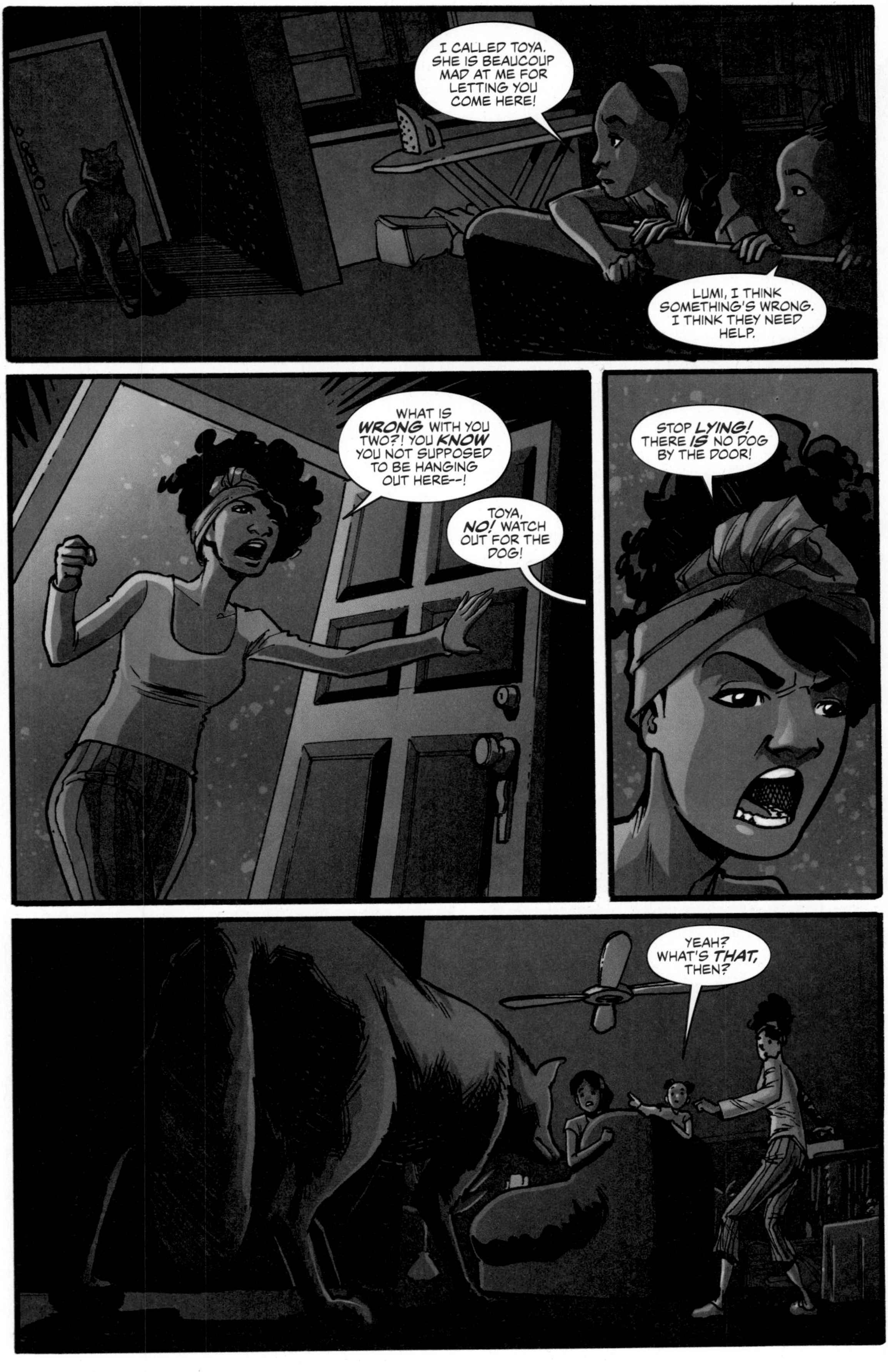
I CALLED TOYA. SHE IS BEAUCOUP MAD AT ME FOR LETTING YOU COME HERE!
LUMI, I THINK SOMETHING'S WRONG. I THINK THEY NEED HELP.
WHAT IS **WRONG** WITH YOU TWO?! YOU **KNOW** YOU NOT SUPPOSED TO BE HANGING OUT HERE--!
TOYA, **NO!** WATCH OUT FOR THE DOG!
STOP **LYING!** THERE **IS** NO DOG BY THE DOOR!
YEAH? WHAT'S **THAT,** THEN?

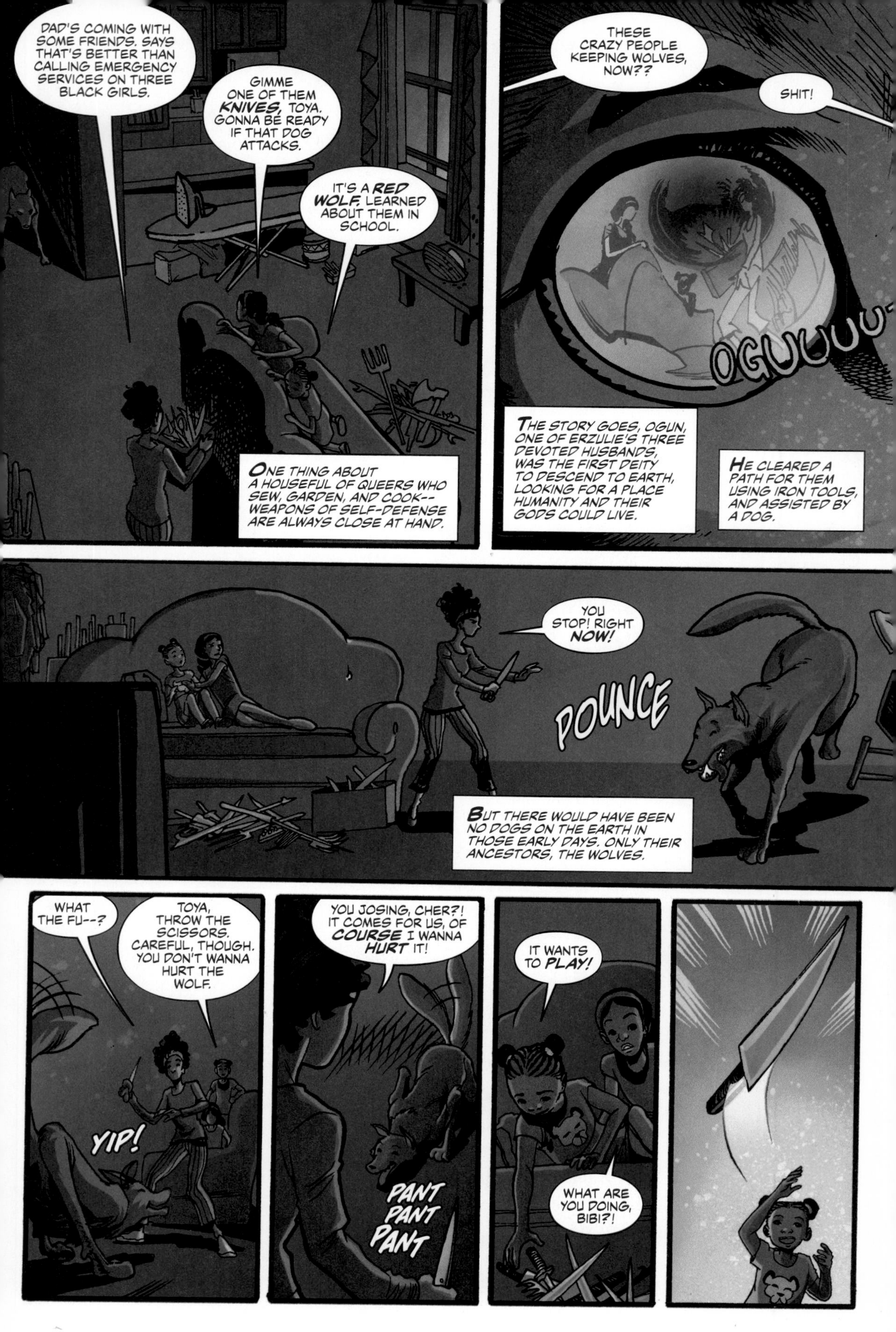
DAD'S COMING WITH SOME FRIENDS. SAYS THAT'S BETTER THAN CALLING EMERGENCY SERVICES ON THREE BLACK GIRLS.
GIMME ONE OF THEM KNIVES, TOYA. GONNA BE READY IF THAT DOG ATTACKS.
IT'S A RED WOLF. LEARNED ABOUT THEM IN SCHOOL.
ONE THING ABOUT A HOUSEFUL OF QUEERS WHO SEW, GARDEN, AND COOK-- WEAPONS OF SELF-DEFENSE ARE ALWAYS CLOSE AT HAND.
THESE CRAZY PEOPLE KEEPING WOLVES, NOW??
SHIT!
OGUUUU-
THE STORY GOES, OGUN, ONE OF ERZULIE'S THREE DEVOTED HUSBANDS, WAS THE FIRST DEITY TO DESCEND TO EARTH, LOOKING FOR A PLACE HUMANITY AND THEIR GODS COULD LIVE.
HE CLEARED A PATH FOR THEM USING IRON TOOLS, AND ASSISTED BY A DOG.
YOU STOP! RIGHT NOW!
POUNCE
BUT THERE WOULD HAVE BEEN NO DOGS ON THE EARTH IN THOSE EARLY DAYS. ONLY THEIR ANCESTORS, THE WOLVES.
WHAT THE FU--?
TOYA, THROW THE SCISSORS. CAREFUL, THOUGH. YOU DON'T WANNA HURT THE WOLF.
YIP!
YOU JOSING, CHER?! IT COMES FOR US, OF COURSE I WANNA HURT IT!
PANT PANT PANT
IT WANTS TO PLAY!
WHAT ARE YOU DOING, BIBI?!

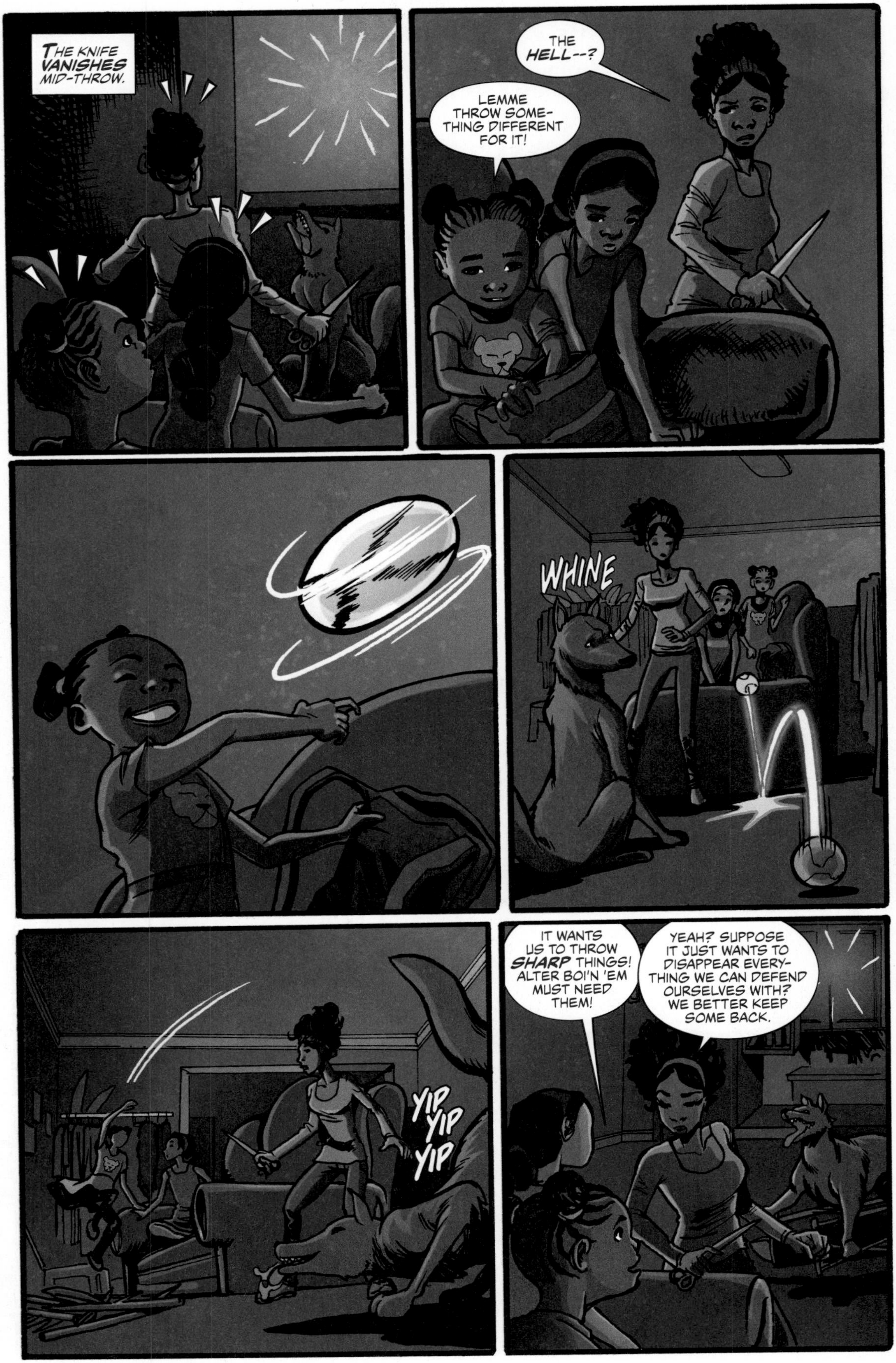

THE KNIFE VANISHES MID-THROW.
THE HELL--?
LEMME THROW SOMETHING DIFFERENT FOR IT!
WHINE
YIP YIP YIP
IT WANTS US TO THROW SHARP THINGS! ALTER BOI'N 'EM MUST NEED THEM!
YEAH? SUPPOSE IT JUST WANTS TO DISAPPEAR EVERYTHING WE CAN DEFEND OURSELVES WITH? WE BETTER KEEP SOME BACK.

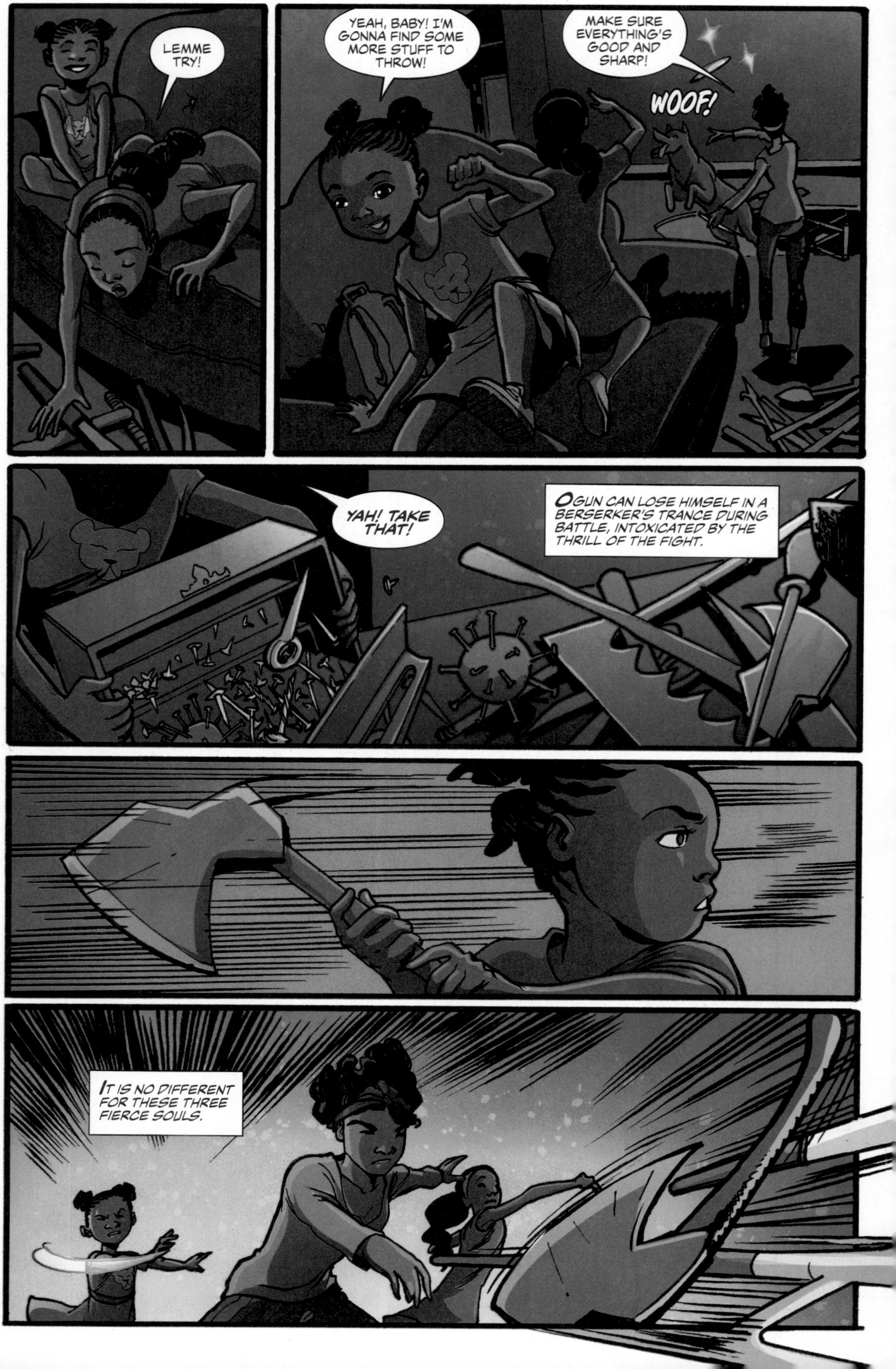
LEMME TRY!
YEAH, BABY! I'M GONNA FIND SOME MORE STUFF TO THROW!
MAKE SURE EVERYTHING'S GOOD AND SHARP!
WOOF!
YAH! TAKE THAT!
OGUN CAN LOSE HIMSELF IN A BERSERKER'S TRANCE DURING BATTLE, INTOXICATED BY THE THRILL OF THE FIGHT.
IT IS NO DIFFERENT FOR THESE THREE FIERCE SOULS.

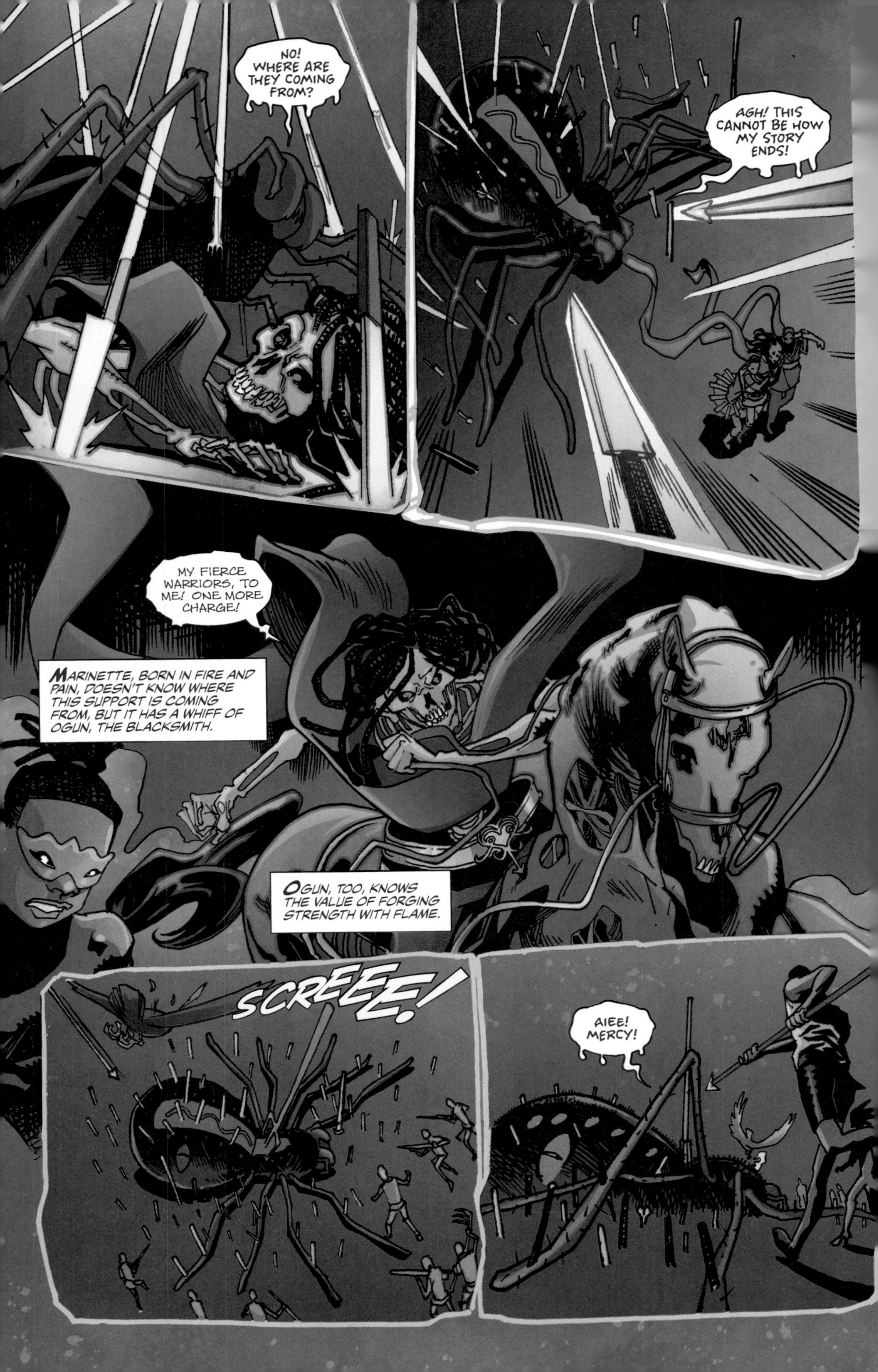
NO! WHERE ARE THEY COMING FROM?
AGH! THIS CANNOT BE HOW MY STORY ENDS!
MY FIERCE WARRIORS, TO ME! ONE MORE CHARGE!
MARINETTE, BORN IN FIRE AND PAIN, DOESN'T KNOW WHERE THIS SUPPORT IS COMING FROM, BUT IT HAS A WHIFF OF OGUN, THE BLACKSMITH.
OGUN, TOO, KNOWS THE VALUE OF FORGING STRENGTH WITH FLAME.
SCREEEE!
AIEE! MERCY!

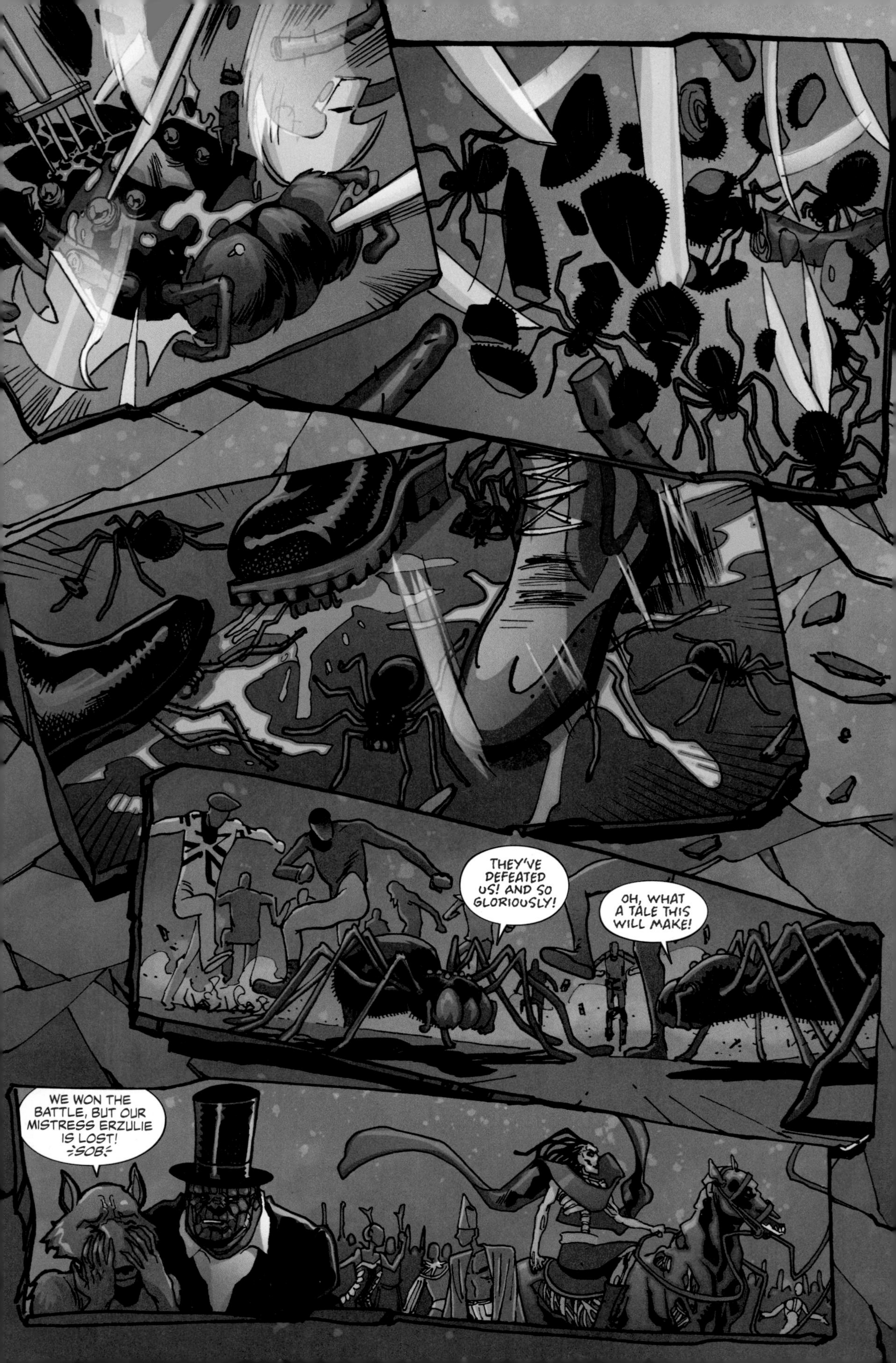
THEY'VE DEFEATED US! AND SO GLORIOUSLY!
OH, WHAT A TALE THIS WILL MAKE!
WE WON THE BATTLE, BUT OUR MISTRESS ERZULIE IS LOST! =SOB=

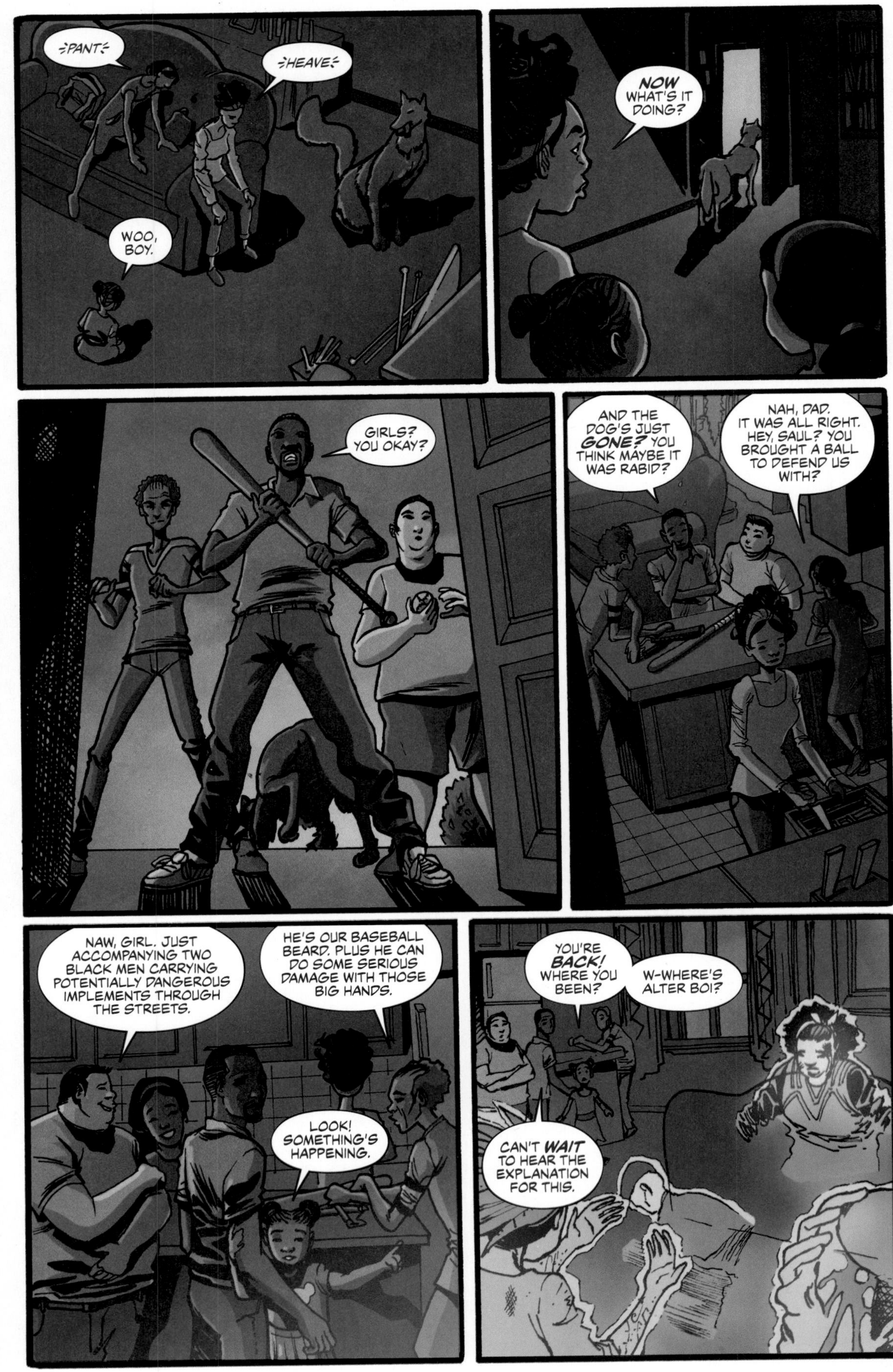
PANT
HEAVE
WOO, BOY.
NOW WHAT'S IT DOING?
GIRLS? YOU OKAY?
AND THE DOG'S JUST GONE? YOU THINK MAYBE IT WAS RABID?
NAH, DAD. IT WAS ALL RIGHT. HEY, SAUL? YOU BROUGHT A BALL TO DEFEND US WITH?
NAW, GIRL. JUST ACCOMPANYING TWO BLACK MEN CARRYING POTENTIALLY DANGEROUS IMPLEMENTS THROUGH THE STREETS.
HE'S OUR BASEBALL BEARD. PLUS HE CAN DO SOME SERIOUS DAMAGE WITH THOSE BIG HANDS.
LOOK! SOMETHING'S HAPPENING.
YOU'RE BACK! WHERE YOU BEEN?
W-WHERE'S ALTER BOI?
CAN'T WAIT TO HEAR THE EXPLANATION FOR THIS.

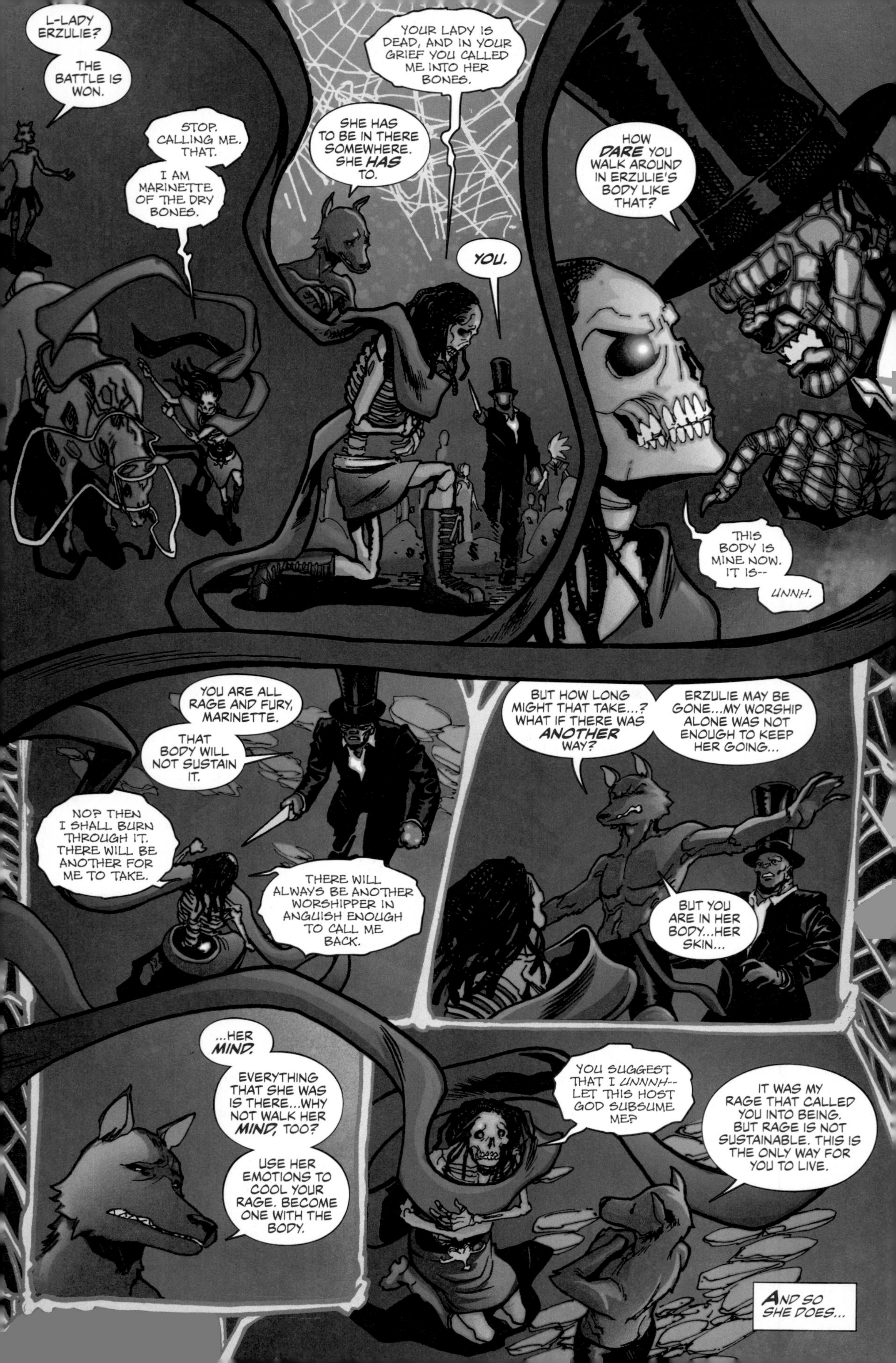

L-LADY ERZULIE?
THE BATTLE IS WON.
STOP. CALLING ME. THAT.
I AM MARINETTE OF THE DRY BONES.
YOUR LADY IS DEAD, AND IN YOUR GRIEF YOU CALLED ME INTO HER BONES.
SHE HAS TO BE IN THERE SOMEWHERE. SHE HAS TO.
YOU.
HOW DARE YOU WALK AROUND IN ERZULIE'S BODY LIKE THAT?
THIS BODY IS MINE NOW. IT IS--
UNNH.
YOU ARE ALL RAGE AND FURY, MARINETTE.
THAT BODY WILL NOT SUSTAIN IT.
NO? THEN I SHALL BURN THROUGH IT. THERE WILL BE ANOTHER FOR ME TO TAKE.
THERE WILL ALWAYS BE ANOTHER WORSHIPPER IN ANGUISH ENOUGH TO CALL ME BACK.
ERZULIE MAY BE GONE...MY WORSHIP ALONE WAS NOT ENOUGH TO KEEP HER GOING...
BUT HOW LONG MIGHT THAT TAKE...? WHAT IF THERE WAS ANOTHER WAY?
BUT YOU ARE IN HER BODY...HER SKIN...
...HER MIND.
EVERYTHING THAT SHE WAS IS THERE...WHY NOT WALK HER MIND, TOO?
USE HER EMOTIONS TO COOL YOUR RAGE. BECOME ONE WITH THE BODY.
YOU SUGGEST THAT I UNNNH-- LET THIS HOST GOD SUBSUME ME?
IT WAS MY RAGE THAT CALLED YOU INTO BEING. BUT RAGE IS NOT SUSTAINABLE. THIS IS THE ONLY WAY FOR YOU TO LIVE.
AND SO SHE DOES...

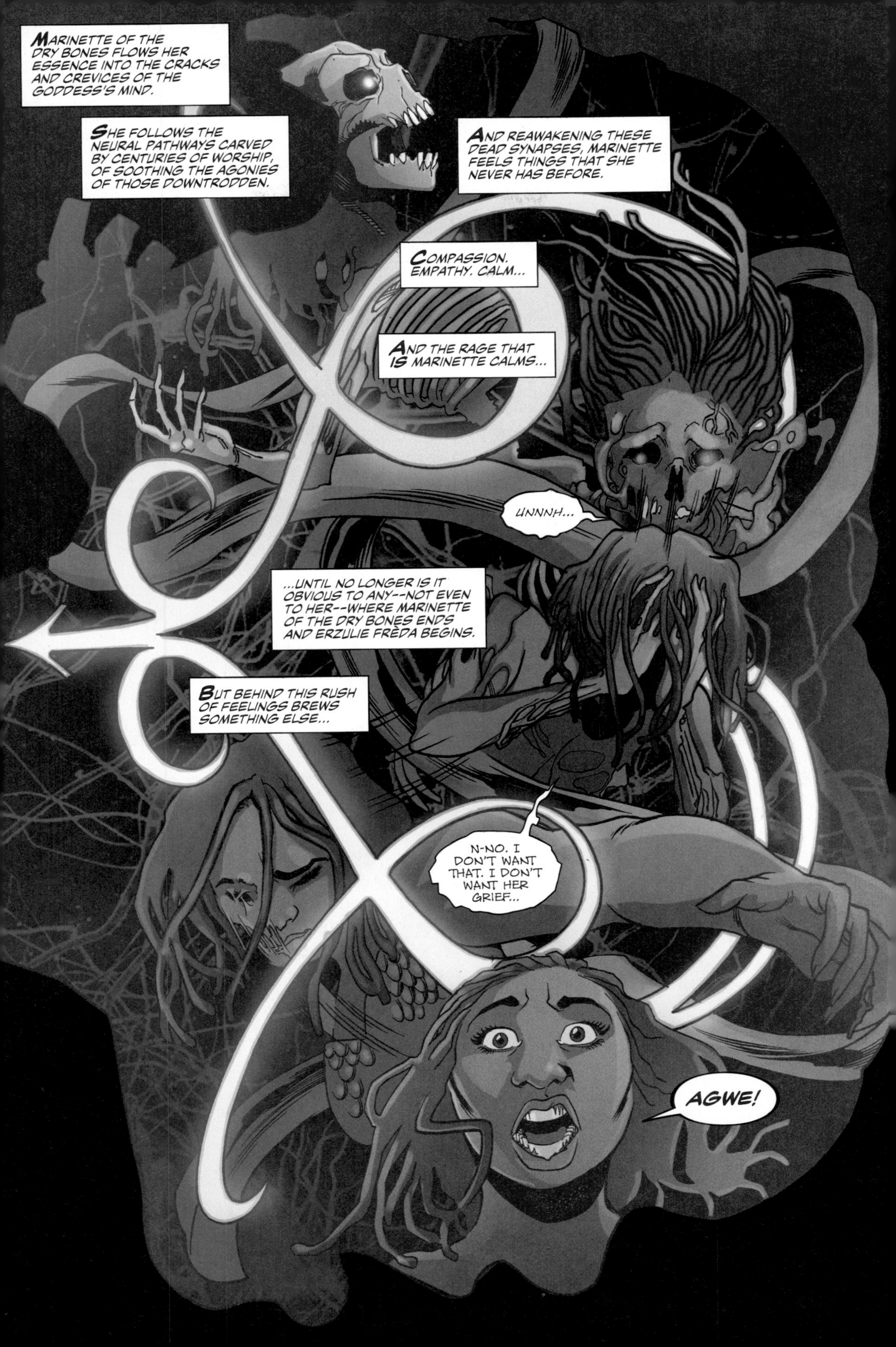
MARINETTE OF THE DRY BONES FLOWS HER ESSENCE INTO THE CRACKS AND CREVICES OF THE GODDESS'S MIND.
SHE FOLLOWS THE NEURAL PATHWAYS CARVED BY CENTURIES OF WORSHIP, OF SOOTHING THE AGONIES OF THOSE DOWNTRODDEN.
AND REAWAKENING THESE DEAD SYNAPSES, MARINETTE FEELS THINGS THAT SHE NEVER HAS BEFORE.
COMPASSION. EMPATHY. CALM...
AND THE RAGE THAT IS MARINETTE CALMS...
UNNNH...
...UNTIL NO LONGER IS IT OBVIOUS TO ANY--NOT EVEN TO HER--WHERE MARINETTE OF THE DRY BONES ENDS AND ERZULIE FRÈDA BEGINS.
BUT BEHIND THIS RUSH OF FEELINGS BREWS SOMETHING ELSE...
N-NO. I DON'T WANT THAT. I DON'T WANT HER GRIEF...
AGWE!

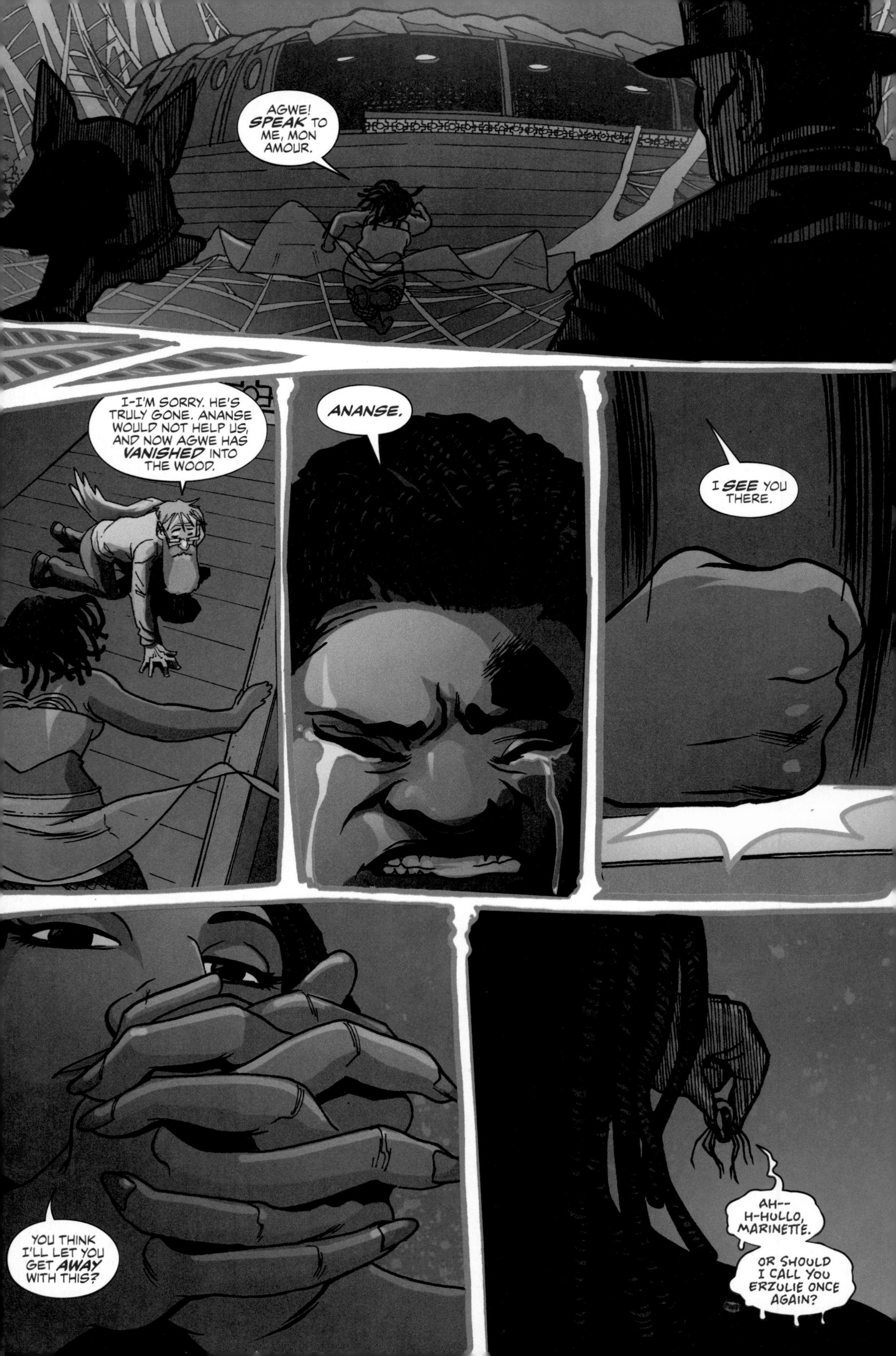
AGWE! SPEAK TO ME, MON AMOUR.
I-I'M SORRY. HE'S TRULY GONE. ANANSE WOULD NOT HELP US, AND NOW AGWE HAS VANISHED INTO THE WOOD.
ANANSE.
I SEE YOU THERE.
YOU THINK I'LL LET YOU GET AWAY WITH THIS?
AH-- H-HULLO, MARINETTE.
OR SHOULD I CALL YOU ERZULIE ONCE AGAIN?

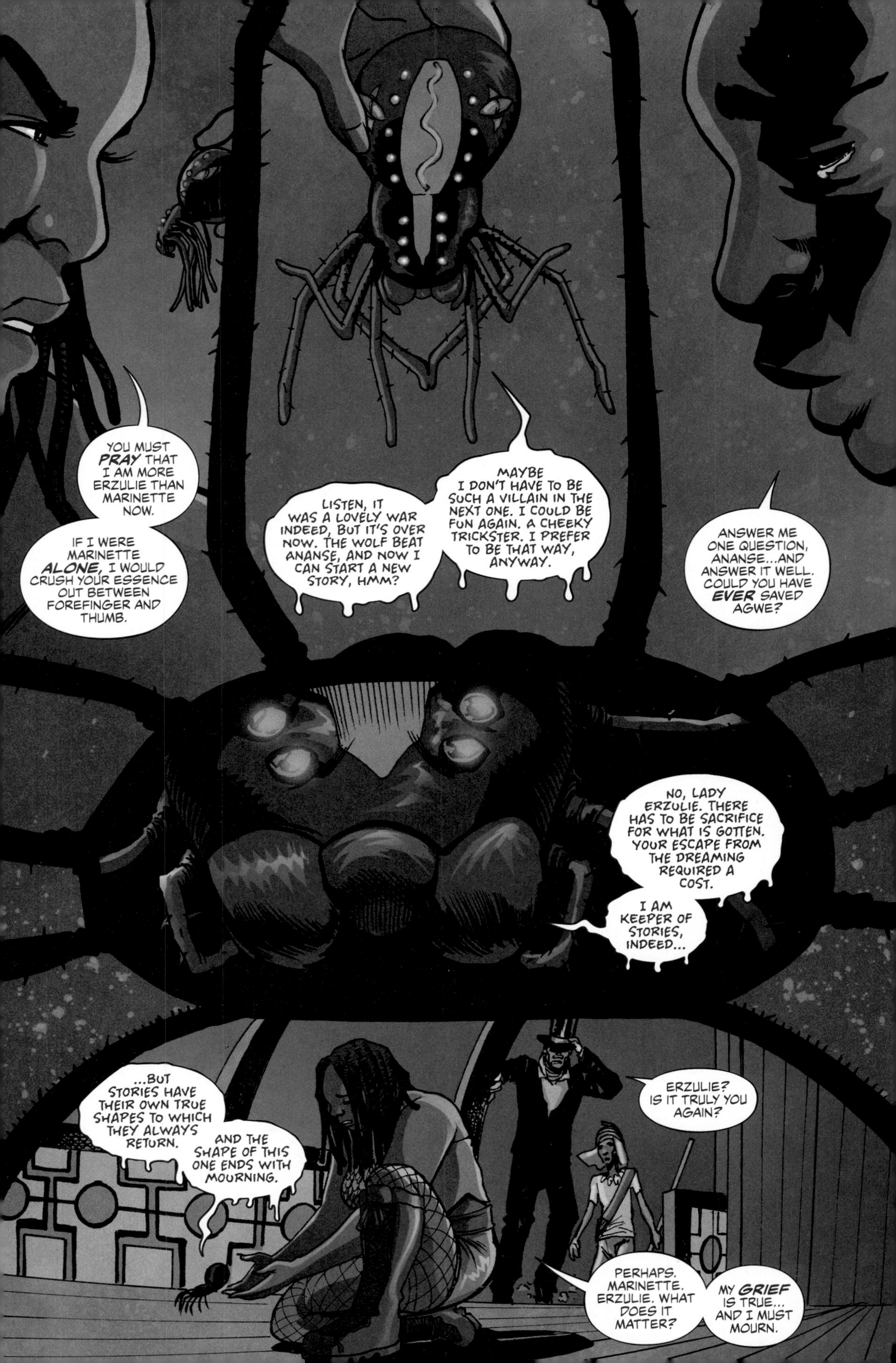
YOU MUST PRAY THAT I AM MORE ERZULIE THAN MARINETTE NOW.
IF I WERE MARINETTE ALONE, I WOULD CRUSH YOUR ESSENCE OUT BETWEEN FOREFINGER AND THUMB.
LISTEN, IT WAS A LOVELY WAR INDEED, BUT IT'S OVER NOW. THE WOLF BEAT ANANSE, AND NOW I CAN START A NEW STORY, HMM?
MAYBE I DON'T HAVE TO BE SUCH A VILLAIN IN THE NEXT ONE. I COULD BE FUN AGAIN. A CHEEKY TRICKSTER. I PREFER TO BE THAT WAY, ANYWAY.
ANSWER ME ONE QUESTION, ANANSE...AND ANSWER IT WELL. COULD YOU HAVE EVER SAVED AGWE?
NO, LADY ERZULIE. THERE HAS TO BE SACRIFICE FOR WHAT IS GOTTEN. YOUR ESCAPE FROM THE DREAMING REQUIRED A COST.
I AM KEEPER OF STORIES, INDEED...
...BUT STORIES HAVE THEIR OWN TRUE SHAPES TO WHICH THEY ALWAYS RETURN.
AND THE SHAPE OF THIS ONE ENDS WITH MOURNING.
ERZULIE? IS IT TRULY YOU AGAIN?
PERHAPS. MARINETTE. ERZULIE. WHAT DOES IT MATTER?
MY GRIEF IS TRUE... AND I MUST MOURN.

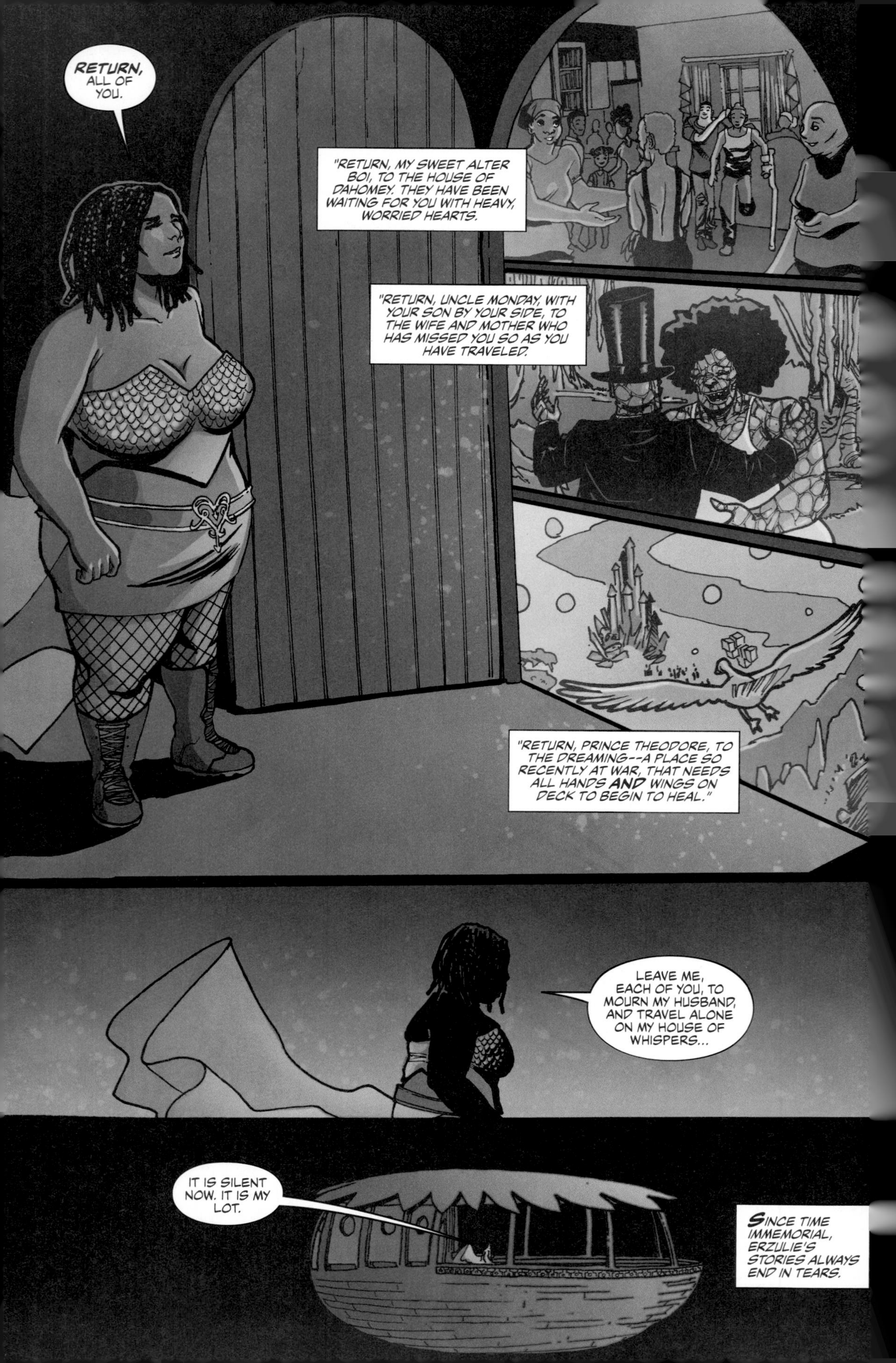
RETURN, ALL OF YOU.
"RETURN, MY SWEET ALTER BOI, TO THE HOUSE OF DAHOMEY. THEY HAVE BEEN WAITING FOR YOU WITH HEAVY, WORRIED HEARTS.
"RETURN, UNCLE MONDAY, WITH YOUR SON BY YOUR SIDE, TO THE WIFE AND MOTHER WHO HAS MISSED YOU SO AS YOU HAVE TRAVELED.
"RETURN, PRINCE THEODORE, TO THE DREAMING--A PLACE SO RECENTLY AT WAR, THAT NEEDS ALL HANDS AND WINGS ON DECK TO BEGIN TO HEAL."
LEAVE ME, EACH OF YOU, TO MOURN MY HUSBAND, AND TRAVEL ALONE ON MY HOUSE OF WHISPERS...
IT IS SILENT NOW. IT IS MY LOT.
SINCE TIME IMMEMORIAL, ERZULIE'S STORIES ALWAYS END IN TEARS.

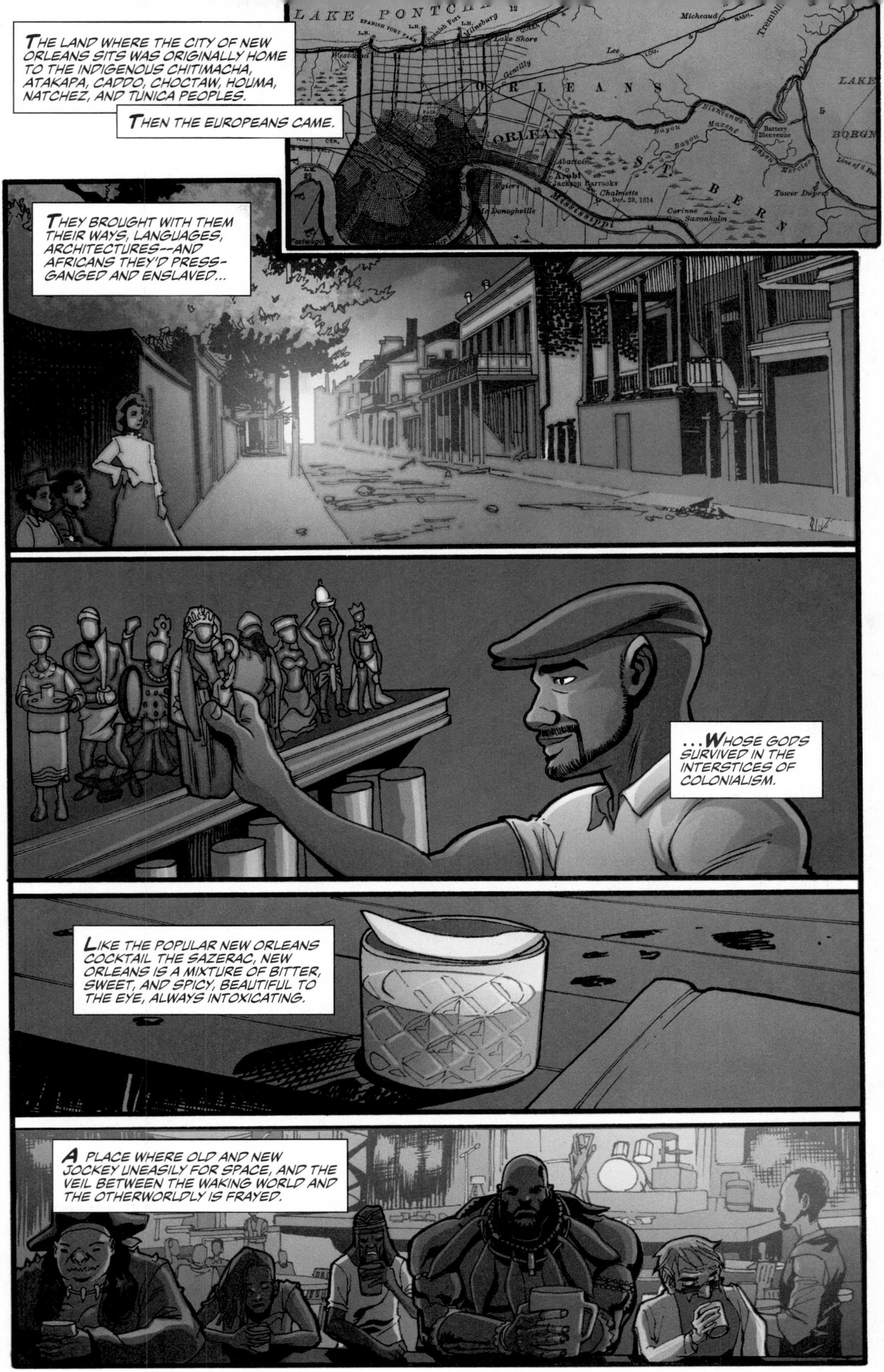
THE LAND WHERE THE CITY OF NEW ORLEANS SITS WAS ORIGINALLY HOME TO THE INDIGENOUS CHITIMACHA, ATAKAPA, CADDO, CHOCTAW, HOUMA, NATCHEZ, AND TUNICA PEOPLES.
THEN THE EUROPEANS CAME.
LAKE PONTCH
ORLEANS
THEY BROUGHT WITH THEM THEIR WAYS, LANGUAGES, ARCHITECTURES--AND AFRICANS THEY'D PRESS-GANGED AND ENSLAVED...
...WHOSE GODS SURVIVED IN THE INTERSTICES OF COLONIALISM.
LIKE THE POPULAR NEW ORLEANS COCKTAIL THE SAZERAC, NEW ORLEANS IS A MIXTURE OF BITTER, SWEET, AND SPICY, BEAUTIFUL TO THE EYE, ALWAYS INTOXICATING.
A PLACE WHERE OLD AND NEW JOCKEY UNEASILY FOR SPACE, AND THE VEIL BETWEEN THE WAKING WORLD AND THE OTHERWORLDLY IS FRAYED.

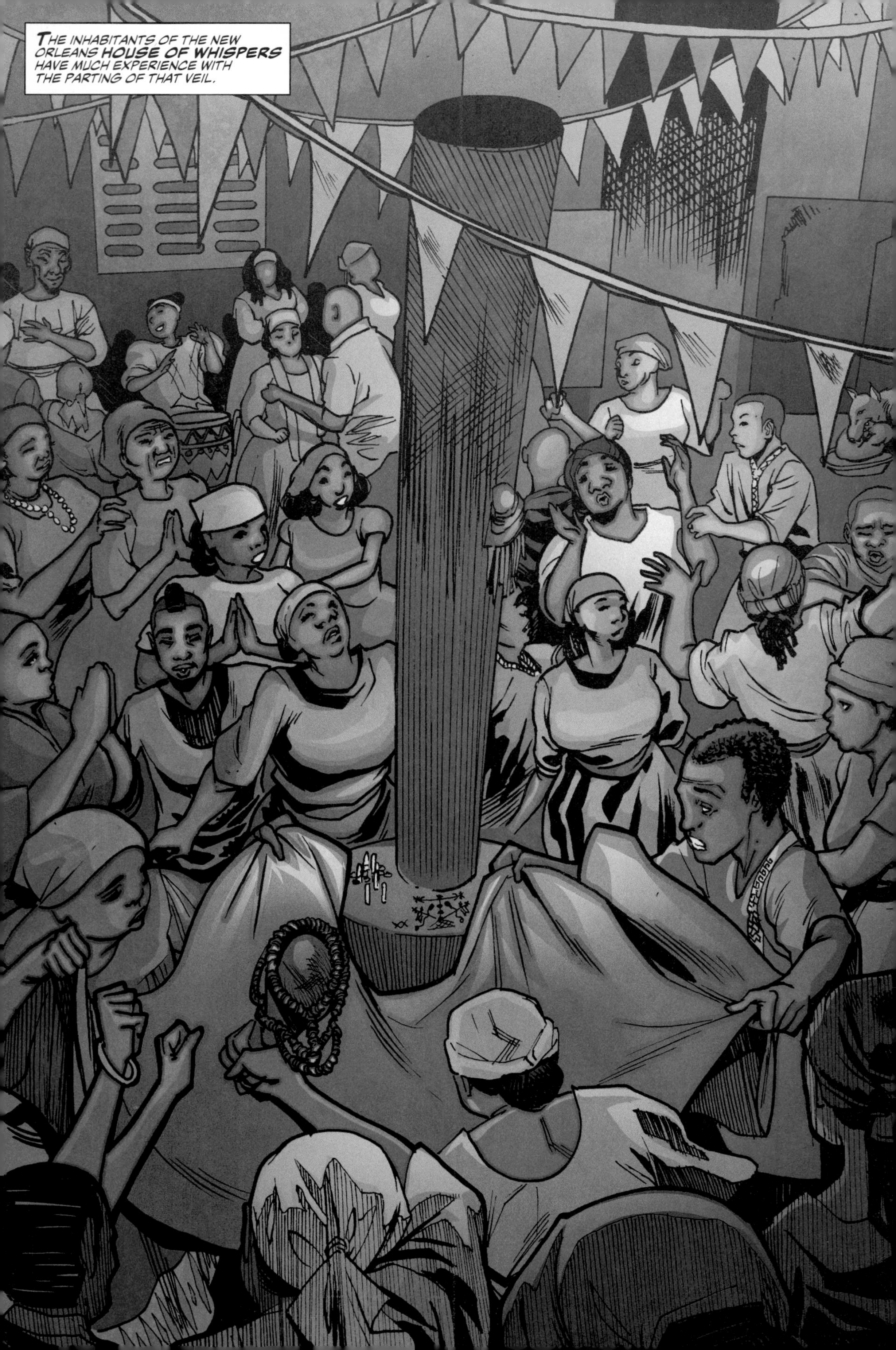
THE INHABITANTS OF THE NEW ORLEANS HOUSE OF WHISPERS HAVE MUCH EXPERIENCE WITH THE PARTING OF THAT VEIL.

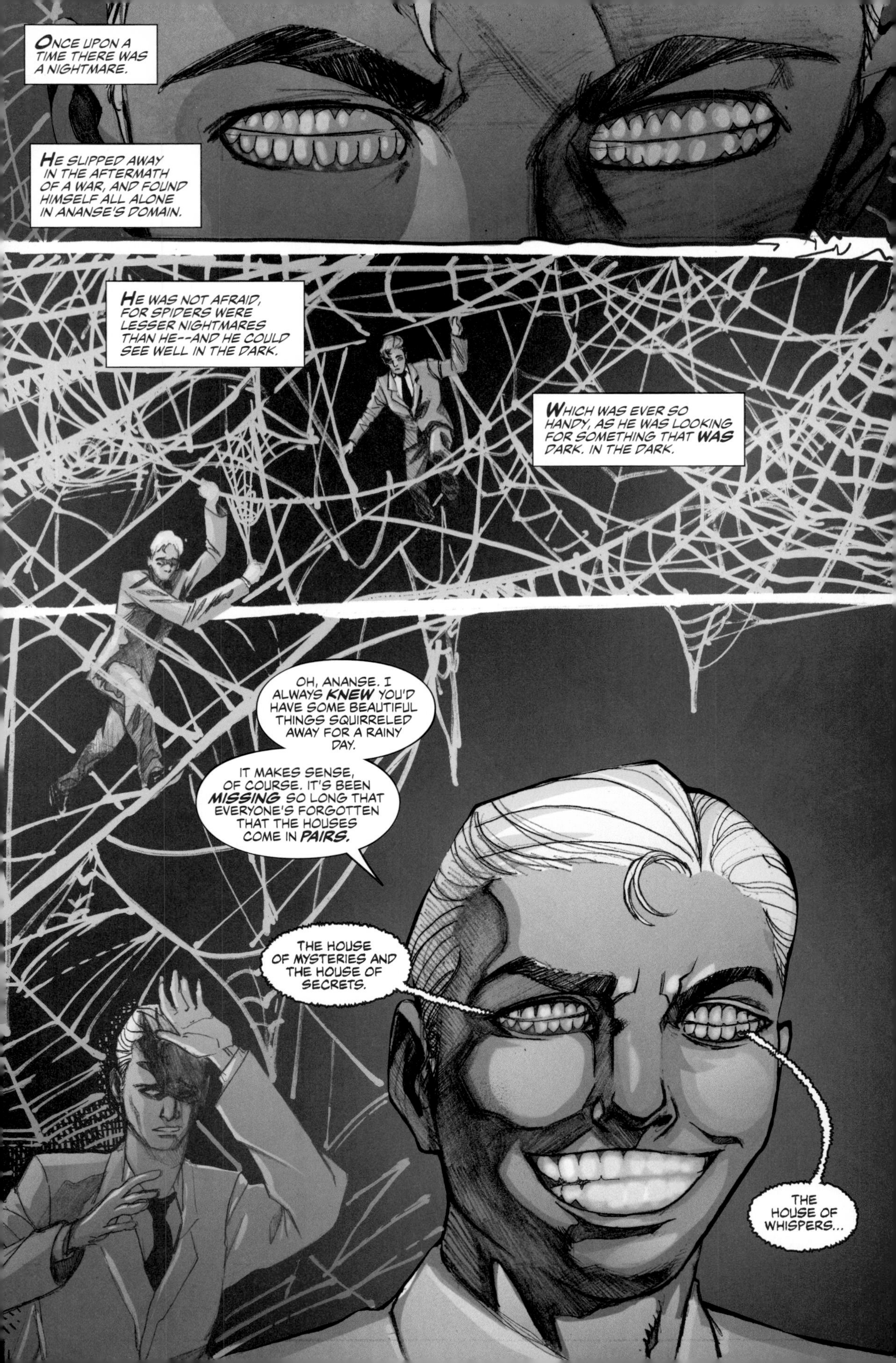
ONCE UPON A TIME THERE WAS A NIGHTMARE.
HE SLIPPED AWAY IN THE AFTERMATH OF A WAR, AND FOUND HIMSELF ALL ALONE IN ANANSE'S DOMAIN.
HE WAS NOT AFRAID, FOR SPIDERS WERE LESSER NIGHTMARES THAN HE--AND HE COULD SEE WELL IN THE DARK.
WHICH WAS EVER SO HANDY, AS HE WAS LOOKING FOR SOMETHING THAT WAS DARK. IN THE DARK.
OH, ANANSE. I ALWAYS KNEW YOU'D HAVE SOME BEAUTIFUL THINGS SQUIRRELED AWAY FOR A RAINY DAY.
IT MAKES SENSE, OF COURSE. IT'S BEEN MISSING SO LONG THAT EVERYONE'S FORGOTTEN THAT THE HOUSES COME IN PAIRS.
THE HOUSE OF MYSTERIES AND THE HOUSE OF SECRETS.
THE HOUSE OF WHISPERS...

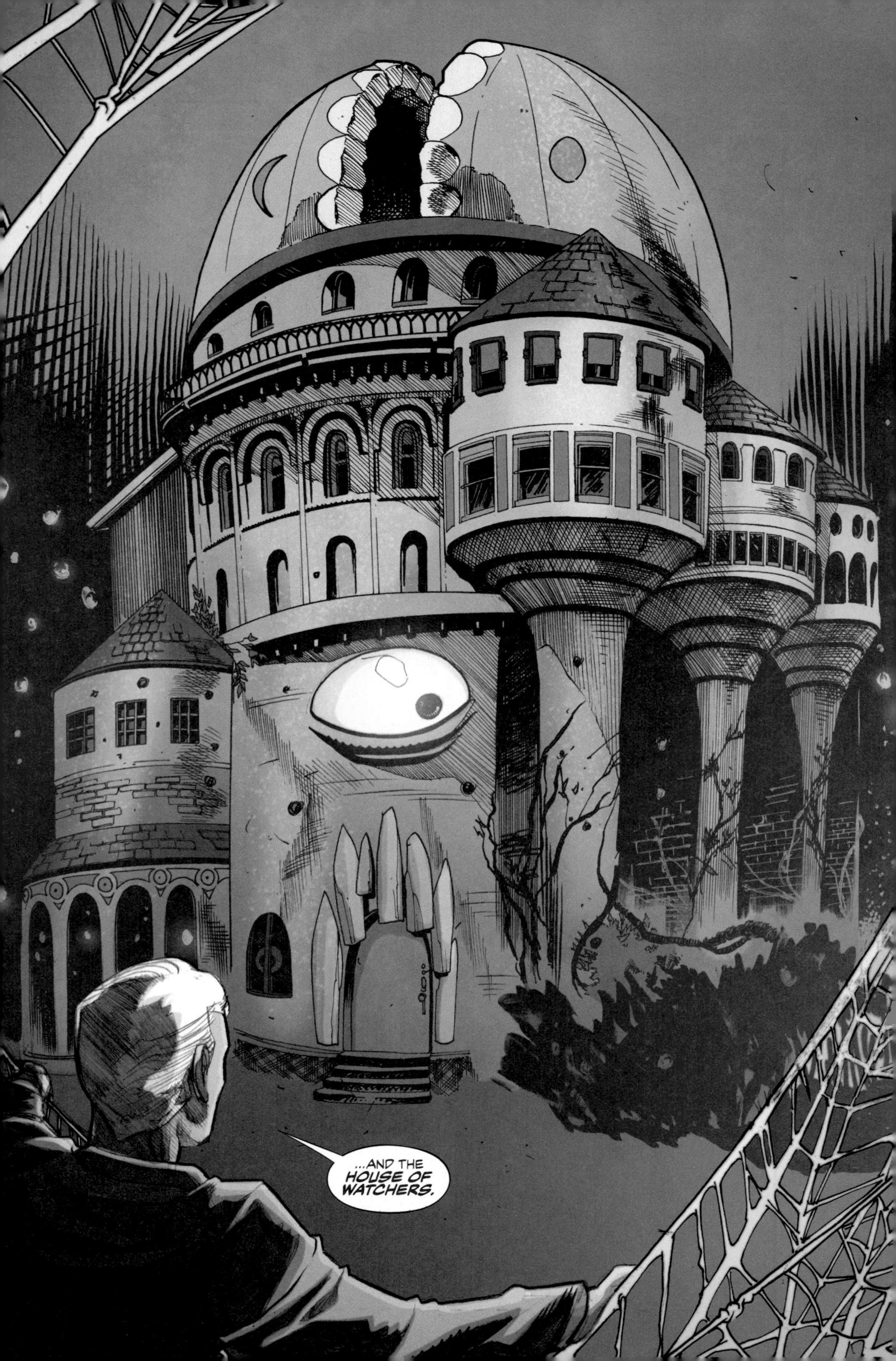
...AND THE HOUSE OF WATCHERS.

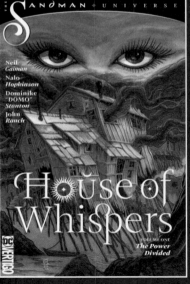

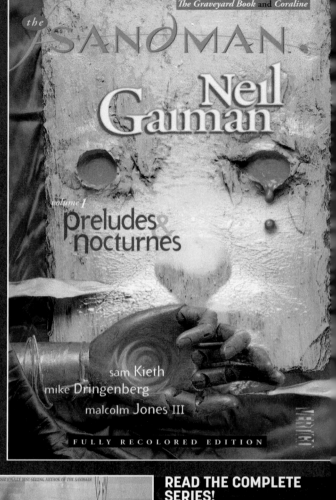

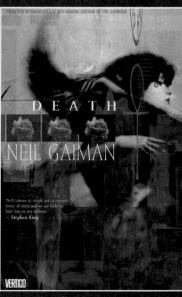

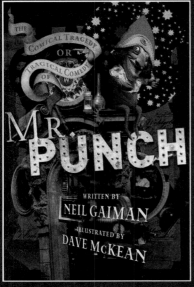

DC VERTIGO

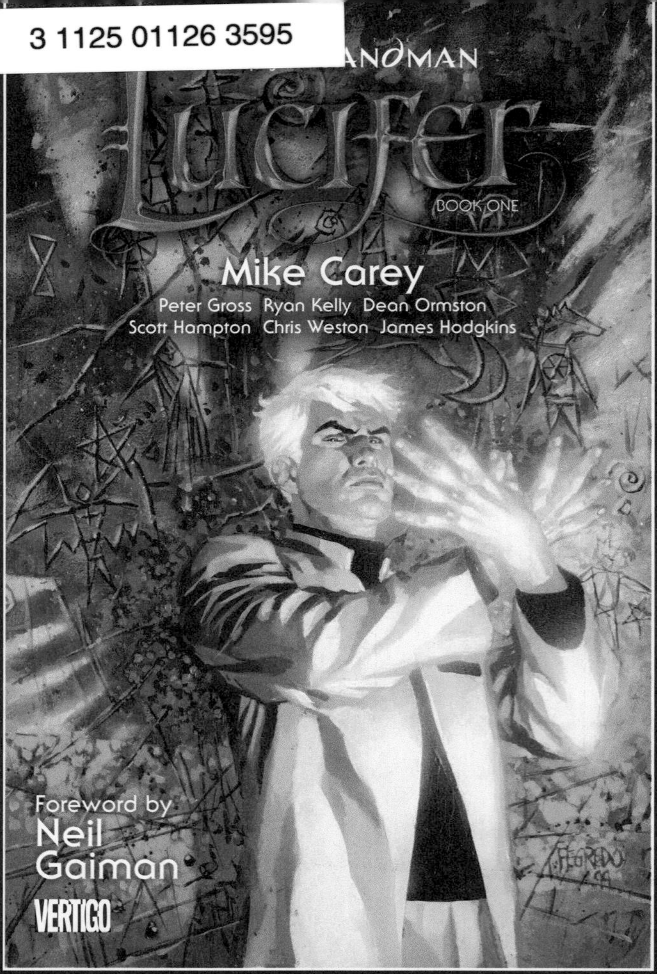
Lucifer
BOOK ONE
Mike Carey
Peter Gross Ryan Kelly Dean Ormston
Scott Hampton Chris Weston James Hodgkins
Foreword by
Neil
Gaiman
VERTIGO

"An original take on the forces of good, evil and beyond evil."
–PUBLISHERS WEEKLY

"Mike Carey's Lucifer is even more manipulative, charming and dangerous than I ever could have hoped."
–NEIL GAIMAN

MIKE CAREY
LUCIFER
BOOK ONE

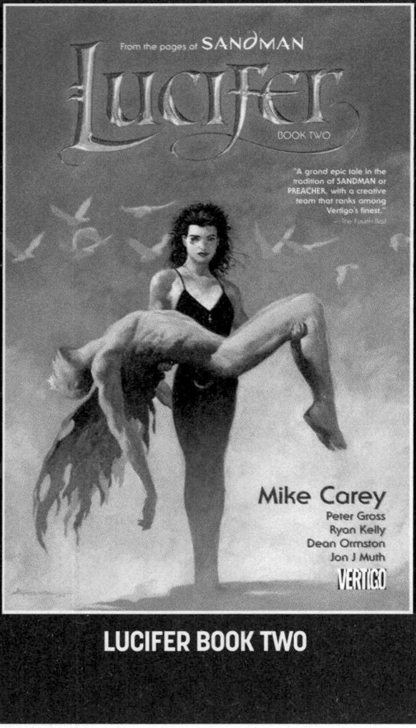
From the pages of SANDMAN
Lucifer
BOOK TWO
"A grand epic tale in the tradition of SANDMAN or PREACHER, with a creative team that ranks among Vertigo's finest."
—The Fourth Rail
Mike Carey
Peter Gross
Ryan Kelly
Dean Ormston
Jon J Muth
VERTIGO

LUCIFER BOOK TWO

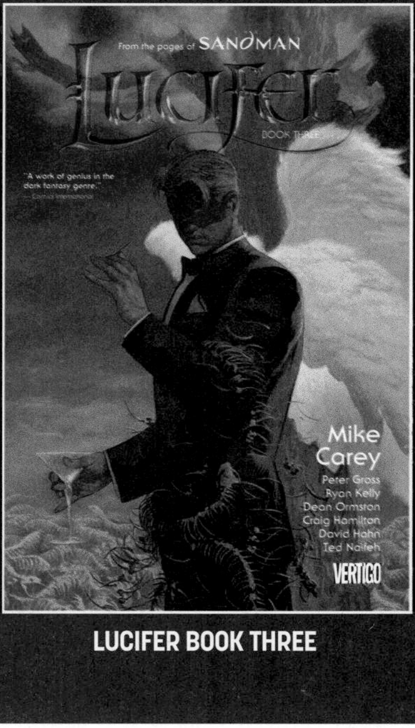
From the pages of SANDMAN
Lucifer
BOOK THREE
"A work of genius in the dark fantasy genre."
—Comics International
Mike
Carey
Peter Gross
Ryan Kelly
Dean Ormston
Craig Hamilton
David Hahn
Ted Naifeh
VERTIGO

LUCIFER BOOK THREE

READ THE COMPLETE SERIES!

LUCIFER BOOK FOUR

LUCIFER BOOK FIVE

DC VERTIGO Get more DC VERTIGO graphic novels wherever comics and books are sold!

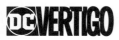